Partial Truths and the Politics of Community

Feminist Approaches to Social Movements, Community, and Power

VOLUME TWO

Partial Truths and the Politics of Community

Edited by

Mary Ann Tétreault and Robin L. Teske

UNIVERSITY OF SOUTH CAROLINA PRESS

Published in Columbia, South Carolina, by the
University of South Carolina Press

Manufactured in the United States of America

07 06 05 04 03 5 4 3 2 1

The Library of Congress has previously catalogued this title:

Feminist approaches to social movements, community, and power / edited by Robin L. Teske and Mary Ann Tétreault.

p. cm.

Includes bibliographical references and index.

1. Social movements. 2. Social change. 3. Community. 4. Feminism. 5. Women in politics. I. Robin L. Teske., 1949– II. Tétreault, Mary Ann, 1942–

HM881 .F45 2000 00-0085212

ISBN 1-57003-331-5 (v.1. Conscious acts and the politics of social change)
ISBN 1-57003-486-9 (v. 2. Partial truths and the politics of community)

This book is dedicated to
the memory of our mothers

Josephine Sagan Hoover Reed
Muriel Ruth Teske

Contents

Partial Truths and the Politics of Community

Introduction

Feminist Community in Postmodern Times

Mary Ann Tétreault

This second volume of *Feminist Approaches to Social Movements, Community, and Power* concludes our formal exploration of women's active engagement in the process of social change. I think of these two sets of essays as addressing complex relationships between agents and structures. Volume one, *Conscious Acts and the Politics of Social Change,* concentrated on agents challenging unjust and oppressive social structures. Social activists specialize in struggle and resistance yet, as Jiřina Šiklová observed in her essay in volume one,[1] what often are far more challenging tasks appear when activist campaigns conclude. How can we consolidate gains so that they persist over time? How can we live together in ways that reflect both our ideals and our obligations? Indeed, can we live together after the excitement and shared commitment to a campaign have dissipated and we realize not only that all of "us" are no longer on the same side but also that some of "them" are in charge?

Volume two, *Partial Truths and the Politics of Community,* considers that aftermath in the realization that results are more difficult to identify than activism. The ways that social movements change our lives are realized gradually and rarely are fully comprehended except perhaps by Minerva's owl. This is "the bird that flies at night," only then able to assess with full knowledge what the daylight activists have wrought. We are not so privileged. Most of us try to evaluate progress and setbacks even while the process of targeted social action continues to create social structures intended to support life in a way more congenial to feminist principles. The most important principle when we think about community is the conviction that there is no global truth, no one "right" way. Individuals and communities are constantly engaged in constructing their living arrangements and, in the process, recreate themselves, even though they may believe that they merely are following tradition.[2]

Part of feminism's link to postmodernist thought generally, the notion of partial truths reflects the realization that all knowledge is situated and incomplete.[3] Although this insight has been part of mathematics and the physical sciences for well over a century,[4] it's been a harder sell in the social sciences where difference and diversity are even now challenging old paradigms and threatening the authority of disciplinary gurus and gatekeepers. Political science, economics, and anthropology are split by struggles over who will control the guiding theoretical and methodological paradigms that are recognized as legitimate ways to understand, teach, and speak about their subjects, and to conduct and evaluate research.[5] Culture wars in the professions parallel conflicts in contemporary politics. In spite of the rumor that we had arrived at the end of history when the Berlin Wall fell, we have not found perpetual peace. This is good news.

In "Perpetual Peace," Kant uses the metaphor of the graveyard to tell us that those who seek perpetual peace will not find it this side of death. Life is a continuous process of negotiation and change. Even though this process gets out of hand when participants cease being reasonable and no longer are willing to see their adversaries as people like themselves, perpetual struggle is a mark of diversity and evidence that the human spirit persists undefeated by what my generation used to call "the power structure." As Karl Polanyi observed in *The Great Transformation,* the appearance of a "united front" signifies the end of politics and the beginning of dictatorship.[6] Today we are more likely to call this "hegemony"; it amounts to much the same thing and evokes the same resistance. *Partial Truths* looks both at ongoing resistance and at home-grown Gramscian strategies to embed opportunities for resistance in the structures of everyday life.

In this introduction, I try to explain what I mean by "feminist community" and "post-modern times"—the latter a phrase borrowed from Ronnie Lipschutz—in the context of the *Feminist Approaches* project. I begin by revisiting a crucial issue guiding our strategy in composing these volumes, the debate over how we define "feminism" and thus what constitutes a "feminist approach." These essays show facets of struggles which Robin Teske and I—the editors—see as feminist, including those taking place within the feminist movement itself. Throughout, our aim has been to locate the ways in which feminists and their allies try to be simultaneously critical, constructive, tolerant, and ethical, particularly with regard to the rights of women and girls to achieve fully realized lives.[7] Consequently, although conflict is reflected in each of these essays, it is not treated as something that can be "resolved" in any permanent way. Rather, it is accepted as a normal outcome of clashes between and among group ideals and private desires, and their necessary consequences expressed as multiple visions of community life.

At the same time, the ensemble of essays in this volume reflects our desire to broaden the effective reach of feminist practice beyond the position we took in volume one, both by tracing feminist influences on a range of strategies for seeking social change and by encouraging feminists and others who share feminist ideals of freedom and justice to seek common ground. This is not a call for unity. Standing on common ground to cooperate on issues where the views of otherwise disparate individuals and groups coincide is not a call to submerge difference. Rather, as Ray Gingerich and Bruce Busching described in their chapter in volume one[8] and Mary Meyer explores in this volume, it is a way to mobilize a larger, more effective coalition for achieving particular social goals at a particular place and time. It also constitutes a forum for what Anne Phillips calls a "politics of presence," which occurs when the range of participants widens to incorporate differently situated viewpoints and interests as explicit elements of political life.[9]

As an egalitarian who values freedom, I subscribe to the definition of feminism offered by Kathy Staudt: an orientation that "recognize[s] power and value imbalances between men and women . . . [and looks] toward active women to foster more balance."[10] I find this definition analogous to what students of U.S. constitutional law might term "substantive" feminism, feminism directed explicitly toward transformative action to equalize the status of women and men. At the same time, I encourage those who might not see themselves or their activities as feminist to consider whether what they are doing might be examples of "procedural" feminism, actions rooted in feminist ethics of intersubjectivity and nonviolence, and intended to further the cause of equality and social justice. A similar perspective on classifying feminist organizations is taken by Patricia Yancey Martin, who suggests that we look not only at what these organizations say but also at what they do.[11] On these grounds, we asked Karen Walch, Marie Deans, and Abigail Abrash to prepare chapters for this volume that we believe reflect such procedural feminist perspectives, even though the motivations for the thoughts and actions each author discusses were not explicitly envisioned as "feminist" when the writers undertook them. We also offer activist chapters by Karla Scheele and by the Cordes-Selbin family that are framed in substantive feminist terms but describe what are more usually seen as "nonfeminist" and even "unfeminist" communities—sororities and homeschoolers, respectively. We hope that readers will consider these examples of efforts to find common ground—along with the more detailed strategies for feminist activism "across borders" described by Beate Gersch, Anne Sisson Runyan, and others in these volumes—as suggestions for future theory-building and activism of their own.

Postmodern Times

"Eras" or "times" are impossible to demarcate neatly regardless of how hard we try and how "scientific" our standards. Dividing one period from another according to "development" criteria applied to social organization and technology is a problem even for archeologists.[12] There seem to be exceptions to every rule. Even so, most writers today assert that modernity is qualitatively distinct from earlier eras, although there is widespread disagreement about whether the modern era is over and, if it is, when "postmodernity" began (not to mention what it means).[13] I believe that we are moving into postmodern times although, perhaps perversely, I also believe that the institutions of modernity persist and the grip of modernity's developmentalist ideologies continues to shape how we perceive the world. Indeed, like Anthony Giddens and Peter Taylor, I agree that we live in an era of "high modernity" marked by the global spread of capitalism and by high, and rising, material standards of living.[14] My main quarrels with this generality are that it ignores how the high life of the few depends on the exploitation of the many, as well as the myriad ways that modernity and its institutions are pervasive and controlling and, therefore, difficult to resist.[15]

It is in the phenomenon of resistance to totalizing systems that I find my understanding of postmodernism. Like Yaron Ezrahi, I see a different consciousness of the self developing, not only in opposition to various collectivisms, old and new, but also in response to hierarchies of values that diverge from the radical utilitarian individualism underpinning modern capitalism. This consciousness is far from what critics have identified as "immoral post-modernism,"[16] a capacity not merely to destroy "incriminating evidence" but actually to create a self-serving "history" complete with invented "chronolog[ies] of events" and casts of characters, a world in which "memory is not what you can remember, but what other people are allowed to tell you that you knew."[17] Rather, I understand postmodernism as an assertion of individuality composed of two ethical strands. One is the radical democratization of a sense of entitlement to live on one's own terms—a position formerly reserved for elites and, even then, mostly male elites.[18] The second stands in sharp contrast to such elite assertions of privilege: an appreciation that a high degree of personal freedom is possible only within a democratically negotiated and universally applicable system of rules.[19] Postmodernity is life on Isaiah Berlin's "shifting, but always recognizable, frontier" which divides that social space where individuals can do as they wish without restraint from the space within which they must honor the rights of others simultaneously with their own.[20] It is the world of the "identified voice" that I described in the final chapter of volume one of this project, a "voice [that] acknowledges its source in a specific person . . . claims authority based on individually grounded knowledge and experience. . . . [and] speaks from an intersubjectivity that seeks to experience another's life as though it were one's own."[21]

Just as I have defined postmodern times in terms of democracy, plurality, and intersubjectivity, contemporary definitions of modernity emphasize hierarchy, instrumentality, and control. These include Anthony Giddens's outline of the institutional dimensions of modernity (military power, surveillance, capitalism, and industrialization);[22] Peter Taylor's definition of modernity as a plurality of projects to impose order on a world characterized by "the incessant change which is the condition of modernity";[23] Jim Scott's picture of the state as, above all, the avatar of "hegemonic high modernism," the producer of controllable standardized units of territory and population[24]—all in aid of taming a modernity which Marshall Berman describes in Marx's words as a place where "all that is solid melts into air."[25] In this Hobbesian world, change is incessant; agents, driven by the imperatives of the various structures within which they interact, are forced to analyze, standardize, monitor, and control to maintain their positions and, if they are clever, to advance over their fellows.[26]

The spread of market relations within and among states is seen from this perspective as the principal engine driving change.[27] Market relations shatter or expropriate[28] most competing forms of social organization and community, detach people from their habitations, and create fictitious commodities such as money and labor.[29] They also create virtual realities such as banking systems, financial exchanges, TV programs, and the Internet.[30] Market relations impose order less through the familial images, nationalist ideologies, and direct coercion associated with state projects[31] than via internalized standards implanted by socialization and advertising—not only are individual products marketed, but consumption itself is packaged as a primary social value and as a way to measure personal worth.[32] Indeed, it is opposition to the convergences in values compelled by expanding and deepening market relations that moves American parents like Helen Cordes and Eric Selbin to school their children at home.

Western feminists exploring the structure and operation of these internalized standards of modernity associate them with masculinist ideologies built around the interests of male persons. Thus, they argue that nationalism, capitalism, militarism, and other hierarchical social ideologies[33] are amplifications of social organizations and systems of thought in which gender is the main ordering principle.[34] The nationalism that puts loyalty to the nation-state at the pinnacle of human attachments, defines sacrifice for the nation-state as the highest form of heroic responsibility, and offers an atomistic vision of equality based on material existence and legal status devoid of moral content can be constituted from the principles and practices of classical patriarchy.[35] This is explored at some length by Ronnie Lipschutz in his essay in this volume. The mechanisms by which hegemonies exercise their control are described by Eric Wolf as those generating a totalizing system.[36] The successful standardization of human beings by states and markets is mediated by the generation and preservation of hegemonic ideologies that articulate "an overall hegemonic pattern or 'design for living' [that is] not so much the victory of a collective cognitive logic or aesthetic impulse as the development of redundancy—the continuous repetition in diverse instrumental domains, of the same basic propositions regarding the nature of constructed reality."[37] This process is endless. We cannot "assume transgenerational continuity, institutional stability, [or] normative consensus."[38] Each of these must be produced and defended continually against alternative conceptualizations of what is normal, natural, and right.

Opposition to the plurality so integral to feminism and other postmodern critiques is a reaction not merely to different ideas or different points of view but, more fundamentally, to the disruption of that "continuous repetition in diverse instrumental domains" which allows the reigning hegemony to renew and reproduce its hold on ideas and institutions over time. It is not only the suggestion that the critic might be offering a better model of the world than the one embodied in conventional, "mainstream" wisdom but, even more, recognition of the possibility that there even could be other models that so frightens the people in charge.[39] Diversity threatens precisely because it undermines standardization and thereby attenuates the authority of elites and their power to control others.[40] Critics who shape their concerns to incorporate the "basic propositions regarding the nature of constructed reality" that constitute their society's "mainstream" views are absorbed into the overall hegemonic vision—they become another one of the boys.[41] Those who insist on the legitimacy of diversity are condemned and sometimes, like other heretics, even liquidated. How to accommodate simultaneously both solidarity and diversity is the chief dilemma that critical theory must address.

A View from the Margins

Feminist critiques of the assumptions and practices of high modernism have focused attention on major institutions: science, the military, politics, and religion. Although less well-known than feminist critiques of the military, politics, and religion, the critique of science is perhaps the most important, both substantively and theoretically, because of the power inherent in the social organization and practices of science and the damage that an unconstrained use of this power has already wreaked and continues to inflict on the planet. Rachel Carson, a biologist, was the first to identify chains of negative consequences for wildlife from the widespread use of organic phosphate pesticides. Her interest in the environment as a complex of interdependent systems was stimulated by her work with the U.S. Fish and Wildlife Service, especially her study of and writings on the sea and wildlife conservation. Her book *The Sea Around Us* (1951) was a popular success and brought her to the attention of *New Yorker* editor William Shawn, who published several chapters of the book in the magazine. A decade later, *Silent Spring* (1962) was serialized in the *New Yorker,* where it was attacked by chemical corporations trying to suppress its publication in book form by Houghton Mifflin. "[T]he reaction was intense not simply because Carson questioned the use and abuse of power by certain prominent interest groups but because she questioned the basic attitudes of our technological society toward the natural world. [Paul Brooks] commented: 'The facts she revealed were bad enough, but it was the point of view behind them that was really dangerous and [had to] be suppressed.'"[42] The facts could stand alone; despite the length of time and the progress of knowledge since the publication of *Silent Spring,* they, as well as the general framework and propositions of the book, remain valid.[43] Feminist critiques of science are good science. They challenge narrow hegemonic visions whose slavish adherence to what Garry Wills sees as perversions of Enlightenment ideals[44] both motivates and justifies the disconnection of theory and controlled experimentation from the wider environment in which the consequences of science work themselves out under uncontrolled conditions. Another female scientist, Barbara McClintock, a geneticist much of whose experimental work dealt with corn development in ecological settings, did not criticize the enterprise of science as Rachel Carson did. But as the first to articulate the connections between environmental conditions and the expression of genes—the relationship between nurture and nature—McClintock provided data and theory to support the proposition that identical genetic blueprints produce very different plants depending on local conditions.[45]

Clark Miller writing in this volume, along with Evelyn Fox Keller,[46] Sandra Harding,[47] and others, emphasizes the importance of a woman's standpoint to explain the prominence of women among critics of science. Keller and Harding argue that women's greater willingness to question science's governing paradigms is a reaction to the way science is practiced.

Women—and both Carson and McClintock experienced this—are excluded or, at best, marginalized by the masculinists who dominate their professions. Miller notes that women are marginalized not only as scientists but also as scientific subjects. He says that in Carson's writings, the "most poignant passages stand out, to me at least, when she is describing the pesticide spraying campaigns in Illinois and the feeling of being the subject of an experiment."[48] Other examples of the objectification of women by science—their treatment as less human than men—include the politics of diseases like breast cancer and endometriosis, where women continue to struggle for treatments that minimize disfigurement and incapacitation, as well as the establishment of appropriate protocols for treating women who present with "male" diseases such as myocardial infarction.

It is common to explain this objectification as a result of conceptualizing "nature" as feminine and rightfully subordinate to men. However, as Angela Argent discusses in her chapter, gender is more fluid than that. Concepts and even persons can be seen as feminine or masculine depending on the circumstances. Ambiguity in "gendering" is complex, especially when it is used to construct and enforce hierarchical ordering. As I note in my chapter on wartime rape, this ambiguity is evident in the treatment of many subaltern groups—especially of men defeated in war.

Marginality also is a complex phenomenon, and it is associated with differences other than gender. Frank Sulloway explores it in the context of birth order, arguing that firstborns are more deeply incorporated into the social realities of their parents than middle children, who not only are less well socialized into the parental world(view) but also have fewer open choices with regard to family roles than their older sibling.[49] Sulloway argues that relatively marginal middle children are more open to social change. He applies Thomas Kuhn's work on scientific revolutions to generate propositions about the impact of birth order on innovation generally and political innovation in particular—who were the French revolutionaries, for example, or who were the U.S. Supreme Court judges most likely to abandon precedent for newly re-visioned conceptions of the law? Countering this perspective, Holocaust scholar Eva Fogelman finds that firstborns and only children predominated among the European rescuers of Jews fleeing Nazi persecution. She argues that parental love and the moral exemplars with whom children identify create caring, ethical human beings capable of defying peer pressure and even the law to be true to fundamental moral principles.[50] Consequently, marginal status may be less important than basic values.

Minority status offers plausible reasons why members of subaltern groups challenge authority in particular ways, but it is even better as an explanation of the reactions of authorities to such challenges. An example comes from the life of Ignaz Semmelweis, a nineteenth-century Hungarian physician. Semmelweis discovered the cause of childbed fever from observing the behavior of medical students and professors in Vienna, where he worked as an unpaid assistant to Johann Klein, the professor of obstetrics at the Vienna General Hospital. Klein's pedagogical innovation had been to replace the leather dummy students had used to learn how to examine women in labor with direct access to living patients—another example of the objectification of women by science. This change was marked by an upward spike in the incidence of childbed fever among the patients at the hospital, for, in line with the accepted medical practices of the day, students routinely went from performing autopsies to examining patients without washing their hands.

Semmelweis is remembered as being unusually compassionate toward his patients, and he was distressed by the sudden rapid rise of illness and death among new mothers in the hospital. He devoted time and attention to observing the patients and quickly noted the similarity between the onset and progression of childbed fever and the pattern of illness and death of a colleague from infection in a wound he had incurred while performing an autopsy. From his ecological observations and as the result of animal experimentation, Semmelweis concluded that the students' dirty hands were transferring "putrefied" matter from the corpses to the living women, thereby causing disease.

As a Hungarian, Semmelweis was a minority professional employed in a relatively menial position in the capital city of the Austrian Empire. He announced his discovery of the cause of childbed fever in the same year, 1848, that he was active in the anti-imperial revolutionary movement. His new theory, a direct challenge to the authority of Johann Klein, was interpreted by Klein as a political attack. Semmelweis had support from a colleague, but this man was a Czech professor of chest diseases—a member of another minority group. Their views were disregarded by Klein, who dismissed Semmelweis from his position.[51] How much Semmelweis's compassion for his patients was due to his own marginality is difficult to say, but the professional retaliation against him was both motivated and facilitated by that marginality. An interesting comparison to the marginal vantage point from which Semmelweis worked is found in Keller's description of Barbara McClintock. Often unpaid and carrying out mostly unfunded research, McClintock was subjected to discrimination with respect to the conditions that governed her admission to and treatment in the institutions where she worked. Keller believes that having to shift her experiments from place to place gave McClintock the opportunity to observe corn development in different ecological settings and also allowed her to see phenomena that lay outside the conceptual framework of then-dominant theories of genetics.[52]

Standpoint and marginality (marginality in the sense of location on an experiential or cultural boundary—a state also called liminality and which Robin Teske and Margaret Hrezo explored in volume one under the rubric of "the inbetween"[53]) are used to explain the contributions of women to critical theories in many fields. They also are linked to the ability of agents to navigate between different worlds. Barrie Thorne writes about tomboys as persons who are "literate" in two genders, able to communicate in the spoken and body language vernaculars of both girls and boys and to switch effortlessly between them depending on the social context.[54] These skills involve an intimate knowledge of how the world is viewed and manipulated from each standpoint, and they are acquired by persons who see themselves as genuinely part of both worlds regardless of whether others see them as full members of either one.[55] Suzanne Fleischman speculates that such skills are self-consciously incorporated into the professional repertoires of feminist scholars, whose intellectual worlds are epistemologically richer than the worlds from which most men operate.[56] Yet standpoint and liminality are not complete explanations as the essays in this volume illustrate. The location of the individual within the communities that she defines and is herself defined by provides a better approximation of the role of critic than a view only from the individual herself.

Equality and Plurality

Feminist theorists have struggled for years to delineate what they mean by "equality" and "difference."[57] This dichotomy, like so many others, is difficult to negotiate. As Angela Argent and Anne Runyan advise in this volume, success requires one to deny both the implied uniformity of equality and the implied essentialism of attributes of identity such as gender, race, nationality, and class, alone or in combination. In the spirit of Runyan's metaphor of the "world-traveling feminist," we are urged to celebrate our singularities and, from them, to construct communities. Without both singularity and community, we cannot survive as a social species. This dilemma is explored in Clark Miller's reading of cautionary parables in stories about technologically advanced dystopian futures and in Robin Teske's essay on feminist spirituality, whose outlook—and reading list—are more optimistic than Miller's. We also would not understand critical aspects of our own presence in this world, such things as how men can be feminists, women masculinists, and interests far more complex than academic theories and conventional wisdom usually reflect. Indeed, among the greatest riches to be found in these essays and in feminist writings generally is an intellectually sophisticated exploration of the range of human possibilities. To return to one of the terms from Hannah Arendt with which we introduced this project, feminists incorporate in their work an appreciation of *plurality* in human existence—that is, the uniqueness of the person and its expression as a vector of action shaped within a particular ensemble of unique persons occupying a particular temporally and spatially defined venue of public life. This is the model of feminist community that is reflected in these essays.

Arendt's conception of plurality incorporates the social context of the identified voice to describe the interplay between agents and structures. In terms of the postmodern framework I sketched earlier, plurality includes both the distinctiveness of persons and the many partial truths that describe how they live together. To the individual feminist, plurality is composed of a realized identity, a community, and a set of choices each of which carries consequences for the chooser as well as for other persons and institutions—rules, structures, and expectations—that affect and are affected by what the chooser decides. This is how experience becomes an explanatory variable, a principle illustrated in Karla Scheele's contemplation of why she joined a sorority and Helen Cordes and Eric Selbin's review of their decision to homeschool their daughters, Jesse and Zoe. However, as these writers note, experience is limited by its attachment to the individual at a particular time and in a particular place. This makes generalizing from experience difficult even for the subject, a problem submerged in the writings of one of the most prominent contemporary feminist writers in central Europe, Jiřina Šiklová, whose essay in volume one was a short memoir of dissident activism in communist Czechoslovakia.[58] As Argent writes in this volume, while the assertion of an experientially located feminism such as Šiklová's invites intersubjectivity, it also constitutes an assertion of the agent's authority to interpret the experience of others. Marianne Marchand suggested in volume one that testimonies be incorporated directly into local knowledge, even when they are mutually inconsistent.[59] As products of identified voices, each can be evaluated and included—or not—in individual and cultural repertoires. Both of these positions affirm plurality as a fundamental feminist value, although Argent and Marchand differ in their identification of the limits to claiming experience as a basis for generalization.

Communities as Structures

Most of the discussion so far reflects significant voluntary components in community. Indeed, human communities seem to form spontaneously. I am sure that I am not the only person to have experienced the bonding that comes from sharing intense experiences, especially stressful experiences like freshman year, basic training, childbirth, even group travel. Linguists speak of "language communities" that grow up around such informally bonded units. Families also create language communities, and authors like Nancy and Jessica Mitford import familial linguistic conventions into popular culture through essays and stories that generate language communities among readers.

Most people belong to more than one community. The intersection and especially the nesting of communities offer activists opportunities to apply multiple strategies to effect social change. Many strategies are "retail"—they apply to a small community over which the activist has authority to change "traditional" ways of doing things. This is the quality of nuclear families that persuades me that the modern bourgeois family, founded on mutual affection and assertions of personal privacy, is a primary site for revolutionary transformation.[60] Few formal institutions, including other family forms, display as high a degree of normatively and structurally protected autonomy. Agda Rössel's essay in this volume reports some of her work as Sweden's ambassador to the United Nations, the UN's first female head-of-mission, including a discussion of female genital mutilation (FGM). As investigations by Alice Walker and others have shown, in most cultures where FGM is practiced, the chief enforcers of this custom are not state agents, clerics, or even mothers but rather grandmothers and other female elders in the community.[61] In Muslim societies, brothers and uncles are more likely than fathers to punish transgressions by young women.[62] All family forms, including the bourgeois family,[63] are associated with child and spouse abuse, but the bourgeois family is structurally organized to favor divergent patterns of social reproduction. Helen Cordes and Eric Selbin epitomize the power of love and civil liberties to create a protected space[64] in which they can educate their daughters to resist the standardization imposed in most public schools. The protected space offered by the nuclear family is a major attraction for activists asserting rights of homosexual couples to marry; they wish thereby to claim its privacy to repel unauthorized scrutiny and coerced conformity to standardized definitions of coupling and parenting.

Other communities and institutions are larger, more formally organized, and self-consciously constructed to reproduce authoritative constraints on autonomy. The Mayflower Compact defined relationships among the Puritans sailing in their tiny ship toward the New World, and between them and their financial backers in England, as binding contracts and thus subject to legal interpretation. Historians like Edmund Morgan regard this as the fountainhead of many U.S. institutions from the town meeting to the constitution.[65] Other early Americans—George Washington is an excellent example—also saw their public actions as establishing institutional frameworks for the future, while their successors used documents, precedents, and rituals to shape politics and behavior in their own times.[66]

Documents, precedents, and rituals reduce the flexibility of communities and provide means for elites to standardize and control them. Spike Peterson's dissertation explores the linkage of early state formation with the subjection of women. She emphasizes the written text as a key to embedding gender and class distinctions in social and political practice during the state-building process.[67] The stranglehold of literate elites on cultural traditions is amply illustrated today, both in the dominance of texts as sources of moral and political authority and in the spirited contestations over control of their interpretation by the respective leaders of establishments (power structures) and revolutionary movements.[68] Wolf's remarks about the diverse instrumental domains in which patterns validating hegemonic dominance are repeated include both church and state, along with the economy and, as I noted earlier, the family.

Protection is a basic human right that is critical to community life, particularly in a diverse or multicultural society. As John Stuart Mill observed over and over again, the state is far from the only institution with the capacity to crush dissent and diversity. Indeed, Mill, along with Tocqueville, argues that society is far more likely to demand and enforce standardization.[69] When we look at the state and its history, therefore, we see a mixed picture that includes not only the repression and embedded hierarchy that Spike Peterson found but also authoritative guarantees of human rights through constitutions and legislative constraints that institute regimes of visibility and legibility not only for the state but also for citizens, however narrowly citizenship might be defined. Consequently, institutions are concerns of feminists engaged in building communities.

In this volume, we look at this construction of institutions on several levels. Agda Rössel's memoir of her pathbreaking UN ambassadorship highlights her efforts to bring international law to bear on the human rights violations associated with female genital mutilation. In my chapter, I examine strategies for employing international law to punish and thereby constrain the use of rape as a weapon of war and genocide. Patricia McCabe's essay describes her work with the Legal Advocacy Fund (LAF) of the American Association of University Women. The LAF contributes financial and legal assistance to women suing institutions of higher education for having discriminated against them. All three chapters emphasize the importance of defining rights in law and then embedding them in precedent, not because it is easy, but because it addresses the plight of the individual at the same time that it promises to replace structures of gender discrimination with more egalitarian institutions.

Mary Meyer and Diane Duffy analyze feminist efforts to effect nonviolent social change in two very different national environments. Meyer looks at feminist contributions to peacemaking and reconciliation in Northern Ireland, while Duffy examines the work of five feminist groups dedicated to improving access to health care and guaranteeing equal social entitlements to female citizens of Poland. Meyer's chapter describes a feminist process which she calls transversalism. This involves "rooting and shifting," a process that simultaneously grounds intersubjectivity firmly in the persona of the identified voice and takes a procedural feminist approach to building coalitions committed to nonviolent resolution of Northern Ireland's troubles. The political environment for feminist activists in Northern Ireland is openly hostile, a situation shared by Polish feminists, whose efforts are belittled both by an uncaring national government and by a strongly anti-feminist religious establishment. Polish feminists use the already established normative and institutional frameworks of international bodies like the United Nations and the European Union to put pressure on the Polish government to improve services for women. They also apply power through a technique that Duffy calls "power as if," taking advantage of the national government's lack of interest in meeting the needs of Polish women to move into unfilled niches at the local level. There they create "facts on the ground" in the form of services provided to Polish women who, along with their economically straitened town and village governments, become constituents and advocates of these programs. The simultaneous creation of global and local constituencies for their activities limits the authority of the national government to reduce their reach or close these feminist organizations down. A similar application of "power as if" can be seen in the protests of Chilean women against human rights violations by their government, a story told in the volume one essay by Craig Warkentin and Beth Daly.[70]

Abigail Abrash takes on an ostensibly pro-human-rights U.S. government in her role as chief organizer of Let Freedom Ring (LFR), an ad hoc campaign to mobilize popular support to urge then-President Bill Clinton to press Chinese leader Jiang Zemin to end human rights violations in China and Tibet. An opportunity structure hospitable to this effort opened with the scheduling of a state visit by Jiang to the United States in 1997. Abrash's chapter tests the utility of procedural feminism as a lens for analyzing coalition building. It offers a "worst case" example, not only because human rights organizations are not noted for their feminist proclivities but also because the LFR included anti-feminist activist Gary Bauer as a coalition member. When we asked Abrash to consider whether the LFR could be described as a "feminist approach" to human rights activism, we sent her a copy of Mary Meyer's chapter on Northern Ireland with its transversalist conceptualization of coalitions in which both Protestant and Catholic women submerged their sectarian identities to pursue a common goal. Illustrating limits to our ability to generalize experience across different kinds of cases, Abrash ends her essay by identifying "feminist traits" in the LFR but remains reluctant to call it a feminist approach.

A third level of action to create liberating structures and liberated agents is dealt with in four additional essays examining education and one that applies a feminist lens to practical deficiencies in international relations theory. In her retirement, Marjorie Zap, a long-time feminist activist, is an energetic proponent of improving the lives of impoverished women and girls in rural Mexico. In her brief report on Mujeres en Cambio, Zap tells about a local NGO engaged in small-scale projects to increase educational opportunities for teenage girls in rural villages in the state of Guanajuato. The group includes nationals and foreigners as members. Unlike microcredit organizations such as the Grameen Bank, Mujeres supplies resources to develop human capital rather than investment capital, thereby adding to individual autonomy. Thus, despite its retail reach, Mujeres features an empowerment strategy that is potentially as or more transformative than one that assigns primary agency to the financier and the local organization supervising operations, as microcredit projects do.[71]

Like nuclear families, the effects of Mujeres and the prison programs described in two other essays in this volume are limited by their small scope. In addition, the prison projects are vulnerable to what Beate Gersch identifies as the prisons' virtually absolute power to define basic rules to which all residents of jails and prisons, inmates, guards, and visitors are required to conform. In contrast to most families and to the quasi-parental qualities displayed by the Mujeres board, prisons are less "communities" than totalizing institutions. They rely on discipline and punishment to prevent inmates from escaping both from the premises and from legible and visible acquiescence to the intense standardization that these institutions require. Yet even prisons, all of which are hierarchical and founded on the authoritative application of violence,[72] are not identical. Some favor punishment: their governors use brutal methods to control inmates, even if these methods impede rehabilitation (a kind of escape even if it is incorporated into the formal goals of these institutions). Other officials see their role as administering disciplinary "correction" to assist prisoners to live safely in the present and to prepare them for a future outside prison walls.

These two essays ask whether feminist approaches can be applied to build plurality and community in the framework of prison settings. The account by anti-death-penalty activist Marie Deans describes the epitome of a prison organized around punishment. Deans is pessimistic about the capacity of inmates and activists to "tilt at closed institutions." She recounts the results of her initially hopeful attempt at empowerment as devastating, both for the prisoners seeking greater empathy, self-control, and capacity to trust others, and for herself. Her experience is a case study of how power-over masculinism can destroy community. Strongly reminiscent of Barbara Welling Hall's essay on the Help Fund in volume one,[73] Deans's chapter confronts the limits of feminist approaches to social change in institutions gripped by totalizing structures, their hopeful human embodiments smashed and sequestered to prevent a successful challenge to the "basic propositions regarding the nature of constructed reality" on which totalitarian control depends. Beate Gersch's essay looks at a jail environment that is less restrictive than the prison environment Deans attempted to ameliorate, and speaks with a self-consciously feminist-identified voice that seeks to reduce socially constructed barriers to community among agents occupying very different status positions. Her story is more hopeful, yet she also describes constraints on agency, internal and external, in her self-critical evaluation of the limits of human beings to put their ideals into practice in real-world situations.

Ronnie Lipschutz addresses agency by engaging in what he himself admits is a "rant," fulminating against professors and texts unable to make the inequalities generated in or exacerbated by today's globalizing world comprehensible to privileged undergraduates living in developed countries. Even more troubling is his picture of how modern people in general fail to see structural impediments to human achievement in the contemporary world. Lipschutz describes it as a variation on the old criticism of Woodrow Wilson: that he loved humanity but hated people. Love or hate notwithstanding, Lipschutz is dismayed by the lack of connection in many people's minds between the mutual constitution of social structures and human lives. In his chapter he draws a roadmap toward a different pedagogy of world politics, one that he and I hope to carry further by writing what we are calling an "anti-text." That this is a daunting project is indicated by the range of issues and perspectives he identifies here as crucial to incorporate. Adding to our difficulties is that we are unlikely to find much help from traditional international relations theory, which Karen Walch criticizes in her essay for its short-sighted dependence on radical utilitarian models of egocentrism, which leaves it unable to explain much more than conflict and competition. Walch's is another essay written by someone who does not normally think of her concerns as feminist. Yet even more than Abi Abrash, she finds through a review of her recent research on international food negotiations that what little she knows about feminist theory comes closer to the reality she and her colleague encountered in their fieldwork than any of the "mainstream" theoretical schools in which she had been so rigorously trained as a graduate student to ground her analyses.

Moral and structural limits to agency are addressed by the last two chapters in this volume: Clark Miller's on attempts by idealistic agents to change the world and Robin Teske's on feminist theology. Although differently framed and argued, both essays confirm the necessity of democratically negotiated collective action to achieve constructive social change. Miller draws on science fiction to show the perils to the planet that arise from self-referential activists attempting to impose their own visions of what science should do on the rest of us. Teske's survey of feminist spirituality reemphasizes the necessity of acting together, not merely for instrumental reasons, but also out of friendship and mutuality and in recognition of the connectedness of living things to other living things and to the earth.

Feminist Approaches to Community

In our introduction to volume one, Robin Teske and I outlined a number of goals we had for this project. Among them were to assess the usefulness of feminist approaches to social movements and community as efforts to achieve social justice; to examine movement strategies, assess their contributions to the structure and operation of informal and formal institutions, and to evaluate the portability of experience to activists in other situations; to revisit the subject of interests and thus the vexed question of what constitutes public and private spheres and whether community even exists; and to reconsider the role of political institutions in the achievement of women's rights. In the remainder of this chapter, I offer my assessment of what both volumes have accomplished in this regard.

Social Justice

Social justice is critical for feminists because of the long history of its absence in women's lives. Even in cultures and within social groups that are relatively privileged, women almost always have less power and authority than men have and are forced to operate in environments more constrained by structural and ideological obstacles than men are. In these volumes we have considered social movements themselves as structures that, to achieve social justice, must also embody it. The accuracy of that assumption is reflected most sharply in the contrast between Welling Hall's essay on the Help Fund and Betty Durden's observations about the 1992 ERA campaign in Iowa in volume one,[74] and in the many chapters in both volumes describing egalitarian social movements that achieved some of their stated goals and, on occasion, social goods the organizers didn't even plan for. From this perspective, I believe it is evident that undemocratic social movements beget undemocratic institutions and communities incapable of achieving substantive justice. Linkages between small-scale communities and larger societies are transmission belts creating redundant patterns across multiple domains, in this case, patterns of hierarchy or equality, and discrimination or inclusiveness. Perhaps the most troubling example, in addition to Marie Deans's and Welling Hall's case studies of attempts to effect social change from below, is Haya al-Mughni's volume one description of social movement activism from "the middle," Kuwaiti feminists caught between patriarchal families and an autocratic patriarchal state.[75] There, justice for women threatens fundamental norms and structures that support and reinforce patriarchal domination in both realms. As Haya al-Mughni points out, recent alterations in the position of the regime on the issue of women's rights has created an opportunity structure for liberal and Islamist women to work for social change. However, insofar as these results import religiously justified authoritarian norms and procedures into feminist activism, they cloud prospects for social justice across the entire range of Kuwaiti plurality. Indeed, this check on democratization in the larger society may well have been one of the aims of the amir's decision to open a political space for female activists.[76] At the same time, enlarging access to public space offers opportunity to engage in a politics of presence, a subject to which I shall return at the end of this chapter.

Strategies and Lessons

Patricia Martin may be correct that feminist scholars have become more comfortable discussing their work in their own identified voices, but it still is unusual to combine academic essays and personal accounts by social activists in the same work. We wanted our volumes to be occasions of conversation between activists and theorists and, to the extent that we have tested this proposition in life, there seems to be some validity to it, although not always in the direction we had anticipated. In the spring of 2001, I taught volume one to a class titled "Gender and IR." More than half of my students used the essays just as I envisioned, taking examples from the activists' accounts to evaluate what the more academic essays had to say about activism as a social phenomenon. However, their conclusions highlighted for me two of the greatest drawbacks of taking "lessons" from the past and applying them to new situations.

The first is something we might term seduction by analogies. In a thoughtful analysis of the decisions leading up to the introduction of U.S. air and ground forces to Viet Nam in 1965, Yuen Foong Khong discusses the prominence of three analogies in discussions among policy makers.[77] The one that, in hindsight, proved closest to the actual American experience in Viet Nam was the analogy to Dien Bien Phu, the siege that marked the defeat of the French and led to their departure from the country in 1954. Undersecretary of State George Ball's detailed analysis of the U.S. predicament in light of this analogy was rejected as a source of useful lessons by every other member of President Lyndon Johnson's inner circle—because it was a French example and because the French had lost. More compelling to some was the analogy of Korea which, by the mid-1960s, had been reconstructed as a U.S. victory and, therefore, a useful precedent for what might happen should the United States become engaged in another "limited war" against Communists in Asia. Most compelling to Johnson and to Secretary of State Dean Rusk, however, was the analogy of Munich, a model predicting the inevitability of world war when democracies fail to resist territorial aggrandizement by totalitarian regimes.

Even this brief sketch indicates problems integral to working with analogies. First, no paradigm fits perfectly in a different situation and, therefore, which analogy is chosen and how it is applied depends on each analyst's interpretation. Second, in addition to the story line applied consciously in the new context, there are submerged "memories" and implied lessons that also influence decision makers' expectations about outcomes whether they are aware of them or not. Munich, for example, carried with it no message about the perils of intervention because it is the story of an intervention that never happened. Thus, the only negative lesson of Munich is that failure to intervene can be dangerous.

The imperfect fit of analogies in these essays is evident in the lessons Cheryl Sparks derived from the suffrage movement and disagreement over their applicability to contemporary movement for equal rights.[78] Betty Durden argued that social and technological changes, ranging from the lack of women with time in their lives for more than one activist campaign to the ability of contenders to attract money from afar to influence public opinion next-door, make many of the lessons of the suffrage movement irrelevant to ERA campaigns today. Robin Teske and I have talked about the possible applications of her experience in Iowa to women's rights campaigns in Kuwait, but the adoption of any analogy as a source of strategic guidance requires systematic inquiry and thought and a more open-minded discussion than characterizes most decision making settings. Finding utility in analogies is not impossible, but it is far more difficult than it appears at first blush.

The second drawback, the limits of experience, was touched on earlier. Although experience for feminists is a rich source of data, it also can be a rich source of misunderstanding and conflict. Angie Argent's close reading of Jiřina Šiklová's writings exposes gaps between Šiklová's images of feminism and how others understand and evaluate their own feminist impulses. Much of the conflict in this instance I think comes out of anger. Argent locates some of that anger in Šiklová's criticism of those whom she calls "Western feminists," foreign women who assumed—without evidence—that Communist rhetoric and legislative quotas were morally and experientially equivalent to democracy and human rights for women in Czechoslovakia and elsewhere in Eastern and Central Europe. I hear an additional locus of anger in Šiklová's volume one essay in words such as these: "There were thousands of women who [worked against Communism] . . . under conditions of . . . terror and harassment. Few of their stories are known to the broad public."[79] Despite her disclaimer that "[women] do not seek publicity and glory, but primarily they were and are interested in 'issues,'"[80] the ease with which their male counterparts moved into the leadership of the post-revolutionary community and took control not only of the stories of dissidents that filled foreign imaginations but also of the "historical memory" of the entire period of anti-Communist dissidence surely also rankles. How much of this Czech feminist's anger is due to "Western feminists" and how much to the ambivalence she feels going back to "normal" life with its full complement of "stereotypes and prejudices"[81] is hard to say. Even so, the wrongs that echo in her tone are audible to the reader. Despite Argent's misgivings, I believe that Šiklová's "experience" is available just as Marianne Marchand predicts, in the story and its telling as much as in its "facts."

Activist accounts in volume two also illustrate this peculiar duality of experience. How large, after all, is the proportion of young women who seek or find feminist community in sororities as Karla Scheele did? (Even she retains a bit of ambivalence about how "feminist" her experience actually was.) Helen Cordes and Eric Selbin argue that homeschooling is a choice they made as feminist activists who wanted to avoid the standardizing influences of public education on their children, but they also admit that the same decision is made by parents whose wish is to reduce the diversity of viewpoints represented in their children's educations. How well did Let Freedom Ring construct common ground when, even though it accepted Gary Bauer as a partner, it surrendered to the demands of Amnesty International and agreed to shut out the Coalition for Taiwan Independence? Durden would applaud the first based on her ERA Iowa 1992–experience but probably not the second. An even more complicated lesson from experience comes in Haya al-Mughni's saga of Kuwaiti women activists, among whom the number of liberals is dwarfed by the large influx of Islamist women hoping to use the movement to discipline Kuwaiti society rather than open it to divergent ideas and lifestyles.

Our students also demonstrate that many readers are "cafeteria" analysts, picking and choosing the elements of the stories they encounter to suit their individual purposes. Catherine Tinker's experience offered words to live by to some of Robin Teske's students, who were inspired by the practical value of what she wrote. Tinker's essay presented social action not only as worthy but also within the realm of possibility for someone who has a "normal" life. It was not so much the issue or the venue that formed the greatest source of attraction. Even more than David Meyer's essay on protest movements, Tinker's story of her NGO was full of practical information about how to make your own political opportunity structure and then what to do once you've got it. I am sure that people seeking directions for building communities will find them in several of the essays in this volume, such as Diane Duffy's account of five feminist groups in Poland, Mary Meyer's of feminist activists in Northern Ireland, Marge Zap's of raising money to send teenagers to school, and Beate Gersch's of teaching inmates in Texas jails.

Interests

The notion of gender interests and their categorization by Maxine Molyneux as practical or strategic[82] is at once essentialism and an argument against it. On the one hand, women do have similar interests arising from broadly, if not universally, shared gender commonalities such as motherhood, sisterhood, and the experience of sex discrimination. On the other hand, few such common interests are either predictable or permanent, and many are as likely to breed conflict as community. Marge Zap reveals that while some mothers struggle to give their daughters the opportunity to live better lives, others treat their daughters as free labor and stunt these girls' chances of escape from poverty and oppression. Although sex discrimination can be turned around, as I noted in my conclusion to volume one, by clever dissidents like Jiřina Šiklová and her daughter-in-law, or the mothers of the Plaza del Mayo, this also helps to normalize discrimination after the dictators have been disposed of.

More important than gender interests for feminists is how to cope gracefully with plurality. Anne Runyan's image of the world-traveling feminist offers a strategy anchored in plurality, intersubjectivity, and the identified voice. "Traveling" is a critical concept. It reflects the fluidity of identity and its dependence on social context. Who we are at any time is, at least in part, a function of whom we are with. This is not "identity" as a costume put on or discarded on a whim. Rather, it is a recognition of identity's multiple and reflexive qualities and its dependence on the community context for expression. Most of us belong to communities whose compositions have changed and, as a result, changed us: our family position altered by the birth of a child; our social circle by the introduction of a newcomer; the ability of the members of our department to work together by the hiring of a new chair. The mutual constitution of individual and community, agent and structure, lends clarity and poignance to the brief glimpses of the personae and situations of the subjects and writers of these essays.

From this perspective, all interests are "special," contingent on the location of a unique individual and the composition of her world. This mutual constitution, this interdependence, also ensures that interests so determined are at the same time general, reflecting the needs and desires of the community that arrived at them through empathy and reason. Karen Walch calls such constructions of interests sociocentric. They are produced by the apprehension of a world in which each ego is the center of a network of similarly organized if not similarly endowed other egos. Each owes obligations and claims security and moral identity on the basis of an individually situated yet mutual inclusion in community life. This is how Margaret Hrezo imagines Simone Weil's multiple plane and how Robin Teske imagines love. A similar vision underlies David Meyer's story of the decision by a handful of black students to rely on the organic reality of their community to support and sustain their nonviolent claim to civil rights.[83]

Community is the necessary environment for a politics of presence. In her 1995 book, Anne Phillips regrets the informal quotas that seem to guide the appointment of female and minority tokens to appellate benches in the United States and Canada.[84] Courts, which do not see themselves as representative institutions, are prevented both by the relative paucity of women and by ethical conventions based on masculinist "neutrality" from representing women's interests or devising a feminist approach to judging.[85] Even so, I believe that Phillips is too pessimistic. To Phillips, the ethical core of democratic politics is direct representation and the consequent legitimacy that arises from citizens satisfied that their interests will be pursued by people like themselves as members of legislatures and courts. Another student of courts, Martha Nussbaum, would predict an improvement in representation from the incorporation of any kind of person sensible of her or his interdependence with others. To Nussbaum, the ethical core of representation is "the literary imagination," the capacity of representatives to perceive meaning from another's viewpoint.[86] The essays in this volume variously term that capacity "intersubjectivity," "empathy," and "sociocentrism." In this view, a politics of presence is possible wherever spaces of appearance include persons able to comprehend and accommodate multiple affected interests in accordance with the community's conception of justice.[87]

Constructing communities with these capacities requires a feminist design for living, one whose "redundancies in diverse instrumental domains" reflect plurality and an ethic of mutual respect and care. Robin Teske argues in the essay that concludes this volume that a community's values shape and are shaped by the nature of its religion, its vision of itself as part of the cosmos. Others engaged in this project have shown that the values by which we live our daily lives also shape our social and political institutions. As my friends and I used to say when we were complaining about the power structure, the personal is political. People exist in multiple domains, in communities linked through the human beings located where these domains intersect. Tocqueville thought that the democracy he observed in the early United States was the public face of the democratic families he encountered on his travels.[88] I argue that embracing plurality in any domain offers an avenue for increasing social justice and protecting human rights in other realms.

The State Reconsidered

As the state threatens to wither away to satisfy the demands of thoughtless globalizers, perhaps we can spare a moment of reflection on what we will miss should their wishes be granted and the state disappear. Not every withered state will be equally mourned, of course. When I regret that the state is being hollowed out and decapitalized, I think of the eroding capacity of democratic states to sustain civil society, those vital communities that incorporate spaces within which citizens can participate in making decisions according to their values and their aspirations. No state has achieved its democratic ideals completely but even those that come close are admonished, along with the rest, to leap into the ashbin of history and make way for the global market. This is more than a tragic waste.

As Barbara Stark argued in volume one,[89] the importance of an authoritative guarantor of women's rights cannot be overstated. Not only because of state collapse but, even more, because of most states' lack of effectiveness in providing basic rights guarantees to women, Stark encourages feminist activism as a means of increasing the protective capacity of international law. Agda Rössel's chapter on the United Nations represents the experience of one activist in this regard, and my essay on wartime rape, in addition to the horrors committed during recent "minor" conflicts, charts efforts to construct regimes able to deter future horrors. Yet international law is not enough. Patty McCabe reminds us that we live in local communities—nation-states and smaller units—whose primary role is to settle day-to-day disputes rooted in conflicts over status and rights. Their failure to exercise this authority fairly, visibly, and legibly leaves us all vulnerable to the whims of the powerful.

As a professor of international relations, I frequently discuss with my students Hobbes's vision of the social contract as a parable of the origin of the state as a protector of populations not only from external attack but, even more, in its capacity to protect us from one another. Looking at the genesis of the nation-state we know today, historians of medieval Europe describe a trajectory that diverges from those traced by many contemporary social scientists, finding that it coalesced around leaders with the capacity to provide superior judicial services.[90] To avoid igniting another ceramics-versus-agriculture argument over which technology inaugurated civilization, I hope that we all can agree that both kinds of protection are necessary social technologies for community life.

Religion offers a different kind of support for community in addition to its historic role as guardian of the rules and practices marking one community off from another.[91] René Girard believes that we misunderstand religion by thinking of it primarily as a medium for celebrating a community's great events and mediating personal life transitions. He suggests that religions, which he describes as regimes built around actual or symbolic sacrifice, are the means by which communities without judicial systems attempt to prevent perpetual cycles of vengeance.[92] I find Girard's argument persuasive insofar as it reflects the embeddedness of religion in how human creatures deal with those aspects of life that we call "sacred." To the two primary institutions, religion and law, that Girard identifies as designed precisely for this purpose, I would add science.

Religion and law remain inextricably intertwined as the result of their joint history, even though the law, along with the state, has become progressively secularized. Even so, the idea that "you can't legislate morality" is cherished only by the ignorant: values lie at the heart of all legal systems. Perhaps in consequence, the history that, going back at least to Galileo, has divorced science from religion has resulted in large numbers of scientists being numbered among the ignorant for proclaiming that science is somehow "value-free." Thinking of science solely as a technical enterprise is to detach it from moral authority. Scientists then can proceed without thought or care for the comfort, modesty, and safety of women in labor or for the health of non-insects living in environments subjected to massive applications of DDT; they can experiment on human beings in concentration camps, nuclear test sites, penal and mental institutions; they can contemplate testing the validity of theories about global warming by waiting to see what happens. Part of the impetus driving some contemporary religious revivals is a reaction to such science-as-enterprise, although, sadly, both subject and object attempt to achieve their goals by colonizing the least democratic and therefore most unjust institutions of the state.

The conflict I see is not between "science" and "religion" but between "enterprise" and "community." Enterprise is centered on divisible gains acquired by enterprising individuals, a desire for what economist Jonathan Nitzan calls "differential accumulation"—I have more than you have—in other words, classical power-over.[93] In contrast, community is centered on the indivisible prosperity and security of the whole. Another economist, Thorstein Veblen, called the tension between these two modes of economic organization a conflict between "business," people seeking profits, and "industry," the working out of the scientific and technological legacy of human beings as complex systems designed to create and supply material goods.[94] Feminist approaches to social change and power speak to this tension. They seek to replace "enterprise" and "business" hierarchies dominated by opportunists with "community" and "industry" where the plurality of unique human beings have equal access to the earth's bounties and to reasonable security in their lives. This volume collects our arguments for plurality and feminist community, and offers a report from the field by those who are laboring to make them real.

Notes

1. Jiřina Šiklová, "Women and the Charta 77 Movement in Czechoslovakia," in *Conscious Acts and the Politics of Social Change,* vol. 1 of *Feminist Approaches to Social Movements, Community, and Power,* ed. Robin L. Teske and Mary Ann Tétreault (Columbia: University of South Carolina Press, 2000), 272.

2. The emphasis on tradition as a defining quality of culture should not obscure the fact that tradition is continually (re)invented to meet contemporary needs. For a rather cynical view of this process, see Eric J. Hobsbawm and Terence Ranger, eds., *The Invention of Tradition* (Cambridge: Cambridge University Press, 1992).

3. Relationships between feminism and various strains of postmodernism are explored at some length by Craig Warkentin and Beth Daly in "Claiming Agency: Chilean Women and the Rescripting of Feminist Activism," in *Conscious Acts,* 150–69.

4. Standard examples include non-Euclidian geometries and wave/particle theories of light.

5. The most prominent professional associations of American political scientists, the International Studies Association and the American Political Science Association, are experiencing deep internal divisions and conflicts over these issues. The APSA rebel leader operates sub rosa, calling her/himself Perestroika (the political science equivalent to El Commandante Marcos?) to protect her/his professional future, although senior scholars engaged in the Perestroika dialogue do sign their names to their contributions. However, other than an article in the *New York Times* in the fall of 2000 and another in the *Guardian* in the spring of 2001, little about these struggles has reached public fora. Centered in France, post-autistic economics is enlivening professional discourse in that discipline through its electronic journal

featuring signed articles. Rebels in anthropology and archeology have "gone public" in spectacular and controversial ways. Several have published books examining the connections between dominant theories and dominant ideologies that reveal how the research of leading scholars produced results compatible with their ideologies and politics. Examples include Derek Freeman, *The Fateful Hoaxing of Margaret Mead: A Historical Analysis of Her Samoan Research* (Boulder, Colo.: Westview Press, 1999); Stephen Jay Gould, *The Mismeasure of Man,* rev. and expanded ed. (New York: Norton, 1996); David Hurst Thomas, *Skull Wars: Kennewick Man, Archaeology, and the Battle for Native American Identity* (New York: Basic Books, 2000); and Patrick Tierney, *Darkness in El Dorado: How Scientists and Journalists Devastated the Amazon* (New York: Norton, 2000).

6. Karl Polanyi, *The Great Transformation* (New York: Farrar and Rinehart, 1944).

7. This is a necessary condition for democracy. See, for example, Carol C. Gould, *Rethinking Democracy: Freedom and Social Cooperation in Politics, Economy, and Society* (Cambridge: Cambridge University Press, 1988).

8. Ray C. Gingerich and Bruce C. Busching, "New Approaches to Power in Grassroots Coalition Building: A Case Study of Common Ground," in *Conscious Acts,* 230–45.

9. Anne Phillips, *The Politics of Presence* (Oxford: Clarendon Press, 1995).

10. Kathleen Staudt, *Policy, Politics and Gender: Women Gaining Ground* (West Hartford, Conn.: Kumarian Press, 1998), 30.

11. Patricia Yancey Martin, "Rethinking Feminist Organizations," *Gender and Society* 4, 2 (June 1990): 182–206.

12. Whether one can say definitively that the development of agriculture precedes or follows the development of ceramics technology is one such uncertainty. See Luigi Luca Cavalli-Sforza, *Genes, People, and Languages* (New York: North Point Press, 2000), 96–98.

13. Perry Anderson, *The Origins of Postmodernity* (London: Verso, 1998).

14. For examples, see Anthony Giddens, *The Consequences of Modernity* (Stanford, Calif.: Stanford University Press, 1990); Peter J. Taylor, *Modernities: A Geohistorical Interpretation* (Minneapolis: University of Minnesota Press, 1999).

15. See, for example, the discussion in V. Spike Peterson, "Analytical Advances to Address New Dynamics," in *Rethinking International Political Economy: Emerging Issues, Unfolding Odysseys,* ed. Mary Ann Tétreault, Robert A. Denemark, Kurt Burch, and Kenneth P. Thomas (London: Routledge, forthcoming).

16. This is Deniz Kandiyoti's term for cultural relativism with regard to the acceptance of anti-woman policies advocated by religious social movements.

17. Stanley Cohen, *States of Denial: Knowing about Atrocities and Suffering* (Cambridge, U.K.: Polity Press, 2001), 130.

18. The ability of elites to create alternative worlds for themselves in premodern times is nicely illustrated in John Boswell, *Same-Sex Unions in Premodern Europe* (New York: Villard Books, 1994). Their ability to do it now is visible everywhere. A rare example of an ancient woman in this position is described by Judith Thurman, "The Queen Himself," *New Yorker,* 5 May 2001, 72–77, which looks at the life of Cleopatra—including her inferior capacity to impose her alternative world as compared to the capacity of Marc Antony or Octavian to impose theirs.

19. This last is the message of the final chapter in Polanyi's *The Great Transformation,* and of Ezrahi's *Rubber Bullets: Power and Conscience in Modern Israel* (Berkeley: University of California Press, 1997). What I mean by the distance between a sense of elite entitlement and the democratization of plurality is sharply drawn in David Brooks, "The Organization Kid," *Atlantic,* April 2001, 40–46, 48–54. Brooks decries the achievement culture of today's student body at Princeton University whose members he describes in terms that we would recognize as encapsulating the ethic of authority based on visible and legible performance within a universal system of rules. Brooks argues instead for the "knightly spirit" that animated the "privileged men from their prominent families" who made up the Princeton student body one hundred years ago (50). He is particularly distressed by the loss of "the language of sin and character-building through combat with evil" (54) in the younger generation.

20. Isaiah Berlin, "Two Concepts of Liberty," in *Four Essays on Liberty* (London: Oxford University Press, 1969), 118–72, quote from 127.

21. Mary Ann Tétreault, "Women, Power, and Politics," in *Conscious Acts,* 282.

22. Giddens, *Consequences,* 59.

23. Taylor, *Modernities,* 17.

24. James C. Scott, *Seeing Like a State: How Certain Schemes to Improve the Human Condition Have Failed* (New Haven, Conn.: Yale University Press, 1998).

25. Marshall Berman, *All That Is Solid Melts into Air: The Experience of Modernity* (New York: Penguin, 1988).

26. See, for examples, Carl E. Schorske, *Fin-de-Siècle Vienna: Politics and Culture* (New York: Knopf, 1980) and Scott, *Seeing Like a State.* Also, Jonathan Nitzan, "Mergers, Stagflation, and the Logic of Globalization," in *Rethinking.*

27. Giddens, *Consequences;* Polanyi, *The Great Transformation.*

28. Such expropriation is called "articulation." See, among others, Eric R. Wolf, *Europe and the People without History* (Berkeley: University of California Press, 1982); Barry K. Gills, "Globalization as Global History: Introducing a Dialectical Analysis," in *Rethinking;* and Nazih Ayubi, *Overstating the Arab State* (London: Verso, 1995).

29. Polanyi, *The Great Transformation.*

30. Peterson, "Analytical Advances."

31. On familial images, see, for examples, Jacqueline Stevens, *Reproducing the State* (Princeton, N.J.: Princeton University Press, 1999) and Anthony Smith, *National Identity* (Reno: University of Nevada Press, 1991). On nationalist ideologies, see in addition Benedict Anderson, *Imagined Communities: Reflections on the Origin and Spread of Nationalism,* rev. and extended 2d ed. (London: Verso, 1991). And on coercion, see among others, Anthony Giddens, *The Nation-State and Violence,* vol. 2 of *A Contemporary Critique of Historical Materialism* (Berkeley: University of California Press, 1987). The market relies on the state for coercive services in the form of institutions and laws conferring and protecting property rights.

32. Susan Bordo, *Unbearable Weight: Feminism, Western Culture, and the Body* (Berkeley: University of California Press, 1993); George Lipsitz, *Time Passages: Collective Memory and American Popular Culture* (Minneapolis: University of Minnesota Press, 1990); Michel Foucault, *Discipline and Punish: The Birth of the Prison* (New York: Vintage Books, 1995); and Richard Wightman Fox and T. J. Jackson Lears, *The Culture of Consumption: Critical Essays in American History, 1880–1980* (New York: Pantheon, 1983).

33. Students of nationalism such as Anderson in *Imagined Communities* argue that it is a democratic ideology, but feminist analysts have exposed the limited "fraternity" of nationalism in a number of works. For examples, see Carole Pateman, *The Sexual Contract* (Stanford, Calif.: Stanford University Press, 1988); and Stevens, *Reproducing the State.*

34. See the essays in Marysia Zalewski and Jane Parpart, eds., *The "Man" Question in International Relations* (Boulder, Colo.: Westview Press, 1998); also Catherine MacKinnon, "Feminism, Marxism, Method, and the State: Toward a Feminist Jurisprudence," *Signs* 8, 4 (1983): 635–58; and V. Spike Peterson, "Sexing Political Identities/Nationalism as Heterosexism," in *Women, States, and Nationalism: At Home in the Nation?* ed. Sita Ranchod-Nilsson and Mary Ann Tétreault (New York: Routledge, 2000), 54–80.

35. See, for examples, the path-breaking volume edited by Nira Yuval-Davis and Floya Anthias, *Woman-Nation-State* (London: Macmillan, 1989), and efforts to integrate these feminist analyses and insights into the literature on nationalism, such as Ranchod-Nilsson and Tétreault's *Women, States, and Nationalism.*

36. The honorable ancestor of this term originates with sociologist Louis Coser, who describes "total" institutions as demanding high and intense levels of effort and allegiance. Here I adapt the word to be "totalizing," to incorporate not only notions of intense efforts and allegiance, but also that these efforts are exacted within a top-down, authoritarian system. The logic and ethic of "totalizing" in the context of the state is laid out in appalling detail in studies on the holocaust such as Irving Louis Horowitz's *Taking Lives: Genocide and State Power* (New Brunswick, N.J.: Transaction Books, 1980); and Cohen's *States of Denial.*

37. Wolf, *Europe and the People without History,* 388. How these redundant patterns are modeled on gender is the subject of Gayle Rubin's essay, "The Traffic in Women: Notes on a Political Economy of Sex," in *Toward an Anthropology of Women,* ed. Rayna Reiter (New York: Monthly Review Press, 1975), 157–210.

38. Wolf, *Europe and the People without History,* 387.

39. Among the classical explorations of the tension between hegemonic visions and multiplicity is Henry Adams, *Mont-Saint-Michel and Chartres: A Study of Thirteenth-Century Unity* (New York: Penguin Classics, 1986). This long essay was first published in 1913 after having been distributed privately for several years. Adams saw the high Middle Ages, with its cult of the Virgin, as a hegemonic unity, and the "dynamo" of modernity as symbolic of multiplicity and chaos.

40. Garry Wills writes of this impulse in the context of papal reactions to modernity beginning with Pius IX, "Pio Nono." See *Papal Sin: Structures of Deceit* (New York: Doubleday, 2000). While I have argued that high modernists seek to impose standardization, they do so from a different ethical perspective, radical utilitarian individualism. The papal perspective is rooted in the Roman imperial ethic of hierarchy blended with medieval, also hierarchical, conceptions of order.

41. Charlotte Hooper, "Masculinist Practices and Gender Politics: The Operation of Multiple Masculinities in International Relations," in *The "Man" Question,* 42–46.

42. Paul Brooks, *The House of Life: Rachel Carson at Work* (Boston: Houghton Mifflin, 1972), 293–94, quoted in Mary A. McCay, *Rachel Carson* (New York: Twayne Publishers, 1993), 80.

43. Carol B. Gartner, *Rachel Carson* (New York: Frederick Ungar, 1983), 93. See also John H. Cushman, "After 'Silent Spring,' Industry Put Spin on All It Brewed," *New York Times,* 26 March 2001, A14.

44. Wills, *Papal Sin.*

45. Evelyn Fox Keller, *A Feeling for the Organism: The Life and World of Barbara McClintock* (San Francisco: W. H. Freeman, 1993).

46. Ibid.; also see Keller's *Reflections on Gender and Science* (New Haven, Conn.: Yale University Press, 1996).

47. Sandra Harding, *The Science Question in Feminism* (Ithaca, N.Y.: Cornell University Press, 1986).

48. Clark Miller, e-mail communication with Mary Ann Tétreault, December 2001.

49. Frank J. Sulloway, *Born to Rebel: Birth Order, Family Dynamics, and Creative Lives* (New York: Pantheon Books, 1996).

50. Eva Fogelman, *Conscience and Courage: Rescuers of the Jews during the Holocaust* (New York: Anchor Books, 1994).

51. I thank my sister, Virginia Dafner, for locating these Internet sources on the story of Ignaz Semmelweis to make up for the loss of my copy of his out-of-print biography in a recent move. Mark Taylor, "Ignaz Semmelweis: 'Please Wash Your Hands,'" *Singapore Microbiologist* April–June 1999, found at http://www.np.edu.sg/dept-bio/ssm/news/apr_jun99/ignaz.htm (10 May 2001); also Encyclopaedia Britannica Online, "Semmelweis, Ignaz Philipp," http://search.eb.com/bol/topic?eu=68455&sctn=> (April 2001).

52. Keller, *Feeling for the Organism.*

53. See Robin L. Teske, "Political Space: The Importance of the Inbetween," and Margaret Seyford Hrezo, "Composition on a Multiple Plane: Simone Weil's Answer to the Rule of Necessity," both in *Conscious Acts,* 72–90 and 91–106, respectively. Historian Lynn Hunt developed the concept of liminality in the context of dwellers on the interface between cultural worlds in *Politics, Culture, and Class in the French Revolution* (Berkeley: University of California Press, 1984), chap. 5.

54. Barrie Thorne, *Gender Play: Girls and Boys in School* (New Brunswick, N.J.: Rutgers University Press, 1993).

55. This disjunction, along with the utility of marginality as a source of capacity to facilitate social change is discussed by Hunt in *Politics, Culture, and Class,* chap. 5.

56. Suzanne Fleischman, "Gender, the Personal, and the Voice of Scholarship: A Viewpoint," *Signs* 23, 4 (1998): 975–1016.

57. See, for example, the extended debate on this issue in response to Rita Felski's article, "The Doxa of Difference," *Signs* 23, 1 (1998): 23–40. Responses are from Rosi Braidotti, Drucilla Cornell, and Ien Ang.

58. Šiklová, "Women and the Charta 77 Movement."

59. Marianne H. Marchand, "Some Theoretical 'Musings' about Gender and Resistance," in *Conscious Acts,* 56–72.

60. Mary Ann Tétreault, "Women and Revolution: A Framework for Analysis," in *Women and Revolution in Africa, Asia, and the New World,* ed. Mary Ann Tétreault (Columbia: University of South Carolina Press, 1994), 14–17.

61. See Alice Walker and Pratihba Parmar. *Warrior Marks: Female Genital Mutilation and the Sexual Blinding of Women* (New York: Harcourt Brace, 1993).

62. See Germaine Tillion, *The Republic of Cousins: Women's Oppression in Mediterranean Society,* trans. Quintin Hoare (London: Al-Saqi Books, 1983). For a contemporary example, see Mary Ann Tétreault, *Stories of Democracy: Politics and Society in Contemporary Kuwait* (New York: Columbia University Press, 2000), 114.

63. See, for example, Miriam M. Johnson, *Strong Mothers, Weak Wives: The Search for Gender Equality* (Berkeley: University of California Press, 1988). Historical examples focusing on Western families can be found in John Boswell, *The Kindness of Strangers: The Abandonment of Children in Western Europe from Late Antiquity to the Renaissance* (New York: Vintage, 1988); and Philippe Ariès, *Centuries of Childhood: A Social History of Family Life,* trans. Robert Baldick (New York: Vintage, 1962).

64. The concept of protected space is developed in Mary Ann Tétreault, "Civil Society in Kuwait: Protected Spaces and Women's Rights," *Middle East Journal* 47, 2 (Spring 1993): 275–91.

65. Edmund S. Morgan, "America's First Great Man," *New York Review of Books,* 12 June 1997, 42–44.

66. Garry Wills has explored this at some length in such works as *Inventing America: Jefferson's Declaration of Independence* (Garden City, N.Y.: Doubleday, 1978); *Cincinnatus: George Washington and the Enlightenment* (Garden City, N.Y.: Doubleday, 1984); *Lincoln at Gettysburg: The Words That Remade America* (New York: Simon and Schuster, 1992).

67. V. Spike Peterson, "An Archaeology of Domination: Historicizing Gender and Class in Early Western State Formation" (Ph.D. diss., American University, 1988).

68. See, for example, Michael Walzer, *The Revolution of the Saints: A Study in the Origins of Radical Politics* (Cambridge: Harvard University Press, 1965); Ellis Goldberg, "Smashing Idols and the State: The Protestant Ethic and Egyptian Sunni Radicalism," in *Comparing Muslim Societies: Knowledge and the State in a World Civilization,* ed. Juan R. I. Cole (Ann Arbor: University of Michigan Press, 1992), 195–236.

69. But from different vantage points. In the fourth chapter of *On Liberty,* Mill argues from a position of radical utilitarian individualism that society is composed of agents ranging from nosy neighbors to legislators and policemen who should refrain from interdicting anything anyone might do that does not in the process directly injure others. Tocqueville rather sees society as structures and observes that American society is boring because democracy as a system commodifies every aspect of life. "When all the members of a community are independent of or indifferent to each other, the co-operation of each of them can be obtained only by paying for it. . . . The [resulting] love of wealth . . . gives to all their passions a sort of family likeness and soon renders the survey of them exceedingly wearisome." Alexis de Tocqueville, *Democracy in America,* The Henry Reeve Edition (New York: Vintage, 1990), 2:228–29. Thus what for Mill is the enabling condition of individual freedom is to Tocqueville a set of Hobbesian constraints that produce uniformity through a process that the IMF used to call "convergence."

70. Warkentin and Daly, "Claiming Agency."

71. The controlling aspects of micro-credit schemes are persuasively identified and analyzed in Josephine Lairap-Fonderson, "The Disciplinary Power of Micro Credit: Examples from Kenya and Cameroon," in *Rethinking Empowerment: Gender and Development in a Global/Local World,* ed. Jane L. Parpart, Shirin M. Rai, and Kathleen A. Staudt (London: Routledge, forthcoming).

72. The deep connection of formal justice systems to rituals of violence is analyzed by René Girard in *Violence and the Sacred,* trans. Patrick Gregory (Baltimore, Md.: Johns Hopkins University Press, 1977).

73. Barbara Welling Hall, "Power and Powerlessness in the Help Fund: Women, Russia, and the Spirit of Totalitarianism," in *Conscious Acts,* 246–64.

74. Ibid.; and Betty Durden with Robin L. Teske and Mary Ann Tétreault, "A Conversation with Betty Durden," in *Conscious Acts,* 209–18.

75. Haya al-Mughni, "Women's Movements and the Autonomy of Civil Society in Kuwait," in *Conscious Acts,* 170–87.

76. I have made this argument in two recent articles, "Women's Rights in Kuwait: Bringing in the Last Bedouins?" *Current History* (January 2000): 27–32; and "A State of Two Minds: State Cultures, Women, and Politics in Kuwait," *International Journal of Middle East Studies* 33, 2 (May 2001): 203–20.

77. Yuen Foong Khong, *Analogies at War* (Princeton, N.J.: Princeton University Press, 1992).

78. Cheryl Logan Sparks, "How Grandmother Won the War: Strategic and Organizational Lessons of the Struggle for Suffrage," in *Conscious Acts,* 188–208.

79. Šiklová, "Women and the Charta 77 Movement," 271.

80. Ibid., 269.

81. Ibid., 272.

82. Maxine Molyneux, "Mobilization without Emancipation? Women's Interests, The State, and Revolution in Nicaragua," *Feminist Studies* 11, 2 (1985): 227–54.

83. Hrezo, "Composition on a Multiple Plane"; Robin L. Teske, "The Butterfly Effect"; David S. Meyer, "Social Movements: Creating Communities of Change"; all in *Conscious Acts.*

84. Phillips, *The Politics of Presence,* 185.

85. Efforts to shift the ideology of jurisprudence from masculinism toward gender egalitarianism are outlined in Caroline A. Forell and Donna M. Matthews, *A Law of Her Own: The Reasonable Woman as a Measure of Man* (New York: New York University Press, 2000).

86. Martha C. Nussbaum, *Poetic Justice: The Literary Imagination and Public Life* (Boston: Beacon Press, 1995).

87. See also Martha C. Nussbaum, "Kant and Stoic Cosmopolitanism," *Journal of Political Philosophy* 5, 1 (1977): 1–25. This is not an argument for virtual representation—see a detailed examination of these issues in Lani Guinier, "No Two Seats: The Elusive Quest for Political Equality," in *The Tyranny of the Majority: Fundamental Fairness in Representative Democracy* (New York: Free Press, 1994), 71–118.

88. Tocqueville, *Democracy in America,* vol. 2, chap. 8.

89. Barbara Stark, "International Human Rights Law, Feminist Jurisprudence, and Nietzsche's 'Eternal Return': Turning the Wheel," *Conscious Acts,* 124–42.

90. Here the history of European state-making as told by sociologists like Charles Tilly, whose ideas are nicely summed up in his article "War Making and State Making as Organized Crime," in *Bringing the State Back In,* ed. Peter B. Evans, Dietrich Reuschemeyer, and Theda Skoçpol (New York: Cambridge University Press, 1985), 169–91, should be compared to that same history—which begins at an earlier point in this reading—as told by medievalists like Joseph Strayer, *On the Medieval Origins of the Modern State* (Princeton, N.J.: Princeton University Press, 1970).

91. I discuss this in more detail in "Contending Fundamentalisms: Religious Revivalism and the Modern World," in *The International Political Economy of Religious Revivalism,* ed. Mary Ann Tétreault and Robert A. Denemark (Boulder, Colo.: Lynne Rienner, forthcoming).

92. Girard, *Violence and the Sacred.*

93. Nitzan, "Mergers, Stagflation, and the Logic of Globalization."

94. Thorstein Veblen, *Absentee Ownership: Business Enterprise in Recent Times: The Case of America* (New Brunswick, N.J.: Transaction Publishers, 1997).

Part One

Family Quarrels

Chapter 1

Post-Communism and "Women's Experience"?

Angela Argent

Almost ten years ago, in a now-famous exchange between two writers, the reply from Slavenka Drakulić, a writer from Zagreb, to the request by an American writer, Nanette Funk, read: "We definitely don't have answers for you. A Critical Theory approach? Maybe in ten years. In the meantime why don't you try asking something else?"[1] The reply, smacking of frustration, stated that the questions to which Drakulić was responding were "cold, artificial, slippery, not touching my reality." And the justification for her refusal read: "But one can hardly blame them. It is not the knowledge about communism that they lack—I am quite sure that they know all about it—it's the experience of living under such conditions."[2]

Funk's request to Drakulić had been for "an analysis about women and democracy, the public sphere, civil society, modernization etc. A kind of Critical Theory approach." For Drakulić, the "innocence" of Funk's questions "trapped" her "like a white mouse in an experimental laboratory."[3] Drakulić's reply was not directed toward Funk alone, but to an unknown plural category, "they." Funk, "hurt, outraged, and angry" as the result of Drakulić's rebuff, later offered her own interpretation of the "risks, tensions, and difficulties inherent in discourse between Eastern and Western women" in the very collection that had first prompted the troublesome questions.[4]

Not surprisingly, since the revolutions of 1989 there have been remarkably few theoretical attempts to bridge the "abyss" between the new feminisms emerging after the collapse of Communist Party rule and other feminisms. Frequently, as the previous instance evidences, arguments founded on claims to discrepant experience have become the basis of consternation, distrust, and mutual recrimination. Ignoring both the geographic and semantic shakiness of the terms, the binary categories "East" and "West" have continued to be reinscribed as if they meant something still.[5] Claims to divergent experience of "Eastern-ness" or "Western-ness" have been regarded as so self-evident that no one has noticed that the term "experience" itself is in need of interpretation. So far, the question of how to think through discrepant experiences has been fastidiously avoided.

At the heart of newly articulated critiques of feminist discourse emerging from writers and intellectuals in the post-Communist states of Central, Eastern, and Southern Europe, is the desire to explain that the experience of women who survived Communism is so fundamentally different from other women's experience that inorganic, eclectic, or imported feminisms are at best irrelevant and at worst invalidate the significance of discrepant experience.

Separate and often unrelated conversations are taking place among feminists in English-speaking countries and in other European contexts. They have attempted to make sense of the transition to post-Communism, to analyze the effect of the transition on women, and to predict the future(s) of feminism(s) in this region. Many writers have lamented the Central and Eastern European "allergy to feminism," first observed by Barbara Einhorn in Prague in 1991.[6] The experience of Western women's precarious existence in market economies is highlighted in order to implore Central European women not to abandon entirely the dubious "equality" engendered by state socialism.

My efforts to comprehend the series of antagonistic debates, contested on the basis of "experience" and premised upon dubiously constructed notions of "Eastern-ness" and "Western-ness," have been discomforting, and were all the more so when I lived in Prague in 1998. Not only does writing this chapter involve representing a dialogue about which I don't and can't know the full history of exchanges, but it means locating myself somewhere in relation to the debates I discuss. In Prague, regarded as unequivocally "Western" by Czech friends, I was simultaneously afflicted with the unsought sorority of educated Americans who assumed that I must conceive of the communication problem in precisely the same manner as they did, if for no other reason than that I spoke English with such ease! Though I recognize the irreducible advantage conferred by the mere facts of being white, speaking English, and having grown up on an affluent and democratic island called Australia, on the map neither Melbourne nor Sydney are Western cities by any stretch of the imagination.

This chapter begins by considering the changing narrative of experience produced throughout the 1990s by a prominent contemporary female Czech sociologist, Dr. Jiřina Šiklová, who is well-known in Prague today as "the grandmother of Czech feminism."[7] In thinking through the implications of the uses to which Šiklová puts experience, I have needed to consider my own relationship to feminism in ways that I previously had not. As part of the generation for whom feminist consciousness was inherited or observed rather than raised,[8] I regard feminism as having been the fundamentally transformative movement that made possible many life choices. I am too young to remember the 1970s invocations of feminism that Šiklová writes about. Hence, I bring a set of theoretical tools that are different from Šiklová's to the discussion. Interpreting "experience" is my attempt to do what Drakulić suggested that Western feminists should do when she commanded Funk to "try asking something else."

Rather than downplaying the significance of dissimilar experience or differentiated subjectivity in the lives of dissimilar women, in this chapter I argue that it is necessary to think through claims to divergent experience and to draw into question the meanings given to experience. From the outset, I want to make it clear that I am not in any sense attempting to seek out harmonious compromise or negotiated consensus, a better or less exclusionary feminism. I regard the incommensurability of difference between dissimilar women as implying that "we would gain more from acknowledging and confronting the stubborn solidity of 'communication barriers' than from rushing to break them down in the name of idealized unity."[9] I borrow from a broad range of feminist perspectives which insist that it remains imperative to locate, contextualize, situate, historicize and problematize every claim to experience on the basis that "there is small advantage in uncritical cultural descriptions, or an unreflective politics of experience."[10] Definitions which imply that feminism is in no sense a "natural" excretion of socially constructed experience, but rather "a controversial political interpretation and struggle" are employed.[11] If experience were to be regarded as merely an interpretation of lived reality rather than as literal fact, the word might begin to possess meaning. I intend to shift the focus of this particular cluster of histories from "one bent on naturalizing 'experience,'" to one that regards it as a category in need of analysis.[12]

Although several Czech feminist intellectuals have had important things to say on the question of what "experience" means in the Czech context, this chapter concentrates primarily on Šiklová's writing because she has concerned herself with the question unrelentingly since the early 1990s. I regard Šiklová as a significant figure in the contemporary Prague landscape because she has helped, as have other women and at least one man, to create a range of spaces, both academic and mainstream, for dialogue about gender relations and the position of women in her country. In addition to her contributions to Czech scholarly journals, Šiklová has engaged in wide-ranging discussions, introduced via *Playboy*, popular daily and weekly newspapers, and television debates that have cemented her name in the minds of general readers and viewers. Well-known and respected in her own country as a principal contact for an illegal literature distribution network during state socialism, as a banned and imprisoned dissident intellectual, as a Charter 77 signatory, and as a self-proclaimed "one-woman broadcasting station" in November 1989,[13] Šiklová remains an influential voice in the Czech Republic today. In the Czech as well as the international context, Šiklová's words have come to possess enormous authority; her ideas are endlessly repeated and reinscribed, and sometimes interdict and marginalize younger and less well-known feminist voices.

Šiklová's changing approaches to feminism and to the importance of experience to feminism are insightful precisely because, as she freely admits, prior to 1989, although she had "written under assumed names about gender problems for many years, [she] did not know anything about modern feminism, or gender, or women's studies."[14] Because of the high profile of the Foundation for Gender Studies, founded by Šiklová in 1991, and perhaps because of her association with several Western-funded feminist initiatives, Šiklová also has become the most frequently translated and esteemed "Czech Feminist" in popular Western imagination. Šiklová has therefore encountered more than her fair share of the fundamental difficulties faced by Czech feminists who have been required to provide explanations "on the run" from the early 1990s onwards, in two languages, for two entirely different audiences. As Czech philosopher and sociologist Hana Havelková explains it: "So far my feminist writing has had two faces: at home I was trying to explain the usefulness of feminist thinking. To western colleagues I was explaining why some of their concepts cannot be automatically accepted without critical confrontation with our very real differences. Today I have this (later) phase more or less behind me, and I'm not so sure whether the so-called 'specifics' are so fundamental."[15]

Discrepant Experience

In recalling the Czech experience of having survived state socialism and what that survival experience would mean for the future, Šiklová conveys a complex range of emotions towards feminism. On one hand, from the early 1990s, Šiklová's writing on the subject of the dialogues between "Western feminists" and "Czech women" have chronicled the sustained existence of a broad range of feelings in relation to the confrontation that has occurred on the "battlefield" of East-West exchanges, highlighting the "tedium of tiresome mutual misunderstandings"[16] and "blame."[17] At that time, Šiklová produced a series of narratives that she called narratives of "emotional resistance,"[18] produced in opposition to what she referred to categorically as "the proclamations of Western feminists."[19] Similarly, English-language essays published in 1998, entitled "Why We Resist Western-Style Feminism" and "Why Western Feminism Isn't Working in the Czech Republic," responded in a very direct sense to questions she perceives as "Western questions" in her country. In a Czech-language essay published in 1999, Šiklová stated, "all those feminisms . . . that consider or understand themselves only as a different ideology for the struggle for the rights of women, are more or less repugnant to me."[20]

In contrast, the best of Šiklová's most recent Czech-language essays sidestep what she terms "the proclamations of Western feminists" to locate feminism among the set of ideas that belong to the twentieth and twenty-first centuries on the basis that, in a global world order, "the difference in power and the economic standing of woman and man is one of the most noticeable differences that still exist in the world."[21] In these most recent essays, Šiklová concedes that feminism "threw the gauntlet at Eurocentrism," and courageously "addressed the current interpretation of the human world from a different perspective."[22] While more receptive to the potential uses of some aspects of eclectic feminisms within the Czech context, here, as in earlier writings, Šiklová argues in favor of the primary significance of experience over other forms of knowledge. In an interview with the editors of a recently founded Czech lesbian journal, *Incognito,* Šiklová's advice is, "Build it on personal experience, because general theory you read today and forget tomorrow. With personal experience you best get to know the depths of a human being."[23]

Experience operates in Šiklová's usage as direct, observed knowledge derived personally from contact with facts or events, a meaning that grants central importance to immediacy or proximity, to having lived, rather than vicariously known, the past. Experience is also the term Šiklová ascribes to the skill or knowledge derived in this way. Experience is inscribed as a verb to suggest an active personal role in observing and sharing in the event that was state socialism. Experience is also summoned to suggest the process of having been affected by aspects of the past. Disregarding entirely epistemological debates about whether all knowledge can be ultimately empirical, that is, based on experience, Šiklová employs experience as not only a cause of, but also as a justification for, the beliefs she has about the world. Experience is summoned to lend support to, and to justify, the beliefs it gives rise to. Within this logic, difference is born of experience itself.

"In Eastern and Central Europe, women have experience with totalitarian systems, and they know that the lone fact of the entry of women into production processes does not fundamentally change women, or free them. . . . Women in this part of the world are not under the impression that being part of the working process will change their position in society,"[24] argues Šiklová. Work denied women the "opportunity for self-realisation and self-determination."[25] "Man for women in post-communist countries was not an omnipotent boss, but only a partner working at the next machine or writing desk. Above him and her the omnipotent Communist Party was making all the decisions for them. . . ." Given such a history, Šiklová argues that, "in contrast to the concepts of American and West European feminism, Eastern European streams are not so leftist, and they don't want to be part of political power and man is not their enemy."[26]

In Šiklová's opinion, "Women in the West are more sensitive and better informed about their rights than women in our country." At the same time, however, "the questions that foreign feminists are asking our women are, from our perspective, very complex, almost incomprehensible."[27] People in the Czech Republic are affected by "low self-esteem caused by their upbringing in the provincial atmosphere of our country."[28] Šiklová laments the reality that "we (Czechs) view ourselves as naive and small-minded which is obviously not beneficial to our mutual understanding."[29] In spite of these admissions, Šiklová insists that the role of women remains "really very authoritative." In the 1990s as in 1975, she argues that "the modern era brings men's crises not women's, woman retained the majority of the social roles but men lost them," and that gender studies today "should also concern itself with this."[30]

On behalf of the nation of women whose sentiments she claimed to represent to Western audiences, the rejection of feminism, Šiklová insisted, should be understood as a "reaction to our own recent past as well as to the indoctrination we were subjected to for decades."[31] "Extreme feminism" was experienced negatively during state socialism,[32] and hence words such as "emancipation," "women's liberation" and "feminism" have a "pejorative meaning for many Czech women, who use them nearly as slander."[33] Šiklová argued that the vocabulary of feminism has lost meaning, become depleted, or exhausted in the Czech context, even before it had taken hold.[34]

Unaware that none of the words to which she referred possessed the comfortable certainty that they once did anywhere, the "Western reader" is reminded frequently that "meanings and terms are encumbered by personal experience and history."[35] Šiklová argued that an experiential "gap in understanding"[36] plays itself out in a plethora of ways, that "you and we from the former communist countries react to different experiences, and our knowledge of each other is distorted," that the gap in experience remains "literally an abyss."[37]

In Šiklová's usage, "we, the people from post-communist countries" from the early 1990s and "us," "those women who experienced and survived socialism,"[38] are contrasted with "you from the West."[39] What was purportedly shared by post-Communist women was "various types of emotional experiences" which differed from those of Western women.[40]

The emotional divide seemed so vast that Šiklová declared the existence of a "two female world,"[41] and asked, "Where is the frontier between Western and Eastern Europe and the rest of the world—from a woman's point of view?"[42] Šiklová's reading of Western feminism paradoxically oscillated between regarding it as having little to offer more "experienced" Czech women, and readings that criticized feminism for scaremongering. Feminism was inscribed as the ideology of "someone who has previously been exploited and oppressed, [and who on this basis] is not necessarily the best leader of society."[43] In rejecting Western feminism Šiklová insisted that

> those of us from the post-communist states have had bad experience with the introduction of a foreign ideology and political education. My personal opinion is that our women possess perhaps a more realistic experience with emancipation than Western women. Consequently they have no need to talk so much about their emancipation. Nor do they constantly need to assert themselves. The "battles" of Western feminists and their sexist jargon sometimes seems ridiculous to them. But quite often they are not aware of their own emancipation and their specific feminism. They do not react to it ideologically and politically. Perhaps I could use an analogy by way of explanation: adolescents need to proclaim their independence, while adults who already know their own worth, no longer have such a need.[44]

"Experience" was used to validate incongruous representations of "adolescent" and, simultaneously, "ferocious, dogmatic feminists from the West, (who) are merely trying to instigate another totalitarian regime."[45] Many caricatures played on the image of "Western-style militant feminists"[46] during the early 1990s. Some were "dangerous;"[47] some expressed "hatred" or represented "ideological manifestations" (usually Marxist ones[48]); some suffered from "delusions about socialism"[49] and were "captives of their own ideology."[50] Others were burdened by their encyclopedic knowledge.[51] In contrast, another pervasive stereotype emerged in which *all* Czech women are strong on a personal level, having gained economic self-sufficiency and relatively high self-esteem during state socialism as a result of their dominant position in their families. Czech society was imagined to be "prevalently matriarchal," and according to this interpretation it was frequently argued that "women's role is in fact undisputable."[52] Images of undifferentiated strong women often served to rebut Western allegations that East Central European society was masculinist or sexist.

In service to the claim to the authority of experience, Šiklová relativized, simplified, and compressed history for the benefit of her English-language readers in order to argue that "over the past two centuries, Czech men and women had more common interests than their Western counterparts."[53] A chronology of "relative cohesion and agreement" asserts that women have remained "men's allies in their joint struggle(s)" since the time of bitter oppression by the Hapsburg Monarchy. During the Czech National Revival, resistance to German occupation, and then to state socialism, "men and women united for a higher purpose." In every epoch women and men remained "allies against the power that manipulated them."[54]

The imagined need for a seamless homogeneity of experience led Šiklová occasionally to claim that "no one in this country is interested in feminism and almost no Czech woman describes themselves [sic] as a feminist."[55] That "both men and women in the region have rejected the language and practices of feminist ideology," and "many people feel the need to denounce feminism as something obnoxious or proudly declare how they disagree with it, even though they don't really know anything about it," were paraded as much more than personal opinions.[56]

Quite reasonably, Šiklová asked "Western feminists" to "please recognize (that) our rejection of many of the ideas supported by feminism is primarily a reaction to our own past, as well as the indoctrination we were subjected to for decades."[57] More problematically, she asked that the "our" of "our past" should justify and legitimate homogeneous and undifferentiated visions of the future.

Protecting Experience

There is a wealth of writing by Czech writers in addition to Šiklová that has attempted to examine critically the desire to protect the authenticity of experience against invading Western feminism. For example, Czech science-fiction writer Eva Hauser self-consciously and humorously parodies the way in which Czech women are often constructed as "wise and sensible," historically "skeptical," and "mistrustful of all ideologies."[58] Czech sociologist Hana Havelková offers the explanation that a "general diagnosis" has been produced by Czech women who, "encouraged by the interest shown by Western countries, and discouraged by the lack of it at home . . . articulate their attempts at a generalization of the experience of Czechoslovak women for their Western colleagues."[59]

Šiklová says of the evolution of her own thoughts about feminism in Czech language essays: "After a few years I understood that there are many feminisms, that it is not a dogmatic teaching, and usually feminists are not as militant as those who were among the first to come to our country, and most are not trying to create some new manual to ease the interpretation of the past, present or future or to provide recipes for all the ills of this world."[60] The most remarkable aspect of Šiklová's more recent writing for Czech audiences is the way in which she is self-reflective about the fundamental difficulties of being that person who at once fell into the position of entering into "their dialogue," that is, of speaking on behalf of Czech attitudes towards feminism in "the West," at the same time as introducing a discussion of feminism at home:

> My first articles and lectures in the West were polemical explanations of why in the post-communist states feminism is not catching on, why it's not known, why it fails to produce enthusiasm in a generation of women who lived through and survived socialism. I needed to orient myself very quickly on this theme, and very often from randomly selected books and journal articles, I generalized about feminism as a whole, I simplified it, and with these simplified versions I polemicized. I tried to understand feminism, to put it into words and to reinterpret it for me and for us, sometimes badly, sometimes correctly. At the same time I developed some kind of schizophrenia in me. When I was in the West, the self-assuredness of the opinions of many feminists really irritated me, all of them immediately had a "recipe and explanation," like our education, which included historical and dialectic materialism. When I returned, I noticed the reduction of feminist ideas in our country to arguments and debates about who is going to wash the dishes or take the children to school, so I was really irritated about that as well.[61]

These explanations for the making of experience reiterate in important ways some significant aspects of a broader critique of Western feminisms. Slovenian philosopher and sociologist Renata Salecl argues that there is a special kind of prejudice at work in the attitude of Western intellectuals in talking to their "Eastern" colleagues. Western writers condemn post-Communist writers to a "performance, a kind of staged behaviour in which people have to act in a certain way." Salecl argues that when Western feminists speak about feminism they can discuss abstract issues such as "women in film noir" or "the notion of the phallus in feminist theory." However, "someone coming from Eastern Europe must speak about the situation of women in her own country because of the 'horrors' going on there."[62] Salecl's criticism reiterates criticisms made by non-Western feminists such as Trinh T. Minh-ha who also observed that feminists have in the past required "The Third World Woman" to "paint herself thick with authenticity":

> Now, i am not only given permission to open up and talk, i am also encouraged to express my difference. My audience expects and demands it; otherwise people would feel as if they had been cheated. . . . We came to listen to that voice of difference likely to bring us *what we can't have* and to divert us from the monotony of sameness. . . .
>
> We no longer wish to erase your difference. We demand, on the contrary, that you remember and assert it. At least, to a certain extent. . . .[63]

Poststructuralist feminists have similarly drawn attention to the reality that Western women "are not gifted in the art of situated knowledges," and that the more centered one's experiences become, the more one's location acquires the greatest abstraction.[64] Havelková's observations on this theme mirror their claims. She suggests that while "women from post-communist countries try to contextualise their theoretical views, to explain, to translate. . . . Women from the West never feel the need to on the basis that they have grown up and lived in contexts which don't require them to contextualise for the purposes of dialogue."[65] Havelková's critique, rather than Šiklová's, makes it clear that the precondition for the emergence of feminist conversations "against this flight into universalistic abstraction,"[66] must be based on situated, located, and contextualized engagements.

The Problem of Oppositionally Constructed Experience

Šiklová's claims to irreducible and incommensurate experience become easier to understand in light of the observations contained in the previous section. Unquestionably, the "Western advice" to which Šiklová claims to have responded is in need of critique, as is Western women's poor record in recognizing that when they speak, they do so from somewhere particular, somewhere "situated." But can undifferentiated "experience" hold up as the sole grounds for its rejection? Specifically, can it do so when oppositionally constructed claims to experience serve to create a reduced, and often bipolar set of positions constructed or evolved through the course of debate?[67]

The first effect of a binary and oppositionally constructed "authority of experience" is that it distorts, reduces, homogenizes, and essentializes all Czech women's experience. Serious interpretive damage is done when the complex and fundamentally different experiences of dissimilar women under state socialism are generalized. This kind of convenient packaging of the past glosses over the ways in which state socialism was experienced differently by different women. There were always lesbian women, Romany women, women of different ethnic origins, socio-economically advantaged and disadvantaged women, and dissimilar women themselves experienced things differently at different times. As Polish-American writer Eva Karpinski argues, there were divisions and inequalities among women, some of whom were more privileged than others.[68] By failing to acknowledge the reality of multiple differences, Šiklová's writing trivializes, distorts, and misreads the history of women in the Czech Republic.

Ironically, Šiklová's insistence on the incommensurability of Czech women's experience means that she at times missed the opportunity to redeploy existing critiques of feminism which would otherwise add weight to her argument. For example, when Šiklová argued in the early 1990s that "sisterhood is nice but . . . sisterhood among Cinderellas and stepsisters is difficult," she overlooked the significance of the theoretical challenges made by black, postcolonial, non-Western, and Third World feminists. Šiklová stated categorically that "the slogans of 'black feminism' cannot be utilized under our conditions,"[69] and failed to acknowledge that it was these critiques that made it implausible to pretend that any totalizing feminist discourse might be adequate for the task of articulating the dissimilar situations or lived realities of dissimilar women. The misrecognition and underestimation of these critiques are made on the false understanding that "in the West, feminism is promoted by minorities, primarily racially different ones."[70] Quite clearly, recognizing the significance of challenges made to feminist theory by nonwhite/non-Western feminists is the first step in the important process of antiracist feminism. Moreover, as Chandra Mohanty and Gayatri Chakravorty Spivak have argued, non-Western feminisms have made redundant the ethnocentric habit of "global feminism" and the unproblematized "solidarity" of dissimilar women. Rather than rejecting these important critiques, Šiklová could have used them to support her quite valid but unnecessarily dismissive claim.

Šiklová's "resistance" also led her to dismiss as irrelevant what she regarded as invading feminism from the West, and also to deliberately misrecognize Western feminism and hold it up for ridicule in her own country. She combined reasonable anti-imperialist arguments, which assert that feminism is "a silly Western import which we don't need," "building blocks from someone else's Legoland," a "luxury for which we have neither time nor the right conditions to think about," with an insistence that Western feminism is premised upon "insubstantial . . . silken worries."[71] "I'd be happy to take on your problems and Rothschild's money,"[72] she insisted.

While there is no doubt truth to Šiklová's claim that feminism in the Czech Republic was inhibited in the early 1990s by a relatively good economic situation and a low level of unemployment, and that the rights for which Western women are fighting, including divorce, abortion, and sexual freedom, are taken for granted there, it is not in any sense true that the "worries" of all or any Western women are by any means insubstantial or "silken." The existence of very real differences among dissimilar women who live in "the West," and the existence of very real systematic discrimination experienced by all women everywhere, was lost in Šiklová's homogenizing treatment. Reiterating the views of émigré Czech/Canadian writer Josef Škvorecký and the media misrepresentation of feminism she elsewhere castigates, Šiklová demeaned the "excesses and discussions at American universities about politically correct statements and affirmative action," and the other "stupid stuff . . . such as, for example, the trial with boxer Tyson in the USA." Rape and sexual assault were regarded as the prerogative of the Western imagination alone. The reality of, the pervasiveness of, and the damage caused to women by these crimes in all societies is trivialized. Šiklová's argument that "many Czech women . . . have already overcome the problems Western feminist programs are dealing with,"[73] was both patronizing and impossible in the sense that the problems of dissimilar women are never the same problems.

A good example of the reification that typifies Šiklová's argument is provided in her dismissal of the "Western" presumption that women benefit from their engagement in the public sphere and in paid employment. According to Šiklová, the experience of women's employment under state socialism did not raise women's self-confidence or promote equality, but rather negatively affected women's expectations and alerted them to the impossibility of managing incompatible home and workplace roles.[74] This interpretation is then used to imply that women in the West place "too much emphasis on work," "overestimate the significance of employment for emancipation," "devalue the meaning of home and domesticity," and risk a "loss of individuality" through choosing to become politically involved.[75]

That which Šiklová perceived as Western women's misrecognition of socialism is and will continue to be the subject of intense and productive conversations and negotiations between women. Less positive was Šiklová's relativistic negation of the possibility that in other contexts, hard-won battles for political and economic participation have achieved significant freedom from economic and emotional exploitation for a substantial number of women, as well as previously unknown freedom and life choices for women of my generation and younger generations still. While Šiklová's narratives offered valid insights into the ways in which public life and politics have discrepant meanings depending on context, she defended her legitimate right to "experience" by deliberately invalidating "other" women's experiences and reality.

The Difference Problem

Atvar Brah argues that "we would be in a better position to address the need for respect for cultural difference, and to circumvent cultural relativism, without recourse to essentialism if cultures were to be conceived less in terms of reified artefacts and rather more as processes."[76] Yet, so broadly entrenched is the acceptance of the binary and monolithic categories "East" and "West" that I think few participants in this particular feminist exchange, including Šiklová, have bothered to observe "how obsolete are the old categories, the tight separations and the comfortable autonomies."[77] It seems to me that the endless naming of "the other" as "other" is probably not conducive to understanding or dialogue.

As Brah and Edward Said illustrate, assertions of difference have become important precisely at the moment of globalization, which leads to a homogenization of cultural consumption across transnational boundaries and simultaneously to greater fragmentation characterized by the resurgence of local aesthetic, political, and ethnic trends.[78] Šiklová's narratives imply but don't ask whether it is possible to accept globalization of economic and cultural processes, as well as cultural conformity in consumerism, lifestyle, and telecommunications, without being influenced by "the Western mindset." It may well be that "experience" is the site of contestation of that ambivalence.

In searching for a strategy to see a way clear of the "reified polarities of East and West"[79] implicit in most writing about the transition to post-Communism, Said's writing is helpful in the sense that he illustrates how in other contexts there has been little scepticism that a monolithic "West" exists. The construction of "the West" has been "totalising in its form, . . . all-enveloping in its attitudes and gestures," the effect of which has been to "shut out even as it includes, compresses, consolidates."[80] The leap to essences and generalizations is an inevitable result of accepting the centrality of the West, and Said's argument that "every opposition to the West only confirms the West's wicked power,"[81] sums up exactly the consequences of the Czech ambivalence. Feminist postcolonial critic Gayatri Chakravorty Spivak has similarly noted how current notions of marginality implicitly validate the center.[82]

Said could have been talking to a room full of East/West feminists when he said that "there seems no reason except fear and prejudice to keep insisting on . . . separation and distinctiveness as if that was all human life was about."[83] When Said declares that his principal aim is not to separate but to connect,[84] he is not implying the need to act in concert, but rather to reject the words that divide. What is rejected is that which is monolithic or reductively compartmentalized, separate, distinct, or homogeneous. It is the "relatively understood domains," "binary oppositions," the "us" and "them," "each quite settled, clear, unassailably self-evident," which are redundant.[85]

Pertinent to the Czech context is Said's argument that experience has sometimes been put to the service of "exclusivity" and "defensiveness" by "inside traders," the effect of which has been to "absolve and forgive a great deal more demagogy than they enable knowledge." Said sees the process of insider/outsider trading as a circle within which "stand the blameless, the just, the omnicompetent, those who know the truth about themselves as well as the others: outside the circle stand a miscellaneous bunch of querulous whining complainers."[86] Said argues that "our tradition" is one of the most debilitating exercises imaginable and that there is no intellectually justifiable reason why "we" should only or mainly be concerned with what is "ours." Said insists that "we must be able to think through and interpret together experiences that are discrepant," "polarized, radically uneven or remembered differently."[87] "Contrapuntal ensembles" are necessary on the basis that while no identity can ever exist by itself and without an array of opposites, negatives, oppositions, the process of naming these oppositions admits to particular knowledges and structures of attitude and reference and those require careful analysis and research.[88] Said argues that it is possible to represent "overlapping experience," "interdependence of cultural terrains" at the same time as expressing an awareness of "rival geographies, narratives (and) histories."[89] By "juxtaposing experiences and letting them play off each other," it is possible "to make concurrent views and experiences that are ideologically and culturally closed to each other," or that attempt to distance or suppress other views or experiences. Far from seeking to reduce the significance of ideology, he argues, the exposure and dramatization of discrepancy highlights its cultural importance: this enables us to appreciate its power and understand its continuing influence.[90]

For Said it is an inadmissible contradiction to build analyses of experience around exclusions. If we "acknowledge the massively knotted and complex history of special but nevertheless overlapping and interconnected experiences . . . there is no particular intellectual reason for granting each and all of them an ideal and essential status."[91] The discrepant experiences of women who lived through state socialism provide the impetus to challenge feminisms in important ways. The valuable insights that might be provided by such a critique have a better chance of emerging if the binary "us" and "them" were to be reconsidered and "experience" itself were to be problematized.

Interpreting Experience

If Šiklová's "resistance" was primarily premised on a belief in the explanatory capacities of experience over theory, it is necessary to interpret her silence on the issue of the broader relationship between feminisms and experience. For this reason, it is pertinent to consider the ways in which "experience" has been employed and problematized in a range of recent feminist scholarship, and offer some suggestions as to the means by which experience might be critically reinscribed.

Despite recent critiques of "experience" as a concept, Western feminist practices have validated, and continue to validate, "female experience." Teresa de Lauretis has gone so far as to argue that "the relation of experience to discourse, finally is what is at issue in the definition of feminism."[92] Notions of otherwise repressed or devalued female experience continually form the basis of new feminist epistemology.[93] Personal narratives have provided "evidence of a world of alternative values and practices whose existence gives the lie to hegemonic constructions of social worlds."[94] Feminism has employed the experiences of women to "unmask all claims to objectivity as an ideological cover for masculine bias by pointing out the shortcomings, incompleteness and exclusiveness of mainstream theory."[95]

This contemporary invocation of experience is only part of the longer history of various changing meanings and usages. For example, Simone de Beauvoir argued in *The Second Sex* that experience was the measure of the attainment of equality. For de Beauvoir, "the doubtful concept of 'equality in inequality,' which the one uses to mask his despotism and the other to mask her cowardice, does not stand the test of experience: in their exchanges woman appeals to the theoretical equality she has been guaranteed; and man the concrete inequality that exists."[96] In spite of de Beauvoir's statement at the outset of her book that "enough ink has been spilled in quarreling about feminism," she contributes seven hundred more pages on the basis that "the fact of being women will affect our lives."[97] That fact of being, according to de Beauvoir, is measurable only via experience.

The women's liberation movement of the late 1960s erupted in a literature of complaint that arose from immediate experience and which sought to change the conception and the experience of what it was to be a woman and a man.[98] By examining individual and overlapping personal experiences, validating shared reactions to social constraints within society and the family, a feminist consciousness was made of a "capacity to theorise from immediate and personal observation." Initially at least, "ideas were checked and connected by new experiences." British socialist feminist

Sheila Rowbotham saw the negative potential of a feminism in which "ideas tended to become split from women's experience," and which risked losing "contact with experience in all its complexity." This kind of feminism, according to Rowbotham, only evidences "partial expressions of a changing reality." Feminism's capacity to "revise repeatedly" on the basis of always changing experience is required if it is to be more than merely an "ideological model . . . a self-justifying system which is then projected back on women's perceptions and culture as a universal quintessence."[99]

Certainly feminism is today still grappling with the fundamental difficulty of "how to handle appeals to experiential knowledge, when, with the advent of post-structuralist thought, experience has been placed so convincingly under erasure." Belief in the truth of experience is recognized to be as much an ideological production as the belief in the experience of truth. Experience has emerged as a "conservative fiction," a product of ideological, social and historical practices, which has also been employed as "evidence" of a sort to validate the production of ideology.[100]

However, far from accepting the erasure of experience, its continual reinscription has been part of a much broader epistemological shift effected by feminism, which also demanded new ways of thinking about culture, language, art, nature, and the boundaries of the political. This reinscription gives validity to ascribing distinctly female ways of experiencing, knowing, gazing, writing, or speaking, and therefore of feminine modes of consciousness and subjectivity.[101] According to Teresa de Lauretis, unlike other postmodernist or philosophically antihumanist visions, feminism remains "not merely a sexual politics but a politics of experience of everyday life, which then in turn enters the public sphere of expression and creative practice, displacing aesthetic hierarchies and generic categories, and which thus established the semiotic ground for a different production of reference and meaning."[102] The shift to which de Lauretis refers is from an earlier reading of woman defined in terms of her sexual difference from man to a more complex and difficult position in which the female subject is the site of multiple differences, "differences that are not only sexual or racial, economic or (sub)cultural, but all of these together, and often at odds with one another." This reading begins and ends with "women's own experience of difference, of our differences from Woman and of the differences among women . . . and within women."[103] Feminist poststructuralist scholarship has drawn attention to the reality that, "'female experience' is never as unified, knowable, universal or as stable as we presume it to be."[104]

Feminist historians have been particularly troubled by the questioning of experience. "Experience," according to Joan Scott, "emerged as a critical term in debates among historians about the limits of interpretation and especially about uses and the limits of post-structuralist theory for history."[105] Feminist historians recognize that "experience" essentializes identity and reifies the subject. They would abandon it altogether except that "experience is not a word we can do without." Denise Riley's interpretation of the dilemma is that "feminism can never wholeheartedly dismantle 'women's experience,' however much this category conflates the attributed, the imposed and the lived, and then sanctifies the resulting melange."[106] Scott asserts that the undeniable appeal of experience is that it "serves as a way of talking about what happened, of establishing difference and similarity, of claiming knowledge that is 'unassailable.'"[107]

Scott's solution to the dilemma has been to assert the need to interpret "all categories of analysis as contextual, contested and contingent."[108] She says that the answer for feminist historians lies in tracking the appropriation of language, in situating and contextualizing language, thereby historicizing the terms by which experience itself is represented, allowing identity to emerge as a contested terrain. The most significant aspect of Scott's analysis for the purposes of this chapter is her insistence that "experience is at once already an interpretation *and* is in need of interpretation. . . . Experience is . . . not an origin of explanation, but that which we want to explain."[109]

Scott's analysis reinterprets earlier analyses by literary theorists Raymond Williams, Gayatri Chakravorty Spivak, and Teresa de Lauretis and by historians R. G. Collingwood, E. P. Thompson, John Toews, and Denise Riley to expose the processes by which writers from a range of disciplines uncritically inscribe experience. Scott exposes the process by which experience and/or the appeal to experience is taken as the origin of knowledge, as the uncontestable "bedrock of evidence on which explanation is built, and on which analysis is based." In this sense, the "evidence of experience works as a foundation providing both a starting point and a conclusive kind of explanation, beyond which few questions can or need to be asked."[110] Scott's analysis, applied to the Czech context, exposes the ways in which the identities of those whose experience is being documented are taken as self-evident and thus are naturalized. Questions about the relationship of experience to the rendering up of that experience as interpretation, questions about difference, subjectivity, "about what counts as experience and who gets to make that determination," are precluded. The evidence of experience becomes evidence for the fact of difference rather than a way of exploring how difference is established or constructed, how it operates, how and in what ways it constitutes subjects who see and act in the world. Accordingly, the evidence of experience reproduces rather than contests the authority of the constructed knowledge of experience, precluding critical examination of that system itself, its categories of representation, its premises about what these categories mean and how they operate, and its notions of subjects, origin, and cause.[111] Scott's critique of E. P. Thompson holds true for Šiklová: "Although his author's voice intervenes powerfully with moral and ethical judgements about the situations he is recounting, the presentation of the experiences themselves is meant to secure their objective status. We forget that Thompson's history . . . is an interpretation, a selective ordering of information that through its use of originary categories and teleological accounts legitimizes a particular kind of politics."[112]

Scott's point is that once the process by which experience is fashioned can be explained and demystified, experience need not act as an origin of explanation or the authoritative evidence that grounds what is known, but rather becomes that which we seek to explain, that about which knowledge is produced.[113] "Woman," Scott argues, is historically and discursively constructed as well as relationally constituted, by which she means that woman is always relative to other categories which themselves change.[114] For Scott, "woman" and "man" are "at once empty and overflowing categories, empty because they have no ultimate, transcendent meaning, and overflowing because even when they appear to be fixed, they still contain within them alternative, denied or suppressed definitions."[115] There is a need to refuse fixed and permanent binary oppositions in favor of "genuine historicization and deconstruction."[116] In Scott's view, describing difference serves only to establish social distinctions as social facts. Conversely, "analysing the history by which these differences have been produced disrupts their fixity and enduring facts and recasts them (and the social hierarchies they organise) as the effects of contingent and contested processes of change."[117]

Rejecting Stability

The renegotiation of experience that Scott proposes is only part of a larger feminist project to contest the theoretical stability of feminism as a discourse. Feminism is frequently regarded as a "highly contested political terrain"[118] in which "almost every category . . . has been problematised or deconstructed." Those "categories we use to understand the world are unstable, constantly shifting under us like a continuous earthquake."[119] As well as illustrating that feminism is the site of continual contestation and repositioning, feminists have also been careful to point out that feminism has no unitary subject. Riley and Scott have argued that "feminism" was and remains troublesome precisely because it can only be conceived of as the site of the systematic fighting out of the unstable category "woman." Riley reveals that depictions of "woman" and "Woman" are always inadequate, "semantically shaky" and ultimately impossible "seductive frauds." By problematizing the neutral and simultaneously loaded term "woman," she shows that feminism is the vague stuff of instability and argues therefore that feminism "cannot but act out the full ambiguities of that category."[120]

By highlighting the paradoxical nature of the ways in which women's sameness and difference (from men) have been reiterated throughout the history of feminism, Scott, like Riley, shows that "in order to protest women's exclusion, they (women) had to act on behalf of women and so invoked the very difference they sought to deny."[121] This required and continues to require that "women" don't exist, while simultaneously maintaining a politics "as if they did." Feminists have therefore "argued in the same breath for the irrelevance and relevance of their sex" which has at times meant that they have been perceived as "unreasonable or dangerously incoherent."[122] Scott's book, the title of which is borrowed from French revolutionary feminist Olympe de Gouges's famous statement that she had "only paradoxes to offer and not problems easy to resolve," shows that feminism has been constituted by the discursive practices of Western democratic politics which have equated universal individuality with embodied masculinity, and that it still bears the traces of these ambiguities.[123] Scott conceives of feminism as a history of complex unresolvable paradoxes which even today can be read as a "politics of undecidability." She makes this clear when she says that "the history of feminism is not a history of available options or of unconstrained choice or the winning plan. It is rather the history of women (and some men) grappling repeatedly with the radical difficulty of resolving the dilemmas they confronted."[124] The impossibility of any reliance on self-evident and unchanging meanings of "women" and "feminism" has moved historians to argue for the need to historicize and conceptually challenge the usage of the terms, and to refurbish them instead of allowing them to be "perversely strengthened by repetition."[125] Šiklová's resistance therefore is not only understandable but also impossible. In grappling to find the authentic, the real, or the definitive "feminism," she implies a stable and fixed understanding of "woman" who is and always was fictitious. Šiklová's favorite claim against feminism, that it "is better at disrupting gender order than in finding solutions to the questions it raises,"[126] can therefore be understood as a frustrated misreading of the contradictions and paradoxes within feminism itself.

Non-Western Feminisms and Situated Knowledges

Chandra Mohanty argues that experience has frequently functioned as an "unexamined, catch-all category" which has instilled a politics of "transcendence rather than engagement."[127] For Mohanty, "one of the tasks of feminist analysis is uncovering alternative, non-identical histories"[128] because it is important to understand how women in different sociocultural and historical locations formulate their relationship to feminism.[129] This aim necessitates "remapping boundaries and renegotiating connections."[130] By highlighting the ways in which Western feminisms have in the past homogenized the experiences and conditions of dissimilar women, and the ways in which Western feminists have taken their own position as normative, Mohanty argues *against* solidifying the identification of feminism with the West. Rather, she argues for the need to challenge the hegemony of specific analytic and political positions with differentiated, more finely articulated and more attentive feminisms. Mohanty suggests that it is possible to express "difference" as a process which refers to the particularities of the experiences of the group without necessarily imposing divisions and impermeable boundaries between groups; that it is possible to express interest in other cultures without expressing inappropriate assumptions of intimacy or celebration or nostalgia for sameness or similarity; and finally, that it is not inevitable that by attempting to demand that a history of difference be respected, cultural practices will be treated as reified symbols of an essentialist historic past.[131]

The naturalization of analytical categories such as "woman" that are assumed to possess cross-cultural validity, end in a mystification of difference.[132] "'Sisterhood,' defined as the transcendence of the 'male' world, thus ends up being a middle-class, psychologised notion which effectively erases material and ideological power differences within and among groups of women, and paradoxically, removes us all as actors from history and politics."[133] Mohanty's alternative to the "harmonious, empty pluralism" of positions that promote benign variation (diversity) is to define difference in terms of "incommensurate cultural spheres situated within hierarchies of domination and resistance (which) cannot be accommodated within a discourse of 'harmony in diversity.'"[134] For Mohanty, "experience" and "difference" are capable of emerging as analytical and political categories precisely at the moment that *specific* locations and histories of struggle are recognized in spaces where "a politics of location" is invoked. I am persuaded by Mohanty's argument that it is precisely the juncture of feminist antiracist/Third World feminist politics and postcolonial studies that "can point the way to a more precise, transformative feminist politics,"[135] materially as well as methodologically. For Mohanty, this is a matter of making connections and asking better questions.

Influenced by Mohanty, Spivak, and Deleuze, poststructuralist feminist theorists have taken up the valuable critique provided by non-Western feminisms and asked, "can worlds be claimed in the name of categories such as 'woman' in all innocence and benevolence, or do these gestures mark the revival of a form of feminist cultural imperialism?"[136] These questions have led to a pervasive difficulty in understanding that "recognition of the common condition of sisterhood in oppression cannot be the final aim; women may have common situations and experiences, but they are not, in any way *the same*."[137] "Situated" practices have become a central criterion in feminist knowledge claims,[138] and "the site at which 'naturalisations' have begun to be deconstructed in the name of anti-imperialist and anti-racist feminism."[139] For Rosi Braidotti, "not only is the situated perspective an important contribution to the analysis of theoretical and political practice after the decline of Marxism, but it also translates into simpler ideas." Havelková certainly, and even Šiklová possibly, might agree with Braidotti "that in intellectual debates, a little less abstraction would be welcome indeed."[140]

The term "politics of location," initially conceived by Adrienne Rich in 1987 and more recently reinscribed by a number of poststructuralist feminists committed to embodied and embedded perspectives, has been newly articulated as "technologies of the self," "situated knowledges," or "nomadic subjectivity." "The politics of location" and its spin-offs provide a theory of the recognition of the multiple differences that exist among women. It stresses the importance of rejecting global statements about all women and attempting instead to be as aware as possible of the place from which one is speaking. It implies attention to the situated as opposed to the universalistic nature of experience and knowledge, and illustrates the importance of situating ourselves and our words. Braidotti argues that "positionality is crucial . . . that the only way of making general theoretical points is to be aware that one is actually located somewhere specific."[141] It is in this sense that feminism may be able to resist what Mary Hartstock has frequently referred to as "the view from nowhere."

Feminist appeals to situated knowledges have illustrated the embeddedness of our assumptions and the specific historical context from which they are derived, locating us within systems of power, geopolitical, and metaphorical sites. Only in this way does it become possible to destabilize unexamined or stereotypical images and work through complex relationships between dissimilar women. By seeking "maps of the circuits of power," feminism becomes a critical practice. As Kaplan argues, "we can turn the terms of inquiry from desiring, inviting and granting space to others to becoming accountable for one's own investments in cultural metaphors and values. Such accountability can begin to shift the ground of feminist practice from magisterial relativism (as if diversified cultural production simply occurs in a social vacuum) to the complex interpretive practices that acknowledge the historical roles of mediation, betrayal and alliance in the relationship between women in diverse locations."[142]

Significantly, the argument for situated knowledges applies not only to feminists who regard themselves to have emerged from "The West." Donna Haraway argues that all knowledge claims, including subjugated knowledges, must be partial, vulnerable, locatable, critical, and responsible, that is, able to be called into question. Haraway shows "there is a premium on establishing the capacity to see from the peripheries and depths" that "the positionings of the subjugated are not exempt from critical re-examination, decoding, deconstruction and interpretation," and that "the standpoints of the subjugated are not 'innocent' positions . . . they are savvy to all modes of denial through repression, forgetting, and disappearing acts—ways of being nowhere while claiming to see comprehensively." Subjugated knowledges, as other knowledges, have "a decent chance to be on to the god-trick and all its dazzling—and therefore, blinding—illuminations."[143]

The possibilities for conversation afforded by situated perspectives also raises important questions about the potential for coalition building between women. I agree with the multitude of writers who have argued that a feminist advocacy on behalf of "untroubled solidarities of women"[144] is an impossible longing. In this regard, and in spite of the fact that I reject entirely the binary, reductionist, and ahistorical means by which Šiklová formulates her argument, I agree with her when she suggests that any notion of "sisterhood" is unpalatable. However, if "facile cultural relativism," can be overcome through critical, multiply differentiated, and situated perspectives, there does still remain "the possibility of alliances made on the basis of affinity, that is, temporary political consensus on specific issues."[145] In Braidotti's understanding, differences can become the stuff of communication, that is, of "multiple literacies." In Kaplan's words, through the careful critical process of "exploring all the differences, keeping identities distinct," it is possible to keep "power differentials from masquerading as universals."[146] Mohanty and Brah similarly stress the importance of analyzing and theorizing difference in the context of feminist cross-cultural work, and also of historicizing and locating political agency as an alternative to formations of the universality of gendered oppression and struggles.[147] Suggesting the need for "repositioning," bell hooks argues that people who are committed to antiracism might be able to understand the way in which their cultural practice reinscribes their own supremacy without promoting paralyzing guilt or denial.[148]

Indeed, many writers contend that momentary "coalitions are possible through the politics of identification as opposed to the politics of identity,"[149] and have therefore argued for a broader set of identifications among women. Kaplan argues that "the insistence on gender alone as a universal system of explanation means that we sever ourselves from other women."[150] For Mohanty, "the experience of being a woman can create an illusory unity, for it is not in the experience of being a woman, but the meanings attached to gender, race, class and age at various historical moments that is of strategic significance."[151] These arguments are consistent with Said's analysis that "no one today is purely *one* thing." "Labels like Indian, or woman, or Muslim-American," he contends, "are no more than starting points, which if followed into actual experience for only a moment are quickly left behind."[152]

Subjectivity and identity are the "hallmarks of contemporary feminist theory."[153] Situated knowledges require feminists to rework and rethink notions of subjectivity as constituted by complex fragmented identities. Non-Western/nonwhite feminisms have drawn attention to the reality that subjects are not fixed embodiments of their cultures but rather are formed within a range of heterogeneous discursive practices occurring in internally differentiated and changing cultures.[154] Not only do we inhabit multiple and changing identities, but these identities are produced and reproduced within social relations of "race," "gender," "class," and "sexuality." Mohanty, arguing for a "politics of engagement rather than a politics of transcendence," urges that "experience of the self, which is often discontinuous and fragmented, must be historicised before it can be generalised into a collective vision . . . experience must be historically interpreted and theorised if it is to become the basis of feminist solidarity and struggle, and it is at that time that an understanding of the politics of location proves crucial."[155]

A broadly based sentiment implies that "figurations of mobile, complex, shifting subjectivity are here to stay," and that "fixed identities must be left behind as the sedentary site that produces reactive positions like greed, paranoia, Oedipal jealousy and other forms of symbolic constipation."[156] Braidotti has called her own version of a situated, culturally differentiated understanding of the subject "nomadic subjectivity," which she argues is about the "decentered and multi-layered vision of the subject as dynamic and changing entity, situated in a shifting context."[157] Similarly, Haraway argues for the production of the "split and contradictory self" that can interrogate positionings and be held accountable. "Splitting" in this context is about "heterogeneous multiplicities" and recognizing that "the knowing self is partial in all its guises, never finished, whole, simply there and original: it is always constructed and stitched together imperfectly."[158] Jane Flax has also argued in favor of what she has called "multiples," by which she means possibilities of fluid, multiple subjectivities whose desires for differences will impel us toward resisting (inner or external) relations of domination. Flax employs "gendering," rather than the singular noun "gender," in order to show that gender is not a fixed or simple identity or set of social relations, but rather functions as complex, overdetermined, and multiple processes which are provisional and reproduced and reworked throughout lives.[159] Rethinking experience ultimately means problematizing identity and subjectivity. This analysis seeks to illustrate that Šiklová's reticence toward problematizing experience is linked to an equally felt resistance to what she imagines are the disquieting implications that rethinking identity and subjectivity raise, but need not.

Conclusion

The significance of the relationship between experience and feminism is in no sense being eroded. The Czech case generally, and Šiklová's writing specifically, both support this view. In the difficult cross-cultural debate about post-Communist feminisms, it is necessary to locate, contextualize, situate, and problematize all claims to experience and knowledge. Claims made on the basis of divergent experience need to be interpreted: experience by itself is not an interpretation, but rather that which is in need of interpretation. Employing Said's argument that we must be able to think through and interpret discrepant experiences together, I have argued that Šiklová's writing for English-language audiences, premised on a binary and antithetical reinscription of "East" and "West" and an unproblematized appeal to "experience," sometimes closed rather than opened opportunities for dialogue. There is no unitary or stable historical female subject; therefore Šiklová's search for "genuine feminism" is as impossible as her hostility to its absence is understandable. After exploring Šiklová's uses of the past and the ways in which she reinscribes universal humanist values for the purposes of the present, I attempted to problematize her uses of "experience." I argued that feminism's long-term theoretical engagement with the notion of "experience," enhanced specifically by theoretical investments by non-Western feminists/Third World feminists, illustrates possibilities for the emergence of more accountable, precise, and transformative cross-cultural feminist encounters. I am not suggesting that Šiklová should uncritically accept eclectic theoretical positions but, rather, that experience does not, and need not, provide a simple defense for nonengagement.

Šiklová explained that during socialism "one achieved quickly the concept of one's identity through the concept of *us and them,* and that this strategy proved to be convenient and uncomplicated."[160] Perhaps a more convenient way of thinking about identity has not emerged, but maybe it should. Czech "male feminist" Mirek Vodrážka has asked the difficult question that Šiklová has so far avoided: "Maybe the fear of feminism is quite justified in our country, because feminism could actually introduce the beginning of the great 'de-construction' of the 'humanity monster' . . . Isn't post-communist society now facing the problem of the great post-feminist exodus from the 'Same' to the 'Different'?"[161]

I agree entirely with Šiklová when she says that feminism is a product of a particular political culture, country, and social system, and that on this basis post-Communist feminism "is certain to be a different hue than other feminisms."[162] Her perception that "our feminist movement is going to develop . . . on the basis of solving concrete, non-political, primary practical tasks," and that it will derive its existence from the (local) interests of women,[163] is no doubt accurate. Similarly, I agree that it is likely that a younger generation of Czech women "will form itself as a political community in opposition to silent and passive masses of women brought up under the socialist regime,"[164] and may thereby form the vanguard of a new feminism. What is much more difficult to accept as "an outsider" is the view that "the specific interests of women will emerge and crystallise in parallel with the change to a capitalist society"[165] if an unproblematized understanding of experience remains the basis of all knowledge. Though I am incapable of being the person who reinscribes a more critical reading of experience in the Czech context, I am able to suggest that reinscription is necessary and potentially beneficial.

I accept Braidotti's definition of feminism as the movement that struggles to challenge the values attributed to, and the representations made of, women in the longer historical time of patriarchal history as well as the deeper time of one's own identity.[166] While Šiklová implies that common human values and feminism are mutually incompatible, I would argue, as have bell hooks and innumerable other writers, that it is not "unauthentic" or "traitorous," and does not amount to "shifting the focus" or "changing the subject"[167] to challenge the values and representations made by, or on behalf of "woman" or her experiences. Experience is the site where, through critical reinscription, Czech female writers may be able to argue successfully for the existence of dissimilar pasts, presents, and futures that command a meaningful respect for difference as a product of discrepant experience.

Notes

1. Slavenka Drakulić, *How We Survived Communism and Even Laughed* (London: Vintage, 1993), 132.
2. Ibid., 125.
3. Ibid., 127.

4. Nanette Funk, "Feminism East and West," in *Gender Politics and Post-Communism: Reflections from Eastern Europe and the Former Soviet Union,* ed. Nanette Funk and Magda Mueller (New York: Routledge, 1993), 318–30.

5. While publishing conventions dictate the use of West and East (capitalized) in this volume, I do not in any sense wish to essentialize the certainty with which this styling seems to endow them.

6. Barbara Einhorn, *Cinderella Goes to Market: Citizenship, Gender and Women's Movements in East Central Europe* (London: Verso, 1993), 6.

7. Šiklová described herself as "the grandmother of Czech feminism" at a meeting at the Foundation for Gender Studies in Prague in October 2000.

8. Australian Democrat, Senator Natasha Scott Despoja coined this description of the generation of female Australians for whom the expectation of structural equality predated their entry into the work place/public sphere.

9. Ien Ang, "I'm a Feminist but . . . 'Other' Women and Postnational Feminism," in *Transitions: New Australian Feminisms,* ed. Barbara Caine and Rosemary Pringle (Sydney: Allen and Unwin, 1995), 61.

10. Teresa Brennan, series preface to *The Spoils of Freedom: Psychoanalysis and Feminism after the Fall of Socialism,* by Renata Salecl (London: Routledge, 1994), vii.

11. Linda Gordon, "What's New in Women's Studies," in *Feminist Studies/Critical Studies,* ed. Teresa de Lauretis (Bloomington: Indiana University Press, 1986), 30.

12. Joan W. Scott, "The Evidence of Experience," *Critical Inquiry* 17 (Summer 1991): 774.

13. Ruth Rosen, "An Interview with Jiřina Šiklová," *Peace and Democracy News,* Fall 1990, 35.

14. Jiřina Šiklová, "Women and the Charta 77 Movement in Czechoslovakia," in Robin L. Teske and Mary Ann Tétreault, ed., *Feminist Approaches to Social Movements, Community, and Power,* vol. 1, *Conscious Acts and the Politics of Social Change* (Columbia: University of South Carolina Press, 2000), 266.

15. Hana Havelková, "Affidamento" (Trust), in *Nové čtení světa, feminismus devadesátých let Českýma očima (New readings of the world: feminism of the 1990s through Czech eyes),* ed. Marie Chřibková, Josef Chuchma, and Eva Klimentová (Prague: One Woman Press, 1999), 59.

16. Jiřina Šmejkalová-Strickland, "Revival? Gender Studies in the 'Other' Europa," *Signs* 20, 4 (Summer 1995): 1000.

17. Jiřina Šiklová, "Women and the Welfare State in Transition," paper presented at the Prague School for Economics/Institut für Gesellschaftspolitik-Abteilung Sozialpolitik, Linz, 29–30 November 1994, 3.

18. Jiřina Šiklová, "Identity and Traditions of Women's Rights in the Czech Republic," unpublished paper, [1994?]; available at the Foundation for Gender Studies, Prague.

19. Jiřina Šiklová, "Únava z vysvětlování" (Tiredness from explanations), in *Nové čtení světa,* 129.

20. Šiklová, "Únava z vysvětlování," 135.

21. Ibid., 129.

22. Ibid., quotes from 130 and 131, respectively.

23. Jitka Kačánová and Jarmila Pávková, "Život může být jako krasohled, Rozhovor s Jiřinou Šiklovou" (The world can be a beautiful kaleidoscope: interview with Jiřina Šiklová), *Incognito* 1 (1999): 11.

24. Šiklová, "O feminismu women a gender studiích u nás a na západě" (About feminism, women and gender studies in our country and in the West), in *Documenta pragensia, Žena v dějinách Prahy,* vol. xiii, ed. Václav Ledvinka. (Prague: Scriptorium, 1996), 24.

25. Jiřina Šiklová, "Moderní feminismus" (Modern feminism), *Playboy* (Czech edition) 1 (1993): 29.

26. Šiklová, "O feminismu," 24.

27. Jiřina Šiklová, "Rozumí Západ našim ženám?" (Does the West understand our women?), *Listy* (Prague) 5 (1991): 15.

28. Jiřina Šiklová, "Moderní doba je krizí muže" (The modern time is a crisis for men), *Právo,* 5 March 1998, Salon section, pp. 1, 4.

29. Šiklová, "Rozumí Západ?" 15.

30. Šiklová, "Moderní doba," 1, 4.

31. Šiklová, "McDonalds, Terminators and Coca Cola Ads and Feminism? Imports from the West," in *Bodies of Bread and Butter: Reconfiguring Women's Lives in the Post-Communist Czech Republic,* ed. Susanna Trnka and Laura Busheiken (Prague: Prague Gender Studies Centre, 1993), 7; reprinted in *Ana's Land: Sisterhood in Eastern Europe,* ed. Tanya Renne (Boulder, Colo.: Westview, 1997), 76.

32. Jiřina Šiklová, "Jiný kraj, jiné ženy—proč se v Čechách nedaří feminismu" (Different region, different women: why feminism isn't successful in the Czech Republic), *Respekt,* 13, 25–31 March 1996, Civilizace section, p. 17.

33. Jiřina Šiklová, "Are Women in Eastern Europe Conservative?" in *Gender Politics and Post-Communism,* 79.

34. Jiřina Šiklová, "The Grey Zone and the Future of Dissent in Czechoslovakia," *Social Research* 57, 2 (Summer 1990): 348.

35. Jiřina Šiklová, "Factors Inhibiting the Development of Feminism in the Czech Republic" (paper presented at the conference Crossing Borders: International Dialogues on Gender, Social Politics, and Citizenship, Stockholm, Sweden, 27–29 May 1994).

36. Eva Hauser, "Mind the Gap! Women from Post-Communist Countries: Conservatism or Progressivism?" *Women: A Cultural Review* 3 (Winter 1992): 242.

37. Jiřina Šiklová, "McDonalds, Terminators," in *Ana's Land,* p. 77.

38. Jiřina Šiklová, "Feminism and the Roots of Apathy in the Czech Republic," *Social Research* 64, 2 (Summer 1997): 1; Šiklová, "McDonalds, Terminators," 8; Šiklová, "Report on Women in the Post-Communist Centre of Europe (Personal View from Prague)," in *She and He in Slovakia: Gender Issues in Public Opinion,* ed. Zora Bútorova et al. (Bratislava: USPO Bratislava, 1996), 11; Šiklová, "Women and Human Rights in Post-Communist Countries, the Example of the Czech Republic," in *Gender, Planning and Human Rights,* ed. Tovi Fenster (London: Routledge, 1999), 153–67.

39. Šiklová, "McDonalds, Terminators," 7.

40. Šiklová, "Factors Inhibiting," 2.

41. Jiřina Šiklová, "Women in Politics in the CSFR" (conference report presented at Women in Leadership: Politics and Business, Vienna, 9–22 November 1992, 49); available at the Foundation for Gender Studies in Prague.

42. Jiřina Šiklová, "Feminism and Citizenship" (paper presented at the Third HCA Assembly, Fourth Commission: Women and Citizenship, Ankara, Turkey, 1993).

43. Šiklová, "McDonalds, Terminators," 10.

44. Šiklová, "Women in Politics in the CSFR," 48–49. Similar sentiments are expressed in her Czech-language article "Rozumí Západ?" 15.

45. Eva Hauserová, "Cosmopolitan a harlequinky: plíživá emancipace ze Západu" (Cosmopolitan and Harlequin books: sneaky emancipation from the West), in *Jedním oken/One Eye Open, Women's Issues in Central and Eastern Europe* (Prague, Gender Studies Centre) 5 (Summer 1997): 13.

46. Jiřina Šiklová, "Why Western Feminism Isn't Working in the Czech Republic," *The New Presence: The Prague Journal of Central European Affairs,* January 1998, 9.

47. Hauserová, "Cosmopolitan," 13.

48. Šiklová, "Parallel Paper," 2.

49. Hauser, "Mind the Gap," 242.

50. Šiklová, "Parallel Paper," 5.

51. Šiklová, "Feminism and the Roots," 5.

52. Ibid., 5, 16, quote from 16.

53. Šiklová, "Why Western Feminism," 9.

54. Šiklová, "Feminism and the Roots," quotes from 7 and 9.

55. Šiklová, "Why Western Feminism," 8.

56. Jiřina Šiklová, "Why We Resist Western-Style Feminism," in *Transitions: Changes in Post-Communist Societies* 5, 1 (January 1998): 30; Šiklová, "Why Western Feminism," 8, respectively.

57. Jiřina Šiklová, "McDonalds, Terminators," 7.

58. Eva Hauser, "How and Why Do Czech Women Organize? (Altos, Sopranos, and a Few Discordant Voices)," *Canadian Women's Studies/Les Cahiers de la Femme* 16, 1 (1995): 87.

59. Hana Havelková, "Abstract Citizenship? Women and Power in the Czech Republic," *Social Politics* 2, 3 (Summer/Fall 1996): 244–45.

60. Šiklová, "Únava z vysvětlování," 134.

61. Ibid., 137, 133, quote from 133.

62. Renata Salecl, *The Spoils of Freedom: Psychoanalysis and Feminism after the Fall of Socialism* (London: Routledge, 1994), 2.

63. T. Minh-ha Trinh, "Difference: A Special Third World Women's Issue," in *Woman, Native, Other: Writing Postcoloniality and Feminism* (Bloomington: Indiana University Press, 1989), 88–89.

64. Rosi Braidotti, "Uneasy Transitions: Women's Studies in the European Union," in *Transitions, Environments, Translations: Feminists in International Politics,* ed. Joan W. Scott, Cora Kaplan, and Debra Keates (New York: Routledge, 1997), 357.

65. Hana Havelková, "Abstract Citizenship?" 244.

66. Braidotti, "Uneasy Transitions," 357.

67. David Cohen, *The Combing of History* (Chicago: University of Chicago Press, 1994), 75.

68. Eva Karpinski, "Do Polish Women Need Feminism?" *Canadian Woman's Studies/Les Cahiers de la Femme* 16, 1 (1995): 91.

69. Šiklová, "Identity and Traditions," 13.

70. Jiřina Šiklová, "Inhibition Factors of Feminism in the Czech Republic after the 1989 Revolution," in *Women, Work and Society,* ed. Marie Čermárková (Prague: Academy of Sciences of the Czech Republic, Institute of Sociology, 1995), 41.

71. Šiklová, "Feminism and the Roots," 6, 19; Šiklová, "McDonalds, Terminators," 10; Šiklová, "Feminism and Citizenship," 1.

72. Marianne Grunell, "Feminism Meets Scepticism: Women's Studies in the Czech Republic," *European Journal of Women's Studies* 2 (1995): 108.

73. Šiklová, "Feminism and the Roots," 6; Šiklová, "Factors Inhibiting," 3.

74. Šiklová, "Why We Resist," 32.

75. Šiklová, "Jiný kraj, jiné ženy," 17; Šiklová, "Why We Resist," 32; Šiklová, "Jiný kraj, jiné ženy," 17, 79.

76. Avtar Brah, "Questions of Difference and International Feminism," in *Women's Studies: A Reader,* ed. Stevi Jackson et al. (New York: Harvester Wheatsheaf, 1993) 33.

77. Edward Said, *Culture and Imperialism* (New York: Vintage Press, 1994), 62.

78. Brah, "Questions of Difference," 30

79. Said, *Culture and Imperialism,* 48.

80. Ibid., 24.

81. Ibid., xix.

82. Gayatri Chakravorty Spivak, *The Post-Colonial Critic: Interviews, Strategies, Dialogues,* ed. Sarah Harasym (New York: Routledge, 1990), 147.

83. Said, *Culture and Imperialism,* 408.

84. Ibid., 15.

85. Ibid., xiii.

86. Edward Said, "Intellectuals and the Post-Colonial World," *Salmagundi* 70–71 (Spring–Summer 1986): 50.

87. Said, *Culture and Imperialism,* 36; Said, "Intellectuals,"45.

88. Said, *Culture and Imperialism,* 61.

89. Ibid., xii.

90. Ibid., 37.

91. Said, "Intellectuals," 56.

92. Teresa de Lauretis, "Feminist Studies/Critical Studies: Issues, Terms and Contexts," in *Feminist Studies/Critical Studies,* ed. Teresa de Lauretis (Bloomington: Indiana University Press, 1986), 5.

93. Diana Fuss, *Essentially Speaking: Feminism, Nature and Difference* (New York: Routledge, 1989), 113.

94. Joan W. Scott, "Experience," in *Feminists Theorize the Political,* ed. Judith Butler and Joan W. Scott (New York: Routledge, 1992), 24.

95. Scott, "Evidence of Experience," 786.

96. Simone de Beauvoir, *The Second Sex* (London: Picador, 1988), 730.

97. Ibid., 13, 25.

98. Sheila Rowbotham, *The Past Is before Us: Feminism and Action since the 1960s* (London: Pandora Press, 1989), xiv.

99. Ibid., 69, 26, 34, 37, 26.

100. Fuss, *Essentially Speaking,* 113, 114, 116.

101. Christine Battersby, *The Phenomenal Woman: Feminist Metaphysics and the Patterns of Identity* (New York: Routledge, 1998), 6.

102. de Lauretis, "Feminist Studies/Critical Studies," 10.

103. Ibid., 14.

104. Fuss, *Essentially Speaking,* 114.

105. Scott, "Experience," 26.

106. Denise Riley, *"Am I That Name?" Feminism and the Category "Woman" in History* (London: Macmillan, 1988), 100.

107. Scott, "Evidence of Experience," 794.

108. Ibid., 36.

109. Scott, "Experience," 36.

110. Scott, "Evidence of Experience," 790.

111. Ibid., 777, 778.

112. Ibid., 785.

113. Ibid., 780.

114. Scott, "Introduction," in *Feminism and History,* ed. Joan W. Scott (Oxford: Oxford University Press 1989), 11.

115. Joan W. Scott, "Gender: A Useful Category of Historical Analysis," in *Feminism and History,* ed. Joan W. Scott (Oxford: Oxford University Press, 1989), 174.

116. Scott, "Gender: A Useful Category," 165.

117. Scott, "Introduction," 9.

118. Chandra Talpade Mohanty, "Feminist Encounters: Locating the Politics of Experience," in *Destabilizing Theory: Contemporary Feminism Debates,* ed. Michele Barrett and Anne Phillips (London: Polity Press, 1992), 83.

119. Barbara Caine and Rosemary Pringle, "Introduction," in *Transitions: New Australian Feminisms* (Sydney: Allen and Unwin, 1995), x.

120. Denise Riley, *"Am I That Name?"* 112.

121. Joan W. Scott, *Only Paradoxes to Offer: French Feminists and the Rights of Man* (London: Harvard University Press, 1996), x.

122. Ibid., 11, 17.

123. Scott, *Only Paradoxes,* 5.

124. Scott, *Only Paradoxes,* 17.

125. Riley, *"Am I That Name?"* 113.

126. Jiřina Šiklová, "Gender and Citizenship: Contentions and Controversies in the East/West Debates" (unpublished paper, 1997), 4.

127. Mohanty, "Feminist Encounters," 77.

128. Ibid., 84.

129. Chandra Talpade Mohanty, "Cartographies of Struggle: Third World Women and the Politics of Feminism," in *Third World Women and the Politics of Feminism,* ed. C. Mohanty, A. Rosso, and L. Torres (Bloomington: Indiana University Press, 1991), 7.

130. Chandra Talpade Mohanty, "Feminist Politics: What's Home Got to Do with It?" in *Feminist Studies/Critical Studies,* ed. Teresa de Lauretis (Bloomington: Indiana University Press, 1986), 193.

131. Brah, "Questions of Difference," 31.

132. Mohanty, "Feminist Encounters," 31.

133. Ibid., 83.

134. Chandra Talpade Mohanty, "On Race and Voice: Challenges for Liberal Education in the 1990s," *Cultural Critique* 14 (1989): 181.

135. Mohanty, "Feminist Encounters," 78, 82.

136. Caren Kaplan, "The Politics of Location as Transnational Critical Practice," in *Scattered Hegemonies: Postmodernity and Transnational Feminist Practices,* ed. I. Grewal and C. Kaplan (Minneapolis: University of Minnesota Press, 1994), 137.

137. Rosi Braidotti, quoted in Mary Eagleton, "The Politics of Location," in *Working with Feminist Criticism* (Oxford: Blackwell, 1996), 209.

138. Braidotti, "Uneasy Transitions," 357.

139. Kaplan, "Location as Transnational Critical Practice," 38.

140. Braidotti, "Uneasy Transitions," 357.

141. Braidotti, quoted in Eagleton, "Politics of Location," 209, 213.

142. Kaplan, "Location as Transnational Critical Practice," 138, 139.

143. Donna Haraway, "Situated Knowledges. The Science Question in Feminism and the Privilege of Partial Perspective," in *Simians, Cyborgs and Women: The Reinvention of Nature* (London: Free Association Books, 1991), 191.

144. Riley, *"Am I That Name?"* 111.

145. Rosi Braidotti, "The Exile, the Nomad and the Migrant: Reflections on International Feminism," *Women's Studies International Forum* 15, 1 (1992): 10.

146. Caren Kaplan, "Deterritorializations: The Reworking of Home and Exile in Western Feminist Discourse," in *The Nature and Context of Minority Discourse,* ed. Abdul R. JanMuhohamed and David Lloyd (Oxford. Oxford University Press, 1990), 359.

147. Mohanty, "Feminist Encounters," 75.

148. bell hooks, "Beyond Black Rage," in *Killing Rage, Ending Racism* (New York: Holt and Company, 1995), 50.

149. Brah, "Questions of Difference," 34.

150. Kaplan, "Deterritorialization," 364.

151. Mohanty, "Feminist Encounters," 75.

152. Said, *Culture and Imperialism,* 407.

153. Mohanty, "Feminist Encounters," 75.

154. Brah, "Questions of Difference," 33.

155. Mohanty, "Feminist Encounters," 87–9.

156. Rosi Braidotti, "Figurations of Nomadism" (keynote address delivered at the 20th conference of the International Association for Philosophy and Literature [SOAS], George Mason University, 8–11 May 1996); also forthcoming in John Burt Foster and Wayne Froman, eds., Series in Philosophy and Literature, Northwestern University Press.

157. Ibid., 77.

158. Haraway, "Situated Knowledges," 193.

159. Jane Flax, *Disputed Subjects: Essays on Psychoanalysis, Politics and Philosophy* (New York: Routledge, 1993), 24.

160. Jiřina Šiklová, "Dilemmas of Transition: A View From Prague," *Peace Review,* (Winter 1992): 26.

161. Mirek Vodrážka, "Před Velkým Exodem, Kořen Českého Antifeminismu" (Before the great exodus, the root of Czech antifeminism), translated by Pavla Slaba and Anne Petrov (lecture sponsored by the University of California–Berkeley and Stanford University, summer 1993), 15–18.

162. Šiklová, "Are Women in Eastern Europe Conservative?" 81.

163. Šiklová, "Parallel Paper," 3.

164. Šiklová, "Are Women in Eastern Europe Conservative?" 81. I began to write an earlier version of the chapter that appears in this volume in the European winter of 1998–89, while I was living in Prague and undertaking doctoral research for a thesis about Czech intellectual women's conversations with feminisms. As the most widely translated of contemporary Czech feminist intellectuals into English, the writing of Jiřina Šiklová was well known to me when I arrived in Prague, and a few

months into my stay I began to read her work and the work of other feminist writers in Czech. Two years later, I continue to believe that Šiklová offers a fascinating series of accounts about the state of feminism. But more recently, Šiklová's feminist colleagues have instigated newer conversations about feminisms in their native Czech language, conversations which, in Hana Havelková's phrase, have attempted to "explain the usefulness of feminist thinking" in their national context for local audiences. For a range of Czech feminist intellectuals, the process of feminist social criticism has come to mean overcoming what they regard as the ostentatious refusal of feminism. In some ways it is this newer enthusiastic defense of local and tailor-made feminisms as legitimate forms of intellectual engagement capable of highlighting intransigent attitudes towards the remaking of gender identities that has become the hallmark of contemporary Czech feminisms. However, ideas about experience discussed in this chapter also remain central to these newer conversations.

165. Šiklová, "Why We Resist," 35.

166. Rosi Braidotti, "Sexual Difference as a Nomadic Political Project," *Nomadic Subjects: Embodiment and Sexual Difference in Contemporary Feminist Theory* (New York: Columbia University Press, 1994), 168.

167. bell hooks, "Revolutionary Feminism: An Anti-Racist Agenda," in *Killing Rage, Ending Racism,* 100.

Chapter 2

World-Traveling Feminisms in an Era of Global Restructuring

Anne Sisson Runyan

> Far from being an essential and ahistorical reflex of women's identity or of gender inequality, feminism is a social movement marked by the particular historical contexts in which it emerges, and it is predicated on a specifically political identity for women that must be discursively constructed.
>
> Susan Gal

Introduction

Much contemporary feminist theory holds that the meanings of and impulses for feminism shift over time and in relation to varying cultural, social, political, and economic contexts. It follows, then, that contemporary feminist formations and debates must be reflexively analyzed through the lens of the massive shifts associated with the rise of globalization. Although much ink has been spilled, including my own, on feminist critiques of and resistances to globalization processes,[1] less attention has been given to how these processes are restructuring feminism itself. Given that the meanings, perspectives, and actions associated with feminism (and other social movements) are dependent upon particular material and ideological conditions in particular historical contexts, feminism cannot just be viewed as an autonomous response to and critique of globalization. Rather, it should be seen as a site of global restructuring itself.

In this chapter, I will be exploring how discursive constructions of feminism are being restructured or reconfigured in an era of globalization and the implications this has for notions of feminist identity and community. I start from the premise that Seyla Benhabib has recently argued: contemporary feminism is undergoing a paradigm shift in relation to the "deeper forces of economic, military, technological, and communications and information integration" of late capitalism that are accompanied by "surface antagonisms, conflicts, and agonisms."[2] In Benhabib's view, "surface" conflicts, such as wars of ethnic cleansing or revivals of nationalist and fundamentalist movements are manifestations of "desperate attempts to recreate" the "naturalistic signifiers in the political and cultural realm" that are "melting down" in the process of global integration.[3] She further argues that these highly visible polarizations account for the preoccupation in feminist theorizing, especially during the 1980s, with postmodernist emphases on differences among women and the incommensurability of their experiences and perspectives as a result of their differing social locations and national and cultural histories. However, as globalization has worn on, there has been a discursive shift in how feminist theorists are apprehending women's identities and feminist politics in the face of both disintegration and integration. In particular, Benhabib observes that discourses of "fragmentation," "incommensurability," and the "clash of cultures" are giving way to discourses of "hybridity," "interstitiality," and "multiculturalism" or "polyglotism" in contemporary feminist thinking about social identities and relations.[4]

This paradigm shift is reflected, for example, in Robin Teske's discussion of "inbetween" politics in the first volume of this two-volume examination of *Feminist Approaches to Social Movements, Community, and Power.*[5] She argues that the dual character of globalization as a simultaneously fragmenting and homogenizing set of forces is making it possible to see that the categories of sameness and difference are not necessarily oppositional. When these categories are brought into relation to each other and experienced at the same time, whether at the level of individual identities or social relations, new understandings about ourselves and our relationships with others can emerge. This conjoining of sameness and difference, the universal and the particular, and the local with the global under globalization opens up a "third" or "hybrid" space for new political connections to be forged.[6] The creation of such a third, connective space has become all the more crucial in the face of the disintegrative forces of globalization. As Aili Mari Tripp has argued, in sites where ethnic and religious conflict continue to rage, such as in much of Africa and the Middle East, "difference has mattered 'too much.'"[7] In these contexts "where the politicization of difference has led to violence," women's movements advocate "the depoliticization of difference and the search for common ground."[8] Thus, Tripp urges a tempering of the politics of difference that has pervaded Western feminist discourse, calling for new, contextualized understandings of difference that do not rule out "unifying strategies."[9]

Lending further urgency to the search for some common ground among women to mount feminist movements in resistance not only to direct but also to structural violence are the integrative forces of globalization. Economic violence is visited upon women by global capitalism in the form of the worldwide feminization of labor and poverty as a result of the rise of flexibilized and casualized global factory and service-industry work and the retreat of social welfare and development funding. These pressures are prompting the development of transnational feminist responses. However, such "unifying strategies" are not without their problems. The difficulty lies in how to actuate a third space, how to conduct a connective politics that neither suppresses difference nor reduces it to "the liberal emphasis on equality" that "fails to recognize injustice, oppression, and power imbalances" among women.[10]

In what follows, I will be further elucidating both the challenges to the construction of feminist identities and communities represented by global restructuring and the trends in feminist theorizing in the context of global restructuring that are resulting from these challenges. I will also be exploring debates over the possibilities of a transnational feminist politics that does not (re)produce the logic of globalization that upholds inequalities and hegemonies (that is, ideological and structural power relations) among women. Finally, I will be examining two forms of transnational feminist practices, "world-traveling" and "faithless translation," which constitute potential methods for actualizing nonhegemonic relations among women. Such practices start from an understanding of the hybrid nature of identities made palpable by the simultaneously conflicting and conjoining forces of globalization, and move us to new conceptualizations of hybrid feminist politics that can walk the "fine line" between "diversity and fragmentation" and between unifying connections and homogenizing hegemonies.[11]

The Global Restructuring of Feminism

As Marianne Marchand and I have argued elsewhere, globalization cannot be reduced simply to top-down economic forces and effects.[12] We prefer the term "global restructuring" because it evokes the far more complex material, ideological, and symbolic "unsettlings" that are simultaneously occurring at all levels from the market and the state to the household and the individual. These destabilizations, as posited in the fast-expanding literature on global restructuring, include the globalization of the economy made possible by developments in communications technology; the spatial reorganization of production that produces a global division of labor; the disruption of the geopolitical categories of West, East, North, and South; increasing economic polarization within the geographical North and the South producing a large economic South in all geographical areas; the internationalization of the state (in which it becomes more beholden to financial and corporate interests than to citizens) and the attendant privatization of public space; and massive cross-border flows of information, goods, services, and people. These technological, economic, and political processes are also related to the rise of globalizing cultural processes associated with two contradictory forces. On the one hand, homogenization is produced by time and space compression, global markets, and global media; on the other hand, fragmentation of political identity is produced as national identities are crosscut, complexly mediated, or hybridized by class, race, ethnic, gender, and sexual identities. According to Roberta Garner, this latter aspect of globalizing culture means "that movements must devote more time, energy, and resources to 'calling' potential supporters in terms of a specific identity."[13] It also means that any single identity, whether based on gender, class, nationality, race, or sexuality, that is called upon or called into being to serve as the basis of a social movement will be a site of contestation.

Under these conditions, new discursive constructions of feminism have proliferated. These include the development of postmodern, postcolonial, and post-Communist feminisms associated with women's situatedness in different parts of the world economy (such as the economic West, East, and South), and a dizzying array of "hyphenated" feminisms based on sometimes surprising combinations of new and old constructions of gender, ethnic, national, class, and sexual identities (Asian-American-queer-anti-racist feminists, French-socialist-lesbian feminists, Egyptian-Islamic-anti-imperialist feminists, ad infinitum). Of course, conflicts in feminism that historically have grown out of competing discursive constructions of a "female" political identity as the basis for political solidarity are not new. For example, debates have raged for at least a century over whether women should organize as mothers, workers, or citizens to bring about social change.[14] Today, however, the particularly destabilizing and fragmenting forces of global restructuring significantly multiply and complicate the range of potential identity formations for women. The sheer proliferation of discursive constructions of women, mediated by ever-shifting meanings of nation, race, ethnicity, gender, and sexuality, increases feminist frictions over the political identities of women able to serve as bases for any single "imagined community" of feminism. This has produced what has been termed the "doxa of difference"[15] in feminist theorizing, which mitigates against any one notion of feminist community and, in some readings, puts into question the very idea of feminism itself.

At the same time, the homogenizing forces of global restructuring produce discourses that reduce women (and men) to depoliticized, economic ciphers, rendering them variously as consumers, service providers, and cheap labor to serve the interests of transnational capital. This legitimizes ever more exclusive communities, whose prosperity depends upon pushing more and more people to the economic margins. One response to these exclusions has been the rise of reactionary ethno/religious nationalisms, which themselves transform economically excluded communities into communities of cultural exclusion. Not only do such movements exclude —often violently—the perspectives of those who are deemed to be "outsiders," but they also rest on homogenizing, reductionist, and problematic constructions of "their" women, thereby silencing and excluding the perspectives of women who do not conform to these constructions. One way is to emphasize women's roles as mothers/symbols/embodiments of (but not equal participants in) the nation or "traditional" culture. Approaches to countering communities of exclusion produced by both global capital and ethno/religious nationalisms include the call for a worldwide community, a "global civil society" based on universalist principles of human rights. This still vague concept, however, has been criticized for its own homogenizing tendencies, both in the degree that it rests upon Western-centric and gender-neutral concepts of rights, and in its failure to acknowledge oppressive forces within civil society itself.

Another approach to countering exclusion as well as insufficiencies associated with the concept of global civil society is the move toward what is termed "transnational feminism," a term intended to distinguish itself from such terms as "international" and "global" feminism. These smack of an older "missionary" model of global sisterhood through which women's diversity was collapsed under "a universalized Western model of women's liberation that celebrates individuality and modernity."[16] Instead, transnational feminist practices seek to "address the concerns of women around the world in the historicized particularity of their relationship to multiple patriarchies as well as to international economic hegemonies. . . . Transnational feminist practices require this kind of comparative work rather than the relativistic linking of 'differences' undertaken by proponents of 'global feminism': that is, to compare multiple, overlapping, and discrete oppressions rather than to construct a theory of hegemonic oppression under a unified category of gender."[17] The development of such anti-imperialist transnational feminist practices, however, is complicated by the fact that transnational feminism is not just a resistance to, but also is a product of global restructuring.

Contemporary transnational feminist organizing emerged, in part, as a response to the growing concentration of power in global economic institutions, including international financial institutions (IFIs) and transnational corporations (TNCs). Women have little say in these transnational institutions and yet bear the brunt of the effects of their policies and practices.

Thus, feminist activism has increasingly "gone global" as evidenced by the growing number of transnational feminist nongovernmental organizations (NGOs) formed to lobby IFIs to adopt gender-sensitive policies. In effect, then, the transnationalization of power created the material conditions that gave birth to contemporary transnational feminist politics. Transnational feminism is also a product of increasing encounters between unequally positioned women in the world economy through processes such as migration and outsourcing production processes, and through the electronic information flows that characterize global restructuring. Both give rise to transnational coalition-building and strategies of resistance to mitigate the negative economic impacts of global restructuring on women. As Chandra Mohanty has argued, global capital ironically produces both the basis for and the necessity to establish a common context for the struggles of "Third-World women workers" North and South. Although they have different histories and live in different national and cultural contexts, such workers are linked "by the logic and operation of capital in the contemporary global arena."[18]

However, Mohanty and others observe that transnational feminist politics themselves reproduce the hegemonies of global capital and Western feminism to the degree that they ignore the asymmetrical nature of the linkages among women that are forged through processes of global restructuring. Gayatri Spivak offers perhaps the most scathing critique of transnational feminism and how it is implicated in global power structures that (re)produce old and new relations of dominance. In her view, the relationship between the rise of globalization and the growth of transnational women's organizing through the succession of large-scale United Nations women's conferences since 1976 is an ominous one. She is critical of the way in which high-level meetings on the status of women speak for "the subaltern—the woman denied access to social mobility . . . defining, not her way of acting, but her suffering others' actions."[19] Spivak is also suspicious of "the effort to bring the world's women under one rule of law, one civil society" at the behest of demands from mostly elite women because it implies a "grand design to bring the world's rural poor under one rule of finance, one global capital" run by the world's capitalist elite.[20]

Spivak's view that transnational feminism is problematically enmeshed in the "power lines" of the United Nations, donor consortia, governments, and elite nongovernmental organizations is echoed in what Zillah Eisenstein, Vandana Shiva, and Jacqui Alexander and Chandra Mohanty variously criticize as "free trade" or "free market" feminism or "feminism for export."[21] These terms characterize forms of transnational feminist politics that they see are too easily coopted by or elided with international financial institutions and business interests. Such interests seek to transnationalize liberal individualist feminism through which women can be constructed as new entrepreneurs and free wage laborers to serve the global economy.

Related to the foregoing critiques are growing concerns about the "NGO-ization" of feminism as the result of so much feminist transnational organizing. As Margaret Keck and Kathryn Sikkink note, transnational advocacy networks develop when channels between domestic groups and their governments are blocked, a particular feature of globalization referred to as the internationalization of the state.[22] They are fostered by international (especially UN) conferences and, increasingly, by the Internet (another globalizing agent). As Gita Sen argues, the development of transnational feminist politics can also lead to the de-democratization of social movements, a result of the professionalization required to participate in international fora.[23] One outcome is to separate professional international organizers from their grassroots bases, both reducing their accountability to movement members and increasing their vulnerability to co-optation. At the same time, the current penchant of international governmental organizations and international financial institutions for "participation" by civil society or NGOs can be read as part of a neoliberal agenda to weaken state accountability and to privilege those elements of civil society (such as private business interests and reactionary cultural and religious interests) likely to deepen relations of domination.[24]

Thus, the uneven and fragmenting processes of global restructuring facilitate the production of significantly different and unequally positioned female subjects, who are, nevertheless, bound together, however asymmetrically, in what Rita Felski calls relations of "complicated entanglement."[25] On the one hand, they confront in varying contexts international economic, national, and local hegemonies; on the other hand, they encounter one another through globalizing processes. At the same time, the homogenizing forces of global restructuring mitigate against nonhegemonic and anti-imperialist transnational feminist practices. The question then becomes how to produce transnational feminist practices that reshape the logic of global restructuring away from hegemony, domination, and exclusion and toward the formation of nonimperialist, equitable, and inclusive relationships among women. Such relationships can serve as the foundations upon which new multivalent "imagined" feminist communities can be based.

World-Traveling Feminist Practices

Transnational feminist politics are embedded in global power structures, but seeing feminism as a site of global restructuring is also to see it as a space marked by constant negotiation and renegotiation of boundaries, meanings, and identities. Under these conditions, no dominant or homogeneous image of "woman" or feminism can prevail. Thus, the idea that there are conflicts *within* feminism over the representation of "woman" or women[26] is giving way to notions of multiple feminist resistances. These are characterized by "a complex array of identifications, partial self-recognitions, and critical refusals, whereby subordinated groups negotiate their ambivalent relationships to the representations that define them."[27] Such resistances are also becoming increasingly and complicatedly interconnected through the process of "metissage," or "borrowing or lending across porous cultural boundaries," which enables the recognition not only of difference within and between female subjects but also of "affiliations, cross-pollinations, echoes, and repetitions."[28] Viewing feminism as a site constantly (re)negotiating its boundaries and meanings rather than as one torn by internal conflict over the merits of its forms also "allows us to conceive of multiple, interconnecting axes of affiliation and differentiation"[29] among women and feminisms. This enables us to think about and to engage in nonhegemonic transnational feminist practices.

A particular nonhegemonic transnational feminist practice is what Maria Lugones calls "'world'-travelling."[30] This is not superficial globe-trotting in which privileged subjects travel to other lands to peer briefly into the lives of subalterns to determine how their oppression should be described. Rather it refers to "a non-arrogant way of seeing and being," a form of "cross-cultural and cross-racial loving."[31] It does not reduce subjects to objects or "others" and does not seek to assimilate women under any common definition of "woman" or negate the particularistic histories, experiences, or perspectives of women. For Lugones, a world is not a fixed geographical place or a singular identity. It can be variously—and often simultaneously—a "whole society," a "tiny portion of a particular society," a construct of memory and imagination, an "incomplete visionary non-utopian construction of life," a "traditional construction of life," and/or a construction of one's life (often purveyed by dominant social and cultural forces) that one does not "understand or accept" but nevertheless enacts unconsciously or out of necessity.[32] Differing worlds exist within as well as outside of ourselves. To "travel," then, means "shift[ing] from being one person to being a different person,"[33] not by adopting a disingenuous pose, but rather in terms of acting out a "plurality of selves."[34] Lugones argues that this plurality of self-knowledge is most available to those from nondominant cultures and social strata who live both in those worlds and the worlds of those who dominate them. Those who experience the "dis-ease" of inhabiting and, thus, crisscrossing multiple worlds are "world"-travelers because it is difficult to claim any single fixed self-identity for the whole of their living. On the other hand, the "agonistic traveller," whose identity is fixed, "imbued with *self-importance,*" and rests upon winning, "*cannot* travel across 'worlds,' though [s/he] can kill other 'worlds.'"[35]

How can an agonistic traveler become a world traveler? How can she learn to travel in ways to find that "others" are "really subjects, lively beings, resistors, constructors of visions even though in the mainstream construction they are animated only by the arrogant perceiver and are pliable, foldable, file-awayable, classifiable"?[36] How can the agonistic traveler disrupt her image of self to make that self open to traveling to the worlds of other subjects? Chilla Bulbeck, drawing upon the work of Lugones and Paula Gunning, argues that the prerequisite to world traveling for those feminists whose privileged perspectives have inclined them most to arrogant perception—that is, white, Western feminists—is "understanding the cultural pressures which created 'us,' the self."[37] This would include critically examining the construction of whiteness, Eurocentrism, Americanism, and so on; exploring how and how much the Western self has been constructed in opposition to "the other," and then interrogating the self about one's white, Western, class, and/or heterosexual privilege. By historicizing, particularizing and, thus, denormalizing and decentering themselves, white, Western feminists are learning to develop the capacity to resist universalizing their own experiences and therefore to avoid prejudging the experiences and practices of women different from themselves. This process of decolonizing identities is uneven due to countervailing global circulations of power that press continually for the reproduction of relations of domination among women; indeed, acknowledgment of these forces and pressures is key to developing a plurality of self-understandings which can resist them.

To conduct a self-examination that is able to open the way to nonarrogant or "loving perception," requires "looking at ourselves as others might see us."[38] Bulbeck recounts multiple examples of how women from South and East Asia view Western feminists. Their perceptions unsettle many comfortable assumptions too many Western feminists have about themselves. Among them are the following:

> Some Japanese women expressed surprise that American women can claim to be feminist in a country with high rates of rape, domestic violence and infant mortality. . . . Luo Ping, although impressed by the gentle Swedish men pushing baby carriages, notes that in the West, "women do not have basic rights to their own surnames . . . they don't even have abortion rights". . . . While one of my Beijing students in 1993 drew an analogy between the beauty myth and foot-binding, my students could hardly come to grips with silicone implants and anorexia, so prevalent in the West. They tentatively suggested that, in contrast to their own stable

> sense of self-worth as females, Western women must be lacking in self-respect and dignity. Similarly Indrani Ganguly noted, "I was really shocked to find out how far very intelligent and otherwise quite independent women would starve themselves, to conform to pretty unrealistic expectations."[39]

Similarly women in post-Communist contexts have questioned the liberatory efficacy of Western feminism for women in the West and, thus, its applicability to women in the East. For example, when Julie Beck interviewed several Czech professional women involved in developing NGOs on a range of women's and human rights issues, she found that the respondents consciously distanced themselves from the images of Western women portrayed in imported media images as "dependent, stupid beings . . . interested only in fashion—just empty, very empty."[40] They also distanced themselves from dominant images portraying Western feminism as antithetical to their own positions that "a woman's power and strength lie in her femininity, her sexuality, and her ability for motherhood."[41] As one respondent, a lawyer who runs a small legal education center for women, put it, "First, calling herself a feminist, to be a feminist here in the Czech Republic, means to diminish or liquidate herself. It's unacceptable, so every feminist here says, 'Oh, I am anti-feminist.'"[42]

Although such perceptions may be based on disinformation purveyed by global media and influenced as well by local and national patriarchies with interests in portraying feminism as a uniform and alien ideology, they also suggest that Western feminists reexamine their own subjectivities and projects by taking seriously the subjectivities of postcolonial and post-Communist women. To simply "constrain, erase, or deem aberrant" these perceptions, or reduce them to false consciousness, would be to jettison some openings for creating "non-imperialistic understanding between people."[43] Adding weight to these perceptions requires, finally, "seeing the other as she sees herself in her own cultural contexts."[44] For example, Bulbeck points to how Western feminist preoccupations with speaking or individual voice as a sign of agency and freedom result in a misreading of cultural practices in which women are seemingly silenced yet are in control of the situation. One such misreading has been made about Maori women who have major roles in welcoming the participants to and setting the tone for ancestral meetings through ritualistic chanting and body language, yet do not "speak" in the Western sense in these meetings.[45] Bulbeck also observes that the assumptions valorizing an opposition between the individual and community in the Western mind are neither shared by nor applicable to cultures in which rights are gained through observing social responsibilities and cultural values, not acting against them.

> A meeting of 600 women from ten Asian and Pacific nations in 1993 agreed to a new definition of democracy, based not on a form of government but as "a question of how we relate to each other and how decisions are made." Although democracy must be an internalised value system, it must "flow through the family, community, society, the State and at the global level." Women's empowerment was to be striven for collectively rather than seeking the empowerment of individual women. In Japan there is a slogan "men superior, women dominant." Equality is measured over a lifetime rather than at any point in time, and Japanese women seek equality through pragmatism and nonconfrontation in a culture which values interpersonal harmony. Similarly, middle class Vietnamese women come to rely on the mutuality of social institutions "out of a sense of rightness rather than fear or submission."[46]

This view that cultural difference need not be a source of disabling division among women and, in fact, may serve to democratize feminism and its meanings is echoed by critics of Susan Moller Okin's essay, "Is Multiculturalism Bad for Women?"[47] Okin takes the position that liberal arguments for group/minority rights are in unhealthy tension with liberal feminist principles because they end up condoning cultural traditions and practices which justify sex discrimination and violence against women, especially in the private realm. A host of largely postcolonial critics argue that her polemic is problematic in that her representations of both feminism and multiculturalism are too narrow, either making the opposition too stark and overdrawn or setting up a false opposition. For some, the issue is not *whether* but *which* cultural ideologies and practices undermine feminist principles. They ask why Okin singles out, in particular, non-Western, minority, and/or "traditional" cultural practices, arguing that they are somehow more patriarchal then Western, majority, and/or "modern" cultural practices. Okin does admit that Western culture sustains various forms of overt and covert sex discrimination. However, she neglects the ways in which Western discriminatory practices are most implicated in sustaining racial, economic, and other structural inequalities that contribute so significantly to women's inequality within and outside the West. She also fails to consider that some of what she claims are traditional practices may be of relatively recent origin, the results of colonial impositions, variegated responses to (neo)colonial contact over time, and/or postcolonial political regimes'—and their oppositions'—manipulations of religious and cultural interpretations. Finally, there is the issue of where to draw the line between practices that are "imposed" upon women and those that are more fully "chosen" by women, as well as which cultural practices, either "traditional" or "modern," serve to enable feminist principles rather than act as barriers against them.

These latter points are addressed to some degree by those who argue that feminism is consistent with a variety of cultural traditions. They point out that indigenous feminist movements have emerged in a host of cultural contexts. They argue further that what feminists share with multiculturalist movements that seek cultural survival and diversity as well as with those members of "traditional" cultures and religions who seek more "authentic" and/or open interpretations of tradition is an openness to difference and a resistance to oppressive impositions by dominant groups. For example, Azizah Al-Hibri argues that far from condoning violence against women, Islamic texts enjoin believers to intervene against such violence, thus sharing, in this instance, a common moral framework with secular feminism.[48] Pointedly, Al-Hibri asks: "Why is it oppressive to wear a head scarf but liberating to wear a miniskirt? . . . Clearly, I could build a limited united front with secular feminists and try to foster popular sentiment against self-oppressive choices. But my Islamic training and knowledge of my community tell me that many of these Muslim sisters have thought seriously about the issue of covering their heads and have reached the conclusions different from mine. Forcing them to abandon their religious choices is not only patronizing but fundamentally unIslamic! Islam has an established etiquette of difference, by which I may explain my position to other Muslims without ever claiming exclusive access to the truth or becoming coercive."[49]

Okin remains skeptical that theocratic regimes allow this level of articulated intra-cultural and intra-religious difference, especially in the absence of the liberal principle that all views can be expressed. She further argues that without educational exposure (preferably mandated by the liberal state) to other cultural and religious ideas, cultural and religious group members cannot be said to be making a choice about their beliefs and practices.[50] However, in her insistence that only a liberal order can ensure equality and choice, she neglects her own and other Western feminists' critiques of liberalism as based on a unitary (male), "privatizing, withdrawalist," and individualist conception of citizenship under which women are not asked "what sorts of institutions or principles" they "would choose." This makes liberalism "at least tensely related to feminism's project of empowering women to act in concert to advance their own aims."[51]

Thus, one can argue that both liberalism and multiculturalism have agonistic relationships with feminism. However, this does not mean that both of these "traditions" need be completely jettisoned from feminist practices. Elements of each can be and are selectively and strategically woven into world-traveling feminist practices. Western feminists' support for greater gender equality within "other" cultures is predicated on holding up their own dominant cultural practices "to the same critical scrutiny they apply to Others, to hear the plural voices of women everywhere and to learn from them, while also refusing to prejudge the merits of practices that are unfamiliar or threatening to those of us raised in bourgeois liberal societies. For the sake of future solidarity of women as feminists, the question of what constitutes gender (in)equality must be kept disturbingly open to perpetual reinterrogation."[52] Such reinterrogations emerge as women "negotiate" between "intracultural gender inequalities" (or local patriarchies) and "intercultural oppression" (or global economic, political, and cultural hegemonies),[53] using necessarily hybrid perspectives and strategies and thereby continually producing new hybridized meanings of feminism.

Faithlessly Translated Feminisms

Negotiations, in which the meanings of feminism are reworked or reconfigured to resist the hegemonic and exclusionary aspects of global restructuring, can be likened to a process of "faithless translation." Whereas, in the popular imagination, "translation" refers to the process by which, for example, "a book is made available, with its original meanings intact, to a new set of readers," linguists are aware that "new meanings are always forged by the interaction of languages."[54] The postcolonial concept of "faithless translation," however, goes further in calling for "a necessarily faithless appropriation, a rewriting of a text"[55] to create not just different, but more just meanings. Anna Tsing finds this method at work when environmental activists in India rewrote a U.S. environmental think-tank report which claimed that all countries should be equally responsible for reducing emissions that lead to global warming. Based on the same statistics used by this Western think tank, Indian environmentalists were able to argue that it is, in fact, mostly the countries of the North that have exceeded acceptable emission standards. Unlike the insistence of U.S. analysts that every country reduce its emissions by the same proportion, the Indian analysts suggest that reductions in global emissions levels are largely the responsibility of developed countries. Even so, rather than taking the position that environmental protection is just a Northern or Western issue, they argue for a Southern environmentalism with very different priorities and commitments: namely, acting upon "grassroots awareness of the dangers of misusing natural resources" and seeking "social equality in resource management."[56] These analysts reject not only the imposition of a Northern environmentalism "which attempts to manage global resources for the benefit of Northern nature lovers and consumers,"[57] but also nationalist Third World claims, such as those advanced by Brazilian officials, that juxtapose development with environmentalism. "Indian radicals stepped in to translate 'development versus environmentalism' into 'two competing environmentalisms.' In this translation, development is still a defining feature of the South, but it is equity- rather than progress-oriented. Not an opponent of environmentalism, equity-oriented development is a *version* of environmentalism. The challenge to the North is not a nation-building agenda but an alliance of grassroots protests. The Indian claim, unlike that of Brazilian leaders, is not nationalist, but anti-colonial. . . . One can see elements of the Brazilian agenda: poverty, participation, resistance to imperial rule. But they have been rewritten into a new framework."[58] Such reframing makes more room for the kind of transnational organizing that confronts transnational power structures while at the same time both giving voice and being responsible to grassroots activists.

Another example of faithless translation comes from Beck's examination of how post-Communist women activists in the Czech Republic are identifying themselves and their projects in the context of transition. She finds in their self-reports that they "borrow" selectively and simultaneously from Western feminism, state socialism, pre-Communist cultural traditions, and liberal individualism to produce a version of feminism she refers to as "gender humanism." This perspective refuses to engage in a Western-style critique of patriarchy by resisting state repression and exploitative global market forces in addition to gender inequality.

> In publicly enacting their own agency, a possibility which the influx of the market and democratic freedoms have offered them, they appropriate aspects of liberal individualism and reject internalized passivity. But in simultaneously drawing upon positive aspects of socialist egalitarianism and waging a sustained critique of materialistic values, these women essentially refuse to embrace liberal individualism, liberal feminism, and many aspects of the new market culture . . . The socialist legacy, then, is Janus-faced, for at the same time that it incites these women to escape from its repressive constraints on personality, its egalitarian principles and achievement of mass education, training, and full employment for women sustain a strain of resistance against new signs of gender discrimination, as well as provide the foundation from which these women differentiate their feminist egalitarianism from Western liberal feminism. This legacy, coupled with pre-socialist Czech forms of gender equality and "European traditions," which boast of complementarity between the sexes, may provide yet another point from which Western market values are contested even as certain aspects of the market system are embraced.[59]

This "metissage" of traditions and ideologies does not erase the contradictions among them. Rather it enables us to see that our histories are "not segregated cultural lines but lumpy and contestable aggregations"[60] in which juxtaposed positions are not collapsed but brought into negotiation to produce reframings of those positions and thus new anti-oppressive meanings and uses for them.

World-traveling, non-Western, and minority women are producing faithlessly translated or reframed feminisms. Such approaches are more meaningful in relation to their own (multi)cultural contexts and particular, albeit complexly aggregated and mediated, histories. They also are more useful in relation to developing local and transnational strategies that address their specific experiences of patriarchies and global capital. Western feminists who embrace such world-traveling feminist practices must, as part of the process, reframe their own feminisms in relation to the new meanings "other" feminists are producing. This also requires that Western feminists acknowledge how the experiences and perspectives of others become distorted through problematic framing when they cross national and cultural borders. Uma Narayan argues that dominant Western cultural frames often act to filter out non-Western information on issues that connect the experiences of Western and Third World women, such as domestic violence or global economic exploitation of women workers.[61] Instead, they focus on what are assumed to be "backward" and "alien" cultural practices such as female circumcision, dowry-murders, and sati, to which Third World women's "problems" then can be reduced. A world-traveling feminist response to such reductionism and exoticization would include asking why, for example, dowry-murders get more statistical attention in India and more media attention in the United States than do far more commonplace and often less extreme forms of domestic violence that women in India and the United States both experience. Even in cases of extreme violence, the murder of women by fire is no more horrific than the murder of women by firearms. It is merely a question of the relative availability of kerosene and guns in households in these two countries. Women would benefit more by challenging the process by which domestic violence in non-Western contexts is reduced to cultural explanations while multiple explanations, few of which attribute blame to national culture, exist for the phenomenon in the West; and by questioning what "kinds of 'contextual information' are often left behind when issues cross national borders" as well as what issues of greater importance to larger numbers of women, such as Western-induced global economic exploitation, "are held up at the border" altogether.[62]

Narayan is pessimistic about the possibility of ever achieving full "cross-cultural understanding." Translations, even by world travelers who can share contextualized knowledges as a result of inhabiting two or more worlds, can never be completely faithful due to the "'multiple mediations' that work to 'shape' issues in different national contexts."[63] But this raises the question of whether completely faithful translations are necessary to produce solidarities, especially in light of the potentials for new understandings of the self and other arising out of the renegotiations of meanings involved in faithless translation. For Lugones, "intimate" knowledge, or "deep knowledge of the other self,"[64] is not a prerequisite for world traveling nor is total transparency or agreement necessary for the development of "loving perception." What is required to build a nonhegemonic transnational feminist politics of loving and more democratized feminist communities is "walking the tightrope of connection, distance and power"[65] to reach a recognition that the divides that make us also bind us.

Conclusion

In the face of the horrendous disintegrative and integrative violence at work in the world that is carried on under the name of globalization, a new urgency to construct political solidarities to counter this violence is emerging. The current paradigm shift in feminist thinking and discourse, from an almost exclusive emphasis on differences among women to a more complicated story about our hybrid identities and our interdependencies, is an outgrowth of this new urgency. It is also a reflection of the simultaneity of sameness and difference that global restructuring evokes. Although forces of difference as fragmentation and sameness as homogenization coexist under globalization, contemporary feminists are rejecting this synthesis in favor of a "'synthesis without violence'"[66] in which there is space for diversity and connection. For Seyla Benhabib, this means building solidaristic communities in which multiple identities are acknowledged and listened to "with respect for the many webs of interlocution that constitute our lives."[67] I have argued that the methods of world traveling and faithless translation hold promise for vitalizing solidaristic feminist communities that can counter the violence of globalization. These methods do not depoliticize difference. Rather, they repoliticize community, making it not a site of naturalistic, exclusivist, or homogenized identities, but a space for connective politics.

Notes

Susan Gal, "Feminism and Civil Society," in *Transitions, Environments, Translations: Feminisms in International Politics,* ed. Joan W. Scott, Cora Kaplan, and Debra Keates (New York and London: Routledge, 1997), 43.

1. See Marianne H. Marchand and Anne Sisson Runyan, eds., *Gender and Global Restructuring: Sightings, Sites and Resistances* (London and New York: Routledge, 2000) for a review of this literature and for a more extensive discussion of reconceptualizing global restructuring through a gender lens as well as a preliminary discussion of the restructuring of feminism, both of which inform my approach here.

2. Seyla Benhabib, "Sexual Difference and Collective Identities: The New Global Constellation," *Signs* 24, 2 (1999): 336.

3. Ibid.

4. Ibid.

5. Robin L. Teske, "Political Space: The Importance of the Inbetween," in *Conscious Acts and the Politics of Social Change*, vol. 1 of *Feminist Approaches to Social Movements, Community, and Power*, ed. Robin L. Teske and Mary Ann Tétreault (Columbia: University of South Carolina Press, 2000), 72–90.

6. Ibid., 73.

7. Aili Mari Tripp, "Rethinking Difference: Comparative Perspectives from Africa," *Signs* 25, 3 (2000): 649.

8. Ibid.

9. Ibid., 673.

10. Ibid.

11. Ibid.

12. See Marchand and Runyan, ed., *Gender and Global Restructuring.*

13. Roberta Garner, "Transnational Movements in a Postmodern Society," *Peace Review* 6, 4 (Winter 1994): 429.

14. See, for example, Marianne Hirsch and Evelyn Fox Keller, eds., *Conflicts in Feminism* (New York and London: Routledge, 1990).

15. See Rita Felski, "The Doxa of Difference," *Signs* 23, 1 (1997): 1–21. See also Penny A. Weiss and Marilyn Friedman, eds., *Feminism and Community* (Philadelphia: Temple University Press, 1995) for a somewhat different, but related, characterization of the problem of difference for feminist theorizations of community.

16. Inderpal Grewal and Caren Kaplan, "Introduction: Transnational Feminist Practices and Questions of Postmodernity," in *Scattered Hegemonies: Postmodernity and Transnational Feminist Practices*, ed. Inderpal Grewal and Caren Kaplan (Minneapolis and London: University of Minnesota Press, 1994), 17.

17. Ibid., 17–18.

18. Chandra Talpade Mohanty, "Women Workers and Capitalist Scripts: Ideologies of Domination, Common Interests, and the Politics of Solidarity," in *Feminist Genealogies, Colonial Legacies, Democratic Futures*, ed. M. Jacqui Alexander and Chandra Talpade Mohanty (New York and London: Routledge, 1997), 28.

19. Gayatri C. Spivak, "Gender and International Studies," *Millennium: Journal of International Studies* 27, 4 (1998): 815.

20. Ibid.

21. Zillah Eisenstein, "Stop Stomping on the Rest of Us: Retrieving Publicness from the Privatization of the Globe," *Journal of Global Legal Studies* 4, 59 (1996): 59–95; Vandana Shiva, *Trading Our Lives Away: An Ecological and Gender Analysis of "Free Trade" and the WTO* (Penang, Malaysia and New Delhi, India: PAN Asia and Pacific and Research Foundation for Science, Technology and Natural Resource Policy, 1995); M. Jacqui Alexander and Chandra Talpade Mohanty, "Introduction: Genealogies, Legacies, Movements," in *Feminist Genealogies, Colonial Legacies, Democratic Futures.*

22. Margaret E. Keck and Kathryn Sikkink, eds., *Activists Beyond Borders: Advocacy Networks in International Politics* (Ithaca, N.Y.: Cornell University Press, 1998), 12. As noted earlier in this chapter, the internationalization of the state refers to national governments becoming more beholden to international financial institutions and transnational corporations than to citizens.

23. Gita Sen, "Globalization in the 21st Century: Challenges for Civil Society" (presented as the University of Amsterdam Development Lecture, 20 June 1997, University of Amsterdam). For similar arguments, see also Mary K. Meyer and Elisabeth Prügl, eds., *Gender Politics in Global Governance* (Boulder, Colo.: Rowman and Littlefield, 1999).

24. See Anne Sisson Runyan, "Women in the Neoliberal 'Frame,'" in *Gender Politics in Global Governance,* 210–20 for a more extensive discussion of this point.

25. Felski, "Doxa of Difference," 13.

26. This approach is codified in Hirsch and Keller, *Conflicts in Feminism.*

27. Felski, "Doxa of Difference," 24.

28. Ibid., 12.

29. Ibid.

30. Maria Lugones, "Playfulness, 'World'-Travelling, and Loving Perception," in *Making Face, Making Soul/Haciendo Caras: Creative and Critical Perspectives by Women of Color,* ed. Gloria Anzaldúa (San Francisco: Aunt Lute Foundation Books, 1990), 390–402.

31. Ibid., 390.

32. Ibid., 395–96.

33. Ibid., 396.

34. Ibid., 398.

35. Ibid., 400.

36. Ibid., 402.

37. Chilla Bulbeck, *Re-Orienting Western Feminisms: Women's Diversity in a Postcolonial World* (Cambridge: Cambridge University Press, 1998), 84.

38. Ibid.

39. Ibid., 212, 213.

40. Julie Beck, "(Re)Negotiating Selfhood and Citizenship in the Post-Communist Czech Republic: Five Women Activists Speak about Transition and Feminism," in *Gender and Global Restructuring,* 188.

41. Ibid.

42. Ibid., 185.

43. Lugones, "Playfulness, 'World'-Travelling, and Loving Perception," 396.

44. Bulbeck, *Re-Orienting Western Feminisms,* 84.

45. Ibid., 60–61.

46. Ibid., 75.

47. See Joshua Cohen, Matthew Howard, and Martha C. Nussbaum, eds., *Is Multiculturalism Bad for Women? Susan Moller Okin and Respondents* (Princeton, N.J.: Princeton University Press, 1999).

48. Azizah Al-Hibri, "Is Western Patriarchal Feminism Good for Third World/Minority Women?" in *Is Multiculturalism Bad for Women?* 45–46.

49. Ibid., 46.

50. See Susan Moller Okin, "Reply," in *Is Multiculturalism Bad for Women?* 117–31.

51. Will Kymlicka, "Liberal Complacencies," in *Is Multiculturalism Bad for Women?* 33; Bonnie Honig, "My Culture Made Me Do It," in *Is Multiculturalism Bad for Women?* 39.

52. Honig, "My Culture Made Me Do It," 40.

53. Saskia Sassen, "Culture Beyond Gender," in *Is Multiculturalism Bad for Women?* 78.

54. Anna Lowenharpt Tsing, "Transitions as Translations," in *Transitions, Environments, Translations,* 255.

55. Ibid.

56. Ibid., 262.

57. Ibid.

58. Ibid., 263–64.

59. Beck, "(Re)Negotiating Selfhood," 190.

60. Tsing, "Transitions as Translations," 269.

61. Uma Narayan, *Dislocating Cultures: Identities, Traditions, and Third World Feminism* (New York and London: Routledge, 1997), chap. 3.

62. Ibid., 101–3; see also Bulbeck, *Re-Orienting Western Feminisms,* 89.

63. Narayan, *Dislocating Cultures,* 104.

64. Lugones, "Playfulness, 'World'-Travelling, and Loving Perception," 401.

65. Bulbeck, *Re-Orienting Western Feminisms,* 221.

66. Benhabib, "Sexual Difference," 353 n. 2.

67. Ibid., 350.

Part Two

Family Values

Chapter 3

Is This the Educational System You Wanted?

Feminism and Homeschooling

Helen Cordes and Eric Selbin
with Jesse Cordes Selbin and Zoe Cordes Selbin

The stereotypes are familiar to many of you, no doubt: homeschoolers equal fundamentalist Christians or, at their most threatening, bunkered survivalists or, at best, hippy-dippy back-to-the-earth types. Another stereotype, perhaps no less pernicious, is that those of us committed to community, to feminism, to activism are necessarily committed to the public school system, commonly, if often misleadingly, read as a signifier of diversity. These notions helped form our view of homeschooling before we—Eric Selbin, a political science professor, and Helen Cordes, a freelance journalist and author—started homeschooling our daughters Jesse (then eleven) and Zoe (then five) four years ago.

Whatever grains of "truth" may be embedded in such stereotypes, they are little more than misleading caricatures which ill-serve anyone who cares about children, about education, about community, and about change. In our four-years-and-running educational experiment, we've found that rather than narrowing our children's sense of community, homeschooling has greatly expanded it for them and for us. In our sample size of two, we've found homeschooling to be a tremendously female-empowering experience, defined in part by activism and rife with the diversity and creativity largely absent from the public schools where we live (and those in much of the rest of the United States as well). As our daughters continue to realize more of the power and potential that should be every girl's (and boy's) birthright, we have come to view homeschooling as part of our activism: helping one-by-one to create new feminists, activist feminists cognizant of and committed to changing themselves and the world around them.

Our own experience and our research on homeschooling in the United States and abroad has shown that the most common stereotypes about homeschoolers are seriously mistaken. Behind the widespread notion that conservative Christians make up the bulk of homeschoolers is a deliberate and aggressive campaign led by a national fundamentalist Christian homeschool group, which seeks to control public perceptions of homeschooling to further its ultraconservative political agenda.[1] In reality, parents who homeschool for nonreligious reasons are now the *majority* of the estimated two million homeschoolers, a group growing at an estimated 15 percent per year. Parents report that the reasons they decide to homeschool include dissatisfaction with academic quality and concerns about safety, drugs, and adverse peer pressure.[2] Our initial reasons had little to do with unhappiness with local schools, but our homeschooling experience has sharpened our sense that institutionalized schools have fundamental problems. Public, private, even well-thought-out and well-intentioned charter schools need to be radically reimagined, restructured, and reconsidered.

To be fair, some children do well at school. There are large numbers of wonderful and dedicated teachers out there (we have had some and we have met some), and staff and other support people are committed to public schools. What we want to raise here are questions about the "big picture," about what people might find if they questioned some of the basic assumptions about the structure and content of education that we all carry with us. In our view, and that of many educational critics, these often crowded institutions, deemed critical for children's socialization, have evolved into places primarily devoted to system maintenance, crowd control,[3] and the production of "model" consumers.[4]

And as for the stereotype that only the privileged can afford to homeschool, we are well aware of and grateful for the privileges that allow our family some leverage—one steady and two reliable incomes from two professions with some time flexibility and that enjoy credibility in many people's minds.[5] However, we've observed that homeschooling can be much more accessible than many assume. Like many homeschoolers, we've downscaled our consumption expectations, trading added income for added time with and more opportunities for our children. Among the options we see regularly are parents who juggle their schedules to have one adult at home or those who choose jobs with hours that allow more at-home presence. Some parents telecommute or start home-based businesses. Many homeschoolers establish, formally and informally, learning and childcare co-ops. We have, by this time, seen an impressive array of variations; there is no "right way," but simply ways that you and your children discover and uncover as you go along. While the economics may be a struggle, the only real limits to progressive homeschooling are the limits of one's imagination.

Thus, we want to suggest—and will try to outline for you here—how and why homeschooling can be feminist in theory and practice, reflect political action and efforts to create change,[6] and be women-centered and transnational.[7] We would add that the practice(s) of homeschooling are necessarily transitional and may well be, whether consciously and intentionally or not, transformative. In keeping with the premise and promise of these two volumes, we want to help "build better theory and . . . persuade activists that theory is not merely 'academic.'"[8] Perhaps most presumptuously, we believe that enabling and ennobling the emergence of happier and healthier people improves the broader society we live in.

That, at least, is our hope, our dream, our aspiration. Here is our story and what we've found.

Helen is a lifelong feminist (of farm stock), and Eric's feminism evolved in stages (albeit fast-forwarded by Helen). We both agree that having a daughter, and then another, put a visceral and urgent edge to feminism's fundamental necessity. Creating a "baby woman" in a world hostile in all too many ways to her very existence brings, after the initial joy and delight, simultaneous waves of grief and relief. While much has changed for the better just in our own lifetimes, many thorny problems remain for our children to suffer and struggle with, including their growing knowledge that while many gender issues have been at least superficially addressed in our society, girls in other parts of the world are still subjected to overwhelming sexism and horrifying abuse.

We have tried to educate our daughters from early on about the realities of a female-hating culture and their abilities to change it, and also to "inoculate" them against its effects. We believe, perhaps immodestly, we've somewhat succeeded: we high-fived when Jess told her kindergarten teacher that the song about "ten little Indian boys" was both sexist and racist; we grinned as Zoe, then barely four years old, scathingly deconstructed sexist toy ads with (yes, still!) active boys and deferring girls. More importantly, we have watched them try not only to embody the notion that "girls can do (and be) anything" but also to educate their often skeptical pint-sized Texas peers about the concept.

While Helen was writing her *Girl Power* books,[9] a course of events began that made the decision to homeschool inevitable. There was nothing dramatic; the sad part is that everything that happened is so "normal." During her fourth- and fifth-grade years at the local public school, Jess was becoming more and more discouraged because she didn't fit in. No overt cruelty or exclusion dogged her; she was even "friends" with some of the most popular girls. Yet she was consistently shadowed by the sense that the person she was—a book-loving, kids'-game-playing nine-year-old—simply did not measure up to the "ideal" informally but insistently enforced by her peers, girls (and boys) immersed in and obsessed with endless talk of boyfriends and girlfriends; makeup; the most popular TV shows, movies, music, and clothes; and acquisition of the latest kid-consumer items. Sadly, these kids were afraid to "act their age" of nine or ten. Instead they were intent on imitating the attitudes and trappings of teens and adults as their avenue to feelings of power and autonomy.

At the same time, Helen observed in Jess's classrooms variants of the problems she'd been researching for the *Girl Power* books. By the time they reached the fourth and fifth grades, girls had clearly internalized the lesson that looks equaled worth and, amid talk of diets and too-big butts, had created a beauty pecking order. Girls we knew who had been outspoken at earlier ages—including Jesse—had begun the self-silencing process documented by Lyn Mikel Brown, Carol Gilligan, and others, growing reluctant to answer questions and offer opinions in classes.[10] Consistent with the research of Myra and David Sadker, Helen noticed that teachers often paid boys more attention: sometimes it was negative attention, because of boys acting out more, but some teachers spent more time challenging boys to higher achievement than they did girls. Some simply allowed boys more leeway than girls in their classroom behavior.[11] We were also troubled by curricula and learning approaches that were uninspiring and chauvinistic—for example, the state-mandated veneration of the Alamo that starts in first grade.[12]

Troubled by these factors and by our daughter's unhappiness, we discussed the situation with her. At the same time, we did what we could to help her fit in—getting her some of the faddy clothes and CDs she "wanted." (Now she can admit that she did not enjoy them but merely wanted them for the potential popularity-boost they seemed to promise or just to fit in.) But nearly every day after school, Jesse would reveal her anxiety and frustration in the time-honored way of children and, let's be honest, adults: being sad and irritable toward her family, who she knew loved her unconditionally.[13]

The situation came to a head as we considered her imminent passage to middle school, where we knew the peer pressure and, most likely, her misery would only intensify. Helen investigated Jesse's designated middle school, visiting for lunch weekly as a mentor to an eighth-grade girl enrolled there. She could see, both through her mentee's experiences and from what she observed, that sixth graders were jockeying—armed with blasé demeanors and skin-tight outfits—over who was most like the eighth graders. Helen routinely heard children dissed and shamed by others; adults were typically absent or not inclined to interfere. Also, the school principal's reputation and stated preference for running an orderly school (read crowd control and discipline) over advocating innovative academic methods strengthened our resistance to the middle school option.

We briefly considered private schools (doubting they'd be much different), but there are only a few conservative Christian schools in our area. They weren't an option for a pair of thoughtful and articulate feminist Jewish/pagan kids with liberal/progressive leanings—or for their parents.[14] A friend, who had homeschooled her children for several years, enthused about it to us.[15] While homeschooling seemed do-able, we both are strong believers in public education and agonized over taking our kids out of public schools. Our friends, almost uniformly, posed the "but how can you stop supporting the public schools" question whenever we mentioned the possibility of homeschooling. This was no small issue, especially for Eric. He had attended the notoriously bad Louisiana public schools during a period when continued enrollment was a profound political statement symbolizing a family's commitment to integration, to redressing class inequities, and to building a strong community.

After much discussion between us and with Jesse, issues became clearer. We realized that even if we homeschooled, we could still be public school advocates. We had been active parents throughout our daughters' school careers, both in public schools and in a local Montessori school that offered education through third grade. We were familiar with the school system and we had known, supported, and worked with principals, teachers, and others invested in the public schools.[16] This encouraged and gave us a basis from which to question some of what we all "know" about public schools: is it really true that the schools represent a melting pot, designed to break down or at least familiarize students with difference and diversity while building strong community bonds? Perhaps not. In our local schools, color and class lines were all but physically drawn. National research shows that while desegregation has been the law for decades, schools are in fact more segregated (formally and informally) now than at any time in the past thirty-five years.[17] And are schoolchildren inspired and motivated by having peers, like Jess, whom they perceive as more advanced in the classroom? Based on our own experiences and Jess's, we were not hopeful: some classmates would dislike her for getting good grades; others would be resigned to, although not happy about, never being able to be "a smart kid like Jesse."

"Going through school will arm her for the 'real world,'" argued some of our friends, family, and peers. "We all toughed it out," implying so should she. But why, we wondered, should we willingly subject our daughter to a situation that any adult would leave at the earliest opportunity? Picture a workplace where employees are made to feel unvalued by coworkers, the work is uninspiring, and everyone is forced to work on the same level (often with the same material and at the same pace) as office-mates. What if, in addition, you were discriminated against as a woman and bombarded with quasi-official religion? Is it time to get a lawyer? While neither of us had been traumatized by our school years (rather amazing given our respective experiences in a small, rural Catholic school and the Louisiana public schools), we pondered whether we might have had a better education and a better time if we hadn't had to "tough it out" against the effects of being too shy/smart/mouthy/Jewish/dorky/not-whatever-was-in-style.

As we worked toward a decision, Helen and the girls checked out the local resources. The most important was the main social support group for nonreligiously motivated homeschoolers (such groups are popularly known as "inclusive" groups, and they, unlike many fundamentalist homeschool support groups, don't require a "statement of faith" or impose other restrictions on participants). Our findings were encouraging: kids met regularly for various occasions, including for twice-weekly informal soccer/chatting sessions, theater classes, chess club, "park days," and other activities. They seemed relaxed and happy, with children of different ages and genders often interacting. Consumerism was considerably muted—unlike Jess's schoolmates' apparent fixation with Tommy Hilfiger, not one sported the logo. We were particularly relieved by interactions with girls around Jess's age: talk tended toward eclectic books and movies, homeschool projects, or general silliness. Even teenagers weren't embarrassed to play the occasional game of chase or dress-up or engage in spontaneous drama. There was a lot of hugging, a lot of laughing (and the requisite giggling), a generosity of spirit with younger children (especially younger girls), and a lot of conversation.

Jess remained hesitant about the homeschooling prospect. "It seemed to me then that if we homeschooled, I would lose all my friends, structure in learning, and sources for finding out what was 'in,'" Jesse recalls. That summer we asked her regularly how she felt about homeschooling. She would respond in percentages, and her homeschool comfort rating slowly inched up from 25 to 47 and finally, after attending a get-acquainted-with-middle-school gathering a few nights before school started, to 50 percent. Zoe, too, seemed satisfied and even a little relieved about the decision. She had not been looking forward to the longer day required by the Montessori school for students at her level.

Apprehensively, we began our homeschooling adventure. In retrospect, no one expected "the polls" to rise so rapidly. After four months, Jesse was happier than she'd been for several years, finding better—more thoughtful and self-aware—friends than those she'd had during six previous years of school. Because our daughters' homeschooling peers have generally been exposed to diverse viewpoints, our children are able to share more of their lives and interests with them without feeling a need to be cautious and self-censoring. For example, when Zoe (then five) proudly reported her participation in *The Vagina Monologues* performances at Southwestern University and explained author Eve Ensler's motivation for her landmark play, her young peers and their parents weren't shocked and disapproving as we'd warned the girls that some in our community might be. When we hosted a gala coming-of-age/thirteenth-birthday celebration for Jesse, her homeschool friends were already versed in the reasons behind the growing trend to honor and celebrate a girl's menarche as the time when she joins the sisterhood of women.

Homeschool children, including our daughters' close friends, aren't cut off from popular culture—some of them occasionally express concern about their appearance, and some are fans of Britney Spears and 'N Sync. But they are also animated about Shakespeare, local and national issues such as light rail and the ethics of vegetarianism, Indian movies, the "game of questions" from Rosencrantz and Guildenstern, chess, and,—well, we could go on and on and on!

Quite simply, our primary motivations for homeschooling—our concerns about Jesse's unhappiness and our wish that she be able to develop her own interests—have been vindicated. Our fears that she'd become another statistic in the trend documented in the *Girl Power* books and other writings that chart girls' plummeting self-esteem, particularly at middle-school ages, have dissolved. Jesse's self-confidence and self-esteem have soared, a phenomenon observed in other homeschooled girls.[18] She's rarely reluctant to offer opinions and provide answers in groups or settings of any kind. And Zoe, who seemed to personify self-esteem from day one, now has the opportunity to offer her many intriguing opinions and narratives to even wider audiences.

As our homeschooling has continued, so has the blossoming of our favorite homeschool component, the ever-mushrooming and often interacting communities growing around our daughters and turbocharging both their learning experiences and self-esteem. Our two homeschool support groups, a large 300-family group in Austin and a smaller group of families nearer our home in Georgetown, give our children more regular and more interactive contact with a far more diverse group than they had found at school.[19] There's ethnic diversity (African Americans, Hispanics, Asians, and various multi-ethnic mixes), diversity in social and economic class as well as parents' occupations (reggae musicians to software engineers, firefighters to architects, and much more), and, given our locale, a surprising array of political perspectives (Democrats, Republicans, Greens,

Libertarians, Socialists, and apoliticals). There also is a delightful range of believers: Hindus, pagans, Jews, Sufis, along with (this being Texas) plenty of Christians, who in this group, are generally of the liberal variety and definitely not proselytizers.

We particularly enjoy the communities of differing ages, ones that schoolchildren rarely experience in their grade-only peer boxes. Mixed-age interplay is common to homeschool get-togethers, with younger children looking up to Jesse and older ones protective and fond of Zoe. These get-togethers foster interaction with adults as well: many parents give informal and formal guidance and mentorship through career fairs and volunteering opportunities.

Our daughters also have many "peers" at Eric's campus—students, professors, and staff who know them well. Jess and sometimes Zoe, too, have been thrilled to sit in on lectures, symposiums, concerts, and plays. The girls have been able to meet and talk with visiting activists and scholars like Rigoberta Menchú, Carlos Fuentes, and bell hooks. Jess has been generously allowed to attend some courses, most recently one focusing on Shakespeare, previously another on acting methodology. Both girls have been in campus theater productions including *The Vagina Monologues* and Lillian Hellman's *Watch on the Rhine*. They've also performed in several plays—including four by Shakespeare—put on by the local theater guild and by a leading Austin theater, which offers a challenging homeschool drama program. Jess has enjoyed a writing course taught by an English professor from Austin Community College as well as a course on the Middle East. Both girls have had wonderful experiences in writing clubs. "I learned, and continue to learn, a lot in these classes that I very likely wouldn't have learned at school," says Jesse. "And in classes like the Middle East one, we explore lots of different aspects and viewpoints. At school, I might just get the teacher or textbook's one-sided point of view."

Since homeschooling's "schedule" is quite flexible, the children have been able to volunteer much more than they ever had before. They've volunteered and participated in two "Girl Day" all-day workshops designed to empower girls, as well as a goal-setting workshop Helen put on for a group of disadvantaged girls in a YWCA program. They've volunteered at a resource room for abused foster children, at the Reading is Fundamental program that promotes literacy and gives away children's books, and at the local public school's annual reading advocacy day.

We've gotten to know our neighbors better. Zoe often visits the 84-year-old retired woman across the street. She also belongs to a mother-daughter book club, furthering her contact not only with girls her own age but also with adult women. "The good thing about homeschooling is that you can have older or younger kids and even grownups for friends," notes Zoe. "In school, you just have to be in a room with everybody your age, but with homeschooling I have friends of all ages." As a much-sought-after babysitter, Jess has had the opportunity to see how other people structure their lives and how they work with their children.

All of this broad experience and interaction with a range of youngsters, teens, and engaged adults leads us to laugh when people share their concern about our children's presumed lack of social skills because they've been "kept out" of school. With homeschooling, our kids have acquired more positive socialization than most children ever get in a school setting with its de facto peer rule occasionally tempered by the one adult currently responsible for twenty to thirty children. And the results of this are evident not only in our children but in most homeschooled children. Accustomed to being treated with respect by multi-aged peers and the large numbers of adults in their lives, homeschoolers generally emulate the mature role models in negotiating relational problems.[20] Bottom line: we've found it's generally much easier to have a conversation with a homeschooled child than a schooled child, simply because the homeschooler is used to making more conversation with more people.

Another commonly expressed concern is whether homeschooled children are learning as much as they could in a school setting. In the quantitative terms that define "education" in our culture, homeschooled children typically perform well on standardized tests.[21] Test results certainly show that our daughters are doing well. At fourteen, Jesse scored "post high school" across-the-board with an overall average of 96 percent on the California Achievement Test. At nine, Zoe's scores average 94 percent, and in four categories she scored "post–high school." The overall average of Zoe's grade equivalents places her roughly halfway through her junior year of high school. Even more important to us and most other homeschoolers is that their enthusiasm about learning and their ability to integrate knowledge from wide-ranging sources has soared. Their learning is broad and deep with a surprising—at least to us—amount of nuance and sophistication.

One factor facilitating both a love of learning and a desire to follow particular passions is the increased "free" time that homeschooling affords. Because of the one-on-one learning, as well as not having to spend time repeating information and engaging in other time-consuming practices mandated by an institutional setting, homeschoolers need much less time to "do school."[22] For our daughters, the extra time means they can follow interests such as Jess's current fascination with acting, the Middle Ages, strong and powerful women (Queen Elizabeth and Cleopatra have been recent favorites), and, yes, fashion design. She's been able to apprentice at directing at the university, sit in on a lecture on women in medieval times, and pore over fashion history and costuming books. Both children have ample time for reading and writing, with Zoe spontaneously churning out plays, stories, and even commercials, while Jess recently published an article on sexism in children's books for *New Moon,* a national girl's magazine.[23]

And there's also more family time with homeschooling. When Jess was in school, she had the worst schedule in the house. Up and out early, she spent long hours sitting and listening, followed by hours doing relatively mindless homework day after day after day. Our increased family time has resulted in increased communication and bonding among our little community of four as well as relieved our concerns that school, with its mandated hours and requisite homework rising along with grade level, would absorb most of our daughters' waking hours and squeeze out family time. Our children are learning and doing incredible things and seem to revel in a world they are making. So we wonder at times, what is it exactly that they are missing? Have we deprived them of anything significant? Our gut feeling is no—affirmed by our extended family and friends who often note, "This homeschooling thing seems to be working out."

Of course, homeschooling isn't perfect. It takes time away from Helen's writing and researching, although it has also given her a good reason for taking on only the most engaging assignments and forgoing those done primarily to generate income. As Jesse's learning material becomes more complex, Helen spends more time working with her. However, we can avail ourselves of the many resources available to homeschoolers, including occasional tutoring, community college "dual credit" classes intended for high-school-aged students, and a multiplicity of interactive on-line classes that are part of an enormous universe of on-line resources. Eric also feels torn between "professional" responsibilities and wanting to be more involved with the girls' day-to-day education. And, once in a while, our children aren't receptive to the learning we've proposed—Zoe would rather play with roly-polys than memorize multiplication tables (who could blame her) and Jesse, while generally self-motivated, has been less than eager to devote time to physical science.

While most homeschooling families we've met have been delightful, homeschooling does attract some strange bedfellows whose approaches we wouldn't necessarily recommend. We have great respect, however, for homeschoolers who are skilled at accepting differences and focusing on commonalities. For instance, students of differing abilities and interests are not marginalized or ridiculed, as a rule, and are appreciated and recognized for what they bring to the mix—soccer skills, math capabilities, musical abilities, obsession with Shakespeare (or Magic cards), fascination with the

Internet, and so on. Instead of a melting pot designed to reduce difference (and creativity) to a common stew, we found a delightful tossed salad, full of different ingredients constantly being mixed and remixed into new combinations.

Sure, we haven't escaped the shallow consumer culture endemic to schools and our society in general, but that's not entirely bad. We realize that such information is not unimportant, especially as children begin to develop their own views of the world distinct from their parents'. But it seems a lot healthier when these messages are coming from a diverse and varied crowd. We also are happy to see that gender issues, including acceptance of nonheterosexual affiliations, are downplayed in a homeschooling community. Few girls are shrinking violets, and boys and girls interact more easily without the schoolyard taunt of "ooooh, that's your girlfriend/boyfriend" branding them from preschool on up.

In fact, the worst thing about homeschooling is that more children aren't doing it. Take community—most kids are afforded few if any opportunities to create and sustain communities of their own choosing or ones that are fulfilling for them. Adults devote a lot of energy trying to surround themselves with people and situations that reinforce a sense of their own value and efficacy. After spending eight hours in school, followed by a regimen of homework and formal enrichment activities, children not only have little opportunity for such community-building but also are likely to be stressed-out and emotionally drained. Studies tell us that children spend more time interacting with TVs, VCRs, computers, and other electronic devices than with the parents who have a pivotal role in their education and love of learning whether it be in school or at home.[24] Schooled children have little free time and opportunity to follow, or even discover, their passions.[25]

In sum, we've come to believe that homeschooling could, in fact *should*, be a profoundly feminist act-ion/ivity/ualization. If feminism is, in large measure, a multifarious, multifaceted array of approaches to the problems confronted in a world inimical to women's interests, desires, hopes, and dreams, what better place than education—a field long dominated by men and designed to (re)enforce the hierarchy/patriarchy such as the Church, the military, and the state—to work with what is at hand by whatever means necessary.[26] This may seem to ignore that "school" is mostly read and written as the province of women,[27] but here we want to distinguish between this stereotype and the overwhelmingly male direction and domination of educational processes and procedures in this (and most) other societies.[28]

Schools as currently constructed and construed em*body* and en*gender* systems of oppression and domination. Why not resist and rework "school" and education into child-friendly, perhaps more importantly, girl-friendly conceptualizations? A profoundly feminist homeschooling will necessarily generate a progressive social movement rooted in notions of resistance, rebellion, and perhaps even revolution all embedded in and reconstitutive of human community.

Every state and every society seeks to socialize citizens. The community building, however dysfunctional, that occurs in the (roughly/vaguely) common experience of the standard educational system is critical to the maintenance and extension of what is commonly referred to as "civil society." But this term can also be seen less positively, as redolent of latent notions of "civilization" and "the white man's burden." For most people most of the time, the "civilizing mission" of education—in the hands of Church or state—rarely seeks to inculcate messages of freedom, of justice, of equality, of diversity in all its glories; rather education's raison d'être is regulation, homogenization, and obedience to priests, politicians, and advertisers. Why not empower children and parents to wrestle with state and society on their own terms instead? How better to realize the immense revolutionary potential of the bourgeois family.[29]

There are indications that educational institutions are looking to integrate some of homeschooling's advantages. Opposition is increasing to the growing reliance on standardized tests as the sole means of assessing a child's learning. This is particularly true in Texas and other states where teachers are being forced to "teach to the test" to the exclusion of other topics. Colleges are reducing their reliance on SATs, ACTs, and other standardized entrance requirements, and relying more on portfolios that illustrate a prospective student's learning and aptitude to learn more. One reflection of this trend is that homeschoolers are being courted by even elite colleges and universities. Multi-age classrooms are proliferating as more educators realize the importance of children learning from and interacting with peers beyond those of their same chronological age. One Austin, Texas, high school has a program that sounds like group homeschooling. Designed to cut "repetition and fluff" from the curriculum, the school offers an individualized study course, a living-room like classroom, and half-day attendance that leaves time for other pursuits.

Paraphrasing the compelling question about democracy posed by Mexico's Zapatista National Liberation Army, one of the twentieth century's most intriguing social movements, we ask: "Is this the educational system you wanted?"[30] If we are to reimagine "theoretical concepts which . . . have great normative importance to feminist theoreticians and activists,"[31] what better place to begin than with one of the most basic—education. We must "act and not merely be acted upon"[32]—the stakes are too high for our children and ourselves. Such dramatic change does not simply come. It is made by real people living in the real world. "It is not necessary to conquer the world," contend the Zapatistas, "It is sufficient with making it new. Us. Today."[33]

Notes

While primarily written by Helen Cordes and Eric Selbin, whose names are listed here alphabetically, Jesse Cordes Selbin and Zoe Cordes Selbin both wrote brief parts as well as read and commented on the entire manuscript; some of their comments are included. Helen and Eric are responsible for any errors.

1. Helen Cordes, "Battling for the Heart and Soul of Home-schoolers." *Salon*, 2 October 2000. http://www.salon.com/mwt/feature/2000/10/02/homeschooling_battle/index.html (25 April 2002).

2. Patricia Lines, "Homeschooling Comes of Age." *Public Interest* 140 (Summer 2000): 74–85.

3. John Taylor Gatto, *The Underground History of American Education* (New York: Oxford Village Press, 2000).

4. Alex Molnar, *Giving Kids the Business* (Boulder, Colo.: Westview Press, 1996).

5. It is striking the number of times Eric has had people allow that "as a professor" he has the "knowledge to homeschool."

6. With the caveat that while "change" most often—especially in our relevant communities—denotes some sort of Enlightenment, male, linear progression, it need not necessarily do so.

7. Mary Ann Tétreault and Robin L. Teske, "Introduction: Framing the Issues," in *Conscious Acts and the Politics of Social Change*, vol. 1 of *Feminist Approaches to Social Movements, Community, and Power*, ed. Robin L. Teske and Mary Ann Tétreault (Columbia: University of South Carolina Press, 2000), 1.

8. Ibid.

9. Helen Cordes, *Girl Power in the Classroom: A Book about Girls, Their Fears, and Their Future* (Minneapolis, Minn.: Lerner Publications, 2000); Helen Cordes, *Girl Power in the Mirror: A Book about Girls, Their Bodies, and Themselves* (Minneapolis, Minn.: Lerner Publications, 2000)

10. Lyn Mikel Brown and Carol Gilligan, *Meeting at the Crossroads: Women's Psychology and Girls' Development* (Cambridge: Harvard University Press, 1992).

11. Myra Sadker and David Sadker, *Failing at Fairness: How Our Schools Cheat Girls* (New York: Touchstone, 1994).

12. Social Studies Center for Educational Development, "Texas Essential Knowledge and Skills—Questions and Answers." http://www.tea.state.tx.us/resources/ssced/teks/teksqa.htm (25 April 2002).

13. Though in fairness to Jesse, she was the most charming-and-sweet sad-and-irritable person you could imagine—which only made it worse, somehow, for all of us.

14. The then seven-year-old Zoe, our house liberal, wrote presidential candidate Al Gore a letter of support during the contested 2000 election which included the following: "I am the only Demo in a house full of socialists."

15. We remain indebted to Laurie Stone for egging us on to join her in home-schooling.

16. During Jess's first stint, in kindergarten, we dutifully filled our prescribed and highly gendered roles, with Helen as a "homeroom mom" and Eric working the athletically based "field day." On Jess's second tour of duty, Eric served as a parent representative on the Williams Elementary School Site-Based Decision Committee for two years and as a parent representative on the Georgetown Independent School District Site-Based Decision Committee for one year. Helen served for one year on the Georgetown Independent School District Gifted and Talented Committee.

17. See, for example, Gary Orfield and John T. Yun, "Resegregation in American Schools," The Civil Rights Project, Harvard University, June 1999. http://www.law.harvard.edu/civilrights/publications/resegregation99/resegregation99.html (25 April 2002).

18. Susannah Sheffer, *A Sense of Self: Listening to Homeschooled Adolescent Girls* (Portsmouth, N.H.: Boynton/Cook Publishers, 1995)

19. While the local schools are at least nominally integrated, most schools in our town and region reflect the increasing national practice of creating schools within schools, for example, honors programs, where different classes and ethnicities rarely mix. Dr. LaVonne Neal, Assistant Professor, Department of Education, Southwestern University, Georgetown, Texas, conversation with Eric Selbin, 28 February 2001.

20. Roland Meighan, "Home-Based Education Effectiveness Research and Some of its Implications." *Educational Review* 47, 3 (November 1995): 275–87.

21. Ibid.

22. Some homeschoolers advocate "unschooling," a learning philosophy totally guided by a child's interest; we do a blend of child-led learning and education that conforms to structural requirements such as future college entrance exams.

23. Jesse Cordes Selbin, "Reading between the Lines: Why Are So Many Books Still Sexist," *New Moon: The Magazine For Girls and Their Dreams* 8, 4 (March/April 2001): 40–42.

24. Helen Cordes, "Kids Who Do Too Much." *Child* 15, 7 (September 2000): 71–74. Also, Cordes, "Overdoing Extracurriculars: How and When to Say 'When,'" *Britannica Online,* 7 September 2000. http://www.britannica.com/bcom/original/article/0,5744,10020,00.html (20 November 2001).

25. Helen Cordes, "Sour Grapes, Anyone?" *Salon,* 6 June 2000. http://www.salon.com/mwt/feature/tues/2000/06/06/homeschool/index.html (25 April 2002).

26. Most commonly associated with Malcolm X, the phrase "by whatever means necessary" is apparently a paraphrase from Shakespeare's *Hamlet* (Roger Protz, "Millions of Britons See Malcolm X In TV Broadcast of Debate at Oxford," *The Militant,* 14 December 1964, 2) and has been widely adopted by progressives around the world. It reflects the strategy(ies) adopted by millions of people for thousands of years when faced with oppression, repression, and lack of social justice.

27. This was brought home on one occasion when our children were enrolled at the local Montessori school. Eric volunteered to help with lunch one day and was greeted with, "Oh, there's a man in the house." All too telling.

28. Worldwide, boys have much more access to education, leaving one-third of the world's females illiterate. The U.S. followed European tradition by barring girls from full participation in schools for nearly two centuries (Sadker and Sadker, *Failing at Fairness,* 15–41). In our nation's early years, only a small minority of wealthy, white girls attended private elementary schools or public schools—which they were allowed to attend only after the boys' school day ended and for a fee.

During the 1800s, girls gradually gained access to public elementary schools, but it took decades for high schools to begin offering equal curricula to girls (as opposed to a home arts–oriented education), amid emotional debate over whether education diverted to the brain blood needed for menstruation and widespread fears that coed schools would shatter the family by erasing the differences between male and female (Sadker and Sadker, *Failing at Fairness*, 230–32).

29. On this "significant revolutionary potential," see Mary Ann Tétreault, "Women and Revolution: A Framework for Analysis," in *Women and Revolution in Africa, Asia, and the New World*, ed. Mary Ann Tétreault (Columbia: University of South Carolina Press, 1994), 11–17; and Tétreault, "Women and Revolution: What Have We Learned?" in *Women and Revolution*, 438–40.

30. The Clandestine Revolutionary Indigenous Committee General Command (CCRI-CG) of Mexico's Zapatista National Army of Liberation (EZLN) sent out a communique 31 January 1994 (thirty days after their uprising began) in which they asked, "Why is everyone so quiet? Is this the 'democracy' you wanted?" Often dated 4 February 1994 in the U.S. (Ejército Zapatista de Liberación Nacional, "EZLN Communique 31 January 1994." http://www.ezln.org/documentos/1994/19940131b.en.htm [25 April 2002]).

31. Tétreault and Teske, "Framing the Issues," 13.

32. Ibid., 14.

33. Ejército Zapatista de Liberación Nacional, Clandestine Indigenous Revolutionary Committee General Command of the Zapatista Army of National Liberation, "First Declaration of La Realidad For Humanity and Against Neoliberalism," January 1996. http://www.ezln.org/documentos/1996/19960130.en.htm (25 April 2002).

Chapter 4

An Activist in "Retirement"

Marjorie L. Zap

I joined the staff of the United Nations as an economist during its early days when it was housed in the Sperry Gyroscope factory in Lake Success, New York. All the members of the staff were automatically members of the Staff Association, which was governed by an executive committee or council. Although I was only twenty-two years old, I was elected chairperson of the staff committee because I had had a lot of organizational experience. As part of this job, I had to act as a liaison between the staff and UN Secretary-General Trygve Lie. This was a difficult assignment because Lie resented being questioned by the council on staff matters. In fact, he would not communicate with us except through his underlings.

I worked in the Department of Economic Affairs. Among the other U.S. citizens in my department were economists who had been recruited from U.S. government positions in New Deal agencies set up by President Franklin Roosevelt, and others who had been working on postwar problems such as refugee issues. Our department established a technical assistance program to help Third World countries, organized the first international conference on the environment, and compiled statistical reports to aid in research on worldwide economic issues.

The New Deal employees especially became targets for senators and representatives in the U.S. Congress who wanted to make names for themselves by eliminating "Communists"—New Dealers—from every aspect of American life. Having already gotten all the publicity they could by targeting U.S. government employees, academics, and people in the film industry, they needed new victims. The secretary-general, under pressure from the U.S. government, required American citizens on the UN staff to testify at congressional and senatorial hearings and then used their testimony as a basis for firing them. Although the UN Administrative Tribunal ruled that the dismissals themselves were wrong, the tribunal also said that the secretary-general had the right to implement them.

I was among those who were eliminated. Mine was a two-pronged dismissal. I was a member of the staff committee that had questioned the decisions of the UN administration—so I was a troublemaker. I also was an economist whose New Deal bosses were particular targets of these congressional committees.[1] In fact, mine might have been a three-pronged dismissal: I had spearheaded the UN staff movement to refuse to contribute blood to the Red Cross while it continued to segregate blood donations by race. Our refusal was reported on the front page of the *New York Times,* after which the Red Cross changed its procedure. These firings had a profound effect on the morale of the staff, but an even greater effect on the United Nations as an organization. Some of the most effective and dedicated personnel were eliminated, representing a loss of energy and idealism from which the United Nations never recovered.[2]

A few years later my husband and I opened an international handcraft business in Orange County, New York. Every year we would spend two months traveling to Third World countries to buy handcrafts, often directly from the producers. This business lasted for thirty years during which time I saw how population increases were creating major problems in the countries we regularly visited. During the ten months each year we spent at home, I devoted as much time as I could to social action, and among my efforts was promoting family planning locally and lobbying our representatives to support family-planning programs nationally and internationally.

When I retired from the business in 1994, I had to decide where I wanted to live since I could not manage a 250-year-old house with twenty-five acres of land that needed a lot of attention. My choices boiled down to two: Ubud, Bali, or San Miguel de Allende, Mexico. Bali lost; I had been an activist all my life and saw no way I could contribute in Ubud given the closed nature of Balinese society. In contrast, San Miguel welcomes newcomers. It has the largest bilingual library in Mexico, two English-language newspapers, and several thousand expatriates, many of whom are retired and have time to devote to organizations that help children, the poor, and the old.

The first organization I worked with was CASA, Centro para los Adolescentes de San Miguel de Allende. I wrote articles for CASA describing its work on family planning in rural communities, and its child care center, hospital, and midwife program. I could not get deeply involved with this organization, however, because I did not speak sufficient Spanish. I have had difficulty learning languages since childhood and although I continue to take Spanish lessons, my conversation skills remain very limited.

I also joined and serve on the board of directors of the Audubon Society of San Miguel de Allende. A major goal of Audubon is population control because increased population destroys habitats for birds. I don't go on bird walks, but I am involved in its program to improve the sewerage system and water supply for the city. Increased population around the world is depleting rivers, lakes, and aquifers, and this is a major problem in San Miguel. Its aquifer is losing water more rapidly than it can be replenished.

Another organization I joined in San Miguel is its Unitarian Universalist Fellowship. This group is deeply concerned about world problems and discusses them at the weekly services. The UUF has joined with other organizations in the county to establish Project Esperanza to give assistance to AIDS patients. We try to get medication for them and help them with daily survival problems. I am treasurer of this organization.

All of these activities take a fair amount of time and do important work for the community. But the work I do that is the most inspiring is giving stipends to young women from the small communities surrounding San Miguel so they can go to middle school, high school, and college. Mexico's education law makes state-supported schooling available only through the sixth grade, and many children fail to attend even for that short time. Some don't have shoes or proper clothing to wear to school, and others are occupied with odd jobs, such as accompanying beggars in the city to sell one-peso chewing gum, to earn extra money for their families. If a family can afford education beyond sixth grade for one or two children, this money is more likely to be spent on boys than girls. Rural parents especially expect their daughters to get married and believe that girls do not need further education to rear children and work on the farm. As a result, most of the girls in the small villages of our area do not attend secondary or preparatory schools. There isn't enough money to send them, and often their mothers want them to help at home. Others get pregnant at an early age despite being taught sex education in school and by workers from a local organization called Departmento de Desarrollar Integral de la Familia, DIF.

The chief executive officer of DIF is always the wife of the mayor of the city of San Miguel de Allende. In 1995 Pakina Fernandez became the president of DIF. During her term, Pakina grew increasingly concerned about the lack of funding for schools in the rural area surrounding the city. Teachers there were poorly paid, and kindergarten classes were held under a tree. Pakina helped form a not-for-profit organization called Mujeres en Cambio (hereafter Mujeres), or Women for Change. Mujeres is committed to helping disadvantaged women increase their education so they can become more independent and get better jobs. A small organization, Mujeres is one of the growing number of voluntary associations in the state of Guanajuato that incorporate non-Mexican members on their boards. These organizations rely on both local activists and the financial and human resources of the growing foreign population.

The woman who helped to put this multicultural group together, Pakina Langensheidt Fernandez, was born in Mexico City of Mexican parents. Her great-grandfather left Germany in the eighteenth century to take the position of consul to the state of Guanajuato. Pakina attended primary and secondary schools in Mexico City, the city of Querétero, and San Miguel de Allende, and also spent one year in a boarding school in Vancouver, Canada, where she had been sent to learn English. On graduation from high school, she married Jaime Fernandez. He has held various government jobs in immigration, the treasury, and tourism. Pakina attended the National Autonomous University in Mexico City, where she majored in biology. When Jaime was transferred to Guanajuato, Pakina transferred to the university there, changing her major to history since there was no biology program. After she graduated, she taught history in a San Miguel high school for three years.

Pakina is involved in many activities. She works as a manager in the restaurant her father established many years ago in central San Miguel, using the income to support both of her elderly parents. She lives on a ranch in the small community of Atotonilco, where she first became aware of the many problems encountered by rural residents who receive few social services and have little income. When she and her husband realized that the schoolchildren in Atotonilco had no place to play, they donated land adjoining the school and built a playground.

At the request of some of the women in the community, Mujeres started a program in another village, Augustin Gonzales, to support education for girls. Its aim was to assist girls who had done well in elementary school so they could attend junior high and, in some cases, high school. In 1995 the first scholarships were awarded. Eight girls received the equivalent of U.S.$20 every month to continue their educations. They were selected on the recommendation of their teachers, and each had to have an academic average of at least 7.5, with 10 being a perfect grade. By the start of the 1999–2000 school year, five other rural communities had been added to the program and seventy-five girls were receiving scholarships. Many applying for grants had averages between 9.5 and 10. The program encourages elementary school students to work harder and rewards those who succeed with an opportunity to continue their educations. Student progress is monitored carefully. Each student has a file with her year-end report cards and/or the elementary school graduation certificate, which records her grade averages. These files also are used to ensure that the scholarship funds are properly awarded.

Today Mujeres is subsidizing junior and senior high school students in nine communities, as well as ten students in college or in specialty schools. During the 2001–2002 school year, subsidies will be distributed to almost one hundred young women. Pakina reminds them on the local radio station of the day they should come to her restaurant in the center of San Miguel for their stipends. The day before, I go to the bank and withdraw the equivalent of about U.S.$1500 in 100- and 50-peso notes. Four of us, two of whom are fluent in Spanish, greet and distribute the money to the girls, each of whom has to initial one form and sign her full name on another. If a girl does not appear for three months, her name is removed from the list.

We allow a girl from a school to sign for several of her classmates. This reduces travel costs for the recipients and also limits the number of girls crowding into the restaurant on stipend days. Nineteen students from Augustin Gonzalez are getting Mujeres subsidies. It is gratifying to meet with these adolescents who are so eager for an education. But success stories are not universal. Since it began, fourteen girls have dropped out of the program. One was kept at home by her family because they were concerned that she had to walk home from school in the dark. A few girls married, and their places were taken by others recommended by their teachers. One new student was recommended by her granddaughter, who asked that her scholarship go to her *abuela,* or grandmother. This woman, Doña Julia Lopez, learned to read at the age of fifty-five and started secondary school at the age of seventy. She has a son and daughter, both of whom are teachers, and two granddaughters, who are studying in a university. Doña Julia is an activist in her community, involved in environmental issues, and she recruits others to learn how to prevent erosion on their farms.

Every August the secondary school scholarship students come to San Miguel, often accompanied by their mothers and their teachers. There they receive a first allowance of about U.S.$50, to be used for purchases that will allow them to start school. After that they are supposed to return to San Miguel during the first week of each month throughout the school year to receive 150 pesos (about U.S.$15), money for shoes, clothing, backpacks, pens and notebooks, and bus fare for the trip to the nearest school. However, some students work after school and cannot come to the city. In those instances also, mothers or classmates come in their places. Those receiving the funds must sign for them. In the case of the mothers, most of whom are unable to read or write, we used to ask that they put their thumb prints on the paper. Now two Mujeres workers simply initial the paper so we don't have to ask the mothers to get ink on their fingers. The mothers invariably shake each of our hands, and some even plant a kiss on our cheeks.

Mujeres keeps track of the girls' progress. In January a form is sent to the teacher of each scholarship student to be returned to Mujeres the following month. The teachers report whether the student's work is good, acceptable, or bad. Completed forms are signed by the teachers and each form is returned with the school seal, a process that vests responsibility for student progress in the student, the faculty, and also the school administration. At the end of the school year, each student brings a copy of her report card to be added to her file.

High school students in the rural communities receive most of their education via television programs that emanate from Mexico City. The teachers attend summer school to prepare to teach from these programs and are given special textbooks to guide them. Each student also works from a textbook designed to accompany the television programs. The second book in the series, for example, includes lessons emphasizing oral, reading, and writing skills and topical analyses, such as how airplanes shaped a new generation. There are chapters on music and on Mexican history. Mathematics instruction focuses on fractions and percentages. There are lessons on classical history, geography, civics, biology and health, and the English language. The texts also contain bibliographies but, unfortunately, the high schools have very poor libraries. We encourage students to come into the city of San Miguel to use the fine library that is so well supported by the foreign population. Sixteen of the students in the Mujeres high school program have already graduated. Half of those are attending a branch of the University of Leon located just outside the center of the city of San Miguel. The classes are held in the early morning and in the evening so the students can work during the day to earn money to pay for their tuition, now about U.S.$100 per semester. The university offers four-year courses in school administration, business administration, public accounting, law, and architecture.

Mujeres has important work to do, but its resources are limited. There are many girls who are technically eligible for Mujeres scholarships, but there is not enough money available at this time to expand the program. Mujeres also runs other projects, such as providing financial support to enable midwives to attend an annual conference incorporating in-service training. All the Mujeres projects reflect the goal of the organization, which is to support women in various roles in the rural community.

Fund-raising is a major Mujeres preoccupation. We hold lunches during the winter, when "snowbirds" from the northern United States and Canada come to escape the cold and ice, and again in the summer, when "sunbirds" from the south and southwest come to escape the unbearable heat. The lunches raise money to support the organization and also alert foreign women about the needs of the people in the rural areas. Relatives and friends of members of Mujeres are asked to help, and grants are being sought from U.S. corporations with plants in the state of Guanajuato. So far we have not had a single response from our appeals to corporations. Indeed, not much money comes directly from the lunches, but they are useful in promoting the project and keeping news of it alive. Some of the diners, on returning home, request funds from their friends and from charitable organizations. Every fall we send a fund-raising letter to potential contributors, and responses to this appeal constitute the organization's main source of income.[3] Each year the funds we receive increase as more and more donors recognize the important role women play in Third World countries. I continue to be a financial supporter of Mujeres as part of my effort to promote population control: educating women leads to delayed first pregnancies and smaller families.

Mujeres relies solely on volunteers, a core group of whom provide continuity to its programs. Membership changes constantly as foreign members come and go, either seasonally or permanently; however, there are enough full-time and part-time residents dedicated to this program to keep it going, and even growing, as our resources expand. The Mexican women on the board are dedicated to the organization and its mission. The communities Mujeres assists and those from which its members are drawn are fortunate to be able to rely on Pakina Fernandez, who serves as a liaison among its various participants. Pakina also attends the cash distribution meetings and gives encouragement to the young women. Since Pakina lives in one of the rural villages participating in the program, she keeps in touch with developments there and is available to assist members of the community directly.

Although many dedicated residents in San Miguel volunteer in organizations to better the lives of women and children, more government involvement is needed to deal adequately with the problems that arise from extreme poverty in Mexico. The new president, Vicente Fox, vows to address these issues, but only time will tell whether his efforts will be productive. When Vicente Fox was governor of the state of Guanajuato, he arranged for small loans to people in the communities to establish micro-businesses. However, there was little follow-up to help these entrepreneurs use the loans effectively. In Bangladesh, where this program was initiated, the Grameen Bank gives small loans at a nominal interest rate, mainly to women. It employs about four hundred supervisors; each supervisor meets regularly with the borrowers, who are organized in "circles" of about ten loan recipients. The recipients help one another with their projects, make sure the loans are repaid from profits, and consult regularly with their supervisor.[4] As the Grameen model shows, money alone is not sufficient to launch a micro-business: advice and supervision also are needed to support inexperienced entrepreneurs. Without them, the Grameen model cannot be replicated effectively.

Mujeres en Cambio has not yet asked for government help, in part because the group wants to see how the new president's announced plans to extend education to the youth of Mexico are implemented. But the government of Mexico could do worse than ask Mujeres en Cambio for its help. To educate its large numbers of young persons, Mexico will require many more classrooms staffed with effective teachers, but it will also require expertise in reaching the rural poor and in eliciting the same sort of cooperative effort that underpins successful projects like the Grameen bank. When the girls in the San Miguel area graduate from high school, they would no doubt benefit from governmental help in establishing small businesses in their own communities, which now depend almost entirely on services in the city of San Miguel. The city itself suffers from a proliferation of businesses trying to attract tourists. Shifting investment to the rural areas seems a far more rational approach.

It has been rewarding for me to work with Mexicans, Americans, and Canadians who are dedicated to bringing about a better Mexico, where women can be productive beyond caring for their husbands and bearing numerous children. From an early age, I have been an activist. Although I worked from the time I was in college until my retirement, I have always found time to be involved in organizations working towards worthwhile goals. Living in retirement in San Miguel, I remain active in four organizations whose goals I believe are laudable. At the age of seventy-eight, preparing agendas, chairing meetings, being a treasurer, keeping files, writing articles, and keeping in touch with other retirees are my way of continuing to lead what has always been an active life with plenty of mental stimulation. I work with a trainer at a gym three hours every week to keep my body in good enough shape, so I don't have to relinquish my responsibilities. All of these activities help promote the ideals that I absorbed during my early days at the United Nations and the hopes I have cherished throughout my life for all the women of the world.

Notes

1. Linda Melvern, *The Ultimate Crime: Who Betrayed the UN and Why* (London: Wilson and Day Ltd, 1995). A retrospective on this period in UN history was produced by Linda Melvern and broadcast in three segments over British Channel Four as "UN Blues" (London: Programme One, January 1995).

2. Ibid. Others also regret the careerism that took root in the United Nations after that time. See, for example, David Rieff, "Nothing Was Delivered," *New Republic,* 1 May 2000, 26–33.

3. For more information about this program, please contact the San Miguel Educational Foundation at either 2415 East Musser Street, Laredo, Texas 78043 U.S.A. or at Apdo #490, San Miguel de Allende, Gto, 37700, Mexico.

4. David Bornstein, *The Price of a Dream: The Story of the Grameen Bank and the Idea That Is Helping the Poor to Change Their Lives* (Chicago: University of Chicago Press, 1996).

Chapter 5

Sex (Roles) and the Sorority

A Story of Feminist Transformations

Karla Scheele

If one were asked to name something feminist, "sorority" would most likely not—realistically, it would almost definitely not—be the first word to come to mind. Few institutions elicit such rigid stereotyping as sororities do, with most people tacitly assuming that the majority of sorority women fall into the familiar snobbish-beauty-with-questionable-brains mold. As I began one of my graduate school visits, for example, my student host pointed out the area of "Greek" housing near campus and facetiously commented, "And this is where most of the fraternities and sororities are, in case you ever want to pledge." I replied, "I already have," evoking a shocked silence.

Such an experience—not an unusual one for many sorority women—illustrates the widespread belief that sororities are not prime places to find women likely to be concerned with more than next weekend's big keg bash or whom they should ask to the formal dance. Sororities are believed to promote social climbing over social change, a sense of style over a sense of self. As a former "sorority girl" myself, I cannot completely debunk these stereotypes. I felt some pressure to reorder my priorities to conform with those of the group. At the same time, however, I can trace much of the self-awareness and self-confidence I developed during my college years to my involvement in a sorority. Although sororities are not perfectly egalitarian institutions—one shortcoming is their de facto discrimination against women who cannot afford the cost associated with sorority membership[1]—their potential for fostering both collective identity and personal growth among their members is real and powerful. As such, sororities may qualify as feminist communities.

Even though I defend sororities in this essay, I often experienced difficulty reconciling my feminist self with the realities of sorority affiliation. In fact, these different aspects of my identity have often been at war, though the *casus belli* changed as time went by. It may seem strange that someone with such internal conflict about her own feelings could argue that sororities can be feminist communities, but I have come to believe that it is exactly the friction I experienced—rightly characterized as tension between feminism and femininity—that is the central issue. How sororities and other female-oriented groups choose to address it will affect the course of feminist progress and dialogue for some time to come.

This idea is not a new one, but it is particularly potent in the context of sororities because they exemplify this divisive pressure more completely than virtually any other women's organization. While many sororities' stated purposes include fostering personal and collective growth,[2] they have more potent reputations as breeding grounds for feminine charms. Through the lens of my own knowledge and experience, I will attempt to explain why sororities have been and can be feminist communities.

First, let me provide my own response to the question "What makes for a feminist community?" All functional communities possess a sense of common identity and purpose, with members committing themselves to seeking agreed-upon aims that benefit the entire group. Feminist communities also should promote the gender interests of their female members by supporting and encouraging them to fulfill their personal aspirations. The promotion of female worth and equality may occur in indirect, personal ways, or it may grow out of action specifically intended to effect social change. This broad outline may seem little more than a way to get around the problem of identifying sororities as feminist communities. However, I believe that the very uniqueness and malleability of communal forms of association require that a measure of subjectivity be infused into their evaluation.

Even this broad definition of community highlights the potential difficulty of reconciling community with autonomy—how to become and remain an accepted member of a group while retaining one's individuality. Women tend to experience the tension between community and individual identities more acutely than men, primarily as a result of their socialization into feminine roles. Carol Gilligan attributes this difference to women's pattern of moral development. Women are socialized into an "ethic of care"; they define themselves in terms of relationships with others. Men, in contrast, are more likely to absorb and exemplify the predominant societal ethics of individualism and justice. While men tend to define themselves and their relationships on their own terms, women tend to see themselves as connected by relational webs and create mosaics of personhood from these associations.[3]

In *Woman on the Edge of Time,* Marge Piercy creates a feminist utopia where gender roles are blurred and society encourages both autonomy and interconnectedness among all its members. The people of this society chose to end live human birthing in favor of gestation in artificial "brooders," to expand the nuclear family to include three "comothers," and to involve the greater community in child-rearing in order to eliminate the biological rationale for gender inequality. As the character Luciente explains: "Finally there was that one thing we [women] had to give up too, the only power we ever had, in return for no power for anyone. The original production: the power to give birth. Cause as long as we were biologically enchained, we'd never be equal. And males would never be humanized to be loving and tender."[4]

Through these conscious acts and concerted efforts toward social evolution, the people of Piercy's ideal future generate a society in which conventional gender roles do not exist. Men are not expected to remain strong and impassive; women are not presumed to be nurturing and communally minded. Instead, all people are free to construct their social universes as they see fit. This softening of gender identities also encourages the pursuit of individual talents and interests because gender "apartheid" no longer limits people's horizons.

While our society has not come to embrace fully the same ideals as those informing Piercy's vision, great effort continues to be invested in equalizing the balance of power between men and women. Although sororities are seldom in the forefront of this quest, they nonetheless have played a significant role. For instance, my sorority, Kappa Alpha Theta, was founded by Bettie Locke Hamilton in 1870. Bettie was spurred to create her own Greek-letter society after she was invited to wear a men's fraternity pin but was not admitted to the fraternity's secrets. She and her three cofounders—Alice Allen Brandt, Bettie Tipton Lindsey, and Hannah Fitch Shaw—were in the vanguard of women admitted to Indiana Asbury College.[5]

Once there, they were subjected to an unimaginable degree of harassment and intimidation by their male classmates and professors. Establishing Kappa Alpha Theta, as Bettie Locke Hamilton once said, "help[ed] the girls win out in their fight to stay in college on a man's campus. We had to make a bigger place for women in a man's world, and the Fraternity was one means to that bigger end."[6] Through their fraternity (the word "sorority" had not yet been coined),[7] these women were able to create not only a network of support but also an outlet for their often-frustrated aspirations for truly equal opportunities—an early feminist community by any standard. Their women's fraternity was not a uniquely female model because it shared many aspects of the male archetype. Even so, my sorority's founders managed to make this form of organization their own by instilling powerful messages of self-worth and determination into rituals still practiced by members today.

I, like many other women, find strength in these ideals of independence and perseverance and attempt to live by them daily.

As in other realms of life, however, practice often does not measure up to theory. Messages of fortitude and individualism can be lost amid the difficulties presented by daily living, both in an operational and a personal sense. Operationally, a group cannot exist if it has no members. Competition for new members among sororities is often fierce. On my undergraduate campus, as on many others around the country, the numbers of women going through formal recruitment or rush[8]—the traditional method of sorority member selection—has been decreasing. This creates a sense of urgency among smaller chapters, which, although they are in the greatest need of members, tend to be at a disadvantage in the recruitment process.

This occurs for two central reasons. First, many potential members feel a greater attraction to large chapters because they appear stronger and more stable than small ones. In the often-brief recruitment process, appearances and impressions are usually the most available information a potential member has. Second, rush procedures on many campuses favor those chapters with ample numbers of members to attend to all the observable and behind-the-scenes tasks necessary for successful recruitment.[9] Given the structural impediments they face, smaller chapters must often work continually to attract new members, while larger chapters are able to dedicate their efforts toward other projects.

My chapter in particular has had a difficult time recruiting new members. After several years of struggle and threats of closure from chapter advisors and national officials, our national organization changed its strategy, sending more national consultants than before to help rebuild our numbers. Many of the younger consultants encouraged us to capitalize on our chapter's unique qualities. Both as individuals and as a group, we seemed unlike a "typical" sorority: we came from diverse socioeconomic backgrounds; we weren't all stereotypically blonde and beautiful; and we embodied a wide array of interests and goals. However, two older women who came to assess our membership situation made it clear that we needed to attract more, well, *attractive* women if we expected to survive. They assured us that women going through rush prefer to associate with beautiful people; therefore, if we could attract more beautiful women, this would lead to exponential growth in our total membership.

This difference in approach strikes at the heart of a change I believe is beginning to occur in the sorority world, one that perhaps is a reflection of a larger societal trend. Many older women—together with those people who subscribe to prevailing sorority stereotypes—imagine sorority life in strictly social and stratified terms. Sorority membership to them is an ascribed, one-dimensional social status. At the same time, increasing numbers of young women going through rush perceive sororities as springboards to achieving academic and personal goals. They appreciate the social aspects of sorority life but seek other benefits from membership as well, advantages like leadership opportunities, academic support, and networks—skills and relationships upon which they can draw throughout their lives.

The relationships and social networks that permeate individual chapters and sororities at large are often lumped together under the heading of "sisterhood." Sisterhood is perhaps the biggest buzzword of sorority life, and it is widely touted as one of its greatest attractions as well as one of its most meaningful rewards. It was this intangible quality that initially drew me to join a sorority. Sorority members often expound at length upon the bonds they feel between themselves and their "sisters," how these ties enrich their lives now, and how they will continue to do so in the future.

Given its centrality in members' everyday lives and in their representations of sorority life, what sorority women mean by "sisterhood" is important to understand. Like many feminist definitions of sisterhood, however, it is fuzzy at best. Sorority women often point to strong friendships, concern for every sister's welfare, and group loyalty as evidence of their chapter's sisterhood. Yet most would confess that feelings of sisterhood escape easy translation into words, adding to frustrations in deriving a definition with any concrete meaning. A universal idea of sisterhood in sororities is as problematic as a universal idea of feminism. Conceptions vary from woman to woman based upon her experience as a member and also upon how she situates her membership within the broader context of her life.

Sisterhood becomes, in effect, the collective expression of members' constructions of what membership and communal life mean to them—a miniature "imagined community."[10] Although Benedict Anderson confines his use of this concept to explaining the creation of communities among people who "will never know most of their fellow-members,"[11] I would submit that imagination also provides a conceptual foothold for understanding the process of community-building among more personal groupings whose members have similarly disparate identities and interests. In the case of sororities, this imagination encompasses both dimensions: the creation of sisterly affinity within a given chapter, and the subsequent extension of this affinity to all members of the national organization.

Sorority members, despite their perceived homogeneity, are women with very different backgrounds and goals brought together by membership in their chapters. Joining a chapter, however, does not entail an instant bond with fellow sisters, nor does it induce a cosmic alignment of interests among members. The realization of sisterhood within a sorority community—like the process of interest aggregation and articulation within all women's groups[12]—is not automatic; it requires both negotiating common objectives and imagining a profound connection to the group's purpose that permits, even encourages, the privileging of certain interests over others.

As a result, sorority sisterhood is something that can only be imagined, lived, and cultivated; it is neither constant across different chapters nor static within a single chapter. As members' interests change, sisterhood is expressed in different ways, from a diffuse nurturing benevolence to a more explicitly goal-oriented commitment to individual and group excellence. These changing interests and group dynamics affect how members treat one another and how they treat nonmembers. The degree of internal and external social leveling this involves, as well as the autonomy afforded to group members, varies accordingly.

The supportive aspects of sisterhood suffer when members place a high premium on conformity or when levels of interpersonal friction are high. All communities—particularly those whose members live in such close contact as members of sororities routinely do—are susceptible to strains under such circumstances. My chapter certainly experienced its share of cliquishness and disharmony, but I believe that most members shared a deep sense of belonging that allowed them to transcend the stresses of daily living and realize a genuine and emotive bond to one another, to sisterhood.

Sorority sisterhood can provide a reserve of friendship and support for women that may be deeper and longer lasting than that found among members of other organizations. In addition, membership in fraternities and sororities fosters campus and community involvement; members tend to build more "social capital" than nonmembers,[13] both during their undergraduate careers and throughout their adult lives.[14] Membership in sororities contributes to building the leadership and interpersonal skills necessary for women to assert strong, independent presences in their personal and professional lives. Sorority pamphlets, magazines, and web sites teem with lists of notable sorority alumnae—including Nancy Kassebaum Baker, Kay Bailey Hutchison, Elizabeth Dole, and Katie Couric—and stories about those who embody female achievement. This personalizes the developmental benefits of sorority life for potential members and other interested parties, including parents.

Anecdotal evidence suggests that sorority women are more likely than other college women to attain positions of power in their collegiate and professional careers. For example, sorority women often "dominate" campus positions, and many sorority alumnae have been elected to national offices.[15] However, I find this to be an imperfect and even a superficial measure of empowerment. For me, the more important question is whether sororities aid the "new sorority woman" I described previously in her quest for self-actualization, or whether she in fact will be constrained by the conventions of sorority life. On the personal level, the support that comes from sisterhood and the confidence-building that comes from opportunities for leadership may increase self-assertion, but more important is the degree of latitude—opportunity space—sorority life opens up and whether a member can define and redefine herself in that space. The protection offered by such spaces allows the exploration of new frontiers of selfhood.

Herein lies the root of my struggle to define what sorority membership meant, and continues to mean, to me. Over the course of my active membership, I often felt torn between the ideals and the realities of sorority life, between individuality and homogeneity, between autonomy and community. I must admit that I initially joined a sorority for more or less stereotypical reasons—to become part of an instant network of friends and to increase my social status. Never having been popular in high school, this seemed an opportune way to find acceptance and happiness as part of an in-group. Of course, no popularity fairy godmother materialized to grant this naive wish. Nonetheless, I settled into the comfortable routine of chapter meetings and house activities, gradually building friendships with my new sisters.

Soon, however, I realized that being cool in the conventional sense was not as important to me as I had thought. I began to experience pangs of "not fitting in" when I chose to put my own goals—particularly academic achievement—above social outings and the unflagging, unquestioning effort routinely demanded for every house project. I was not ostracized for this choice, but I was generally not supported either. As this pattern continued, my awareness of ideas and actions incompatible with my own value framework was inexorably heightened. I came to be all but obsessed with debasing and deconstructing what I saw as the oppressive ideas held by my sisters.

Cognitive dissonance reached its zenith during and immediately after my junior year. I was both fascinated and repelled by my sisters' attitudes about themselves, their bodies, their futures, their men (or lack thereof). I believed that their brand of femininity was so centered on pleasing men that they often lost themselves in the process. I inwardly—through rarely publicly[16]—decried their vacuous lifestyles and self-repression, once tapping my inner turmoil for a feminist philosophy term paper that critically explored the ramifications of sorority culture. I felt marginalized for challenging group norms—even when my challenge was more implicit than direct—and, in reaction, began distancing myself from many of my sisters. How, I wondered, could I be a part of a group that so clearly endorsed what I saw as a vainglorious and empty conception of self, inimical to my ideals of female empowerment?

Yet I stayed. I still ask myself why, and I am not sure I can give an entirely satisfactory answer. Part of my decision probably stems from my Midwestern ethic of "not being a quitter"; part was simply path-dependent behavior fostered by familiarity and reinforced by the costs of change. However, having had some time away and having traveled some distance from my sorority experience—and its dialectical relationship to my conception of feminism—I can appreciate that my reasoning encompassed much more than that.

Following my junior year, I began steadily moving away from a categorical denial of the feminist potential in sororities. At the time, I had only a vague sense of the underlying changes accompanying this shift. After I began my graduate school career, my sorority affiliation seemed to be more of an anomaly than ever. Members of my graduate-school cohort, like that aforementioned student host, were generally surprised to discover this part of my identity, and I tried to explain away my somewhat unconventional past by saying I had not been a "typical" sorority girl.

Then I had a realization: who *is* a "typical" sorority girl? And who was I to say who is or is not typical—or who is or is not oppressed—as I had so often done? The full import of false consciousness came back to haunt me. If the "typical" sorority girl deludes herself into thinking she is anything but the ultimate pawn of the patriarchy, I too was deluding myself by thinking that by joining a sorority I could—or should—raise my social status to a level comparable to that of my feminist consciousness.

Should I agonize over this inconsistent thinking? Maybe not. My latest "click" moment also made clear that feminism is not a simple concept. This seemingly banal realization has reordered my worldview, allowing me to evaluate my sorority experience without relying on essentialism with respect to either feminism or femininity. I see that I had been holding my sorority sisters to an unreasonable and unjust standard: to choose between feminism and femininity is as impossible as choosing between autonomy and community. Indeed, it is a choice one need not make.

My uncompromising stance against what I judged to be the pathological femininity and the overdependence on others that I observed in many of my sisters led me to oversimplify the process by which each woman defines her own womanhood and the nexus she negotiates between herself and her community. I assumed both to have a single, maximized point of feminist utility at which women would be most fully liberated, and as the earlier discussion makes clear, my liberated woman was one who was strongly, though not slavishly, feminine and generally independent and un-embedded. In actuality, there can be no such universal because each woman's life experience leads her to different understandings of herself and her relationships to others.

Given our gendered world, femininity is not in and of itself an obstacle to self-fulfillment. It becomes problematic only when a narrow conception of womanhood is used to evaluate all women. Sororities can offer women the latitude in which to construct their identities, not in response to societal demands, but as they themselves see fit. Sororities can also assist in this process both by providing young women with strong role models and by buoying them up through mutual support.

I observed many of my sisters defining themselves in terms of their boyfriends or other members of the sorority. This identification was often self-reinforcing. Members usually looked favorably upon, if they did not openly encourage, relationships with men and close friendships within the house. This is by no means a uniquely "Greek" phenomenon as Gilligan's work illustrates.[17] In favoring autonomy over community, I was too quick to dismiss the ways our sisterhood empowered us, both as individuals and as a collective, how it gave us the opportunity to influence each other's lives positively, and how it anchored us within a close-knit community as we spread our figurative wings. Sorority women are famous for their networking prowess; they create opportunities for members to obtain leadership positions on campus and in the "real world." More integral and lasting, however, is the confidence that an older member can inspire in a younger one simply by suggesting a potential outlet for her particular talents. I, certainly, thrived on this sort of recognition.

"Activism by accident," I thought, before I was suddenly struck by its truly purposive nature. That I nearly attributed this exercise of agency to chance is indicative of how the constructive role sororities play in their members' lives is undervalued. Older, more respected chapter members do not spontaneously begin to dispense wisdom and guidance to their younger charges. This behavior is conditioned by observation of the actions and lives of previous generations of leaders. A virtuous circle is thereby perpetuated: younger members are taught how to be active and, over time, they are transformed into mentors and activists themselves.

Countless women believe that being a feminist goes beyond personal activism and commitment to sacrificing not only the fun of femininity but also dependence upon others. I unconsciously applied this logic in reverse in my internal debate on sorority life. Such reasoning leads many women, including many of my sorority sisters, to reject the feminist label even if they agree with feminism's central objectives. I see this as perhaps the most pressing issue for the future progress of feminism. One step toward a more inclusionary feminist program would be to recognize and explore the potential balances between feminist individualism and feminine embeddedness.

Just as there is no single "sorority girl," there is no monolithic feminism. Each female individual and each strain of feminism manifests unique combinations of attachments, beliefs, and values. Each attempts to strike a balance among myriad social and personal pressures. Each woman, then, must reach balance on her own terms, just as I have been struggling to do with respect to myself and my conception of feminism over the last few years. While this may be a never-ending process, I believe that every woman who desires gender equity should feel that feminism holds a place for her and her concerns. Feminist communities, including sororities, can and should play a key role in these feminist transformations. With these multiple networks of support in place, we can change the world—one person at a time.

Notes

1. It might seem obvious that another egalitarian shortcoming of sororities would be segregation, but this issue is more complex than it might appear. There are myriad social, cultural, and personal factors that play into a woman's decision to join a particular sorority, including its historical racial or ethnic orientation. To adequately examine these factors would require analysis that lies beyond the scope of this essay, which—as a reflection of my own knowledge and experience—is confined to "traditional," and traditionally white, sororities.

2. Some examples: "Alpha Omicron Pi is an international women's fraternity promoting friendship for a lifetime, inspiring academic excellence and lifelong learning, and developing leadership skill through service to the fraternity and community" (Alpha Omicron Pi, "Mission," http://www.alphaomicronpi.org/ AOΠToday/ Ideals/Mission [6 June 2002]; "Chi Omega is a sisterhood that provides a network of friends and lifelong development for collegiate and alumnae members. Chi Omega is committed to: personal integrity, excellence in academic and intellectual pursuits, inter-generational participation, community service, leadership opportunities, social enrichment" (Chi Omega, "Chi Omega's Vision and Mission," http://www.chiomega.org/chiomega/ About XΩ/Vision and Mission [6 June 2002]); "Yesterday, today, and tomorrow, Kappa Alpha Theta exists to nurture each member throughout her college and alumnae experience and to offer a lifelong opportunity for social, intellectual, and moral growth as she meets the higher and broader demands of mature life" (Kappa Alpha Theta, "Kappa Alpha Theta Facts," http://www.kappaalphatheta.org/ What Is Theta/Theta Facts [6 June 2002]); "The mission of Zeta Tau Alpha is to make a difference in the lives of our membership by developing the potential of each individual through programming which emphasizes leadership development, service to others, academic success and continued personal growth for women with a commitment to friendship and the future based on the values and traditions of our past" (Zeta Tau Alpha, "Mission Statement," http://www.zetataualpha.org/mission.htm [26 April 2002]).

3. Carol Gilligan, *In A Different Voice: Psychological Theory and Women's Development* (Cambridge: Harvard University Press, 1993).

4. Marge Piercy, *Woman on the Edge of Time* (New York: Fawcett Columbine, 1976), 98.

5. Now DePauw University.

6. Kappa Alpha Theta, "Theta through the Decades—1870s," http://www.kappaalphatheta.org/ What Is Theta/Theta through the Decades/1870 (6 June 2002).

7. My sorority, Kappa Alpha Theta, never adopted the sorority moniker and remains a "women's fraternity."

8. The National Panhellenic Conference, the advisory body representing twenty-six international women's fraternities and sororities, now uses the word "recruitment" to refer to the selection process traditionally known as "rush." However, rush remains a colloquial staple among sorority members and nonmembers alike, and as such I use both terms in this essay.

9. The formal recruitment process often consists of a number of events, or parties as they used to be known, taking place over a few days. Sororities host potential members for conversation and refreshments, then extend invitations to a certain number of women for the next day's events, and the women decide whether to accept or decline these invitations. The process reduces the number of events each day until the women choose the house they wish to pledge.

For sorority members, the formal rush process takes a great deal of planning and effort, both before and during the formal recruitment period. Members are needed not only for conversation with potential members but also for the preparation of refreshments and other organizational and administrative tasks. For these reasons and others outlined above, smaller chapters tend to add fewer members during formal rush while the larger chapters often take quota—the largest number of new members allowed each chapter during formal rush—and therefore are more likely to reach total, the maximum number of members each sorority is allowed to have. Smaller chapters must continue working to build their membership through informal rush while the larger chapters can turn their attention toward other activities.

10. Benedict Anderson, *Imagined Communities: Reflections on the Origin and Spread of Nationalism,* rev. and extended 2d ed. (London: Verso, 1991).

11. Anderson, *Imagined Communities,* 6.

12. For a more extended treatment of the disparate nature of "women's interests," see Maxine Molyneux, "Mobilization without Emancipation? Women's Interests, the State, and Revolution in Nicaragua," *Feminist Studies* 11, 2 (1985): 227–54.

13. In *Bowling Alone: The Collapse and Revival of American Community,* Robert D. Putnam writes that social capital theory rests on the "idea . . . that social networks have value. Just as a screwdriver (physical capital) or a college education (human capital) can increase productivity (both individual and collective), so too social contacts affect the productivity of individuals and groups" (New York: Simon and Schuster, 2000), 19. For a consideration of social capital in the Italian context, see Putnam's *Making Democracy Work: Civic Traditions in Modern Italy* (Princeton, N.J.: Princeton University Press, 1993).

14. The National Panhellenic Conference and the National Interfraternity Conference sponsored a research initiative on the impact of Greek affiliation on college graduates. This study, conducted by the Center for Advanced Social Research at

the University of Missouri–Columbia, found that Greeks ranked high in social capital during both their collegiate and alumni years. See Esther Thorson, *Summary Report: The Impact of Greek Affiliation on College and Life Experiences* (Indianapolis, Ind.: National Interfraternity Conference and National Panhellenic Conference, 1997).

15. I was unable to locate much statistical evidence supporting my claim of "campus domination" by sorority women. The one example I did find—a study conducted at Indiana University—found that sorority members were more involved in university organizations than nonmembers; the personal backgrounds of women surveyed were not significant predictors of their levels of involvement. See Judith P. Abrahamson, *The Influences of Student Involvement by Sorority Membership* (Bloomington, Ind.: Center for the Study of the College Fraternity, 1987).

However, most leadership claims made by sorority, Panhellenic, and Greek Affairs websites are made in generalized terms; as such, examining the institutional conditions that promote these outcomes may be helpful. In doing this, I will rely upon my college experience and my conversations with people from other chapters and other campuses. At my alma mater, Iowa State University, involvement in all-campus organizations such as VEISHEA and Homecoming tended to be heavily (though by no means exclusively) Greek. Campus involvement is often a high priority for chapters; many houses have officers in charge of external affairs or public relations who collect information on upcoming openings for campus positions, promote these opportunities to the entire chapter, and provide assistance and advice to members seeking these positions. As a result, this institutionalized promotion and support often leads sorority members to enjoy a larger presence on campus than their non-Greek counterparts.

Similarly, there is little data on sorority women in elective office; most information encompasses both fraternity and sorority alumni. For example, the 1996 Congress was approximately 29 percent Greek, and the 1996 Senate was 43 percent Greek. One list of Greek facts commonly employed at Iowa State includes the following: "All but two U.S. Presidents since 1900 have been Greek; seven out of ten people listed in *Who's Who in America* are Greek; three-fourths of the U.S. Congress is Greek; 85 percent of Fortune 500 executives are Greek; and since 1920, 85 percent of the Supreme Court Justices have been Greek." (Iowa State University Dean of Students Office, "Greek Affairs: Greek Facts . . . Did You Know?" http://www.dso.iastate.edu/ DSO Departments/Greek Affairs/Did You Know?/Greek Facts [6 June 2002]).

While Iowa State sororities make ready use of the preceding list, I nonetheless recognize the male bias inherent in these indicators of Greek prowess; this list, however, does serve to highlight both the paucity of reliable information on sorority women's activities beyond their in-chapter involvement and the Panhellenic community's apparent acceptance of this lacuna.

16. Though this choice may appear contradictory and not entirely feminist in spirit, I can only explain it as an outgrowth of the common human reluctance to threaten one's core of friendships and social stability.

17. Gilligan, *In a Different Voice.*

Chapter 6

Reflections on Doing Feminist Research in a County Jail

Beate Gersch

> Although I have visited the County Jail on a weekly basis as a volunteer teacher for almost a year now, today is different: I am here as a researcher intent on doing feminist research, although what exactly this entails still is a bit fuzzy. I walk up to the guard. He knows me and already has my purple badge ready. He merely glances at my transparent backpack and pays no attention to the beep of the metal detector as I walk through. Approaching the metal door, I already hear the buzz. The door slams shut behind me, and I make my way down the long corridor to what I call the "glass cage." The first set of double glass doors slides opens. I am now in the holding area, from which I can only be released through another set of double glass doors after being identified by cameras or, if necessary, after a brief communication with what I think of as the voice from nowhere. The time in the glass cage seems endless. Then the doors open at last. I pass the booking area and follow the yellow line to the elevators. I have to let the first two go without me because no officer is present: civilians are not allowed to ride alone with inmates. I finally catch a ride crammed in between a medicine cart, several male inmates in orange jail garb, and an officer. The voice from nowhere asks where we are going. The doors close, and we are transported to our various destinations without ever pressing a button. I get off on the seventh floor. The guards greet me and offer coffee for the long day ahead. They have twelve interviews scheduled for me in the "conference room," which has dirty white walls, a big dark brown table, and several ugly green plastic chairs. I take out my note pad and tape recorder, and patiently wait for my first interview partner. Eight and one-half hours later I leave the fifty-some-degree room with cold feet, hands, and nose, and a headache.

This experience is not part of *my* everyday life; rather, it serves as a "point of entry" into the everyday world of the inmates, a world that I enter only intermittently as a researcher. Referring to Dorothy Smith's discussion of feminist research strategies,[1] Marjorie DeVault states that the researcher "must make her bodily existence and activity a 'starting point' for inquiry."[2] Few studies of correctional institutions exhibit any evidence of "bodily existence or activity" of the researcher.[3] These studies, many carried out by the authorities who control the jails and prisons, are accompanied by impressive statistical tables that do not offer a "point of entry" into the everyday world of inmates. The numbers themselves, of course, are grim: in the last decade the rate of incarceration in the United States has increased from 1 in every 218 to 1 in every 147 U.S. residents.[4] At the end of 2000, 3.1 percent of all adult residents of the United States (or 6.5 million people) were on probation, on parole, in jail, or in prison.[5]

When I decided to investigate media use in correctional institutions for my dissertation,[6] I knew that I wanted to meet some of the faces behind those numbers. Neither as a scholar nor as a private person had I ever had any contact with correctional facilities and/or their inmates.[7] Initially, my research was to involve only female inmates. I wanted to study women in prison for several reasons, foremost, because I thought of myself as a feminist researcher. While I did not believe that feminist research could only be conducted *by* women, I did, at that time, subscribe to the conventional belief that it should be *about* and *for* women. This seemed particularly pertinent, as an increasing number of women have entered the correctional system over the past decade. Between 1990 and 2000, the total number of female prisoners increased 108 percent, compared to a 77 percent increase for males.[8] A second reason for focusing on women was the general consensus among researchers that female inmates' experiences in correctional institutions are different in many ways from those of males. Since many of the women are mothers and have been the primary caretakers of their families, these roles shape how they build and maintain social relationships in jail or prison. Researchers repeatedly point out that, while male inmates are more likely to organize in gangs and cliques, women are more likely to establish quasi-family relationships. One of the goals in my research was to explore these women's "standpoints" to see if the way in which women were "socially situated" would influence the way in which they used media in jail or prison.[9] Finally, I naively assumed that, being a woman myself, I would be able to establish a rapport with them more easily than with male inmates. I believed this to be very significant because, at least initially, being female seemed to be the only thing I would have in common with female inmates.

I was both nervous and excited about embarking on this project. I intended to approach it with a great deal of self-reflexivity and self-awareness of my role as a white, German, educated, woman who never had been, and hopefully never would be, incarcerated.

My research was to be guided by the insights I had gained through immersion in the literature on standpoint theory and feminist methodologies. Since Dorothy Smith's groundbreaking work in developing a "sociology for women,"[10] which takes into account the everyday life of women and questions traditional notions of science and research, standpoint theory has developed into a complex body of literature encompassing multiple, and often opposing, perspectives. Parallel to the epistemological debates, feminist researchers have also given attention to the more practical aspects of doing feminist research, such as developing research methods that attempt to break with hierarchical relationships evident in traditional research grounded in the dualisms of Enlightenment philosophy. In what follows I would like to highlight a few of the recurrent themes in these debates that have been pertinent to my own research.

In her analysis and critique of standpoint theory, Susan Hekman describes its assumptions as follows: "All knowledge is located and situated, and . . . one location, that of the standpoint of women, is privileged because it provides a vantagepoint that reveals the truth of social reality."[11] She quickly points out that this theory must necessarily falter, since the first assumption implies the deconstruction of the second and, thus, the concept of *a* truth does not hold in light of "situated knowledge [which] is, by definition, plural."[12] Inextricably connected to this dilemma is the issue of objectivity. Should we discard the view from nowhere as impossible to attain, or should we strive for what Sandra Harding calls "strong objectivity" (the sum of all subjectivities), by coopting existing research methods for the improvement of women's lives? Those who believe that there can be no objectivity are criticized for creating meaningless relativism devoid of any political impact. In contrast, strong objectivity and feminist empiricism are accused of buying into the male-defined patriarchal research paradigm and upholding existing hierarchies that often leave women powerless.

I believe it is exactly the insistence on this dichotomy that is, in fact, detrimental to meaningful feminist research and political action. We should keep in mind Pertti Alasuutari's advice that by choosing a certain method researchers don't have to buy a whole concept of science.[13] In the same vein, Justin Lewis argues that qualitative/critical researchers have rejected quantitative methods based purely on their epistemological underpinnings.[14] In research with inmates, for example, one must work within the dominant, quantitative, paradigm—and provide objective, empirical, research results—if one is to have any influence on policies that will actually affect inmates' lives. At the same time, I firmly believe that it is impossible for this research to be meaningful unless we gain insight into the "situatedness" of inmates, and give voice to the complex ways in which they attain and construct their knowledge as "insiders."

No matter which methods we choose, they all imply a complicated network of power relations. For many feminists the term "power" has acquired a predominantly negative connotation—the power of the researcher *over* the research subject—as it is manifested in much of so-called traditional research. While feminist empiricists still work within, but attempt to improve, this paradigm, feminists working within the qualitative paradigm[15] strive to diminish the imbalance of power between themselves and their research participants in various ways: by building friendships, sharing information about their personal lives; reciprocating in the form of gifts, friendship, financial and material help, and counseling; offering participants a significant part in designing and/or carrying out the research, and even in evaluating the final written product. These researchers reject the "missionary approach" of much conventional research, that is, research from the top down;[16] instead they promote research that is "emancipatory" through linking the personal lives of women to political activism that will end "social and economic conditions that oppress women."[17] However, numerous accounts by feminist researchers point to the limitations of such attempts, which often bring a new set of frustrations and misunderstandings, while leaving the power imbalances essentially unchanged.[18] Judith Stacey, in an early reflection on feminist ethnography, asks "whether the appearance of greater respect for and equality with research subjects in the ethnographic approach masks a deeper, more dangerous form of exploitation."[19] Diane Wolf's collection of essays on "feminist dilemmas in fieldwork" also attests to the difficulties of attempting to transgress the boundaries of race, gender, class, religion, and other identity-forming characteristics separating researchers from participants in their projects.[20]

I believe that by speaking of power imbalance, we are, once again, caught in a dichotomous/hierarchical pattern of thinking which, not surprisingly, leaves researchers with the option of either taking top-down, hierarchical, and missionary approaches, or "going native" to try to rid ourselves of any notion of superiority. In the end, both approaches must necessarily fail to overcome the power imbalance. What we need to overcome, in fact, is the notion of power imbalance itself, and acknowledge the fact that power, like truth, is only partial. In the first volume of this collection the editors define power as "various ways in which one or more human beings shape the behavior and beliefs of others."[21] This points to the fact that power and the creation of partial truths are inextricably connected.

In the context of my research in correctional facilities, power is most obvious in the ways it permeates the relations between the administration, the inmates, and myself. At first glance, these power relationships seem very clear and simple. For the members of the administration power certainly lies in the control they exercise over granting me access to their institution.

At the same time, they also have control over the inmates' participation in the project. Although not directly involved in my study, this "institutional power" defines the basic rules; they schedule my visits so they do not interfere with everyday routine[22] and, although they don't tell me what to wear, they do tell me what *not* to wear: nothing sleeveless, no shorts, no low necklines, no short skirts, no excessive jewelry. Of course, no matter how plainly I dress, I still stick out among the inmates, whose jail uniforms—simple pants and shirts—are color-coded to reveal their positions: bright orange for general prisoners, white for those working in the laundry, beige for those handling food. "You are what you wear," and in here the dress code divides people into two classes, inmates and non-inmates.

While the inmates are stripped of any power to design their everyday lives, they nonetheless have power in the research process. They control whether to participate in the first place. They control how much information they provide or withhold; they can purposely mislead or lie to me. Each perspective denotes a partial truth that reflects a particular moment and place of an individual's experience as an inmate in a correctional institution. However, I believe that the role of the researcher does not lie in the mere *collection* of partial truths but in providing an interactive "knowledge space" which is created in the moment of communication between researcher and participant. Here, knowledge is not simply transferred from one to the other; rather, it becomes a collective activity that subsequently binds the researcher and the participant as allies in attaining a new level of knowledge and another partial truth. This potentially creates a new consciousness on both sides that can be transformed into (political) action. For the inmates this could mean initiating discussion among themselves and, possibly, generating a dialogue with the administration. The latter is also a possibility, if not an obligation, for the researcher, who constitutes a vital link to the "outside world" and can thus contribute to discussions regarding policy changes, or simply provide a voice for inmates through dissemination of her or his research.

While I am dependent on the participant to share his or her knowledge with me, most inmates are aware that I am in a position to take this knowledge outside the prison, to their families and friends, to the media, or to the policy makers who control their lives. As a researcher, I have the choice to transform my newly gained (partial) knowledge into action. This concept of reciprocity, practiced by many feminist ethnographers, can take various forms, from building a much-needed well in a small village to providing art supplies for a mural project in a dilapidated urban neighborhood. The idea is to give back to the community from which we take what for us, as researchers, is the greatest treasure: knowledge. I don't necessarily regard reciprocity as "fair trade," but rather as an expression of mutual respect, understanding, and support of each other's needs and desires. The concept of reciprocity is by no means limited to material assistance. It can also mean giving back by sharing *our* knowledge and partial truths with participants, which, in turn, they can transform into action themselves if they choose. This act of sharing can take various forms depending on the research context. It can be part of the conversation between researcher and participant; it can mean becoming a part of the community, if only momentarily, outside of the intimate dyad of researcher and participant. In the context of the county jail, of course, both the inmates' and my own actions are limited by the rules and regulations imposed upon us. However, to transform knowledge into meaningful action does not always, or only rarely, entail a grand act; it might simply be reflected in a newfound consciousness. This process is a mutual effort by participants and the researcher, and thus defies the label of a missionary approach.

When I first contacted the local jail to inquire about research possibilities, I offered my services as a volunteer teacher, as a way to familiarize myself with the institution, its inmates, and their everyday lives. The administrative staff was very supportive, but logistics and scheduling made it impossible to offer classes to female inmates at that point. As a result I started teaching an introductory media class to a group of about twenty men. I was very apprehensive at first. What had happened to my goal of doing feminist ethnography?

Most of my students were Hispanic and, with few exceptions, had no more than a high school diploma. Most were in their mid-twenties to late thirties and had one or more children. Some of the fathers were involved in "Papas and Their Children" (P. A.T.CH.), a program offered by the Bexar County Jail to strengthen relationships between male inmates and their children.[23] Most of my students also took other classes offered through the educational program. While there was great fluctuation in class attendance (due to transfers, releases, attorney visits, and medical appointments), a core of about ten students regularly attended and faithfully completed their homework assignments. My initial nervousness and insecurity about how to handle a group of male inmates was quickly alleviated by the immense gratitude and appreciation I encountered. A few students went beyond their regular assignments and started bringing in newspaper or magazine clippings related to the issues we were discussing in class. In the classroom, some of them not only engaged in conversation about media topics but also brought their personal "standpoints" into the discussion. This was quite surprising as I had read and heard from the inmates themselves that it is uncommon for male inmates to open up to a larger group of peers. A few began staying after class—risking a clash with some of the guards—to share some of their personal stories or ask for my advice. They also asked me personal questions: Was I married? Did I have children? At times it was difficult to balance my desire to be personable, adherence to the security restrictions and guidelines (such as not to get personally involved in the lives of inmates) that the administration required, and my own need to set boundaries about what I would share with them.

Male acquaintances and colleagues never failed to point out that my being a woman was the *only* reason that my students were attentive and engaged. While I would have liked to think that the attention was based solely on my merits as a teacher, I have to admit that being able to look at a woman once a week for almost two hours likely kept students coming to my classes. But even so, I'd like to think that my presence in the classroom went beyond mere appearance. Perhaps being the ultimate Other (female, white, and German) actually contributed to my success as a teacher. I developed a good rapport with the students—not on the basis of sameness (as I had hoped with female inmates) but, rather, on the basis of difference—and soon felt comfortable sharing my personal views, which I often prefaced with "Well, as a woman . . .," or "In Germany. . . ."

Fearing they would "tune out" if I mentioned the word "feminism," I tried to use empathy to introduce feminist perspectives on media. For example, I used a discussion about representation and images of crime and inmates on television to draw parallels about the misrepresentation and stereotyping of women and other groups. Since most of the students felt very much misrepresented by the media, it was not difficult to evoke empathy—perhaps even understanding—for the misrepresentation and stereotyping of other groups.

I often voiced my opinion "as a woman," as, for example, when we were discussing images of women in advertising. Not surprisingly, I felt much more offended than my students by some of the ads. When I analyzed what I understood to be the dominant reading of an ad, they had a hard time understanding why I would be offended by a scantily clad, unnaturally skinny model, used as mere decoration for a product that only enhances her vulnerability to the male gaze. I did not expect these male inmates to turn into devoted feminists after taking my class, but I felt encouraged by the respect that this captive audience offered me week after week as I continued presenting perspectives they were unlikely to encounter anywhere else in their lives.

At the same time, they presented perspectives—both within and outside the classroom—that were new to me. Almost all of my students were from Texas and, whether or not they were local, knew the city of San Antonio and its surroundings much better than I. They often told me how "it used to be in the old days." They also said how important it was for them to watch or read the local news while in jail to keep up with what was going on in their communities. Some expressed worries about family and friends when there had been a drive-by shooting since, according to them, these were common in their neighborhoods. The inmates also complained about guards turning off the TV or changing the channel when there was coverage about a crime that might be related to a particular group of inmates, or a criminal justice issue of interest to them. They often voiced their dissatisfactions about the jail, certain officers, and other inmates. They knew they could count on my sympathy when complaining about the awful air and terrible temperatures in the building, since I often mentioned these things myself. At times it got very quiet in the class as, for example, when one inmate talked about his brother being on death row and ultimately being executed, and how this influenced his reading of media coverage of related topics. Some students added personal notes to their homework assignments (a poem, a 'thank you' note) or "adjusted" the assignments to share a personal story. They were both very protective of that information (making sure that they were the last ones in the classroom to hand me their assignment; sometimes pulling a poem out of their socks, because they didn't want the guards to find it) and at the same time eager to share it with me. I occupied an interesting position, perhaps something like a confidant, not one of "us" (the inmates) but not one of "them" (the administration) either.

At times it was quite a balancing act to reveal my empathy without violating any of the administration's rules. A couple of inmates, for example, asked me if I could help them set up a contact with the media. They felt they had been wrongly accused and wanted to make their story publicly known. I knew I could not get involved with their cases without risking my teaching position and the opportunity to do research. My solution was to provide them with information (especially about inmates' interest groups) that they could pass on to families and friends, who could make the contacts. I also encouraged one student to send his poem off for publication and, when I came back from summer break, he told me that it would be published by one of the prison presses.

I found myself becoming very committed to my students, teaching even when I was sick because I knew how disappointed they would be if I didn't show up. When they had court dates, I kept my fingers crossed for them and eagerly awaited their reports. Although my classes changed about every ten weeks and I only taught once a week at the jail, the inmates' faces and their stories have stayed with me.

After about ten months of teaching, I started collecting data through surveys and personal interviews with both male and female inmates. Response rates were higher among the male than the female inmate population for two reasons: first, the number of female inmates is far smaller than that of males; second, fluctuations in the population of female inmates are even greater than for males due to shorter sentences. Thus, many of the women who signed up for the research initially had been released by the time the project started. I held several survey sessions in which inmates filled out a questionnaire and had the opportunity to sign up for a personal interview. I was very excited about the prospect of finally being able to talk with female inmates as well.

To my disappointment, the women, unlike the men, were reluctant to talk and nonresponsive in the personal interviews. Perhaps they thought that they didn't have anything "interesting" to tell, since I was asking them "only" about watching television and reading magazines, activities that most people don't reflect on in their everyday lives. Some were skeptical about my project. They asked questions about it, which I appreciated because it gave the interview more of a conversational character. Most of the women were in their early twenties and came from a variety of ethnic backgrounds. Most had children and were in jail for the first time, usually serving short sentences averaging three months. Although some mentioned tension among the inmates about program choice for the one television shared by thirty to forty women, most described their media experience in jail as uneventful.[24] When asked about their media use prior to incarceration, the answers hardly changed and were often accompanied by shrugs. Overall, I gained the impression that many of these women regarded their period of incarceration as a mere inconvenience. Yet while for some it was just part of life, others vowed that this would be their one and only time in jail. A white middle-class woman, in jail for the first time, carefully analyzed her experience and pledged to become an activist for incarcerated women once she got out. She expressed concern about the lethargy among her fellow inmates and said that more needed to be done by the administration to offer these women some direction and food for thought.

Overall I felt that, while my experience with the male inmates had been very positive, I had failed in doing research *for* and *about* women. Both groups were similar in many ways: although the age range among the men was greater (eighteen to fifty-six), the majority of them, like the women, were in their twenties. The ethnic make-up of the groups was essentially the same—a Hispanic majority, a handful of blacks, and a minority of whites.[25] The majority of participants had at least one child. Although I did interview some of my students,[26] I had not previously met the majority of my interviewees.

The differences in my conversations with male and female inmates were striking. The men were more elaborate in their answers, often to the point where I had to intervene to get them back on track. To my surprise they also often became more personal during our conversations than the women, telling me about themselves, their families and children, something I had expected to hear from the women but rarely did. I especially remember one young man who asked my advice. It was his first time in jail, and he felt embarrassed about it. He was very worried about losing his wife and children due to being separated from them for a considerable period of time. It was a very emotional conversation—he was so distraught—and I certainly did not remain "objective." I felt that I had to give him the "right" advice since this was the only conversation I would ever have with him and my only chance to influence his behavior in a positive way.

Although not all of my interviews with the men were as "involved" as this one, each lasted much longer than my interviews with any of the women. Overall, I felt more comfortable in my interviews with the men, partly because I was more familiar with the facilities at the main building, where most inmates are housed and where I had been teaching, than with the annex where the women and only a small number of men are housed. The guards in the main building already knew me and helped make the interview process go smoothly, for example by bringing in the next interviewee immediately after I finished with the previous one. The guards in the annex, although cooperative, did not make me feel particularly welcome and also seemed less friendly toward their inmates than the guards in the main building. At times there were long waits between interviewees. Also, the room next to the one where I was interviewing was being torn down, and the construction noise at times made it hard to carry on a conversation.

One of my initial explanations for the seeming lack of rapport with the women was that I am white and middle class. I am not the first one to conclude that rapport with other women cannot be established on the basis of gender alone. As feminists from Third World/postcolonial countries have articulated, white middle-class Western feminists cannot speak for *all* women. Race and class play equally important, if not sometimes larger, roles than gender. But shouldn't that have been a factor with the male inmates as well, the majority of whom also were not white? Although I do not want to dismiss the importance of race in any interaction between researcher and participants, in retrospect, I now believe that other factors contributed much more to my failure to "connect" with the women.

One factor was that I did not take into account that "researchers need to interview in ways that allow the exploration of incompletely articulated aspects of women's experiences. . . . Eliciting useful accounts of women's experiences is not simply a matter of encouraging women to talk."[27] Rather, it is to engage in "woman talk" rather than "survey talk." For my research this means I need to adjust my interview protocol so that it actually "speaks to" women. However, it is not only about speaking but also about listening. DeVault further argues that we need to "develop methods for listening around and beyond words," because women often "translate" those parts of their experiences that do not fit the hegemonic (male) language paradigm.[28] This means that women might not provide us with material that fits neatly into existing (male-defined) categories. For example, while men are very clear in defining their television preferences by genre (sports and news) women might categorize their preferences differently, as some of my interviewees did by saying they like to watch "something that makes me forget where I am." As researchers we then need to invent new categories to articulate women's particular experience. This also means that interviews with women often require more listening work to detect commonalities and differences than do interviews with men. In retrospect, when I look at my transcripts, I see that there are many instances in which I should have been a better listener. I could have probed more instead of simply waiting for the familiar keywords (such as "program choice," "effects of media use," etc.) in my research language paradigm. This tactic had worked well with the men, but with the women I often ran into a dead end.

The most obvious difference between interviewing female and male inmates was my previous interaction with the men through teaching. Although I have no evidence of this, there is a good chance that my students actually helped advertise my project in their units (I know that some advertised my class and recruited new students). Additionally, through teaching I had already developed a method, albeit unconsciously, for getting the male inmates to talk freely in class. I may have applied this method in my interviews with them as well, but I was unable to transfer this method to my interviews with the women. In retrospect, I ascribe this inability to apply the same method to both men and women to the difference in the ways that certain concepts are articulated, as I discussed above. Also, while this seemed insignificant to me at the time, in retrospect I realize how much more comfortable I felt in the by-then familiar surroundings of the main building with the familiar faces of the guards than at the annex, which always seemed much more "clinical" and unfriendly.

I believe that the best way to develop the same warm rapport with the female inmates would be through teaching. Teaching female inmates in the annex would make me feel more comfortable in those surroundings and would also give the guards a chance to get to know me, which is a significant factor since I depend on their cooperation. Furthermore, through teaching the women, I could explore—in a nonthreatening setting—the ways of "women talk" among female inmates. I could learn about the women's perspectives and personal backgrounds, and also reveal myself to them as a person (albeit still a teacher) rather than a researcher. I also would need to adjust my teaching strategies and methods to fit their needs. For example, given the greater fluctuation and shorter periods of incarceration among female inmates, offering weekend or weeklong workshops, rather than ten- to fifteen-week classes, makes more sense. In a more concentrated time period, focusing on just a few topics is likely to be more useful than trying to cover many. Through the interviews I learned that many of the women have the same favorite television show. I believe that centering certain topics and issues around something they like to watch is likely to evoke discussion. Even if my experience teaching the women turns out to be completely different from teaching the men, I am confident that it will be both a valuable experience and, eventually, a point of entry into the world of female inmates.

In sum, despite, or perhaps because of, my frustrations, I feel that a feminist methodology is still the most useful approach to my research with inmates. The practices and perspectives it offers "share . . . a desire to locate the researcher firmly at the centre of the research activity, both as change agent and as a living exponent of a specifically feminist praxis."[29] In retrospect I can see that my interactions with the female inmates were far from being feminist research, unlike my experience with the male inmates. This experience also taught me that I no longer can subscribe to the notion of feminist research as being *exclusively* for and about women. Feminist research methods also are applicable in research about men. Feminist research entails the examination of existing power inequities and a desire to change these power relations in order to create social structures that are not oppressive to anyone, women or men. It means lending a voice to those who have no voice in political spaces to which they have no access. And to critics who dismiss this as patronizing, I ask in Karen Ross's words: "Should researchers who *can* enable that voice to be heard be criticized for doing so, simply because they can provide the conduit for articulation where their 'subjects' would otherwise remain mute?"[30]

In my work, I have encountered many of the dilemmas and frustrations of feminist ethnography described by other researchers. However, we as researchers cannot let ourselves be paralyzed by them. Instead, we should embrace them as feedback honing our capacities for more holistic research. While some might view my teaching as a "missionary" project, I regard it a necessary entry point for gaining an understanding of the standpoint of inmates and for achieving strong objectivity in the sense that Harding describes it: "To enact or operationalize the directive of strong objectivity is to value the Other's perspective and to pass over in thought into the social condition that creates it—not in order to stay there, to 'go native' or merge the self with the Other, but in order to look back at the self in all its cultural particularity from a more distant, critical, objectifying location."[31] To me this means that we as researchers form communities, if only temporarily, with the participants in our research. While these communities eventually must dissolve, they are key to laying the groundwork for changing consciousness and initiating political action.

Notes

The experiences described in this essay occurred over the period of one year, when, in January 2000, I started teaching a 'Media and Society' class at the Bexar County Jail in San Antonio, Texas. In November and December of that year, I conducted survey sessions and interviews with a sample of inmates.

1. Dorothy Smith, *The Everyday World as Problematic: A Feminist Sociology* (Boston: Northeastern University Press, 1987).

2. Marjorie DeVault, *Liberating Method: Feminism and Social Research.* (Philadelphia: Temple University Press, 1999), 39.

3. Examples of those that do include Andi Rierden, *The Farm: Life Inside a Women's Prison* (Amherst: University of Massachusetts Press, 1997); Barbara Owen, *"In the Mix": Struggle and Survival in a Women's Prison* (Albany: State University of New York Press, 1998) ; and Kathryn Watterson, *Women in Prison: Inside the Concrete Womb,* rev. ed. (Boston: Northeastern University Press, 1996).

4. U.S. Department of Justice, Bureau of Justice Statistics, "Prison and Jail Inmates at Midyear 1999," http://www.ojp.usdoj.gov/bjs/abstract/pjim99.htm (2 August 2002).

5. U.S. Department of Justice, Bureau of Justice Statistics, "Correction Statistics," http://www.ojp.usdoj.gov/bjs/correct.htm (2 August 2002).

6. "Media use" in my project refers to the use of television, radio, newspapers, magazines, and, to a limited extent, the Internet. Although my questionnaires and interviews include questions about all of the above mentioned media, most of the responses refer to television, as it is the medium most used by inmates. This can be explained in part by the fact that radios and newspapers have to be purchased by the inmates, whereas television is readily available; another reason is the low level of literacy among many inmates.

7. So, how did I get on this subject? The credit goes to *The Shawshank Redemption,* a movie whose depiction of the relationship between a young white inmate and an older African-American inmate sparked all kinds of questions. Aside from the issue of race, however, it also led me to contemplate the importance of access to media in prisons, as one of the focal points in the movie is the installation of a prison library.

8. Based on U.S. Department of Justice, "Prisoners in 2000," *Bureau of Justice Statistics Bulletin* (Washington, D.C.: Government Printing Office, August 2001); available on-line at http://www.ojp.usdoj.gov/bjs/abstract/p00.htm (2 August 2002).

9. One of the questions I wanted to explore, for example, was whether television characters would provide them with pseudo-roles such as the role of spouse, lover, mother, breadwinner, and so forth, that they are unable to fulfill "properly" while incarcerated.

10. Smith, *Everyday World.*

11. Susan Hekman, *The Future of Differences: Truth and Method in Feminist Theory* (Cambridge, U.K.: Polity Press, 1999), 38.

12. Ibid.

13. Pertti Alasuutari, *Researching Culture: Qualitative Method and Cultural Studies* (London: Sage, 1996).

14. Justin Lewis, "What Counts in Cultural Studies?" *Media, Culture and Society* 19 (1997): 83–97.

15. Here defined as the use of interpretive methods and in-depth studies that are informed by critical theories and often take a decidedly political stance.

16. Diane Wolf gives credit to Anne Opie for coining the term; see Diane Wolf, ed., *Feminist Dilemmas In Fieldwork* (Boulder, Colo.: Westview Press, 1996), 29.

17. Joan Acker et al., "Objectivity and Truth: Problems in Doing Feminist Research," in *Beyond Methodology: Feminist Scholarship as Lived Research,* ed. Mary Margaret Fonow and Judith A. Cook (Bloomington: Indiana University Press, 1991), 134.

18. See Acker et al., "Objectivity and Truth"; Elaine Lawless, "'I Was Afraid Someone Like You . . . an Outsider . . . Would Misunderstand': Negotiating Interpretive Differences between Ethnographers and Subjects," *Journal of American Folklore* 105, 417 (1992): 302–14; Judith Stacey, "Can There Be a Feminist Ethnography?" *Women's Studies International Forum* 11, 1 (1988): 21–27.

19. Stacey, "Feminist Ethnography?" 22.

20. Wolf, ed., *Feminist Dilemmas.*

21. Mary Ann Tétreault and Robin L. Teske, "Introduction: Framing the Issues," in *Conscious Acts and the Politics of Social Change,* vol. 1 of *Feminist Approaches to Social Movements, Community, and Power,* ed. Robin L. Teske and Mary Ann Tétreault (Columbia: University of South Carolina Press, 2000), 6.

22. I would like to point out, however, that the administration at the Bexar County Jail of San Antonio, Texas, was extremely accommodating in meeting my needs as well.

23. Inmates in the P. A.T.CH. program have to attend five hours of P. A.T.CH. classes during the week and maintain good behavior to earn a one-hour contact visit with their children on Saturdays.

24. By "media experience" I mean when and where they used what type of media, and why; for example, do they find it annoying to watch television with a large group, often unable to hear the soundtrack due to the surrounding noise of other inmates talking; do they prefer to read magazines in the "privacy" of their bunk, and so forth.

25. These terms of ethnic identification are those used by the inmates themselves. They categorized themselves—and others—as black, white, Hispanic or Mexican.

26. I scheduled my students all on the same day, after I had interviewed everyone else.

27. DeVault, *Liberating Method,* 65–66.

28. Ibid., 66.

29. Karen Ross, "Unruly Theory and Difficult Practice: Issues and Dilemmas in Work with Women Politicians," *International Feminist Journal of Politics* 2, 3 (Autumn 2000): 321.

30. Ibid., 322.

31. Sandra Harding, *Whose Science? Whose Knowledge?* (Ithaca, N.Y.: Cornell University Press, 1991), 151.

Part Three

Discordant Instruments

Chapter 7

Theorizing Global Political Economy *Because* People Matter

Ronnie D. Lipschutz

> The first man who, having fenced in a piece of land, said, "This is mine," and found people naive enough to believe him, that man was the true founder of civil society.
>
> —Jean-Jacques Rousseau (1754)

> Ownership is one of the characteristic institutions of human society. A people to whom ownership was unknown, or who accorded it a minor place in their arrangements, who meant by *meum* and *tuum* no more than 'what I (or you) presently hold' would live in a world that is not our world.
>
> —A. M. Honoré (1961)

Introduction

Why are international relations and international political economy made to seem so special and abstract when they really are so ordinary? Why do people disappear (or never appear) except as homogeneous "populations"? And why, despite our best intentions, do we find it so difficult to escape the suffocating theoretical embrace of the state? Why, indeed. If we were to theorize a global political economy in which people rather than states and corporations are central, what might the study of global political economy look like? What kind of methodological, epistemological—and, indeed, ontological—approaches could provide the kind of insight, sensitivity, and particularity necessary to understand the global politics of a world of six billion people in contrast to the international relations of a world of 190 nation-states?

An attempt to answer such questions is particularly relevant, indeed crucial, to a volume on feminist approaches to community. The increasingly hegemonic discourse of globalization that dominates the study of international political economy treats community not only as nonproblematic but almost as nonexistent. As I have suggested elsewhere,[1] the liberal vision of a world of six or ten billion individualized consumers, each constituting her or his own self-referential "state," is a dystopian nightmare that, to recall Karl Polanyi, is likely to be self-annihilating.[2] By eliminating all *emotional* bonds between people—a quintessentially patriarchal and property-ridden move as we shall see—people are also eliminated except, perhaps, as statistical data (or "populations") distributed along bell-shaped curves.

In this chapter, I develop an approach to global political economy in which people *matter.* I begin with a short discussion of the ontological status of property in our theories and practices of social life, arguing that property relations obliterate human relations. I then examine aspects of four foundational elements central to my framework: critical feminist theory; historical materialism; the social individual; and the construction of political space. With these pieces in place, I propose that to develop a people-based framework for global political economy (GPE), three steps are necessary. First, we must become aware of the beliefs and behaviors underlying the reproduction of structures and the ways in which individuals are socialized into accepting them as "natural." This involves, as well, understanding how each social individual comes to find herself in a particular place and time, doing particular things, and how such placement and behavior is relationally linked to other social individuals and, ultimately, to global political economy. Second, we must ask how we, as social individuals, might confront such socialization and placement in theoretical terms and how we face both constraints and opportunities; this is followed by engaging in similar analysis for other social individuals. I suggest that we would begin this second step ethnographically, constructing a "political economic autobiography" that maps out our own life trajectory in terms of agency and structure. The third step is social action, that is, acting as social individuals. In this chapter, I take up only the first step by offering a brief example; the last two steps are left to the reader and to future chapters.

The Properties of Everyday Life

There are two "blind spots" in the way that we conventionally explain and engage in social and political life, one epistemological, the other ontological. Epistemologically, the abstractions we use to explain global political economy conceal the ways in which power is routinely exercised. Ontologically, the primacy of property, expressed in terms of rights to both real property and property in the self, helps to obfuscate and naturalize critical aspects of human social relations. It is not by accident that power and property trump our ability to theorize about people (and everyday practice), for they are so foundational to liberal politics that they become like the air we breathe: always present, yet largely unnoticed (until someone fears they are threatened).

Consider, for example, the state, state system, and international economy. They are really only complex social institutions, the patterned, structured results of people acting on their beliefs and interests over periods of time in patterned and structured ways. Through these institutional structures and specific practices—by which I mean both the state and its intellectual defenders—some individuals and groups become powerful, wealthy, safe, and comfortable while others remain weak, poor, and in want. That this great disparity is so widely accepted as natural is both evident and a question to be explored empirically. It is evident in that challenges to the arrangements that produce the disparities fail to provoke most people to question them. It is an empirical question because the growing contradictions ought to generate more resistance and opposition than they seem to at the present time

This disparity in power and wealth does not justify ignoring the vast numbers of people who are not powerful, wealthy, safe, and comfortable yet are integral to these institutions. Neither does it justify concentrating almost exclusively on the beliefs and activities of states and leaders and the ways in which their actions play out structurally. Yet, much of the international political economy (IPE) literature does precisely this, treating it as a "true" picture of the "real" world. Such naturalization is one example of the way in which a particular kind of power—the power to specify certain theoretical parameters and suppositions while excluding others—serves to reproduce other kinds of power, here the unchallenged power of states and leaders.

It is, of course, much easier to accept and act to reproduce structures and institutions than to change them because we tend to believe and act as though what we have been told is true: our economic beliefs and practices are not only natural but also the only ones possible (thus, "after 1989, there are no alternatives to capitalism"). And even those who struggle to find alternatives seem continually to return to variations on the same theme.[3]

Consequently, failure under such conditions is normalized as the fault of the individual rather than the result of a stacked institutional deck, and even efforts to reform or change institutions and practices come to have the same form as the institutions and practices being criticized. Moreover, those who challenge these structures are marginalized through ridicule and ostracism ("idealists! utopians!"), and thereby made to appear either impossible or threatening. Institutional resilience, resistance, and absorbency buffer elites and systems from opposition and rebellion. None of this is very surprising.

There is, however, an even more basic foundational principle that trumps the everyday naturalization of power and weakness, of wealth and poverty, and helps to maintain hierarchies of power and wealth: liberal (capitalist) property rights and human rights. It is one of the paradoxes of contemporary life and politics that the very discourse routinely invoked on behalf of individual liberty and freedom from state power—the discourse of "human rights"—also functions as a primary means of discipline and, I would argue, a crucial obstacle to meaningful social change. After all, human "rights" are, on the one hand, declared to be "natural" while, on the other hand, it is understood that they can be granted and guaranteed only by a state, as what for all practical purposes are property rights in the self. Just as the nineteenth-century wage contract of the "free" laborer was deemed to reflect the individual's right to sell that labor as property, so are contemporary human rights framed in terms of the individual's contractual relationship with the state as the grantor of property rights and guarantor of contracts.

Such a conceit is possible only within a philosophical framework in which the material self is somehow construed as a form of "real" property to which the self-possessive individual holds certain kinds of institutionalized privileges (subject to restrictions imposed by the state). This leads to several paradoxes. First, that which should be available to all people—shelter, food, work—is expressed in terms of "rights" offered via the social contract rather than as goods all human beings deserve as a matter of being. Second, it leads to the kinds of debates we see around, for example, abortion, in which property rights in the self are juxtaposed against the state's property rights in the fetus. As I will argue below—and not with any great originality, I might add—it is this conversion of people into forms of property that performs the ontological trickery of naturalizing power relations and rendering people irrelevant to international relations (IR) and IPE. Property, after all, has no emotions, no feelings, indeed, no existence except insofar as it is surveyed, described, named, and inscribed on state-sanctioned documents. Regarded as property, the individual does not exist unless similarly inscribed.

Critical Feminist Theory

With this argument as a basis, how might we begin to think about a global political economy centered on people? Without wishing to fall into essentialism, I begin my framework-building with a critical feminist approach, precisely because feminist theory's initial rebellion was *against* the essentializing of women's role in household reproduction (as an element of household *property*) and *for* the politics of women's involvement in the public sphere (as active subjects). If production and reproduction begin with the individual, rebellion against the hegemony of IR theory and the politics it produces should begin where the political is not only local, but also personal (again, however, not in terms of the liberal individual).

In using the term "critical feminist theory," I do not refer to theories and standpoints that criticize. Rather, I mean theories that examine, with skepticism, not only the subject positions in which individuals find themselves—positions that are a consequence of gendered divisions of labor—but also the developmental premises on which explanations of those positions are based. These premises are not only gendered but also, as I have suggested above, rooted in specific naturalized propositions about power, authority, and human nature. I also mean being sensitive to the ways in which everyday ideas and practices are permeated not only by masculinist systems of power that reproduce themselves and produce the subjects they control, but also by a naturalized and gendered ontology of human subjectivity.[4] Such an approach goes beyond more familiar notions of gendering (at least, for me) by making specific claims about the constitution of the subjects which they claim to describe objectively.

Thus, for example, the very concept of the liberal "individual"—whether person or state—that is so central to international political economy is gendered. This is not only because in classical liberalism the individual is so often construed as male but also because the very concept of the "individual" in liberal theory obliterates from memory and consciousness those bonds and relationships among people that are so fundamental to each person's social development and behavior, and which ought to continue to develop throughout one's life. Christine Di Stefano offers a broad overview of the way psychoanalytic theory's "object relations account of modern masculinity" explains the seemingly natural differentiation between male and female arising from the dynamics of the nuclear family.[5] Di Stefano points in particular to Nancy Chodorow's explanation of the male child's objectification of his mother as a central element in the production and reproduction of masculinity. According to Chodorow, "[Male] domination begins with the mother as object, extends to women, and is then generalized to include the experience of all others as objects rather than subjects. This stance, in which people are treated and experienced as things, becomes basic to male Western culture. Thus, the 'fetishism of commodities,' the rigid self-other distinctions of capitalism or of bureaucratic mass societies all have genetic and psychological roots in the structure of parenting and of male development, not just the requirements of production."[6]

While Di Stefano is attentive to the cultural and historical specificity of the object relations account she discusses,[7] there is nonetheless a sense that the gendered separation of male and female is somehow fundamental to virtually all human societies and an invariant characteristic of patriarchy. Chodorow, however, links male objectification specifically to male Western culture, that is, capitalism and property. It is this last point that I wish to explore further.

Patriarchy is not merely a set of unequal relationships or the exercise of male power over the female; it is also the means whereby particular men accumulate social, material, and political power. The institution of patriarchy is thousands of years old, although its specific manifestations differ among cultures and over time as both Di Stefano and Chodorow would remind us. But the basic goal of patriarchy was and continues to be the diminishing of both matrilineality and "nonrational" social bonds. This is accomplished through the disruption and displacement of emotional relations between and among people—especially between mother and child—by a hierarchy of constructed loyalties to father, to sovereign, to nation. In this displacement, moreover, relations of property come to dominate other social and emotional relations inasmuch as the male head of household, being the sovereign patriarch, is granted property rights in the other members of the household. Just as the subject is linked to the sovereign through relations of property, so historically have members of a family been linked to the patriarch through similar relations.

The most fundamental of emotional relations is that between mother and child. The very first act of mother and newborn—confirming the bond created in utero—is undeniably biological, but it is also foundational to the social (which is clearly seen in the psychopathologies that develop in children who, in infancy, never had a chance to bond closely with another person). As the child gets older, the original emotional bond is extended to others in the child's immediate circle, even as the mother remains the primary focus. Such emotional bonds are a challenge to the exercise of power by men. Power is acquired by isolating individuals from each other and creating loyalties through rational contracts and exchanges rather than through "irrational" emotions, through bargains and benefits rather than love and commitment. These latter bonds are of a different character and do not respond to the calculating logic of power's manipulation and the Hobbesian threats it wields. It is not altogether surprising, therefore, that fathers, sovereigns, and states seek continually to weaken the mother-child bond, capture it, and reproduce and bend it for other purposes, such as military service. Through oaths of loyalty, military training at an early age, and the beliefs and practices of nationalism, all in return for privileges denied to others (especially women), father, sovereign, and state implant rationality and displace emotion. Much of this weakening and capture comes through the use of gendered language and practice, especially that directed toward male children, but it also depends crucially on property rights.

The very concept of the liberal individual has a similar genealogy and social ontology although it is expressed in a somewhat different fashion. Through naturalization of the free, autonomous subject as an objective "fact" bereft of all but the most deracinated social relations—a process and belief that permeates Western politics and economics—the historical, social, and emotional constitution of the person is at best obscured and at worst wholly eliminated. This end is accomplished via the reification of contract as the basis for relations between individuals (indeed, the concept of contract underpins the founding mythology not only of the state *and* the nation-state, as found in both Hobbes and Locke, but also the family). Family members are turned into property and families into a micro-expression of the so-called social contract. As noted earlier, historically, males were deemed the only legitimate holders of property. Unmarried women and widows who came into possession of property acquired the juridical character of men, even though they were never accorded the same social recognition granted to even unpropertied men. These hardly recognized features of the liberal state and society are much more deeply embedded in our life practices than the more obvious aspects of patriarchy to which we usually point.

In another context, Judith Butler has written about this problematic, arguing that

> the question of "the subject" is crucial for politics, and for feminist politics in particular, because juridical subjects are invariably produced through certain exclusionary practices that do not "show" once the juridical structure of politics has been established. In other words, the political construction of the subject proceeds with certain legitimating and exclusionary aims, and these political operations are effectively concealed and naturalized by a political analysis that takes juridical structures as their foundation. Juridical power inevitably "produces" what it claims merely to represent; hence, politics must be concerned with this dual function of power: the juridical and the productive.[8]

The result is, as Butler puts it, that such structures "*produce* the subjects they invariably come to represent."[9] The Western legal system purports to protect individual rights yet, in expressing such rights as forms of property in the self, both Western law and culture admit of no other possible constitution of either individual or society, such as one that would acknowledge the primacy of emotion over rationality or even the equality of the two.

The consequence of such naturalized gendering at the ontological level must be considered a highly pernicious one that leaves this particular form of juridical power virtually invisible. Within the global political economy, the person is treated not as an integral part of the whole, deserving of respect and support, and expected to respond in kind. Rather, each person is regarded as an individual who confronts a set of objectively given opportunities and constraints that must be handled strategically and tactically so as to generate maximum individual utility (usually measured in terms of income or "happiness" based on individualized consumption). One who fails in this mission is considered to have failed to meet the standards of full-fledged huMANity—a standard that excludes most of the world's people, by the way—as presented through liberal epistemology. Of course, were this scenario in any sense "true," we would find ourselves in a really existing Hobbesian State of Nature.

Historical Materialism

The second element in my framework-building is to be found in historical materialism. By this I mean not a crude instrumental Marxism in which substructure dominates superstructure, but a materialism sensitive to the relationship between production (understood as subsistence and livelihood) and reproduction (understood as social and cultural survival and continuity). My intent here is to avoid the idealism inherent in both neorealism and neoliberalism, while acknowledging the constitutive interplay between "ideas" and material conditions. As Marx put it, "We erect our structure in imagination before we erect it in reality,"[10] although once we have erected our structures, our imaginations are constrained by them. Through this form of historical materialism, I mean also to comprehend the genealogies of the physical and social arrangements that people confront when they wish to act.[11] Thus, John Agnew, a geographer, argues that "[People] are *located* according to the demands of a spatially extensive division of labour, the global system of material production and distribution, and variable patterns of political authority and control."[12] Those patterns are the result not only of existing relations of power and wealth largely determined through property, as I have argued above, but also the histories (or genealogies) through which those relations have developed. The implications of this point go beyond the generally understood limits to the "making of our own histories." Rather, the point to recognize here is that even the ways in which we *conceptualize* the making of our own histories, and the constraints on those possibilities, are already a consequence of histories of production and reproduction conditioned by the naturalization of the constructed individual.

Indeed, the legal construction of the liberal individual alluded to earlier is one result of the exercise of such material power. Western legal and political systems are organized around the notion of the liberal individual (historically, a male citizen) to whom rights, duties, and liabilities are granted and assigned. These abstract rights, duties, and liabilities are made manifest through various forms of documentation, whose material existence testifies to the constitution of each particular individual and turns subject into object. Thus, in the United States as in many other countries, to work *legally* one must possess and present on demand documents inscribed with the authorization of the state, testifying to the property rights in the self that are conventionally called "citizenship."[13] It is understood that without such authorization one cannot collect certain entitlements from the state. Without it, one does not even *exist* in the eyes of the state.

In order to acquire representation as a "real" person—as an object of real property, in other words—the liberal individual must engage in specifically prescribed practices that generate the documents testifying to her legal and material existence. In order to travel outside of the U.S. territorial borders (an abstract right), a resident must obtain a passport (material documentation) granting title to that right. To demonstrate one's entitlement to a passport, the prospective traveler must produce a birth certificate (or comparable document) "proving" the occurrence of an historical and material event (one's birth within the United States). But any single individual's birth certificate exists only by virtue of the duty of parents—and there are spaces on the birth certificate for both mother and father; the child without a documented father is regarded as somehow less than fully legitimate—to register each birth as the legal issue of two liberal individuals, the very act that generates the material document proving existence. (A failure to do this might result in the paradox that one does not exist legally and has no objectified identity, which might account for the seemingly pervasive fear of "identity theft"). Moreover, this very act of registration by two liberal individuals, an act required by law, produces in the eyes of the law the object whose material existence is undeniably (but not legally) demonstrated by virtue of her having been born as a subject. Puzzling questions arise. How is it that such documentation—a form of title to property in the self—has come not only to signify but also to substitute for the individual's physical existence? And what has been lost or ignored in this construction of the liberal individual?

The Social Individual

In place of the legal, gendered, liberal individual, I propose that we rebirth the "social individual" as both subject and agent.[14] By this term and the relations it implies, we recognize people as *social beings* born with and socialized into the experience of emotions that should be allowed to grow over a lifetime, creating and relying on mutual relations with and responsibilities to each other, developing through their own histories, acting historically, materially, and in groups. Whereas the liberal individual is an object produced through rational law—a law that is so deeply naturalized as to be regarded as unremarkable—the *social* individual is a subject constituted by emotional relations among people as subjects rather than by contractual relations among people as objects. It might be objected that such emotional ties, when permitted to develop in certain ways, lead to illiberalism and xenophobia, indeed to ethnic cleansing; my response is that such emotions and behaviors are often the product of liberalism and fetishized property relations.[15]

The concept of the social individual has major implications for the construction of a people-centered approach to global political economy. The common liberal conception of the individual's place in politics and economics treats her as no more than one part interchangeable with millions or billions of others—except, of course, for those deemed to be "movers and shakers." The individual is a participant in already existing institutions, whose rules, roles, and relations are predetermined by the functional needs of societal reproduction. Thus, for example, one "voter" is indistinguishable from any other, and her vote (unless it is rejected as invalid) cannot be told apart from any others. Moreover, by the time a vote is cast, most of the important decisions have already been made. There is no opportunity to select from the broad range of other possible choices, including those having to do with the structure of the institution itself or, for that matter, the principles and material forces that constituted the institution in the first place. Whether consumer or voter, the liberal individual is offered only the opportunity to ratify the institution, not to challenge it, while those who fail to vote are chastised not for their rejection of the institution but for their "apathy." In other words, the "politics" in international political economy originates at a shallower level than the "politics" in people-centered global political economy.

The social individual's material existence does not rely on the inscriptions of the state, or any other authority, for that matter; the very event of birth is an occasion of experience, pain, and joy to be shared and often witnessed by those close to both parents and child. Hearing parental testimony of pain and reward even decades after the event, who can question that a birth has happened? Every social individual develops by virtue of the presence and actions of other social individuals. Ultimately, we become who we are not by our beliefs and actions alone but by virtue of our embeddedness in webs of social relations that constitute our identities. The fully autonomous and atomized individual, however well-documented, is not a human being except in the legal sense; we become and remain human through our sociality.

Power does not disappear, of course, but what is involved here is the power of microspaces rather than macrospaces.[16] Such power is not about the "ability of A to get B to do what A wants." Whether conceived as violence, threat, authority, or hegemony, that kind of power—the power of macrospaces—is fundamentally coercive and treats people as no different than objects to be moved through space by mechanistic forces. As a constructive force, operating in the microspaces of everyday life, power is amenable to being utilized relationally, as a means of treating people as ends in themselves rather than merely as instruments for the ends of production or desire. There is no guarantee, of course, that power *will* be used constructively; it could merely serve to reproduce patriarchy, as is often the case.

Constructing Political Spaces

Must political life be reduced to nothing more than a vote for the status quo? Perhaps not. The efflorescence of social movements over the past two decades, although not without problems and contradictions, suggests that new spaces for political life are constructed continuously. The creation of such political spaces results from the productive use of power, based on relationships of action and emotional commitment among social individuals. It is by now a cliché to claim that human institutions are "social constructions," a claim that is regarded by some as tantamount to a threat to rationality and by others as the sheer denial of "reality."[17] Such defensive maneuvers—usually mounted by those whose vocation approximates mindless protection of the authority of the prince—clearly represent a gross misunderstanding of the concept of social construction but, nevertheless, reflect awareness of the political implications of such ideas acquiring widespread currency. In my approach to global political economy, I want to examine the ways in which social individuals construct the political spaces within which they have agency. While this might appear a banal exercise, it actually facilitates an understanding of why, even as structures constrain, agents can act.

The concept of "political space" is a fairly old one[18] although it has usually been restricted to territories within which politics takes place. In the interstate realm, political space has been treated largely as one that is "full" yet anarchic, lacking rules yet requiring the imposition of "order" by great powers. The state is, of course, the archetypal political space for our time. Aside from "international regimes," institutionalized politics have been, for the most part, restricted to those practices considered legitimate within the territory of each political space. When "politics" is defined as encompassing only those practices permitted by the structures that organize and constrain political space (rules, beliefs, laws, acts, agencies, etc. created and disciplined through dominating power), other forms of political practice become marginalized and are even suppressed by force.

Thus, for example, social movements that challenge institutionalized practices and for which there is no legitimized framework, such as labor movements during the late nineteenth and early twentieth centuries, the peace movement during the Vietnam War, or the indigenous and antiglobalization movements of today, are usually dismissed as unrepresentative, irrelevant, illegal, and so on. Nevertheless, such social movements exist and continue to emerge and proliferate. Over time, some are legitimized (labor unions, for example) or co-opted into institutionalized politics (the German Greens), while others are not. And some of the issues and organizations that emerge from social movements are institutionalized through bureaucratized nongovernmental organizations, many of which have become ancillary to the continued hegemony of liberalism. But it is the engendering of these unauthorized political spaces and movements that makes clear the inadequacies of institutionalized politics. Social movements are not the products of rational calculation as it is commonly understood, and this is their great strength. If they were "rational," they could be anticipated, obstructed, and coopted by the defenders of the faith. Because they are based on emotional commitment to certain ends, however, their logic is opaque to the practitioners of institutionalized politics. As the result of the collective action of social individuals, united not by contract but by emotional commitment, movements have objectives but no cost-benefit calculus; they offer satisfaction but no remuneration.

In light of the constraints imposed by institutions on the creation of political spaces, how do social individuals create and move into political spaces and generate support and legitimacy for their projects? How are social individuals constrained, limited, or marginalized by political projects and spaces already in existence (sometimes for decades if not longer)? In other words, what is it that enables some but not others to open political space and achieve their political projects?

John Agnew (quoted earlier) is something of a determinist when he locates individuals in specific places in the global matrix. In doing so, he seems to limit the possibilities of agency. A more expansive view of the possible comes from Joan Scott, a political theorist, who tells us that "subjects have agency. They are not unified, autonomous individuals exercising free will but rather subjects whose agency is created through situations and statuses conferred on them. Being a subject means being 'subject to definite conditions of existence, conditions of endowment of agents and conditions of exercise.' These conditions enable choices, although they are not unlimited."[19] While Scott's arguments are not explicitly rooted in feminist or materialist theory or practice, she argues from a perspective fundamental to critical feminist theory: identifying the presence of power in everyday life and becoming sensitive to its consequences.

Elsewhere, I have suggested that the acquisition of agency rests on a recognition of both context and contingency.[20] As John Walton has argued:

> The constitution of local society . . . is far more than an imposition or small-scale reflection of the national state. On the contrary, it is the evolving product of multiple influences—the people, the economy, natural resources, intermediate levels of state authority, local accommodation to some broader designs, determined resistance to others and, perhaps above all, collective action founded on cultural meaning. Action takes place within social structures that forcibly shape experience, yet people live in local societies where particular customs, exigencies, and choices mediate structural constraints. On the ground people construct their lives in consciously meaningful ways that cannot be read from state-centered directives any more than they can be deduced from modes of economic production.[21]

Under these circumstances, agency is a matter of becoming aware of alternatives and helping to foster conditions under which meaningful choices can be made. More than awareness does, action also involves collective *social* agency, a form of group behavior that conventional economistic theories of collective action cannot explain, as I suggested above. Social agency relies on the creation of political spaces within which established structures—especially discursive ones—can be simultaneously resisted *and* used in pursuit of group goals.

In established contexts governed by patterned rules, relations, and behaviors, social individuals seeking agency must bring to bear two kinds of resources on their project; let us call them "social" and "material." Social resources include intellectual arguments, social capital, and structural knowledge. Material resources include authority, wealth, goods and commodities, and offers of benefit. "Getting things done" involves wielding both types of resources as well as knowing "rules" for action (structural knowledge) and relations that can be tapped (social capital). Having devised an objective or a project, the social individual must map out a strategy. This is not necessarily a well-designed plan; many "strategies" are more ad hoc than fully developed schemes or "business plans." Such a strategy involves using the two forms of resources (social and material) to mobilize supporters through intellectual argumentation and dissemination of goods and promises. Most analyses (including economistic ones) of social action focus on the latter because material effects are easier to observe and measure, but intellectual resources are at least as important. Ultimately, as Norman Long points out, "Effective agency . . . requires organizing capacities; it is not simply the result of possessing certain persuasive powers or forms of charisma. . . . *Agency (and power) depend crucially upon the emergence of a network of actors who become partially, though hardly ever completely, enrolled in the 'project' of some other person or persons.* . . . It becomes essential, therefore, for social actors to win the struggles that take place over the attribution of specific social meanings to particular events, actions and ideas."[22]

A People-Centered Global Political Economy

Putting these four foundational elements together helps us to organize an understanding of a people-centered GPE. As I suggested above, I am especially concerned here with the way in which, on the one hand, power ordinarily "produces" isolated individuals regarded as objects and, on the other, the way in which power might be used productively for emancipating them as social subjects. In most of the international relations and international political economy literature, juridical power—that is, the structural power wielded by and inherent in dominating institutions—becomes the guiding light of explanation. Like the fabled story about the drunk and the lamppost, questioners look only where the light is brightest and regard the penumbra as both uninteresting and unimportant. As one moves farther away from the lamppost, the light dims and so, it appears, does power. This is why, I would suggest that discussions of international politics always contrast "states" with "other" actors, ask whether the latter possess any juridical power, and dismiss them when it becomes clear that they do not.[23]

But productive power—what Mary Ann Tétreault and Robin Teske argue is a "function of the distribution and strategic location of capacities"[24] —is of an entirely different character. It is, first of all, relational in that social bonds among them play a major role in individuals' constitution: productive power acknowledges that emotions and bonds marginalized by juridical power and dismissed by liberalism are actually constitutive of human life. Second, productive power operates in the microspaces of everyday life, not through domination but rather through the *respect* that individuals give to each other and the *empathy and love* they have for each other. Finally, using such productive power, the individual can also be an agent of resistance to structures of domination.

It is in this context that we can ask "who acts." For most students of IR and IPE that question is a relatively simple one. Their ready answer obscures not only the complexity of whatever they ascribe the action to—whether state or individual—but also the very meaning of the term "action." It is often noted that, strictly speaking, corporate organizations such as the state do not "act" in the generally understood meaning of the term which, at its simplest, connotes cause and effect (and at its most complex, is much more complicated). Nonetheless, it is also evident that corporate behavior is not the sum of the individual behaviors of the organization's members. Historically, we have elided this difficulty by "assuming the spherical cow,"[25] that is, by pretending and behaving as if the proposition of methodological individualism for corporate units is accurate enough for analytical purposes.

But what do we lose as a result of such idealization of individual action? And how can we conceive a principle of nonindividual social action? Here is where the concept of "social agency" becomes central, not as applied to social movements but rather as a product of the histories and social relations of each person who acts, alone and together. Lest this seem a contradiction in terms, just as no one is an isolated individual, no one acts in isolation from others. The social contexts in which each person lives are products of complicated histories and relations with other persons and, of course, with structures. Such relationships remain important throughout the individual's life, even though they have been marginalized by both patriarchy and liberalism.

The locations of social individuals in the GPE are the result of unique social histories. The social relationships within which people live are different from one place to another, and the possibilities for agency, though similar, are never identical. Because of the dynamism of the global economy, some types of change are ubiquitous but, at the same time, these changes have different impacts in different places and on different people. Only by mapping out the life choices and trajectories of particular social individuals in a range of different social contexts can we begin to comprehend both the complexity of the GPE and those conditions experienced by different people in different places. What a people-centered GPE analysis would look like in practice is less than evident (and is a project in progress), but I will hazard here an imagined example that draws elements from some of my earlier work.[26]

Rolling Down the River

An Imagined Case Study of People-Centered GPE

Our setting is a smallish city that has grown up along a mid-sized river that flows out of a nearby mountain range. The city has gone through an industrial phase and is now also home to a mid-sized university. The river has, over the years, played a number of economic and aesthetic roles in the area:

food source, recreational area, small-scale transport, waste dump. There are, of course, public agencies whose responsibilities for the river extend to pollution control, land use, and species diversity, but they are resource-constrained, staff-limited, and regarded with some hostility and disdain by local residents.

Taking a leaf from the environmental movement, one resident decides to establish a watershed group to protect and clean up the river. Her motivation does not spring from her brow as Athena did from Zeus's but rather is the result of many years of social interactions with others both inside and outside of her city. She is aware that there are numerous like-minded individuals living in the city, loosely associated by virtue of normative beliefs and values as well as periodic social interactions in small and large groups. These people also have a commitment to the area that goes beyond pure rational calculation and self-interested behavior; it is an emotional bond to both place and people that rests on experience and meaning. Our agent approaches several of those acquaintances, who she believes will be receptive to the idea of a watershed group, and proposes that they spend the next four weekends cleaning a stretch of the river's banks. These *social* individuals agree, even though they will receive no direct economic benefit from the work, and sign on to the project. They, in turn, mention their project to others so that, by the time the fourth Saturday arrives, several hundred people are participating in the cleanup.

There is no official stamp of approval on this activity. No municipal agency has sponsored it, no local business is paying for refreshments, no existing NGO has publicized it. In fact, some people oppose the project because it involves what they believe is a violation of *their* property rights. Some agency staff criticize the group because members have not followed the administrative regulations devised for such cleanups. City council members view the group with some trepidation, fearing that it might become another nucleus of municipal political activity opposed to them. And business people are concerned that one result will be further regulation that will somehow impinge on their profits (this is especially true for one operation that has been surreptitiously dumping its wastes into the river). At the end of the four weeks, the participants decide to establish an organization dedicated to protection and maintenance of the watershed. In time, this group finds itself engaged with many others, in many other locations, who have organized similar programs. Ultimately, such watershed conservation programs become the basis for a transnational network composed of both bureaucratized organizations and informal social movement groups.

It is evident that I have left a great deal out of this story; a complete telling and analysis would require a monograph, if not a book.[27] But we can envision three steps to developing such a story in full, three steps that can also provide a blueprint for social agency. First, a material genealogy of the physical area is required. To account for the creation of this political space, we must examine the industrial and environmental history of the river and its watershed, the ways in which capital has moved in and out over time, the nature of the material interests that contributed to the river's degradation, and their resistance to or support of restoration.

Second, we have to spell out a critical feminist analysis of the structures of power surrounding both social context and social individuals engaged in this project. What are the microspaces of localized political and economic power that produce social individuals as well as action and inaction in this place? What are the impacts of power emanating from the macrospaces, including emergent global environmental discourses and practices that affect global politics and economics?

Third, we have to develop individual genealogies. We have to examine the individual histories of at least some of the social individuals participating in this movement-cum-organization: How long have they lived in the area and where? What kind of production and reproduction are they engaged in? What are their intellectual histories? What has moved them to act in this place and at this time?

At the end of this analysis, we might begin to see how we act and are acted upon by the variety of structures and power relations that constitute and constrain, but do not close down, everyday life. More to the point, "normalizing" such people-centered analyses would have useful and productive epistemological and methodological consequences. It would illustrate the enormous diversity of people's lives and life trajectories and how they have come about, and it would go a long way to delegitimating those knowledges and practices that Foucault called "biopower,"[28] that is, the manipulation of people through instrumental power. It would shed light on the productive side of power within life's microspaces and heighten awareness of the possible relationships between agency and structure. It would empower people, students, activists, and academics by demonstrating how to construct political spaces and how to challenge biopower effectively. Finally, and most of all, it would implicate and involve our students in the production of *their* histories.

The End of Universalism As We Know It

There are no universal theories here. There cannot be. Universal theories are presented as universal truths, applicable in all places, for all time even though they are contingent and limited. A people-centered GPE cannot and should not aspire to such status. Capitalism is a social structure whose effects are discernable all over the world, but capitalism articulates with people in myriad different ways. Accumulation and profit are the drivers behind corporate behavior but neither occurs without conscious and deliberate action (the invisible hand notwithstanding). Poverty and inequity are not the consequence of inaction by the poor and weak but rather of action by the strong and wealthy. Universalist approaches to understanding these problems induce us to ignore responsibility and become fatalists, and liberalism is especially well-organized to achieve this effect.[29]

But the particularism of defining all situations as unique and relativistic is not helpful, either. Constructing and acting on a theory of global political economy *because people matter* is different; it is better understood as involving "transversalism," that is, an understanding of how and why people, places, and situations differ without trying to force them to conform, either analytically or in real life.[30] This does not mean that there are no categories, or that no generalizations can be made about the life conditions of many people. It does mean that to speak only in terms of categories such as populations or consumers is to rob people of their agency. This means that individuals are not the free-ranging atoms of liberalism or, as Margaret Thatcher put it, "There is no such thing as society!" but rather that our choices are constrained, often by "things" of which we are unaware. But, I would argue, there is greater political freedom—individual and collective—in comprehending how social structures constrain our choices than there is in the blind fatalism of international relations and political economy as they are conventionally taught. Moreover, in becoming aware of the juxtaposition of individual and social structures, we can begin to see the possibilities of collective political action to resist and to change those structures.

Notes

1. Ronnie D. Lipschutz, *After Authority: War, Peace and Global Politics in the 21st Century* (Albany: State University of New York Press, 2000).

2. Karl Polanyi, *The Great Transformation* (New York: Farrar and Rinehart, 1944; Boston: Beacon Press, 1957).

3. David Newstone, "Democracy, the State, and the Political Imagination: The Power of Sovereign Stories in the Context of 'Globalization'" (paper presented at the 42nd annual convention of the International Studies Association, Chicago, 20–24 February 2001).

4. Marysia Zalewski and Jane Parpart, eds., *The "Man" Question in International Relations* (Boulder, Colo.: Westview, 1998).

5. Christine Di Stefano, *Configurations of Masculinity* (Ithaca, N.Y.: Cornell University Press, 1991), 30–55.

6. Nancy Chodorow, "On *The Reproduction of Mothering:* A Methodological Debate," *Signs* 6 (Spring 1981), cited in Di Stefano, *Configurations,* 48.

7. Di Stefano, *Configurations,* 42n. 20.

8. Judith Butler, *Gender Trouble: Feminism and the Subversion of Identity* (New York: Routledge, 1990), 2.

9. Ibid.; emphasis added.

10. Karl Marx, *Capital* (New York, 1967), 178; cited in David Harvey, *The Condition of Postmodernity: An Enquiry into the Origins of Cultural Change* (Cambridge: Blackwell, 1989), 345.

11. Ronnie D. Lipschutz, "Environmental History, Political Economy and Policy," *Global Environmental Politics* 1, 3 (Fall 2001): 72–91.

12. John Agnew, "Representing Space: Space, Scale and Culture in Social Science," in *Place/Culture/Representation,* ed. James Duncan and David Ley (London: Routledge, 1993), 262.

13. Yasemin N. Soysal, *Limits of Citizenship: Migrants and Postnational Membership in Europe* (Chicago: University of Chicago Press, 1994).

14. This concept is explored in Charles Taylor, *Sources of the Self: The Making of Modern Identity* (Cambridge: Harvard University Press, 1989), chap. 2, 25.

15. Beverly Crawford and Ronnie D. Lipschutz, eds., *The Myth of "Ethnic Conflict": Politics, Economics, and "Cultural" Violence* (Berkeley: International and Area Studies, University of California, 1998).

16. Michel Foucault, "Truth and Power," in *Power/Knowledge,* trans. Colin Gordon (New York: Pantheon, 1980).

17. See, for example, Bruno Latour, *Pandora's Hope: Essays on the Reality of Science Studies* (Cambridge: Harvard University Press, 1999), chap. 2.

18. One discussion of "political space" can be found in Robin L. Teske, "Political Space: The Importance of the Inbetween," in *Conscious Acts and the Politics of Social Change,* vol. 1 of *Feminist Approaches to Social Movements, Community, and Power,* ed. Robin L. Teske and Mary Ann Tétreault (Columbia: University of South Carolina Press, 2000).

19. Joan W. Scott, "Experience," in *Feminists Theorize the Political,* ed. Judith Butler and Joan W. Scott (London: Routledge, 1992), 34. Embedded quote from P. Adams and James Minson, "The Subject of Feminism," *m/f* 2 (1978): 52.

20. Ronnie D. Lipschutz, with Judith Mayer, *Global Civil Society and Global Environmental Governance* (Albany: State University of New York Press, 1996), chap. 7; Ronnie D. Lipschutz, "From Place to Planet: Local Knowledge and Global Environmental Governance," *Global Governance* 3, 1 (January–April 1997): 83–102.

21. John Walton, *Western Times and Water Wars: State, Culture, and Rebellion in California* (Berkeley: University of California Press, 1992), 287.

22. Norman Long, "From Paradigm Lost to Paradigm Regained? The Case for an Actor-Oriented Sociology of Development," in *Battlefields of Knowledge: The Interlocking of Theory and Practice in Social Research and Development,* ed. Norman Long and Ann Long (London: Routledge, 1992), 23–24; emphasis added.

23. Lipschutz, *After Authority,* chap. 8.

24. Mary Ann Tétreault and Robin L. Teske, "Framing the Issues," in *Conscious Acts,* 6. See also Michel Foucault, "Two Lectures," in *Power/Knowledge.*

25. The joke is rather too long to tell here. Suffice it to say that it involves a physicist modeling a cow's failure to produce milk by "assuming a spherical cow."

26. Especially Lipschutz, *Global Civil Society.*

27. As in Walton, *Western Times and Water Wars.*

28. Michel Foucault, "Governmentality," in *The Foucault Effect: Studies in Governmentality,* ed. Graham Burchell, Colin Gordon, and Peter Miller (Chicago: University of Chicago Press, 1991).

29. Sheldon Wolin, "Fugitive Democracy," in *Democracy and Difference: Contesting the Boundaries of the Political,* ed. Seyla Benhabib (Princeton, N.J.: Princeton University Press, 1996).

30. See, for example, Nira Yuval-Davis, *Gender and Nation* (Thousand Oaks, Calif.: Sage, 1997), 125–33, as well as the chapter by Mary K. Meyer in this volume.

Chapter 8

Feminist Ideas on Cooperation and Self-Interest for International Relations

Karen S. Walch

The Reengineering of Self-Interest
An Introduction

In this volume, I have been invited to participate in a discourse applying aspects of feminist approaches on cooperation to the theory of self-interest in international relations. From this perspective, I find I can mount both a critique and an explanation of the dangers of blind reliance on theories positing the autonomous, discrete, and independent nature of self-interest when parties cooperate. Here I build a case and appeal to feminist scholars for guidance so that I may pursue my research on self-interest with a richer theoretical treatment of cooperation than can be found in traditional international relations literature. My desire is to achieve a reimagination of the orientation and nature of self-interest in international relations by drawing on what I understand from feminist and psychological perspectives about cooperation.

Egoism, individualism, and liberalism dominate the theory and practice of international relations (IR). Throughout my IR career, I have been fascinated and puzzled by the conviction that egoistic self-interest prevails as a cornerstone of state decision-maker orientation and behavior, and have struggled to find ways to explain why this concept is a dysfunctional and inadequate normative and empirical assumption. This critique has become more salient in the IR literature since the proliferation of theories on cooperation, whose premises clash with the continued reliance on egocentric self-interest as the model for decision making. In this essay, I describe my misgivings about this fundamental assumption and show how inadequately it explains behavior and thought in contemporary international relations.

I offer as an alternative the concept of sociocentrism, which is utilized in psychology to describe an orientation that incorporates cooperative values in the definition of self-interest. The contrast between sociocentrism and egoism can be illustrated in international relations through examining regime behavior, such as in the world food trade arena, which will be discussed below. Understanding the complex and functional nature of sociocentric self-interest can provide insight into the nature and meaning of community building, motivation, and survival in an interdependent global political economy. By uncovering these formerly implicit norms and intersubjective frameworks as they operate in international relations practice, we can better understand the dynamics of negotiation, conflict management, dispute resolution, and regime behavior and, from this perspective, build better theory.

Reengineering Self-Interest Using Feminist Theoretical Frameworks on Cooperation

Feminist scholars often are critical of the liberal frameworks used in political theory.[1] These critiques provide opportunities to insert the concept of sociocentric self-interest into IR's theoretical discourse.

The feminist critique of liberal frameworks provides an opportunity to expand the notion of self-interest through emphasis on *intersubjectivity* and psychological awareness. Such an approach emphasizes the need to incorporate consciousness, identity, and preferences. In contrast, conventional IR approaches conceive of states as autonomous subjects acting on static preferences, and thus as interchangeable rather than unique.[2]

A second critique of liberal frameworks argues that all political theory must be grounded in a *social context*. Feminist theories in particular emphasize the need to incorporate aspects of individuals that result from their being embedded in various social settings. This is in opposition to the traditional IR assumption that actors in the international system are independent of social context. Feminists consider the concept of a "pre-social" individual an unsuitable—unrealistic—starting place for political theory.[3] Consequently, any theory of self-interest must place the self not prior to or separate from its collective or social relationships, but rather within them. Feminist approaches place the decision maker in a social context and assume that explaining cooperative behavior requires an understanding of the interdependence among actors in that context.

Another critique finds deficiencies in the binary nature of arguments utilized in liberal approaches explaining theory and practice in international relations. This fundamental either/or orientation underlies dichotomies such as agent/structure, autonomy/dependence, individual/community, and self/other phenomena. Feminist approaches reconstruct liberal frameworks by taking issue with this simplistic dualist approach.

My assumptions concerning social constructions of the self, those dealing with identity and intersubjectivity, for example, diverge from conventional static themes in traditional IR. Responsiveness and attentiveness[4] in the context of interdependency, reciprocity, and community in international regimes—or in parts of regimes such as trade groups—can be explained more adequately as cooperative behaviors in IR if the concept of self-interest is conceived in a more inclusive and dynamic way. It is specifically in these categories that I believe that the work on cooperation in feminist thought can contribute to re-imagining the assumptions of self-interest in IR. I use these frameworks to reconceptualize self-interest as a more complex concept embracing multiple commitments, relationships, desires, and roles than now can be found IR theory.

I do not offer a new feminist theory, but rather view this essay as a way of accepting an invitation to participate in feminist IR discourse. The concept and practice of cooperation form only one aspect of this discourse, and I draw on a very limited portion of feminist literature to examine them. Even so, the concepts of intersubjectivity, social context, and responsiveness utilized by feminists enhance the themes of self-interest and cooperation in IR. Even the most tentative beginnings of such a discourse can be "socially viable."[5]

Discourse on the Intersubjectivity of Self-Interest

I begin with the notion that one's intersubjective orientation is critical to explaining cooperation. I focus primarily on themes in feminist thought that explore definitions of self-interest which include an awareness of interdependency in social relationships and look at the practical impact of these themes on motivation and behavior in an interdependent social and political context. This is in contrast to IR theories, classical economic theories, and other theories of judgment and choice that assume the "engine" of action to be fueled by egocentricism. I argue that the functional and rationalistic assumptions of narrow egoism in IR theory and practice describe and produce motivation and behaviors that result primarily in individual achievement, conquest, and a need to obtain "power over" another in international relations. Competition, violence, intransigence, territoriality, aggression, and rivalry are primary in IR theories. Theories of cooperation address motivations and behaviors that lead to moderation, compromise, and pacifism, thereby describing and driving tolerant approaches to relations among states and communities.[6] IR's focus on abstract egoistic, bureaucratic, and organizational motivations is in sharp contract to feminist discourse on more versatile and complex behaviors. Feminist theories expand the idea of motivations in international relations to include care for others, preferences for harmonious human relations, empathy, and nurturing approaches to international political, economic, and social problems.[7]

A primary feminist critique of IR frameworks asserts that a purely individualistic orientation in assessing problems in international relations results in stereotypical and one-sided behaviors. Feminist writings on cooperation highlight the significance of egoism on motivations to behave in either cooperative or competitive ways. Thus, the notion of self-interest in IR can be enriched and made more enduring if the orientation of actors is understood as intersubjective, a term that describes a dialectic of interaction and responsiveness between the embedded social context of the self and the contemporary interdependent environment.

The conventional IR literature has begun to address cooperation. Current theory defines cooperation as the form of institutional designs and state negotiations present in the context of structural interdependence. The increase in the numbers of international organizations, regimes, and agreements has spawned significant interest in and research on *why state egoists* are motivated to cooperate—why, for example, they build institutions and regimes to produce trade security agreements. Expanding the notion of self-interest to include a feminist perspective can significantly enhance the practice of and scholarship on cooperation in international relations.

IR motivational theories argue that states' interests become entangled and extend over multiple interactions over time, leading to predictions that states will become motivated to cooperate and even become altruistic. The puzzle is that if cooperation is indeed a behavior found in international relations, why do IR theorists continue to assert that *egoists* cooperate? In fact, *egoists do not.* Egocentric individuals, by definition, perceive themselves as socially isolated and independent.[8] Egoists cannot understand, much less accommodate themselves to, the interests of others.[9] Research in cognitive psychology has shown that the perceptions of egocentric individuals are seriously distorted, and decisions derived from these perceptions cannot cope effectively, except by pure chance, with an interdependent social reality.[10] As a consequence, the relationships of such egoists are inevitably contentious, and interpersonal collaboration is virtually impossible.[11]

In contrast, the psychological construct of sociocentrism requires both continuous cognitive assimilation (psychological incorporation) of new information concerning social relationships and context, and accommodation to new social realities. This concept illustrates the themes of cooperation from feminist thought which argue that learning or psychological change occurs as one becomes aware of one's demonstrable connectedness with others and becomes capable of understanding the points of view of these others. As individuals perceive their interests relative to those of others and express regard for others by assimilating and accommodating to interdependencies determined by social context, their intersubjective framework shifts from egocentrism to sociocentrism. Sociocentric orientations encourage reciprocity in relations, realism in viewing human existence as social rather than individual, and efforts to cooperate and to resolve conflict. Clearly, if participants in international negotiations consistently maintained an egocentric orientation, they would be unable to understand (and hence cope effectively with) economic and political interdependence. Consequently, if actual negotiators attempted to coordinate policies solely on the basis of egoistic interpretations of the reality of their social environment, successful conflict resolution, cooperation, and responsive problem solving would be rare or nonexistent.

Cooperation in regime policy coordination, and shared norms expressed in agreements concerning trade nonproliferation, global warming, and human rights all have been observed in "real" IR. Therefore, we cannot conclude that actors are egocentric in a "clinical" sense. If they were, how could negotiators assimilate information from their environment and accommodate to global social realities? They can if, as feminist perspectives on cooperation would suggest, their perceptions and orientations about their own self-interest become sociocentric and are seen as part of a broader social context. The theories associated with the concept of self-interest and cooperation in feminist writings appear to be more capable than IR theory of explaining cooperation in a politically and economically interdependent world.

Discourse on the Social Context of Self-Interest

Governments are composed of actors whose perceptions of values and interests change over time depending on the social and political context.[12] An improved theory of self-interest in IR could be developed if we were to use a model based on sociocentric self-interest in a framework that recognizes that international regimes, institutional practices, and interests are conditioned (but not solely determined) by the global structures and international interactions of which they are a part. Indeed, as feminist theories of cooperation suggest, interests and practices are modified and adapted continuously, the result of a dynamic interaction between the social context or exogenous structural factors, and the endogenous social/psychological orientation of decision makers' self-interest.

By placing decision makers in a social and political context, theoretical insight can be enhanced, for example, with respect to the practice of conflict management. Psychologists claim that if the cognitive framework of egocentric self-interest dominates thought and behavior, social conflict will be inevitable and irreconcilable in social relationships.[13] If egocentric individuals or states perceive themselves as isolated and independent entities, they will have no regard for others. From the psychologists' perspective, an egocentric orientation is what prevents individuals from understanding the viewpoint of others. Egocentrism inevitably and dangerously conditions actors to assign meaning to events in the world strictly from one limited perspective. According to research in cognitive psychology, egocentric individuals' realities are distorted because the information they use to make decisions about events does not include the viewpoints of others or any accurate assessment of their social environment and relationships.[14]

Feminist assumptions about cooperation emphasize the need to incorporate aspects of individuals' perceptions as representative of an *understanding of the self within a social context.* In contrast, if negotiators develop policies based on limited, egoistically interpreted information without adequately understanding the reality of their social environment (as classical realists would predict), prospects for conflict resolution and responsive problem solving are at best limited and at worst impossible. By relying on models based on egoistic self-interest, beliefs that conflict is normal are reinforced and codetermined not only by the structural situation of international anarchy but also by social-psychological processes.

Feminist perspectives on cooperation offer a critique of neorealist and neoliberal institutionalist theories of IR, some of which assume that states' interests are narrowly defined in an egoistic way.[15] Neorealist IR approaches consider interstate cooperation to be structurally constrained by the anarchic (not socially interdependent) international environment, which itself inevitably engenders conflict among states.[16] Neoliberal institutionalists are more optimistic than realists about the ability of egoistic states to cooperate because they believe that interdependence leads states to create and sustain regimes that enable them to pursue common interests and coordinate international policies.[17] Even classical Lockean liberals see egoism as essential to social existence.[18] What all of these perspectives share regarding functional egoism in IR theory is the view that states define their self-interest narrowly in terms of maximizing their own power and wealth (relative power and wealth for the realist and neorealist, absolute power and wealth for the liberal or neoliberal institutionalist).[19]

From a feminist perspective emphasizing cooperation in social contexts, we can envision contemporary state negotiators as defining self-interest broadly (that is, sociocentrically) so as to incorporate more than the state's own power and wealth maximization. This approach changes conventional understandings of the theory and practice of cooperation and negotiation in the international environment. Despite the centrality of egocentrism in IR theory, neither neoliberal institutionalists nor neorealists have examined with sufficient exactitude the implications of egoism for cooperation, conflict management, and international negotiations. Neorealists and some neoliberal institutionalists assume that egoism is a functional response to the exogenously determined conditions of anarchy and resource scarcity.[20] However, if the international system is viewed as interdependent, cooperation becomes functional, requiring IR theory to address critically how *constructive* conflict management in trade, security, and environmental issues at the global level is achieved in practice.

Discourse on the Responsiveness and Dialectic of Self-Interest

Feminist theories of cooperation align with IR constructivists, who build on the notion that interests are determined by the reflexive responsiveness of social-psychological and institutional processes.[21] Constructivists assert that social interactions between state actors, and interactions between them and system structures mutually constitute and codetermine identity and interest formation.[22] However, IR constructivists, along with neorealists and neoliberals, have not fully explored the nature of self-interest in a dynamic —sociocentric—way. I suggest that better theory would result from incorporating feminist and psychological views on the cognitive construction of self-interest as neither objective nor immutable, but rather as intersubjective and flexible *as negotiators respond to* structural interdependence and their country's relations with other states.

Sociocentric self-interest in IR can be understood as a collective identity, a conceptual framework for state actors who find themselves in a complex interdependent context in which it is both desirable and necessary for them to reach agreements. As regime negotiators perceive their self-interest in sociocentric ways, they adapt their frameworks and behaviors to generate and maintain the networks, regimes, and institutions found in the contemporary interdependent global economy. Viewed through feminist and psychological models of cooperation, sociocentrism can be said, in practice if not in theory, to have become both an embedded norm and an engine of *transformation between agent and structure* at the international level, that is, an important source of the "power to create."

Students of IR have observed multilateralism, negotiated agreements, cooperation, and regime formation, even in the context of severe structural and social constraints.[23] Political and economic interdependence give rise to regimes that encourage interstate cooperation and coordination of various international policies.[24] It is a central contention of this essay that interactive exchange and reciprocity produce not only practices of cooperation (as neoliberals have long recognized), but also the intersubjective construction of sociocentrism by negotiators as they take into account the perspective of other—interdependent—regime interests.[25] As a consequence, the outcome of such interactions often integrates the concerns of weak and passive players whose interests could be ignored if the process were merely one of egoistic strategic reciprocity, exchange, and structural bargaining power

The outcome of the General Agreement on Tariffs and Trade (GATT) agriculture talks, for example, illustrates that states do not always define their self-interest in purely egoistic terms. If they did, there would have been no references to the dangers of agricultural trade liberalization for less developed countries, much less a commitment to protect these countries from economic damage. A study Michael Contarino and I did of the Uruguay Round food negotiation case, along with other examples of multilateral behavior, illustrates the responsiveness by state negotiators to interdependent political and social contexts.

The Uruguay Round represents a case where negotiators who had structural power as food exporters—European Union (EU) members and the United States, for example—to dominate food importers—the least developed countries (LDCs)—did not do so, but rather worked to integrate the concerns of the LDCs in the final agreement. This attentiveness and responsiveness pattern is a feature often seen in the contemporary political economy and illustrates the superiority of sociocentric self-interest to egoistic self-interest as an explanation of cooperative behavior. The Uruguay Round agreement is known for the protracted and difficult negotiations it required between the United States, the EU, and other developed-country food exporters. The agreement, and the GATT regime in general, both reflect efforts to reconcile the divergent concerns of the powerful developed countries that dominated the negotiations. We concluded that despite this dominance by developed-country exporters, the final agreement, like earlier intermediate documents such as the Dunkel Draft of 1992, incorporated a number of provisions specifically directed toward LDCs and developing net food importing countries (DNFICs).[26] Although some might consider these measures a small portion of the entire agreement, the outcome does reflect explicit consideration of the interests of these several overlapping groups of states despite the fact that their negotiating power and direct participation were extremely diverse.

The final agreement, for example, includes an entire section, entitled "Decision on Measures in Favor of Least-Developed Countries," which contains a number of specific references to the special needs of extremely poor countries.[27] The section provides that LDCs "will only be required to undertake commitments and concessions to the extent consistent with their individual development, financial and trade needs, or their administrative capabilities"; and calls for "substantially increased technical assistance in the development, strengthening and diversification of their production and export bases."[28] Another section of the GATT agreement, entitled "Decision on Measures Concerning the Possible Negative Effects of the Reform Programme on Least-Developed and Net Food-Importing Developing Countries," explicitly recognizes that, as a result of agricultural trade liberalization, these countries "may experience negative effects in terms of the availability of adequate supplies of basic foodstuffs from external sources on reasonable terms and conditions, including short-term difficulties in financing normal levels of commercial imports of basic foodstuffs."[29] The agreement thereby recognizes that liberalization could lead to higher international food prices and smaller developed-country food surpluses, supplies that hitherto had served as important sources of food aid.

Free-trade advocates may call these concerns overstated, but this view is not universally held. Several studies by the United Nations Commission on Trade and Development (UNCTAD) and others have suggested that the harm is real and potentially extensive. The UN Food and Agricultural Organization (FAO) had warned that global food reserves were dangerously low and grain prices extremely high. Although price increases are not solely the result of liberalization, when world food prices rise, liberalization (especially subsidy reduction) reduces the size of publicly held stocks that could be released to reduce prices. The Uruguay agreement includes attention to the fact that higher food prices may not have the positive effect on direct producers expected in the long run because the proceeds are not always passed on to them. In addition, it is politically difficult for governments to devalue their currencies, because it would cause food prices to rise for consumers. The agreement also recognizes that there is no guarantee that other obstacles to increased production will be eliminated as domestic producers respond to higher prices.

The accord commits GATT signatories to undertake several measures to help the DNFICs and LDCs cope with adverse consequences of liberalization. These include a commitment to ensure that food aid levels do not decline sharply, and that an increasing proportion of basic foodstuffs will be provided to these countries in grant form or on "appropriate concessional terms in line with Article IV of the Food Aid Convention." The section also states that aid programs should "give full consideration . . . to requests for the provision of technical and financial assistance to least developed and net food-importing developing countries to improve their agricultural productivity and infrastructure."[30] Special and differential treatment in favor of these countries was also provided for regarding any agreement relating to agricultural export credits. The fact that the GATT agreement should have addressed the concerns of the LDCs and DNFICs so explicitly is interesting insofar as neither group of poor, economically vulnerable countries had any real bargaining power in the agriculture talks.

Extensive interviews with eighteen GATT agriculture sector participants revealed that the vast majority of DNFICs played no role whatsoever in the talks. Those few DNFICs that did participate were a heterogeneous lot, incapable of articulating a common line much less of pursuing it aggressively from a position of strength. The GATT Secretariat claims that "the low-income countries almost never participate in the GATT talks. They see GATT as a rich man's club, and lack the resources to participate in a meaningful way. They also have little choice but to accept the outcomes the rich countries dominate. They have nowhere else to go."[31] Of the ninety-three DNFICs, eighty-six were inactive—rarely or never present at meetings—despite the fact that numerous quantitative studies showed that agricultural trade liberalization could have a dramatic impact on these economies by raising world food prices, reducing the size of publicly held food stocks which serve as food aid reserves, and eroding the value of the Generalized System of Preferences (GSP).[32] Only seven DNFICs (Egypt, India, Jamaica, Mexico, Pakistan, Peru, and Tanzania) were active in the negotiations, but they were unable to agree on a common set of objectives much less a common strategy.[33] As a consequence, the DNFICs (unlike the Cairns group of developed and developing exporters) failed to form an effective lobby with any real bargaining strength in the Uruguay Round.

In sum, while the GATT agreement includes a series of specific commitments to LDC food importers, *none* of these countries possessed any bargaining power and virtually all of them were either passive or actually absent throughout the negotiations. Of the LDCs, only Tanzania appears to have voiced concern about the possible impact of agricultural trade liberalization. Even so, all eighteen interviewees agreed that Tanzania's role in the talks was minor, sporadic and, ultimately, unimportant. It is also worth emphasizing that all eighteen interviewees responded negatively when asked if they thought that "concessions" to DNFIC and LDC interests were needed to get these countries to sign the GATT agreement. It was generally accepted that these countries were in no position to walk away from any agreement reached among the major players. In the words of a trade representative from the Food Importers' Group of the LDCs, "LDCs cannot force the developed countries to do anything. The EU and USA can, and often do, just ignore us. But not always. We can bring up issues and get them to see our perspective, and sometimes they see that in the long term it is not in their interest to ignore us. We have to inhabit the same planet, you know."[34]

Some developing country interviewees claimed that they could not explain the inclusion of DNFIC and LDC concerns in the agreement; others agreed with an EU food sector negotiator who stated that the major players had agreed to recognize a global interdependency among food importers and exporters. They understood that potential damage to the economies of food-importing developing countries caused by liberalization would have implications for food exporting countries and, ultimately, an undesirable impact on the world economy as a whole. A GATT secretariat official suggested that, although inclusion of the "concessions" was pushed by Jamaica and Egypt, ultimately the USA and EU could have said no if they had chosen to do so.

Reengineering the Concept of Self-Interest for IR

The outcome of the GATT negotiations in general and the agriculture talks in particular can be dismissed as marginally responsive to the interests of LDCs and DNFICs. Nevertheless, the fact that these interests were recognized and addressed at all challenges two of the central assumptions of mainstream IR theory, that is, that states define their interests in narrowly egoistic terms and that the interests of weak and passive actors are accordingly ignored in international bargaining. Given the weakness and passivity of most developing countries and the limited negotiation interaction between food importers and exporters, both neorealist and neoliberal institutionalist theories would have predicted that the negotiations would not reflect the interests of the weaker countries. The negotiation outcome here suggests that responsiveness and attentiveness by state actors can be more adequately explained by feminist theories of cooperation and self-interest. The GATT outcome and other multilateral agreements at the core of diverse trade, security, environmental, and human rights regimes make it difficult to reconcile conceptions about egoistic self-interest and cooperative behavior as currently defined in the IR literature.

Multilateralism has become part of an "architectural form," a deep organizing principle of international negotiation, an on-going, taken-for-granted understanding of international life and problem solving.[35] How can an egoistic orientation serve as the foundation for legitimate, functional, and effective collaboration? The food regime case could potentially be explained by IR constructivist theories that challenge neorealism by emphasizing structural impediments to cooperation. However, constructivism also has shortcomings in explaining how states can be essentially "egoistic," striving to maximize power, and yet "cooperate" and be responsive to more vulnerable states. Neoliberal institutionalism and regime theory see cooperation as emerging from reciprocity amongst egoistic and efficacious partners, but *not* as gratuitous concessions from the powerful to the weak. As conventionally understood, egoism should lead to the complete neglect of the concerns of weak and passive actors.[36]

By enhancing the scope of what we mean by self-interest in international relations, self-conscious international actors will be able to see themselves as capable of devising and practicing behaviors that are realistic if not "realist." Sociocentric actors, unlike altruists, do not sacrifice their own self-interests in order to benefit others. Rather, embedded in their perceptions is an attention to the social reality of structural interdependence and a perception that their own well-being depends upon the well-being of other components of the system. This perspective also has an impact on current security challenges. Global terrorism, the denuclearization of the former Soviet Union, agreements on conventional force deployments in Europe, new security partnerships, control of technology diffusion, conversion of excess defense capacity, and conflict prevention and mediation procedures are just a few examples where "cooperation is not and can never be based on even the appearance of coercion."[37] Denuclearization, for example, can be accomplished only within the context of international accommodation and a commitment to provide assistance for a peaceful transition to an enduring stability for the former Soviet Union.[38]

Pre-negotiation processes[39] and interactive problem-solving workshops focusing on various security matters encourage negotiators to examine the origins of conflict, to create commitments, to design conflict management approaches, and to redefine relationships in constructive ways. Through these efforts, fundamental common interests can be perceived and evaluated by these negotiators. In addition, preventive diplomacy, peacemaking, peacekeeping, and post-conflict peace-building efforts have expanded beyond traditional UN terminology to include assessments of problem-solving dialogue and reassessments of self-interest.[40] These processes provide an opportunity to probe the human relationships that underlie conflict and to design steps to change them.[41] Self-interest also can be reconceptualized through discovery, formation, and redefinition derived from such negotiation and problem-solving interactions.

In the trade area, World Trade Organization (WTO) rules require states to acknowledge the protection of intellectual property and terms of trade in services, agricultural trade, and the phase-out of textile structures. They also have to agree to the integration of developing countries into the WTO system, and to increased market access and standard codes for subsidies involving all member states. The WTO represents an institutional and procedural reflection of the sociocentric assumption that greater international economic activity and growth require a reevaluation of egoistic concerns.[42] As Clyde Prestowitz claims, "there will be a loss of sovereignty. You can argue whether that is good or bad, but it is reasonable to say that in a world of integrating economies there needs to be some institution under which integration takes place, and inevitably, that carries with it some degree of loss of sovereignty."[43] In other words, the sovereign state loses some degree of independence or egoistic self-protection and interest, and is understood (both psychologically and institutionally) to be a member of a larger component system, whose security and economic well-being depends on the strength of other states.

Conclusion

I have barely begun to explore the complex contributions of feminist scholarship to studies of international cooperation and the contributions that can be made to international relations theory and practice. This essay is an invitation to further conversation on the notions of cooperation and self-interest as I have outlined them here. Meanwhile, I continue to search for ways to enhance contemporary conflict management education. Constructive conflict resolution requires a commitment and acceptance of feminist perspectives on cooperation with their emphasis on adaptive self-interest, relationships, systems, and institutions. It is increasingly critical to state policies that probing and understanding the partners in a regime, system, institution, or relationship involve not only an examination of physical and structural characteristics but also of experiences that have shaped decision makers' views of the social world and of themselves. The contemporary global situation requires a richer conception of national interest and a broader picture of how interests are defined in international negotiations and regime formation. States are inevitably drawn together by their interests, and as they discern interdependencies they begin to identify interests that they cannot achieve without cooperation from others. This is how a sociocentric conception of self-interest develops and becomes embedded as a transnational norm, and why trade negotiators come to perceive their state's self-interest as linked to that of others.

Further exploration of feminist approaches to conflict management and community promises to reveal how cooperation and coordination are possible in the absence of a hegemon or a world government. A sociocentric orientation may offer suggestions for rule enforcement where "coercive cooperation" is not possible, guiding global communities to intervene in the internal affairs of sovereign states through constructive international agreements, policies, and institutions. The time has come to pursue further research in the areas of relationships, caring, community, creativity, and integration, all of which have been underexplored in traditional international relations scholarship. IR theory and practice both would be enriched as a result.

Notes

1. Elizabeth Frazer and Nicola Lacey, *The Politics of Community: A Feminist Critique of the Liberal-Communitarian Debate* (Toronto: University of Toronto Press, 1993).

2. Stephen D. Krasner, "Structural Causes and Regime Consequences: Regimes as Intervening Variable," in *International Regimes,* ed. Stephen D. Krasner (Ithaca, N.Y.: Cornell University Press, 1983), 1–21.

3. Joan Tronto, *Moral Boundaries: A Political Argument for an Ethic of Care* (New York: Routledge, 1993).

4. Frazer and Lacey, *Politics of Community.*

5. Mark Tessler and Ina Warriner, "Gender, Feminism, and Attitudes toward International Conflict: Exploring Relationships with Survey Data from the Middle East," *World Politics* 49, 2 (January 1997): 250–81.

6. Ibid.

7. Ernst B. Haas, "Words Can Hurt You: Or, Who Said What to Whom about Regimes," in *International Regimes,* ed. Stephen D. Krasner (Ithaca, N.Y.: Cornell University Press, 1983), 23–60.

8. Jean Piaget, *The Moral Judgment of the Child* (New York: Free Press, 1965).

9. John Marshall, "Why Rational Egoism Is Not Consistent," *Review of Metaphysics* 45, 4 (June 1992): 713–37; Elliott Sober, "What Is Psychological Egoism," *Behaviorism* 17, 2 (Summer 1989): 3–25.

10. Piaget, *Moral Judgment;* Donna Hicks, "An Analysis of Global Security from the Perspective of Cognitive Development" (paper delivered at the annual meeting of the International Studies Association, Washington, D.C., 10–14 April 1990); Donna Hicks and Karen Walch, "Quality Relationships: Personal and Political" (paper delivered at the annual meeting of the International Society for Political Psychology, San Francisco, 4–8 July 1992); Norman Alexander and Mary Glenn Wiley, "Situated Activity and Identity Formation," *Social Psychology: Sociological Perspectives,* ed. Morris Rosenberg and Ralph Turner (New York: Basic Books, 1981), 22–50.

11. T. Jerdee and Benson Rosen, "Effects of Opportunity to Communicate and Visibility of Individual Decisions on Behavior in the Common Interest," *Journal of Applied Psychology* 59, 5 (Summer 1974): 5–77; Samuel S. Komorita and C. William Lapworth, "Cooperative Choice among Individuals versus Groups in an N-prisoner's Dilemma Situation," *Journal of Personality and Social Psychology* 42, 3 (March 1982):

487–96; Piaget, *Moral Judgment;* John Burton, *Resolving Deep-Rooted Conflict: A Handbook* (Lanham, Md.: University Press of America, 1987); Burton, *Conflict: Human Needs Theory* (New York: St. Martin's Press, 1990); Herbert Kelman, "An International Approach to Conflict Resolution and Its Application to Israeli and Palestinian Relations," *International Interactions* 6, 6 (Spring 1979): 25–40; Jay Rothman, "Negotiation as Consolidation: Prenegotiation in the Israeli-Palestinian Conflict," *Jerusalem Journal of International Relations* 13, 1 (March 1991): 22–44; Rothman, *From Confrontation to Cooperation: Resolving Ethnic and Regional Strife* (Newbury Park, Calif.: Sage Publications, 1992).

12. Alexander Wendt and Raymond Duvall, "Institutions and International Order," in *Global Changes and Theoretical Challenges: Approaches to World Politics for the 1990s,* ed. Ernst-Otto Czempiel and James N. Rosenau (Lexington, Mass.: Lexington Books, 1989), 51–71; Alexander Wendt, "Anarchy Is What States Make of It: The Social Construction of Power Politics," *International Organization* 46, 2 (Spring 1992): 391–425; Wendt, "The Agent-Structure Problem in International Relations Theory," *International Organization* 41, 3 (Summer 1987): 335–70; Robert Keohane, "International Institutions: Two Approaches," *International Studies Quarterly* 32, 4 (1988): 379–96; Emerson Niou and Peter Ordeshook, "Realism vs. Neoliberalism: A Formation," *American Journal of Political Science* 35, 6 (Spring 1991): 481–511; Robert Axelrod, *The Evolution of Cooperation* (New York: Basic Books, 1980).

13. Robert L. Selman, *The Growth of Interpersonal Understanding: Developmental and Clinical Analyses* (New York: Academic Press, 1980); Selman, Charles Stone, and Edward Phelps, "A Naturalistic Study of Children's Social Understanding," *Developmental Psychology* 19, 15 (1989): 92–102; Robert Trivers, "The Evolution of Reciprocal Altruism," *Quarterly Review of Biology* 46, 2 (1990): 35–50.

14. Marshall, "Rational Egoism," 713–37; Sober, "Psychological Egoism," 3–25.

15. Kenneth Waltz, *Man, the State and War* (New York: Columbia University Press, 1959); Waltz, *The Theory of World Politics* (Reading, Mass.: Addison-Wesley, 1979); Hans Morganthau, *Politics among Nations: The Struggle for Power and Peace* (New York: Alfred Knopf 1948); Arnold Wolfers, *Discord and Collaboration: Essays on International Politics* (Baltimore, Md.: Johns Hopkins University Press, 1962).

16. Robert Keohane, *After Hegemony: Cooperation and Discord in the World Political Economy* (Princeton, N.J.: Princeton University Press, 1984); Keohane, "Realism, Neorealism and the Study of World Politics," in *Neorealism and its Critics* (New York: Columbia University Press, 1986), 22–36; Keohane, "International Institutions"; Keohane, "Multilateralism: An Agenda for Research," *International Journal* 45, 8 (Autumn 1990): 731–50; Robert Keohane and Joseph S. Nye, *Power and Interdependence: World Politics in Transition* (Boston: Little, Brown, 1977); Charles Kindleberger, "On the Rise and Decline of Nations," *International Studies Quarterly* 27, 6 (1983): 5–10.

17. Krasner, "Structural Causes"; Oran R. Young, "The Politics of International Regime Formation," *International Organization* 43, 3 (Summer 1989): 349–75; John Ikenberry and Charles Kupchan, "Socialization and Hegemonic Power," *International Organization* 44, 5 (1989): 283–316; Peter Haas, "Do Regimes Matter? Epistemic Communities and Knowledge in World Politics," *International Organization* 43, 4 (1989): 377–404; Helga Haftendorn, "The Security Puzzle: Theory-Building and Discipline Building in International Security," *International Studies Quarterly* 35,

1 (1991): 3–17; Gilbert Winham, "GATT and the International Trade Regime," *International Journal* 45, 4 (Autumn 1990): 796–882.

18. Jane Mansbridge, *Beyond Self-Interest* (Chicago: University of Chicago Press, 1990).

19. J. Grieco, "Anarchy and the Limits of Cooperation: A Realist Critique of the Newest Liberal Institutionalism," *International Organization* 42, 3 (1988): 485–507.

20. Keohane, "International Institutions"; Young, "International Regime Formation"; John G. Ruggie, "Multilateralism: The Anatomy of an Institution," *International Organization* 46, 6 (Summer 1992): 35–46.

21. Ernst Haas, *When Knowledge Is Power* (Berkeley: University of California Press, 1990); Ikenberry and Kupchan, "Socialization and Hegemonic Power"; Nicholas Onuf, *World of Our Making* (Columbia: University of South Carolina Press, 1989); Robert Cox, "Social Forces, States, and World Orders," in *Neorealism and Its Critics,* 69–80; Richard K. Ashley, "The Poverty of Neorealism," in *Neorealism and Its Critics,* 44–60; R. B. J. Walker, "Sovereignty, Identity, Community: Reflections on the Horizons of Contemporary Political Practice," in *Contending Sovereignties,* ed. R. B. J. Walker and Saul Mendlovitz (Boulder, Colo.: Lynne Rienner, 1990), 159–95.

22. Alexander Wendt and Raymond Duvall, "Institutions and International Order."

23. Ruggie, "Multilateralism"; Miles Kahler, "Multilateralism with Small and Large Numbers," *International Organization* 46, 6 (Summer 1992): 33–40; James A. Caparaso, "International Relations Theory and Multilateralism: The Search for Foundation," *International Organization* 46, 6 (Summer 1992): 45–66; Steve Weber, "Shaping the Postwar Balance of Power: Multilateralism in NATO," *International Organization* 46, 3 (Summer 1992): 633–80; Robert Jervis, "Realism, Game Theory, and Cooperation," *World Politics* 40, 3 (1988): 317–49; Charles Kupchan and Clifford Kupchan, "Concerts, Collective Security, and the Future of Europe," *International Security* 16, 1 (Summer 1991): 114–61.

24. Keohane, "Multilateralism"; Keohane and Nye, *Power and Interdependence;* Krasner, "Structural Causes"; Young, "International Regime Formation"; Keohane, *After Hegemony.*

25. Keohane and Nye, *Power and Interdependence;* Krasner, "Structural Causes"; Young, "International Regime Formation."

26. United States Trade Representative, *Final Act Embodying the Results of the Uruguay Round of Multilateral Trade Negotiations* (Washington, D.C.: U.S. Government Printing Office, 1993).

27. The WTO's agreements often are collectively termed the Final Act of the 1986–1994 Uruguay Round of trade negotiations that were carried out under the now-superseded General Agreement on Tariffs and Trade. Strictly speaking, however, the Final Act is only the first of these agreements. The text of the Final Act can be found at: http://www.wto.org/wto/english/docs_e/legal_e/final_e.htm (5 August 2002).

28. WTO, "Decision on Measures in Favour of Least-Developed Countries," http://www.wto.org/wto/english/docs_e/legal_e/31-dlldc.pdf (5 August 2002), pp. 386–86.

29. WTO, "Decision on Measures Concerning the Possible Negative Effects of the Reform Programme on Least-Developed and Net Food-Importing Developing Countries," http://www.wto.org/wto/english/docs_e/legal_e/35-dag.pdf (5 August 2002), p. 395.

30. Ibid.

31. The material in this section is based largely on eighteen interviews conducted in January 1983 and March 1994 by Michael Contarino, who spoke with GATT officials and trade negotiation representatives from several developed and developing countries in Geneva. The majority of the interviews were with representatives of developing net food-importing countries, including some LDCs, and all interviews were conducted on a not-for-citation basis.

32. Food and Agricultural Organization data pertaining to the dollar value of all food imports and exports for the two-year period preceding the Uruguay round (1984–86) are used to define this term.

33. See, for example, United Nations Commission on Trade and Development (UNCTAD), *Agricultural Trade Liberalization in the Uruguay Round: Implications for Developing Countries* (New York: United Nations, 1990); Steve Golden and Jim Knudsen, eds., *Agricultural Trade Liberalization: Implications for Developing Countries* (Paris: OECD/World Bank, 1990); Michael Contarino, "Agricultural Trade Liberalization and Food Security: Implications of the Quantitative Studies," United Nations World Food Council discussion paper (Rome: World Food Council, 1990); Contarino, "Implications for Food Security of the Uruguay Round of Multilateral Trade Negotiations," United Nations World Food Council document (Rome: World Food Council, 1991); Abdelkadar Lecheheb, "Les problèmes des pays en développement importateurs nets de produits alimentaires dans le cadre des négociations de l'Uruguay Round sur l'agriculture," UNCTAD report, 1993.

34. Interviewees attributed this widespread passivity to a lack of both financial resources and skilled personnel able to follow and participate in highly technical and time-consuming talks in Geneva, and to a lack of policy instructions from national governments to their Geneva representatives. Poor nations believed they could not influence the outcome of the talks and that their only course would be to accept whatever the rich nations decided. In addition, their weak governments were not eager to antagonize domestic groups which might oppose a more explicit position.

35. Interviews with country representatives suggested that the inability of the seven activist DNFICs to unite behind a common strategy was the result of objectively different interests. For example, the two most active DNFICs were Jamaica and Egypt. Jamaica was most concerned with preventing liberalization from eroding the Lome preferences for African, Caribbean and Pacific (ACP) exports, whereas Egypt, the biggest non-oil-exporting food importer, sought financial compensation for possible losses due to higher food prices and/or reduced food aid. Additionally, Mexico was most interested in insuring that liberalization cover its own exports, while Pakistan and Peru wanted liberalization *not* to affect their domestic agricultural programs.

36. Caparaso, "International Relations Theory."

37. Some readers might reasonably view the commitments made to the food importers as too nonspecific to be considered the result of any real incorporation of DNFIC and LDC concerns. This point is debatable; some DNFIC and LDC representatives expressed satisfaction with the proposals, while others were skeptical. However, I emphasize that even *verbal recognition* of the risks of liberalization to countries lacking power in the negotiations (and generic commitments to mitigate possible negative effects of liberalization on these countries) would *not* be predicted by neorealist or neoliberal institutionalism's theories, which, on the contrary, predict the *neglect* of weak actors.

38. Janne E. Nolan and John D. Steinbrunner, "A Transition Strategy for the 1990s," in *Global Engagement: Cooperation and Security in the 21st Century,* ed. Janne E. Nolan (Washington, D.C.: Brookings Institution, 1994), 573–93.

39. Ibid.

40. William Zartman, "Prenegotiation: Phases and Functions," in *Getting to the Table: The Process of International Prenegotiation,* ed. Janice Stein (Baltimore, Md.: Johns Hopkins University Press, 1989), 55–70.

41. Report of the Secretary General on the work of the United Nations Organization, "An Agenda for Peace: Preventive Diplomacy, Peacemaking and Peace-Keeping," made pursuant to the statement adopted by the Summit Meeting of the Security Council on 31 January 1992 (United Nations, New York, 17 June, 1992).

42. Harold H. Saunders, "Enlarging US Policy Toward 'Ethnic' Conflict: Rethinking Intervention" (paper presented at the symposium "Ethnic Conflicts: Threat to Domestic and International Peace," jointly sponsored by the National Defense University and the Joint Center for Political and Economic Studies, Washington, D.C., November 1993).

43. Senate Committee on Foreign Relations, Subcommittee on International Trade, *The World Trade Organization Dispute Settlement and Codes of Conduct: Hearing before the Subcommittee on International Trade,* 103d Cong., 2d sess., 14 June 1994, 336.

Part Four

Altered States

Chapter 9

Gender Politics in the Northern Ireland Peace Process

A Case Study of the Transversalist Politics of the Northern Ireland Women's Coalition

Mary K. Meyer

> Identity is not a prison; it is an appeal for dialogue with others.
> —Václav Havel

Feminist activists, journalists, and scholars have noted the patriarchal political culture that exists in Northern Ireland and severely constrains the roles and life choices of women and men. Scholars have begun to measure and analyze reasons for the dearth of women in Northern Ireland's formal political arena and their greater, but still marginalized, participation in community and voluntary organizations.[1] Others focus on the common radicalization of republican and loyalist women who have borne the brunt of the Troubles in working-class areas of Belfast and Derry, cleaning up after the violence, holding their families and communities together, and engaging in political struggles. Still others have revealed the largely silenced topic of domestic violence in the region and its link to the cycles of political violence during the Troubles.[2] While studies of gender and community identity have begun to appear recently,[3] no one yet has seriously analyzed women and gender politics in the Northern Ireland peace process.

This chapter begins that analysis, exploring gender politics in the Northern Ireland peace process by examining the role, strategy, and impact of a unique coalition of women that is transforming the political landscape in Northern Ireland. Since the spring of 1996, the Northern Ireland Women's Coalition (NIWC) has been a significant and highly effective feminist player in the difficult search for peace.[4] Its history is directly tied to the emergence and progress of cross-community women's and peace movements in the region and to the emergence of the peace process. Its feminist critique and its political strategy have injected a new discourse, a new agenda, and new methods into Northern Ireland politics.[5] Although some are threatened by and others still resist this new approach, it is clear that the peace process could not have come as far as it has—and its contours would not look the same—without the Northern Ireland Women's Coalition.

The NIWC's participation in, strategy for, and contributions to the peace process have both revealed and challenged the "gender troubles" that are embedded in the "armed patriarchy" of Northern Ireland's politics.[6] Studying this organization can lead to a better understanding of the changing roles of women in politics in Northern Ireland, the gendered structures of conflict during the Troubles, and the gendered nature of conflict resolution in Northern Ireland and beyond.

The Women's Coalition and the Northern Ireland Peace Process

In early February 1996, the seventeen-month Provisional IRA[7] cease-fire ended with the bombing of London's Canary Wharf. A number of other bombings and bomb scares in central London followed. These attacks were major setbacks to the tentative steps toward peace taken by the British and Irish governments (and involving Sinn Féin/IRA) with the Downing Street Declaration (1993) and the Framework Documents (1995).[8] The Tory government of British Prime Minister John Major had squandered the opportunity to build a serious peace process during the cease-fire because its narrow parliamentary majority depended increasingly on the votes of unionist MPs.[9] The ending of the IRA cease-fire reminded everyone that the military stalemate between the IRA and the British army still existed and that negotiation was the only way forward. With support from the Clinton administration, Major announced a scheme for special elections to two bodies aimed at restarting the peace process: the Northern Ireland Forum for Peace and Reconciliation, which would give political parties a place to air their views on a wide range of issues, and the All-Party Talks, which would be the locus of actual peace negotiations. The election rules stipulated that the ten parties with the largest number of votes would be included in both the Forum and the All-Party Talks. These rules also ensured that small parties, particularly those linked to smaller paramilitary organizations, had a chance at being involved in the talks provided that they embraced the "Mitchell Principles," which included adherence to the principles of democracy and nonviolence.[10]

A group of Irish women activists and intellectuals had already come together in preparation for the Beijing Women's Conference of September 1995. They had identified reasons for the lack of women in politics and highlighted the myriad social issues neglected by male politicians during the Troubles. The call for elections gave them an important political opening: they reminded the Northern Ireland Office (NIO) that, given Northern Ireland's overwhelmingly and undeniably male-dominated political parties, any special election for "all-party" talks would deny women representation. How could "all-party" talks aimed at building a new political future for Northern Ireland proceed without women's voices participating in the debates? A return phone call from the NIO asked the name of the "women's party" that would compete in the special elections scheduled for the end of May. Soon thereafter, the Northern Ireland Women's Coalition was born as a cross-community, multiclass women's organization drawing support from across the women's movement in Northern Ireland. The NIWC utilized existing networks of women's organizations and sought to organize women who previously had been politically "homeless" into an effective political voice in Northern Ireland politics.[11]

A "kitchen campaign" was quickly organized to run one hundred women candidates across the region. If each could get one hundred votes from family, friends, and neighbors, the Women's Coalition might garner enough votes to qualify for representation in the Forum and All-Party Talks under the "top-up" electoral system that would provide for some of the smaller parties to participate. With 7,731 votes from across the region, the Women's Coalition won two seats at the talks. Monica McWilliams, a university professor and Catholic originally from a rural area of County Londonderry, and Pearl Sagar, a working-class activist and Protestant from East Belfast, represented the Women's Coalition at the Forum and Multi-Party Talks.[12]

Some observers saw the Women's Coalition as merely a media darling reminiscent of the "peace women" of the 1970s, and its electoral success as just a fluke of the top-up system. Others—including other women—criticized the Women's Coalition for not working inside existing political parties and toeing the established party lines. Once the talks began, McWilliams and Sagar encountered blatant sexism and harassment, with male representatives from the unionist side (the Democratic Unionist Party, DUP, in particular) mooing, haranguing, and insulting them. Epithets like "silly women" and "whinging women" were the least of the insults. The press soon came to focus on this harassment in its otherwise limited coverage of the Coalition, but McWilliams and Sagar faced the verbal assaults bravely and determinedly. Their principles, senses of humor, and political determination aimed at changing the very model of Northern Ireland's politics. Indeed, the campaign slogan for their first election was, "Say Good-Bye to Dinosaurs." Their professionalism and negotiating skills soon won them attention and respect from others involved in the peace talks, including their critics.

A year later, in the May 1997 British parliamentary elections, the Women's Coalition ran three candidates; although none was elected, the total number of votes for the NIWC increased significantly over the previous year's election.[13] Later that month, the NIWC stood twenty candidates in town council elections, and Ann Carr won a seat on the Newcastle (County Down) District Council. For the rest of 1997 and the first four months of 1998, the Women's Coalition worked hard in the Multi-Party Talks that finally led to the Good Friday Agreement of 10 April 1998. For the next six weeks, the NIWC campaigned vigorously for the "Yes" vote in the referendum to approve the pathbreaking peace agreement. A month later, the Women's Coalition organized its fifth election campaign in two years and successfully elected Monica McWilliams and Jane Morrice to the Northern Ireland Assembly, one of several new institutions created by the Good Friday Agreement. Their campaign slogan this time around was "New Voices, New Choices; Vote for Women for a Change." In this election the NIWC's regionwide vote again increased, winning important transfer votes from other parties (see further discussion below).

The Northern Ireland Women's Coalition has indeed proven to be a new voice on Northern Ireland's political stage. In its determined work to "change the model" of Northern Irish politics, it insists on genuine dialogue among all voices, especially those committed to the future rather than the past. Its internal dynamics as well as its participation in the peace process and the wider political community are based on transversalist politics and a process of "active accommodation," embracing the principles of inclusion, human rights, equality, respect, and common sense. This politics and these principles have been crucial to the success of the peace talks that produced the Good Friday Agreement; they will be equally crucial to the survival and implementation of the rest of the peace agreement.

Transversalist Politics and the NIWC

In a seminar in January 1997, Monica McWilliams described the politics of the Women's Coalition as based on transversalism, that is, on "rooting and shifting." McWilliams defined this as "being rooted in one's own identity, but moving to appreciate another's position." Transversalism is "a process of dialogue across differences, a respect for differences." It leads to "a different kind of coalition politics" where participants "respect rather than bury differences."[14] Nira Yuval-Davis provides a useful elaboration of transversalist politics, noting its origins in Italian feminists' work with the Women in Black movement in which Israeli and Palestinian women sought dialogue, respect, and understanding without abandoning their own identities or differences.[15] Transversalism is a feminist politics that rejects universalism, which assumes unity and homogeneity and denies the value of difference (all women suffer the same oppression). Transversalism also rejects relativism, which assumes that no common understanding or genuine dialogue across difference is possible (all women suffer different oppressions) and risks uncritical solidarity with the marginalized or exploited, leading to a politics of victimization. Instead, transversalism is a form of dialogue in which each participant "brings with her the rooting in her own membership and identity, but at the same time tries to shift in order to put herself *in a situation of exchange* with women who have different membership and identity."[16] The point is not to lose one's own identity by putting oneself in the other's "place" (although the empathy, trust, and respect required by transversalism may approach this). Indeed, "the process of shifting should not involve self-decentering, that is, losing one's own rooting and set of values. There is no need for it." Rather, shifting is about putting oneself into genuine dialogue(s) with the Other whose specific positionings and "unfinished knowledge" can be recognized and engaged. It does not require that all conflicts of interest be resolved or be reconcilable, and in fact accepts that agreeing to disagree is legitimate. But transversalism does work to articulate "common value systems" that "can exist across differential positionings and identities." It seeks to distinguish between the messenger and the message, between "social identities and social values," between differences of context and terminology, and differences of values and goals. This form of politics leads to the "multiplicity of forms and intensities of coalition politics."[17]

The Northern Ireland Women's Coalition is a unique and significant example of the operationalization of transversalist politics, both within its own organizational and decision-making processes and within the wider context of the Northern Ireland peace process. The Coalition is made up of women and men, young and old, working-class and privileged, rural and urban and, most importantly in the Northern Ireland context, Catholic/nationalist/republican and Protestant/unionist/loyalist members.[18] One Coalition member described it as "not really a party of the middle ground but a party of extremes." Its members are "all feminists" (although some reject the label) who are "challenging a dysfunctional political system by asking the right questions and seeking to rebuild" through a process of "active accommodation."[19] From its formation in the spring of 1996, the NIWC has incorporated transversalist politics and feminism in significant ways. Its original purpose was to get women elected to the Forum and Multi-Party Talks no matter what their community or party identity. However, the

Coalition soon identified inclusion, equality, and human rights as its underlying principles, and it developed a method of open, democratic, and feminist dialogue as key to implementing transversalism inside the Coalition.

One of the best stories about how this works in practice is Pearl Sagar's account of the Róisín McAliskey case. Róisín McAliskey, daughter of Bernadette Devlin McAliskey, was arrested in Germany and held first in a German and then a British prison while she was pregnant. Her case became significant for nationalists and especially for republicans throughout Ireland. The Women's Coalition discussed the case in an open but tense forum. According to Sagar, she had a difficult time getting her mind around who Róisín's mother is—the very name Bernadette Devlin McAliskey and the past she represented recalled painful, bitter memories. Yet Sagar recognized that she had to confront her own fears and bigotry. Through the discussion, she realized that the case was about equality and human rights, specifically prisoners' rights, and that had anyone else been in Róisín's place, who her mother was would not have mattered.[20] By focusing on common values, Pearl (and others) agreed that the McAliskey case represented an injustice and that the pregnant woman in prison deserved her rights to due process and adequate medical care.

The rooting and shifting went even further. A Women's Coalition member who is a doctor and a Protestant visited the prisoner and subsequently presented her "findings" and the NIWC's position about the case to the press. This made it difficult for unionists to dismiss the Women's Coalition position as just another pro-republican statement. The NIWC often makes use of this practice: positions that may sound favorable to the Catholic/nationalist/republican side of the conflict are usually delivered by members from Protestant/unionist backgrounds, while positions that could be interpreted as favorable to unionism are delivered by members from Catholic/nationalist backgrounds.

A second example of the NIWC's transversalist politics centers on the constitutional question at the heart of the conflict in Northern Ireland. Other political parties are defined and divided by their stand on the region's political status and future—that is, as committed to the union with Britain or to an all-Ireland state—and entered the peace talks to defend their fixed positions. The NIWC, on the other hand, decided that this question diverts attention from pressing issues that affect the daily lives of women, men, and children but have been pushed aside by the conflict—and by male politicians. Even though the NIWC's unionist and nationalist members might disagree on their preferences for the region's political status, they agree that a peaceful and prosperous future is what matters most. They came to the peace talks to seek solutions through dialogue rather than to restate problems and fixed positions. They agreed that to resolve the conflict in Northern Ireland it was more constructive to introduce "forgotten" issues to the agenda: housing, community development and social inclusion, victims of violence,[21] domestic violence, women's and minority rights, transportation, employment, education and training (especially for women), healthcare, child care, and so on. By pressing for dialogue on these issues, the NIWC sought both to alter the nature of the question and to change the shape of the outcome, thus building a new kind of politics for Northern Ireland.[22] In other words, the NIWC not only wanted to broaden the political agenda to address the region's neglected economic, social, and policy problems. It also worked to draw the other parties into a situation of exchange on these issues, where common values and goals—and perhaps new coalitions—might emerge through dialogue. The NIWC thus introduced a new political process in Northern Ireland guided by transversalism.

A third example of the practical use of transversalist politics and open, consensual decision making comes from a membership meeting on 4 July 1998, shortly after the elections to the new Northern Ireland Assembly and just a week before the annual and deeply divisive Drumcree Orange Order march in Portadown.[23] The packed agenda of the meeting focused on the successes and failures of the Assembly election campaign in which eight NIWC candidates had run and two were elected (Monica McWilliams from South Belfast and Jane Morrice from North Down). The meeting also considered whether to reorganize the Coalition more formally as a political party rather than remaining as the "political wing of the women's movement."[24] Just before the lunch break, a member asked if the NIWC might issue some sort of statement in support of the nationalist women on the Garvaghy Road in Portadown who were organizing a street festival and peace camp on the eve of the Orange march through their neighborhood. The meeting's full agenda made this new item difficult to fit in. Discussion ensued about what it might mean for the NIWC to take too strong a stand (or, for that matter, any stand) on the Drumcree conflict. It was both fascinating and inspiring to observe the honesty, respect, and "shifting" that occurred; nevertheless, the discussion was difficult, even painful, for some party activists. In the end, it was decided that a NIWC member from the Portadown district would compose and deliver a message to the Garvaghy women's peace camp. The message would convey the sense of the discussion and reiterate the NIWC's principles of nonviolence, inclusion, equality, and human rights, including the right to be free from sectarian harassment. With this consensus, the meeting broke for a spirited and good-humored lunch before returning to the rest of its agenda.

These are just three of many examples of transversalism inside the NIWC. This politics is deeply informed by a feminism that is brilliant at turning things "inside-out" (for lack of a better phrase), for stepping through the mirrored images to reveal the partialities, absurdities, and the oppressive boundaries that define identity and division in this bitter conflict. It is full of humor and, at the same time, deeply serious. It is built on dialogue and respect without asking anyone to abandon or apologize for her or his identity. It is self-critical and constantly concerned with developing women's political skills and insights. It struggles to dismantle patriarchal structures and political culture in Northern Ireland and break through the profound political and ideological barriers that divide Northern Ireland's society. As Monica McWilliams once put it, there are two major difficulties for the NIWC: "a culture of self-righteousness and a culture of resistance. . . . Therein we try to negotiate a path."[25]

Transversalist Politics and the Northern Ireland Peace Process

Its origins in feminist approaches to women in conflict (the Women in Black movement) and its adoption by the NIWC illustrate that transversalism is a "peace politics" that has worked for feminist women committed to conflict resolution. However, this politics should not be essentialized as a means of conflict management or conflict resolution for women only, even if feminist consciousness and commitment do facilitate the search for common values and active accommodation.[26] Many women and men in Northern Ireland are so deeply rooted in their community identity (which is also gendered[27]), that they are unable to make the kind of shift toward dialogue and the search for common values that transversalism requires. Yet it is significant that in a political culture as deeply patriarchal, gendered, and divided as that of Northern Ireland, hundreds of women and men are able to make such a shift to construct a feminist politics that unites women from both sides of the divide in a common but suppressed struggle. These women have come to see that their liberation as women in Northern Ireland requires a radical reconstruction of society away from sectarianism, violence, and patriarchy and toward a new politics of equality, dialogue, and coalition for all members of society, not just for women.

This political project might appear not only essentialist but also utopian. But dialogue and shifting are not exclusive properties of women or feminist politics, even if such capacities tend to be gendered in a patriarchal system based on violence, subordination, and zero-sum outcomes. Interestingly, in the international relations (IR) literature on negotiation and conflict resolution (where such "feminine" characteristics as talking, cooperation, and accommodation are part of the study and practice of international relations), shifting appears as a key term in the prenegotiation phase of successful conflict resolution. William Zartman explains that prenegotiation is a necessary step to success, and that the "necessary substance of the prenegotiation period" involves a series of shifts wherein the parties in conflict move from conflicting, unilateral perceptions and behaviors to cooperative, multilateral perceptions and behaviors. That is, they shift from a "winning mentality" directed *against* an "enemy" to a "conciliatory mentality" directed *towards* an adversary with whom one can find a solution. This generally requires settling for an "attainable second-best rather than hold[ing] out for an unattainable victory. These are significant shifts, often greater than anything involved in finding the agreed outcome, but necessary preconditions to that search."[28]

Another necessary element to successful conflict resolution is for parties in conflict to abandon "positional bargaining." Positional bargaining stakes out firm stands that rarely can serve as the basis for a satisfactory—or stable—compromise. In contrast, "principled" or "integrative bargaining" leads parties in conflict to focus on common principles and values, attainable next-best outcomes, and a genuine problem-solving approach.[29] Louis Kriesberg discusses both the interpersonal/psychological and structural factors necessary to effective conflict resolution, employing such key terms as "altering," "tolerance and mutual respect," "reframing" the conflict as a "shared problem," and finding "alternative ways" of "converting" the conflict into a problem to be solved. This is an interesting language: mutuality, requitement, altering, sharing, integrating, converting, and so on are quite unlike most concepts found in the IR literature.[30] Remarkably it is not far from the core ideas of transversalism's rooting and shifting.

Inside the Northern Ireland peace process, the Women's Coalition's skills of rooting and shifting, its guiding principles of inclusion, equality, and human rights, and its commitment to the process of active accommodation through dialogue as "social therapy" have made it a highly effective and focused player. NIWC members have earned respect, trust, and praise from all but the most intransigent. Indeed, the NIWC has contributed to the progress of the peace talks, both during the prenegotiation phase (roughly June 1996 to August 1997) and during the formal negotiations phase leading to the Good Friday Agreement (roughly September 1997 to April 1998), in three substantial ways.[31] First, it insisted on the talks being all-inclusive. Second, it played a crucial role as mediator between parties that do not speak to each other directly. Third, it placed other issues besides the constitutional conflict on the talks agenda. Even today it continues to play these roles.

From the beginning of the Forum and Multi-Party Talks, the NIWC argued, cajoled, and insisted that all political parties be included, particularly

Sinn Féin, linked to the Provisional IRA, and the Progressive Unionist Party (PUP) and the Ulster Democratic Party (UDP), linked to the loyalist paramilitary organizations. Not only had these parties won seats through the special Forum elections but, the NIWC argued, no genuine resolution of the conflict would be possible without dialogue among all parties, especially those linked to the paramilitary organizations. During the heated debate over whether Sinn Féin ought to be included without a renewed IRA cease-fire, Monica McWilliams put the matter succinctly when she said that Sinn Féin may as well be included because, with so much mention and debate about the party, "the ghost of Sinn Féin" was already present in the chamber. Although this clever phrase was picked up by others, Sinn Féin continued to be excluded during the prenegotiation phase. However, the NIWC maintained its own dialogue with the republicans, shared information with Sinn Féin about the progress of the Forum and Multi-Party Talks, and put forward arguments sympathetic to Sinn Féin's inclusion in the process. At the same time the NIWC pressed Sinn Féin to sign on to the Mitchell Principles of nonviolence and to work for a new IRA cease-fire.

After the IRA renewed its cease-fire (July 1997) and Sinn Féin joined the formal negotiations process (September 1997), the NIWC was one of the few parties willing and able to talk directly to Sinn Féin. At that point, Ian Paisley's Democratic Unionist Party boycotted the formal negotiations. However, the NIWC continued to engage the DUP as best it could. In February and March 1998, the Northern Ireland Office suspended Sinn Féin and the Ulster Democratic Party from the talks in response to an upsurge of paramilitary violence during the previous January. The NIWC protested strongly, arguing again that no peace could be achieved without those parties being fully included in the talks. "Inclusion" has been a key principle for the NIWC; significantly, it soon became an important word in the political lexicon of the nationalist Social Democratic and Labour Party (SDLP) as well.

In addition to insisting on the inclusion of Sinn Féin, the Progressive Unionist Party, and the UDP as a matter of principle, the NIWC was also the only party willing and able to talk to all other parties throughout the peace talks. In this role, the "gender" of the NIWC was as much of a negotiating strength as it was a target for harassment. Although women have been devalued and politically marginalized in Northern Ireland, particularly in more conservative quarters, they are also seen as relatively unsullied by politics. If some male politicians nearly gag at the word "women" as though it were dirty, the "ladies" of the Women's Coalition occupied an "innocent" position in the peace process that allowed them to play a less threatening mediating role. The NIWC recognized its position as the "double Other" (Catholic/Protestant and women), or better yet as the "triple Other" (as "not men," "not Us" or "not on our side" in the conflict, but also as "not quite Them" either). For example, the NIWC's vigorous support for Sinn Féin's inclusion in the talks, while criticizing their intransigence, destabilized the unionists' (and especially the DUP's) attempts to peg or dismiss the NIWC as republicans in sheep's (women's?) clothing. Rather than getting bogged down in resenting the double and triple othering of the Coalition by the "dinosaurs," the NIWC's transversalism (and their sense of humor) overcame it, allowing its negotiators to move about in the peace process as translators and mediators between parties, and to form new coalitions based on principles that go beyond the deeply rooted identity politics of Northern Ireland. Throughout the peace process, the NIWC also worked to bring the smaller parties (for example, the PUP, UDP, Workers Party, and Alliance Party) into coalition and developed an excellent working relationship with the PUP and UDP in particular.

Beyond insisting on the inclusion of all parties and acting as translator, mediator, and coalition-builder inside the peace process, the NIWC placed a number of issues on the talks agenda which expanded the dialogue beyond the "United Kingdom versus United Ireland" debate.[32] For example, equality and human rights were important issues negotiated in the Good Friday Agreement. While the traditional parties usually think of these issues in terms of equality of religion or cultural tradition (called "parity of esteem" in Northern Ireland), the NIWC was able to broaden the discussion to include not only freedom from sectarian harassment but also the right of women to full and equal political participation, along with guarantees for a broader antidiscrimination policy with respect to age, ability, and other minority status.

Another important part of the negotiations leading to the Good Friday Agreement dealt with releasing prisoners and how to reintegrate them back into society. This issue was controversial because many prisoners eligible for release under the Agreement were serving sentences for having paramilitary links or participating in paramilitary violence. Unionist politicians were particularly opposed to the release of republican prisoners. The NIWC's transversalism was able to support the bridge between republican and loyalist parties on this issue and helped persuade others of the centrality of prisoner releases, both for getting an agreement and for beginning the process of reconciliation at the grassroots level. The NIWC extended the issue by pressing to include in the Good Friday Agreement mechanisms of reconciliation and support for victims of the violence, matters that other parties had not considered.[33]

The peace talks also dealt with the creation of new political institutions for the region, including the new Assembly. However, the NIWC insisted that the Good Friday Agreement also create a Civic Forum, where community (grassroots) organizations, churches, business associations, trade unions, and other social groupings might establish a fuller dialogue among themselves as elements of civil society, where peace and reconciliation still needed to be built. Indeed, the NIWC was (and remains) the only party to see clearly that a peace agreement among top party leaders and the British and Irish governments would not be enough to bring about real peace in such a deeply divided society. Its origins in cross-community neighborhood organizations and its transversalist method meant that the NIWC knew there had to be a forum for other social groups to meet face-to-face and begin the kind of dialogue that transversalism requires. While other parties, particularly the Alliance Party, resisted such a forum, the NIWC's vision won and the Civic Forum is one of four new political institutions outlined in the Good Friday Agreement.[34] The Civic Forum finally began its work in October 2000.

These examples illustrate the NIWC's ability to take issues that other parties may have embraced but defined in their own positional terms (for example, equality, prisoners, victims of violence, social dialogue, peace), and expand them to include deeper issues, new definitions, and broader mechanisms than had earlier been imagined. Moreover, the Women's Coalition continues to be tireless in placing other issues—some long overshadowed by the conflict—on the political agenda: jobs, economic development, transportation, schools, children's rights, healthcare, and domestic violence are among the issues it has raised.

Inside the peace process, most parties faced few costs and many benefits by "allowing" the NIWC to participate. Taken without much seriousness at first, the NIWC soon proved itself a worthy and skillful participant and a useful ally on different issues. It played an important but not uncritical bridging role in the negotiations and modeled the kind of shifting necessary to conflict resolution. Although other parties, especially the Ulster Unionist Party (UUP) and the DUP, have a long way to go in learning to shift from positional win-lose to integrative win-win mentalities, the NIWC had a crucial impact on the peace process in Northern Ireland and has made a discernible dent in the old model of politics. This impact can be measured not only in the clauses supporting victims of violence, women's rights, and the Civic Forum in the Good Friday Agreement but also in the June 1998 elections for the new Northern Ireland Assembly. In this campaign, voters from all political parties gave clear signs that the NIWC is a real player on the changing political stage in Northern Ireland.

Women and Gender Politics in Northern Ireland

In negotiating the Good Friday Agreement, the NIWC worked very hard to get other parties to agree to an electoral system for the new Assembly as inclusive as that used for the Forum and Multi-Party Talks to ensure that small parties would continue to have a voice. Despite support from the British and Irish governments, the Women's Coalition could not get agreement from the larger parties except for Sinn Féin; instead a somewhat more restrictive proportional representation and single transferable vote system was adopted.[35] This meant that the Women's Coalition would need between 5 and 7 percent of all first preference votes cast to stay in the race and be eligible for transfer votes to win a seat in the new Assembly. The party's average poll in previous elections had been just under 2 percent.[36] The NIWC ended up winning two seats in the Northern Ireland Assembly.

The success of the NIWC's original goal of getting more women into politics can be measured in the victories of its own candidates as well as in the increased number of women candidates other parties felt they must put forward. On the nationalist side, the Social Democratic and Labour Party issued a "Women's Manifesto" on the eve of the June 1998 Assembly elections and, for a time, raised questions in voters' minds about the Coalition's stand on abortion. This issue was also raised by pro-choice activists who criticized the Coalition's lack of an official stance, and by more conservative religious and political groupings that assumed the NIWC to be pro-choice.[37] But the SDLP's "Women's Manifesto" and its use of the abortion issue signify that the NIWC's entrée and participation in the Northern Ireland political landscape were being taken seriously. A more humorous indication is a joke popular in nationalist circles that asks, "What is the name for the Women's Coalition in Ulláns (the Ulster-Scots dialect)?" The answer: "The Wee Women's Clique." This joke is a double dig, both at the NIWC and at the loyalist community that claims "Ulster Scots" to be a bona fide language. Despite its "Women's Manifesto," however, the SDLP ran only six women in the Assembly elections, three of whom won seats (Brid Rodgers, Carmel Hanna, Patricia Lewsley) among its twenty-four-member delegation.

Sinn Féin (SF) has had a better—indeed, until the NIWC the best—record of incorporating women into its party structure and of putting forward women candidates since it adopted an electoral political strategy in the mid- to late 1980s.[38] Yet many republican (and other) women were deeply disappointed that the SF male leadership relegated women's issues to the back seat, behind SF's constitutional challenge and United Ireland agenda. Since that time notable republican women have moved the party forward on women's issues and have helped to broaden the equality agenda to include women's rights as part of SF's rights discourse, but the "woman question" remains subordinate to or submerged in SF's larger political goals. Some SF women, such as Bairbre de Brún and Mary Nellis, are close to the top of the party structure, yet women activists inside SF remain a clear minority. In the Assembly elections, SF ran eight women, five of whom won seats in its eighteen-seat Assembly delegation. Their participation in the Assembly and their seating at and near the front bench of SF's delegation help to make SF's (especially Gerry Adams's and Martin McGuinness's) image less threatening to those who link SF directly to the Provisional IRA. Significantly, SF voters transferred some of their second and third preference votes to NIWC candidates in some constituencies, suggesting that the NIWC does not represent an electoral threat to SF and is an acceptable choice to some republicans. These transfer votes may also have been a reward for the NIWC's steadfast insistence on SF's inclusion in the Multi-Party Talks.

The Alliance Party occupies the center of the political spectrum, where the NIWC is both a challenge and an ally. Both parties are based on a cross-community philosophy and appeal to similarly minded voters. Yet Alliance seems to want to erase or deny the legitimacy of identity politics in Northern Ireland, while the NIWC accepts and embraces the legitimacy of both unionist and nationalist identities through its transversalism. Both parties seek an end to political violence and the construction of "normal politics" in the region, yet Alliance's middle-class orientation tends to ignore the political struggles of the working class whereas the NIWC's cross-community grassroots base does not. Feminists perceive Alliance to be very patriarchal; it has recruited and put forward few women as serious candidates. In the spring of 1996, the party squandered an opportunity to recruit Jane Morrice and put her forward for the Forum elections. Instead she joined the Women's Coalition as a founding member. She now represents the NIWC in the Assembly and was elected its interim Speaker in January 2000. Alliance ran six women out of twenty-two candidates in the June 1998 Assembly elections, but only Eileen Bell, the sole woman among senior party members, was elected as part of Alliance's six-seat Assembly delegation.

Alliance blamed the NIWC for the decline in its percentage of the vote in the Assembly election; however, this decline may be based on other reasons. Alliance has never won more than 10 percent of the vote, and it is seen as irrelevant from both the loyalist and republican sides of the divide. Its party leader, Lord (John) Alderdice, is disliked and ridiculed by both sides, and the party lacks strong, professional, and imaginative staff to handle day-to-day party business (for example, the party's website is inaccessible). It ran a lackluster campaign in June 1998: its election posters, featuring black letters on yellow backgrounds without pictures of candidates or other artwork, looked more like traffic signs than campaign posters. Alliance also lacks the political organization and grassroots activist base of the NIWC. During the June elections, Alliance's middle-class and professional supporters were unwilling or unable to carry out a door-to-door campaign to ask for votes.[39]

Its faceless, directionless campaign was outclassed by the grassroots energy of the Women's Coalition. Unless and until Alliance can address its own gender gap as well as some of its other gaps, it will fail to attract women as new voters or party activists, and may continue to lose ground with male voters as well.

The NIWC appears to have made the fewest inroads on the unionist side. Yet even within the Ulster Unionist Party, the appearance and participation of the NIWC has had some observable impact. As the father of the "unionist family" and with close ties to the Orange Order, the UUP is a highly patriarchal political machine that has been effectively closed to women—other than wives or daughters of prominent unionist politicians. Nevertheless, in February 1997, the UUP presented an articulate spokeswoman, Arlene Foster, Honorary Secretary of the UUP, for a *Spotlight* documentary by the BBC on women and politics in Northern Ireland. More significantly, women attending its party conference in October 1998 forced it to address the lack of women's recruitment, inclusion, and participation in the party structure. The *Irish Times* quoted UUP party activist Elaine McClure on 29 October 1998 as saying, "This party is perceived as an all-male bastion; that should change so that our public image reflects our membership and our electorate more accurately." The party conference even heard arguments in favor of adopting a quota system for women candidates in future Assembly elections.

The UUP ran only four women in the June 1998 elections, two of whom won seats in its twenty-eight-seat Assembly delegation. Both UUP assemblywomen remain distant from any connection with "women's groups" and especially with the Women's Coalition. Pauline Armitage delivered a sharp attack against Monica McWilliams and the Women's Coalition in her 15 December 1998 maiden speech in the Assembly. Moreover, in a brief telephone conversation regarding an interview that a colleague of mine tried to arrange with her, Armitage emphatically stated to me—twice—that she was "*not* a woman. I don't *want* to be a 'woman.'" She said she had "nothing to do" with women's groups or women's politics.[40] During the Assembly plenary on 18 January 1999, she sat next to the only other UUP assemblywoman, Joan Carson, the two of them surrounded by a sea of UUP assemblymen wearing dark suits and grim faces.

The Democratic Unionist Party (Ian Paisley's party) has been least affected electorally by the emergence and growth of the NIWC. It is arguably the most patriarchal and conservative of the main political parties in Northern Ireland. Even Ian Paisley's daughter, Rhonda Paisley, criticized the DUP "brotherhood" for its "dismissive" and "chauvinistic" attitude towards women's involvement in the party. She also criticized unionism more broadly for its "rut of 'reaction to' feminist issues."[41] The DUP remains the staunchest anti-Agreement party, even though it participated in the 1998 Assembly elections. It ran four women in the Assembly elections, but only Iris Robinson (wife of DUP zealot Peter Robinson) was elected to its twenty-member Assembly delegation. Women's issues are not part of her political agenda. Iris Robinson has also launched personal attacks against Monica McWilliams and the Women's Coalition, such as in her speech in the Forum debate on 11 July 1997 concerning that year's bitterly controversial Drumcree Orange march: "Finally I say to her: Do not lecture Members of the Forum who have a mandate to speak on behalf of the electorate, unlike her and her little party, and, please, in the world of real politics, do not throw tantrums to the press at every turn about silly incidents. Sadly, this has the negative effect of putting women off from involving themselves in the political arena."[42] These digs at the Women's Coalition were among the more engaging DUP remarks.[43] In the Assembly elections, however, a surprising number of DUP voters used their transfer votes to support NIWC candidates, though much of this was interpreted as an example of tactical voting.[44]

Unlike the other unionist parties, the Progressive Unionist Party (the political wing of the loyalist paramilitary Ulster Volunteer Force) has built an interesting and respectful working relationship with the NIWC. Both parties squeezed into the Forum and Multi-Party Talks with two representatives each through the top-up electoral system, which allowed smaller parties with sufficient votes to participate in the talks. The NIWC's insistence on inclusion of all parties, especially those connected to paramilitary organizations on both sides, as well as its capacity for transversalist politics, opened the door to NIWC–PUP mutual support and cooperation. Although the PUP backed away from the Coalition's demand for a more inclusive electoral system for the new Assembly in the Good Friday Agreement,[45] the PUP has been a congenial and supportive partner on a number of NIWC issues, and vice versa. In the June 1998 Assembly elections, transfer votes from PUP voters to NIWC candidates were significant in many constituencies. The PUP also shared its temporary office and—generously—one of its computers in Belfast City Hall during the election count with the NIWC. The PUP ran one woman candidate (Dawn Purvis) in the elections, but the small party won only two seats (both male) in the Assembly. PUP activists and canvassers during the elections were publicly and genuinely friendly to NIWC canvassers and the Coalition's political agenda, displaying the PUP's own grassroots progressivism and its capacity to root and shift in the process of building a new model of politics in Northern Ireland. The PUP exemplified this capacity most visibly—and interestingly—in the Assembly itself on 18 January 1999. When PUP spokesman David Ervine rose to speak, he began by admonishing the "macho men" of the DUP and UUP for their relentless efforts to wreck the Agreement and bring down the Assembly. He condemned their intransigent opposition to forming a power-sharing executive to which, under the terms of the Agreement, governmental powers would eventually devolve.

The Limits of Transversalism in the Northern Ireland Peace Process

A cautious political optimism emerged with the elections for the new Northern Ireland Assembly in June 1998 which, as it happened, resulted in fourteen women being elected to the 108-seat Assembly.[46] However, this optimism quickly faded as a difficult political stalemate emerged in implementing the rest of the Good Friday Agreement and persisted for the next three years. The unionist family, led by the UUP, blocked the formation of a power-sharing executive and, with it, the devolution of governmental powers to Northern Ireland from Westminster, until the IRA began to disarm.[47] Republicans (and many nationalists) responded that the letter of the Good Friday Agreement did not require the decommissioning of arms until May 2000 and argued that all aspects of the Agreement must be implemented, including the formation of the power-sharing executive. The "no guns, no government"/"no government, no guns" stalemate emerged as a mimetic contest of positional politics and prime-time sound bytes. It was waged primarily by UUP leader David Trimble and SF leader Gerry Adams, with frequent interjections from DUP and SDLP male leaders. Hardliners on both sides made it difficult for Trimble and Adams to talk to each other directly to resolve the political stalemate.

Efforts by British, Irish, American, and South African mediators to break the stalemate in April, July, and autumn of 1999 focused on how to get a deal between the UUP, SF, and to a lesser extent SDLP leaders.[48] Significantly, the NIWC, the PUP, and other small parties were sidelined in these efforts, both by the local media and by the outside mediators. As the UUP and SF clung tight to their zero-sum negotiating strategies, the transversalist negotiating strategies of the NIWC were ignored or forgotten. The peace process in Northern Ireland appeared to reach the limits of transversalist politics in 1999 as media and mediators focused on getting the "big boys" to compromise through crisis talks rather than involving other political voices directly in the process of problem solving.

Surprisingly, after a tense two-month long "review" of the Good Friday Agreement, George Mitchell, along with British and Irish government mediators, succeeded in brokering a fragile deal between the UUP and SF leaders at the end of November 1999. Within days, a power-sharing executive was finally named and ten ministerial portfolios were distributed among the four largest parties.[49] In exchange for the new executive, the IRA named a representative to the Independent International Commission on Decommissioning (IICD) as a start to the arms decommissioning process. On 6 December 1999, Westminster devolved broad (but not complete) powers to the new government, which soon began to deal with everyday issues like funding for hospitals, schools, and roads. By early January 2000, even the political news in the local media had turned to the mundane coverage of a functioning government while jokes and political cartoons lampooned the spending proclivities of the new government's politicians.

Yet just as "normal politics" seemed to take shape in Northern Ireland, the familiar no guns/no government stalemate reemerged with a new game of brinkmanship, throwing the peace process back into serious crisis. UUP leader David Trimble threatened to resign as First Minister (prime minister) and force a return to direct rule by Westminster if the IICD could not report significant progress on IRA arms decommissioning by the end of January 2000.[50] Republicans continued to argue that the Good Friday Agreement did not recognize any deadlines for decommissioning other than May 2000, saying that decommissioning was a matter to be handled by the IICD as per the Agreement. In any case, the guns remained silent. The IICD report did not reassure unionists or the British government,[51] and in mid-February 2000, just seventy-two days after its formation, the new Northern Ireland government and Assembly were suspended. The entire peace process seemed on the verge of collapse as Northern Ireland again teetered on the edge of a patriarchal political crisis based on zero-sum positioning, threats, lack of trust, and recriminations conveyed through the media between, primarily, the UUP and SF.

For the next three months, British and Irish government mediators tried to get the "big boys" to talk to each other, but the laddish game of brinkmanship persisted. Mediators pressed each side to bend a little privately, but were unable to get them to put the details on the table, much less talk to each other directly. In March, President Clinton's mediation efforts led Trimble to indicate he was willing to consider a sequence of events and statements that stopped short of demanding IRA guns "up front." In response, and with added pressure on members of the IRA Army Council by a respected South African politician, Adams helped work out the text of a statement offering to put IRA weapons "beyond use" and that provided for verification by independent third parties.[52] Yet neither side wanted to be seen as weakening its position prior to the other, and certainly not without the other side reciprocating. The impasse continued until 6 May 2000 when, for the first time in months, Trimble and Adams held direct talks buttressed by British and Irish government mediators. In less than an hour they made a new deal. Within days, the IRA issued a statement naming former Finnish president Martti Ahtisaari and former African National Congress secretary-general Cyril Ramaphosa as the independent arms inspectors who would verify that IRA arms were completely and verifiably "beyond use." The British government restored devolved powers to the Northern Ireland at midnight on 28 May 2000. The Assembly and its Executive soberly resumed their work in the first week of June. Yet the moment Trimble and Adams agreed on a guns-for-government formula, Trimble placed new demands on the British government for concessions on a proposed police reform package, thus laying the groundwork for the next round of political brinkmanship. Worse still, despite two positive reports by the independent arms inspectors, Trimble took steps in November 2000 to block Sinn Féin's participation in the North-South Ministerial Council (one of the institutions created in the Good Friday Agreement) until IRA arms were destroyed. "Beyond use" was no longer good enough.

Conclusion

The cautious optimism that emerged first with the successful negotiation of the Good Friday Agreement and then with the election of the Northern Ireland Assembly gave way to a series of political crises over the implementation of the rest of the Agreement. The political situation continues in deep crisis, and the future of the peace process remains in doubt. Meanwhile, the deeply gendered nature of the conflict in Northern Ireland persists. More than guns, many people's minds still need to be decommissioned.[53]

The emergence and participation since 1996 of the NIWC in Northern Ireland's political arena has helped to force open important spaces for women not only inside the Coalition but also in other parties, particularly in SDLP and Sinn Féin. Several accommodated the NIWC's presence and arguments in the political process, responding positively to its transversalism and coalition-building efforts. The electoral successes of the NIWC came at the expense of some parties more than others, but by "allowing" the Women's Coalition to participate in the peace talks and the new Assembly, all gained a skillful translator and mediator at a historic political juncture in Northern Ireland. The other parties in Northern Ireland remain patriarchal and are overwhelmingly dominated by men. Even so, the impact of the NIWC is clear if one looks at the political shifting that took place through the Multi-Party Talks and if one reads the Good Friday Agreement. The

NIWC expanded the peace agenda beyond the timeworn constitutional conflict, injecting new terms, ideas, issues, and methods into the Multi-Party Talks phase of the peace process. It pressed for new institutions based on inclusion, human rights, and equality. In the process, the Women's Coalition used, challenged, and inverted the essentialized notions of women's relationship to the Troubles, and mobilized women politically in unprecedented ways.

The wider impact of the NIWC is also clear if one listens closely to the evolving political agenda and discourse in Northern Ireland. The NIWC continues to work both in the Assembly and behind the scenes, engaging with all the parties in the region and voicing the cross-community, grassroots concerns of the politically homeless. It continues to seek to expand issues and debates in the Assembly beyond narrow conceptualizations and dichotomous positions (for example, by framing the abortion debate as part of the larger issue of reproductive health). Despite its exclusion (along with the other smaller parties) from the ad hoc crisis mediation efforts after the 1998 elections, the NIWC continues to press for inclusion, human rights, and equality, and to place *process*—the process of dialogue and active accommodation, both in government and at the grassroots level—at the center of conflict resolution.

If the ongoing political crisis about guns-for-government (and now policing reforms) demonstrates the limits of transversalist politics in Northern Ireland, the Women's Coalition demonstrates transversalism's possibilities. Transversalism is a politics based on what the NIWC refers to as "active accommodation," a conscious effort to enter into dialogue with the Other in order to begin the process of rooting and shifting. Transversalism sees identity, as Václav Havel put it, as "not a prison," but "an appeal for dialogue with others."[54] It requires self-knowledge and self-confidence, and also a certain humility and sense of incompleteness in order to find the readiness to solve problems (rooting). Transversalism also requires recognition that the Other's values and interests are legitimate, and trusts that the Other can be engaged in dialogue (shifting). Its willingness to engage with the Other is essential to building a process of conflict resolution. But transversalism is also about process itself: rooting, shifting, talking, listening, being inclusive of all voices, recognizing that one's own knowledge or truth is incomplete without hearing the voices of others, and, above all, focusing on the "bigger picture." Through transversalism, one seeks to enter into a dialogical exchange with the Other to discover shared values and goals despite—or beyond—the differences of identity and position that obscure possible commonalities. Transversalism in practice also seeks to rethink the existing terms of debate by going beyond the received words or even the structure of the language of conflict to find a new language, a new grammar, that parties can use to solve common problems. It recognizes that just as conflict is shared, its resolution must also be a shared engagement.

From the very beginning, the NIWC saw process and inclusion as the keys to conflict resolution. From early in the peace process its analysis rested on the conviction that an "eventual deal could not be a deal of the center"—meaning the big parties alone.[55] Kate Fearon, political advisor and negotiator for the NIWC, asserted further that dismantling the negotiating framework of the Multi-Party Talks after the Good Friday Agreement and electing the Assembly was a significant flaw in the subsequent phase of the peace process. It prevented the parties from talking to each other in a problem-solving manner to resolve issues in the implementation of the Agreement.[56] Prior to devolution, occasional parliamentary debates in the Northern Ireland Assembly, which met intermittently between June 1998 and July 1999, were not sufficient to keep the UUP and SF leadership and the other parties engaged in a problem-solving process on the guns versus government stalemate. Instead, the professional mediators stepped in to sponsor a series of crisis talks between UUP and SF leaders, but they still could not resolve the impasse.

The best the outside mediators could achieve were fragile deals between the big parties. In fact, it appears that the professional mediators from the British and Irish governments (who are also parties to the conflict) contributed to the long game of brinkmanship between Trimble and Adams. By framing the problem as one between unionists and republicans, and therefore between these two men as their political leaders, the government mediators shut out the possibility of conflict resolution. Instead they created a situation that sacrificed process to position, evacuated space for real shifting to occur, and sidelined those parties *inside* Northern Ireland whose experience with transversalist politics could help to find a solution to the no guns, no government/no government, no guns mimesis.

This situation reflects a flaw not only in the analysis of the outside mediators but also in the current state of the literature about conflict resolution generally. Shifting should be understood not only as a necessary "prenegotiation" event, but also as a process that continues throughout conflict resolution. Professional mediators and diplomats must resist the temptation to limit the peace process to the "big boys," who are then pressured to reach a compromise. Such an approach prevents the process from being extended to the grassroots level, where conflict resolution and reconciliation processes need to occur, and it locks out grassroots organizations, whose experiences with transversalism are better geared to finding stable resolutions to conflict. Instead, building negotiations around the "big boys" results either in dependency on the mediators to solve problems or in ongoing stalemates, brinkmanship, and recurrent political crises. It also reinforces the old model of patriarchal politics by male politicians and professional male mediators, a model from which women and others with fresh ideas and transversalist capacities remain excluded, silenced, and invisible.

After four and a half years of experience inside the peace process in Northern Ireland, Monica McWilliams explained it best when she stated: "We cannot go on like this where Sinn Féin and the Ulster Unionists have become so dependent on the two governments to deal separately with each of their problems. . . . They have failed to engage with the rest of us in finding our own solution. . . . Politicians need to learn not to bring their own internal solutions to the table but focus on the bigger picture, a stable prosperous and peaceful future for Northern Ireland."[57] By failing to recognize and re-engage the transversalist politics and processes of the NIWC, British, Irish, and American mediators, not to mention the old dinosaurs of patriarchal politics in Northern Ireland, cannot find a way out of the ongoing conflict. They risk continuation of "armed patriarchy"—and perhaps a return to violence—for a long time to come.

Many factors—economic, social, demographic, political, international—are responsible for the very real progress that has been achieved in the peace process since 1996. The transversalist politics of the NIWC were crucial in helping to shift the terms of debate, reframe old questions and raise new ones, and build new bridges and coalitions among most of the other parties prior to the Good Friday Agreement. Through its own modeling of active accommodation, the NIWC has made a dent in the old model of politics for women and men in Northern Ireland. However, for progress to continue and the peace process to survive, others, including professional mediators and crisis managers, need to recognize the contributions and skills of the NIWC in building a new and lasting transversalist politics for everyone in Northern Ireland.

Notes

1. See Rick Wilford, "Representing Women," *Democratic Dialogue,* Report No. 4 (Belfast: Democratic Dialogue, 1996): 48–55; Rosemary Sales, *Women Divided: Gender, Religion and Politics in Northern Ireland* (London and New York: Routledge, 1997); Valerie Morgan and Grace Fraser, *The Company We Keep: Women, Community, and Organisations* (Coleraine: Centre for the Study of Conflict and Centre for Research on Women, University of Ulster, 1994).

2. See Monica McWilliams, "Women in Northern Ireland: An Overview," in *Culture and Politics in Northern Ireland, 1960–1990,* ed. Eamonn Hughes (Philadelphia: Open University Press, 1991), 81–100; Monica McWilliams, "Struggling for Peace

and Justice: Reflections on Women's Activism in Northern Ireland," *Journal of Women's History* 6/7 (Winter/Spring 1995): 13–39. Monica McWilliams of the Northern Ireland Women's Coalition notes an inverse relationship between reported incidents of domestic violence and political violence. During the 1995–96 IRA cease-fire, reported incidents of domestic violence increased owing to the fact that victims were more likely to report such crimes to police than during periods of armed conflict and street violence. During the current paramilitary cease-fires, although paramilitaries on both sides continue to "police" their neighborhoods, it may be easier for victims of domestic violence to call the police than previously. According to an article in the *Irish News* (Belfast) on 13 January 1999, in 1998 (a year of paramilitary cease-fires and substantial progress in the Northern Ireland peace process) the Royal Ulster Constabulary (RUC) dealt with 10,448 domestic incidents, 4,604 of which were violent, whereas in 1997 police handled 8,509 incidents, 3,005 involving violence. Women's Aid also received 14,000 calls from women in 1998.

3. See Mary K. Meyer, "Ulster's Red Hand: Gender, Identity, and Sectarian Conflict in Northern Ireland," in *Women, States, and Nationalism: At Home in the Nation?* eds. Sita Ranchod-Nilsson and Mary Ann Tétreault (New York: Routledge, 2000); Elizabeth Porter, "Diversity and Commonality: Women, Politics and Northern Ireland," *The European Journal of Women's Studies* 4 (1997): 83–100.

4. I wish to thank the women of the Northern Ireland Women's Coalition, particularly Ann McCann, Monica McWilliams, Kate Fearon, Pearl Sagar, Eliz McCullough-Byrne, Judith Cross, and Robin Whitaker, whose openness, hospitality, and inspiring action have made this research possible.

5. See Kate Fearon and Monica McWilliams, "The Good Friday Agreement: A Triumph of Substance over Style," *Fordham International Law Journal* 22 (April 1999): 1250–72.

6. According to Monica McWilliams, Cathy Harkin coined the term "armed patriarchy" when working with Women's Aid in Derry between 1977 and 1981. See McWilliams, "Struggling for Peace and Justice," 34n. 7.

7. Or Provisional Irish Republican Army, the principal republican paramilitary force in Northern Ireland fighting against British rule during the thirty years of the Troubles. Hereafter referred to as the IRA.

8. See Joseph Ruane and Jennifer Todd, *The Dynamics of Conflict in Northern Ireland: Power, Conflict and Emancipation* (New York: Cambridge University Press, 1996), especially chapter 11, for an excellent analysis of the dynamics of the conflict and the steps toward its resolution.

9. John Major's slim parliamentary majority narrowed in the mid-1990s with the deaths or resignations of Conservative Party members and successes of other parties in by-elections. Major thus became more dependent on support from unionist MPs in Parliament and, according to many observers, more beholden to unionist opposition than interested in moving ahead on peace talks with Sinn Féin/IRA.

10. The Mitchell Principles were part of the January 1996 report of the International Body on Decommissioning appointed by the British and Irish governments to seek a way forward in peace talks in Northern Ireland. The commission was chaired by former U.S. Senator George Mitchell, retired Canadian General John de Chastelain, and former Finnish Prime Minister Harri Holkeri—who went on to chair the All-Party Talks. The Mitchell Principles required that participants in any all-party

negotiations affirm their commitment to democratic and exclusively peaceful means of resolving political issues, the total and verifiable disarmament of all paramilitary organizations, the renunciation of the use or threat of force to influence the negotiations, and to abide by the terms of any agreement reached and to use exclusively peaceful and democratic means to alter any aspect of the outcome of talks with which they might disagree. See George J. Mitchell, *Making Peace* (New York: Alfred A. Knopf, 1999), 35–36.

11. Kate Fearon, *Women's Work: The Story of the Northern Ireland Women's Coalition* (Belfast: Blackstaff Press, 1999); Fearon and McWilliams, "The Good Friday Agreement."

12. After the elections, Sinn Féin's seventeen elected representatives were barred from the talks until six weeks after the IRA's second cease-fire was announced in July 1997. In protest of Sinn Féin's exclusion, the SDLP boycotted the weekly Forum Talks, although it did participate in the Multi-Party Talks throughout the period. Because of Sinn Féin's exclusion, the All-Party Talks became the Multi-Party Talks. When Sinn Féin joined the peace talks, the Democratic Unionist Party walked out.

13. The three candidates in the May 1997 parliamentary elections were Bronagh Hinds, North Antrim; Annie Campbell, Belfast South; and Jane Morrice, North Down. Compared to their votes in the May 1996 elections, the votes increased in South Belfast, doubled in North Antrim, and trebled in North Down. Interestingly, an estimated one-third of the NIWC's votes in the parliamentary election came from men. These estimates were noted by Barbara McCabe (address to the Women's Studies Centre Seminar Series, University College Galway, Ireland, 15 May 1997).

14. Monica McWilliams, "Women and Society in Northern Ireland" (address to the CIEE International Faculty Development Seminar: Conflict Resolution: On the Threshold of Peace in Northern Ireland, Council on International Educational Exchange and University of Ulster, Coleraine, Ireland, 7 January 1997).

15. Nira Yuval-Davis, *Gender and Nation* (Thousand Oaks, Calif.: Sage, 1997), 125–33.

16. Ibid., 130; emphasis mine.

17. Ibid., 130–32.

18. The NIWC has around five hundred members, approximately 40 percent of whom are men. See Todd R. Nicholls, "Breaking Barriers for Political Acceptance," *Irish News,* 11 December 2000. http://www.irishnews.com/archive2000/11122000/politics1.html (11 December 2000).

19. Barbara McCabe (address to the Women's Studies Centre, University College Galway, 15 May 1997).

20. Significantly, Sagar's own daughter was pregnant at the time.

21. The Women's Coalition was the only political party to put the question of acknowledging and seeking to redress the rights of victims of violence on the agenda of the peace process. Moreover, it was the only party in January 1999 to submit a policy statement on victims of the violence and their families to a commission working on this issue as part of the peace process. While the other political parties (particularly the UUP and DUP) politicize this issue and trot out IRA victims' families to appear with leading politicians for the television cameras, none seems to be very interested in developing real policies to address the needs and problems of victims of the violence and their families.

22. Thanks to Kate Fearon, NIWC talks negotiator, for clarifying this point for me.

23. Founded in 1795, the Orange Order is a Masonic-style organization dedicated to the defense of the Protestant faith in Northern Ireland and the region's continued union with Britain. Historically, it is closely linked to the unionist political parties in Northern Ireland. Its lodges hold thousands of local marches, primarily in the summertime, commemorating Protestant or British victories in past wars. While most of its marches are not controversial, a number of them commemorating the victory of Protestant forces over Catholic forces during the Williamite wars of the 1690s pass through Catholic or nationalist neighborhoods along what members claim are "traditional routes." Nationalists see these marches as a form of sectarian harassment. The Drumcree march in Portadown has been the focus of serious conflict and violence, both historically and in recent years.

24. Until then the NIWC had thought of itself as an organized social movement or, as one member remarked to me with subtle humor, as "the political wing of the women's movement" in Northern Ireland. The Coalition is still rather uncomfortable with the label "political party" given the negative connotation parties have in the Northern Ireland context as hierarchical, patronage machines. Yet, the Coalition is in the political game to stay and recognizes that it must reorganize itself more formally to survive and remain effective in the new Assembly. The NIWC is now registered as a political party under recent United Kingdom legislation.

25. McWilliams, "Women and Society in Northern Ireland."

26. My point in this section is that transversalism is neither "for women only," nor is it some utopian dream—some of its principles can be found in other parts of the international relations and conflict resolution literature. Nevertheless, transversalism is a feminist peace politics insofar as women and feminists (in particular, Italian feminists working with Middle Eastern women and, now, the Northern Ireland Women's Coalition) have embraced and developed it. Transversalism connects the theory of conflict resolution with practice in a way that appeals to these women and feminists who are interested in dialogue across difference. Perhaps this is because women's imposed Otherness under patriarchy makes them more experienced in—and more accomplished at—rooting and shifting, active accommodation, and dialogue on a daily basis. Transversalism provides an attractive, even a familiar, praxis for women seeking conflict resolution.

27. Meyer, "Ulster's Red Hand."

28. William Zartman, "Prenegotiation: Phases and Functions," in *Getting to the Table: The Processes of International Prenegotiation*, ed. Janice Gross Stein (Baltimore, Md.: Johns Hopkins University Press, 1989), 7–8. These shifts are brought about by clarifying the risks and costs of negotiating or not, by "requitement"—establishing a belief in reciprocity (exchange), by consolidating a supportive internal coalition willing to shift its public image of the adversary, by identifying alternatives for a supportable solution, by identifying and including the necessary participants to the negotiations, by building bridges (cease-fires) to facilitate other shifts, and by creating frameworks that redefine the conflict as a problem that can be solved.

29. J. E. Dougherty and Robert L. Pfaltzgraff Jr., *Contending Theories of International Relations*, 3d ed. (New York: Harper and Row, 1990); David P. Barash, "Diplomacy, Negotiation, and Peaceful Settlement," in *Teaching about International*

Conflict and Peace, ed. Merry M. Merryfield and Richard C. Remy (Albany: State University of New York Press, 1995), 185–216; Janice Gross Stein, ed., *Getting to the Table: The Processes of International Prenegotiation* (Baltimore, Md.: Johns Hopkins University Press, 1989); John W. Burton, "Resolution and Conflict," *International Studies Quarterly* 16 (March 1972): 5–30; Roger Fisher, William Ury, and Bruce Patton, *Getting to Yes: Negotiating Agreement without Giving In,* 2d ed. (New York: Houghton Mifflin, 1991).

30. Zartman, "Prenegotiation," 170–73. Another interesting term used in this literature is "mutually hurting stalemate," which refers to the point reached in a violent conflict when parties face a "plateau and a precipice" of recent or impending catastrophe, and it becomes clear to at least one of them that continued violence will not break the stalemate but rather will lead to more hurt. It is at this point that parties "shift from unilateral solutions toward multilateral or negotiated ones." See Zartman, "Prenegotiation," 5–6. Such language (hurting, requitement, etc.) in this part of the IR literature contrasts sharply with the realist language that dominates the rest, suggesting interesting gendered constructions in the discourse of IR that deserve closer analysis.

31. This delineation of the phases of the peace process is tentative and admittedly problematic. A case could be made that only with the formation of the new Northern Ireland Assembly have we entered the real "negotiating phase" involving all political parties, including the DUP, with the implementation of the rest of the Agreement still in the balance (see further discussion below). Moreover, the "prenegotiation" phase can be marked as having begun in the mid-to-late 1980s. Then, both the Provisional IRA and the British government recognized the existence of a "mutually hurting stalemate," and feelers went out to begin a dialogue about building a peace process between them. The Downing Street Declaration (1993) and the Framework Documents (1995), followed shortly by the first IRA cease-fire, mark the beginning of the "prenegotiations" among the armed players in Northern Ireland and the start of the current peace process.

32. Fearon and McWilliams, "The Good Friday Agreement."

33. Questions relating to prisoners—their rights, status, prison conditions and treatment, and so on—were central to the course of the Troubles from the beginning. Resolving how to deal with prisoners thus became a serious issue in the peace talks. Republican and loyalist parties (Sinn Féin, PUP, and UDP) found common ground in supporting the idea of prisoner releases, and the NIWC nurtured this point of agreement. However UUP and DUP politicians staunchly opposed releasing republican prisoners with presumed links to the Provisional IRA as part of a peace agreement. These politicians periodically posed for photo opportunities with victims of republican paramilitary violence (but not with victims of loyalist or state violence) as the issue was debated but failed to think of including support for victims of the violence as part of the Agreement until the NIWC pressed the issue.

34. The other new institutions are the Northern Ireland Assembly, the North-South Ministerial Council(s), the Council of the Isles (British-Irish Council, or East-West Council), and the British-Irish Intergovernmental Council. In addition to these, the Agreement provides for a number of international commissions addressing such issues as policing and the decommissioning of paramilitary weapons.

35. The proportional representation and single transferable vote electoral system is one in which voters rank party candidates in order of preference. A mathematical

formula based on the total number of ballots cast in each constituency and the number of seats to be filled determines a threshold of votes needed to win a seat. Voters rank their party preferences and once one party wins enough votes to win the first seat, any additional votes it receives are returned—or transferred—for a new round of counting for the next seat. In each subsequent round of counting, the next party preference indicated on transferred ballots is counted but at a diminishing percentage of a whole vote. Several rounds of counting occur before all seats in a constituency are filled. A voter should use her "whole vote" by ranking her preferences all the way down the ballot list. In the Multi-Party Talks, the NIWC pressed hard for an inclusive system of "eighteen constituencies each with six seats, with an additional ten seats allocated in proportion to the parties' first preference votes [across] Northern Ireland as a whole." Only Sinn Féin supported the NIWC's more inclusive electoral vision in the peace talks. Instead, the 108-seat Assembly is made up of eighteen six-member constituencies. See Fearon, *Women's Work*, 115. Under this system, the Ulster Democratic Party (UDP), a small but important party linked to loyalist paramilitaries, was unable to win a seat in the Assembly. It had been an important voice in the Multi-Party Talks.

36. Fearon, *Women's Work*, 136.

37. It was not until November 2000 that the NIWC officially adopted a party stand on the abortion issue. But in doing so, it moved the issue away from the narrow "pro-life versus pro-abortion" terms of debate prevalent in Northern Ireland by reframing it in terms of the broader question of reproductive health. Abortion was debated in the Assembly in June 2000 after the Democratic Unionist Party (DUP) put forward a motion to continue to prevent the extension of the UK's 1967 abortion legislation to Northern Ireland. This was seen as a move to put the Women's Coalition on the spot and also to force open divisions in largely Catholic SF and SDLP about the abortion prohibition. The NIWC introduced an amendment that would have referred the issue, along with the larger issue of reproductive health, to the Assembly's Health Committee for study; however, its amendment failed. Surprisingly, the UUP's Joan Carson, rose to speak eloquently in favor of a woman's right to choose, and pointedly asked the men in the Assembly when had they ever had to make a decision about pregnancy. The DUP's motion was passed. However, the debate revealed divisions within unionism on this issue as well.

38. After the 1981 Hunger Strike in which ten republican prisoners starved themselves to death in Long Kesh prison for the right to be recognized as political prisoners, the republican movement began to rethink its strategy of boycotting electoral politics in Northern Ireland. The most famous of the hunger strikers, Bobby Sands, had surprised many when he won a seat to the Westminster parliament shortly before his death. The hunger strike itself—its causes and the way Margaret Thatcher's government had handled it—was centrally important in galvanizing republican and nationalist opinion about the illegitimacy of direct rule. Soon thereafter, leading republicans, particularly Gerry Adams, saw the strength of anti-British opinion as an opportunity to develop a new political strategy for the republican movement. This new strategy included building a stronger party, Sinn Féin, that would eventually compete in elections both north and south of the border. By the mid-1980s, Adams had persuaded the republican leadership to give this new strategy a chance alongside the Provisional IRA's military strategy. By this time, both

republicans and the British government recognized that the conflict had reached a mutually hurting stalemate, thus opening the door to the British-Irish Agreement and the beginning of the present peace process.

39. The Alliance Party floated an idea in January 1999 that it and the NIWC join forces to elect a candidate to the third open seat for the European Parliament elections in June 1999. This idea indicates the Alliance Party's interest in harnessing the NIWC's grassroots campaigning energy. The NIWC passed.

40. Pauline Armitage, telephone conversation with Mary K. Meyer, 12 or 13 January 1999.

41. Rhonda Paisley, "Feminism, Unionism, and 'The Brotherhood,'" *Irish Reporter* 8, 4 (1992): 32–33.

42. Northern Ireland Forum for Political Dialogue, *Record of Debates,* No. 38 (Friday, 11 July 1997) (Belfast: Castle Buildings, Stormont), 61.

43. At the Forum talks, McWilliams and Sagar withstood childish and hostile insults from the DUP (and like-minded United Kingdom Unionist party) members, including mooing sounds from Ian Paisley Jr. The NIWC eventually introduced a motion to incorporate into the Forum the same anti-sexual harassment rules used in business and the civil service. The DUP got nervous, sent contacts to talk to NIWC members, and ended up filibustering for a full day when the motion was scheduled for debate. Finally, at the end of the day's session, the DUP introduced a motion that diluted and effectively deleted the NIWC motion. DUP behavior improved a bit, but its public disrespect for the NIWC (for example, talking to each other while one of the Women's Coalition's representatives is speaking) has continued. In fairness, the DUP shows similar disrespect (such as, coughing, blowing noses loudly, clearing throats, giggling, and so on) when speakers from other parties, particularly Sinn Féin, have the floor.

44. Tactical voting could prevent a certain party from winning a seat. Under the single transferable voting system, some DUP supporters would sooner vote for *any* party other than Sinn Féin, the SDLP, or even pro-Agreement unionists. Given that DUP is officially "anti-Agreement," many of its voters see the UUP as having sold out unionism through the Good Friday Agreement and might even deny their vote to pro-Agreement UUP (or PUP) candidates. In constituencies where large pro-Agreement parties have a good chance of winning a seat, it would be in the interest of a staunch DUP voter to vote for the DUP as her first preference and then for a smaller party like the NIWC as her second or third preference. Some voters fail to rank all the parties listed on the ballot, thus wasting a part of their vote.

45. This resulted in the exclusion from the Assembly of the Ulster Democratic Party, linked to the loyalist paramilitary organizations UDA/UFF (Ulster Defense Association/Ulster Fighting Force) and LVF (Loyalist Volunteer Force), for lack of sufficient votes. The exclusion of the UDP has led to concerns about the stability of the loyalist paramilitaries' cease-fire. Loyalist violence (punishment beatings, sectarian shootings, and firebombings) linked to the LVF and other loyalist paramilitaries increased in January 1999, and an open feud developed in the Portadown area between the LVF and the UVF (Ulster Volunteer Force). By summer 2000, loyalist violence had spread to Belfast and other areas, contributing to serious concerns about the stability of the loyalist cease-fires—not to mention that of the peace process.

46. In December 2000, SDLP leader John Hume resigned his seat in the Assembly and was replaced by Anne Courtney, the party's leader on Derry City Council. This brought the number of women in the Assembly to fifteen.

47. An attempt to form an Assembly executive occurred on 15 July 1999; however a UUP boycott of the proceedings and the refusal of other unionist parties to nominate ministers resulted in the collapse of the effort in less than an hour. Only the SDLP and SF appointed ministers to the hapless ten-member executive. Bairbre de Brún of SF was appointed minister of enterprise, trade and investment. Brid Rodgers of SDLP received the higher and further education, training and employment portfolio. Following this, the Assembly was suspended, sending the entire peace process into a critical stalemate that lasted until late November 1999 (see further discussion on pages 197–98).

48. The DUP has remained firmly in the "No" camp and continues to work to undermine the Good Friday Agreement and its institutions.

49. Three ministries each went to the UUP and the SDLP; two ministries each went to the DUP and SF. Significantly, two women took ministerial posts: Brid Rodgers (SDLP) took up the Agriculture portfolio; Bairbre de Brún (SF) took up Health. A committee structure was also set up to provide oversight of the new ministries. The NIWC, PUP, Alliance, and the Workers Party took seats distributed across the ten oversight committees and formed a coalition to share information with each other concerning committee and ministerial business.

50. Trimble faced growing pressure from hardliners within his party who were impatient that IRA decommissioning had not started following the fragile deal. Unionist impatience was further stretched following the British government's decision in December 1999 to accept most of the recommendations of the Patten Commission Report on Policing in Northern Ireland. The report envisions both structural and philosophical reforms of the Royal Ulster Constabulary (RUC). This included a change of name and insignia, a significant reduction in size, and a significant increase in the percentage of Catholics serving in the force. Moreover, the report embraces a shift to "community policing" and reforming Northern Ireland's police "force" to a police "service." The RUC, created at the time of Partition (1921), has a long history of close ties to the unionist parties and to the Orange Order; as such, it has had very little legitimacy in the eyes of many nationalists, particularly since the Troubles erupted in the late 1960s. Following the Good Friday Agreement, republicans organized a strongly vocal campaign to "disband the RUC." Unionists reacted strongly against the Patten Commission report, forcing the British government to water down a number of its recommendations in legislation to implement the reform. This legislation has become a serious new source of conflict between unionists and nationalists.

51. At the end of January 2000 the Independent International Commission on Decommissioning (IICD) reported that no IRA decommissioning of arms had yet occurred, nor had the IRA furnished any timetable for decommissioning. The report also indicated that the Commission believed the IRA was still committed to the peace process, stating it was "particularly significant" that the IRA would consider how to put its arms and explosives beyond use in the context of the Good Friday Agreement. This was not enough to reassure unionists and the British Government.

Despite a last-minute visit on 11 February by republicans to General John de Chastelain, chair of the IICD, the British government suspended the Northern Ireland Executive and the Assembly soon thereafter, just 72 days after the Executive had been formed.

52. "Making the Crucial Leap to Mutual Trust," *Irish Times,* 8 May 2000. (http://www.ireland.com); Adrian Guelke, "Goodbye To All That," *Fortnight* (Belfast) 386 (June 2000): 10–11.

53. This clever turn of phrase belongs to the Women's Coalition.

54. Václav Havel, "A Sense of the Transcendent," in *The Art of the Impossible: Politics as Morality in Practice,* eds. Václav Havel and Paul Wilson (New York: Alfred A. Knopf, 1997), 202.

55. Fearon and McWilliams, "The Good Friday Agreement," 1260.

56. Kate Fearon (lecture delivered to the Eckerd College Study Group on the Northern Ireland Peace Process, Institute of Irish Studies, Queens University Belfast, Northern Ireland, 20 January 2000).

57. Róisín Ingle, "Meeting of All Pro-Agreement Parties Urged," *Irish Times* (http://www.ireland.com) 20 November 2000.

Chapter 10

Let Freedom Ring

Recharging and Consolidating "Inside the Beltway" Activism

Abigail Abrash

Amid a towering Goddess of Democracy and a sea of television cameras, a crowd of nearly five thousand people were chanting, "Let freedom ring." In the background, an enormous Tibetan drum was beating, and prayer flags and protest banners were flying. Addressing the crowd, Chinese and Tibetan former prisoners of conscience joined U.S. human rights activist Kerry Kennedy Cuomo, aspiring Republican Party presidential candidate and social conservative Gary Bauer, Hollywood actor Richard Gere, and members of the U.S. Congress from both major political parties to call for an end to human rights violations in China and Tibet.

The 29 October 1997 rally—the culmination of eight weeks of organizing—was sponsored and supported by a "strange bedfellows" coalition of human rights and environmental organizations, Chinese and Tibetan support groups, U.S. labor unions, and religious groups. This remarkably diverse coalition had united behind a single message calling on the U.S. and Chinese governments to uphold freedom of expression, religion, and association in China and Tibet. Across the street from the demonstration, U.S. President Bill Clinton was giving a twenty-one gun, red-carpet welcome to Jiang Zemin, president of the People's Republic of China (PRC). Jiang's White House visit was the first by any Chinese leader since June 1989, when the Chinese government had ordered a brutal crackdown on thousands of peaceful Chinese civilians demonstrating in Beijing's Tiananmen Square.[1]

As a primary organizer of the rally, what most inspired me about this intense experience was the power that diverse communities unleashed by coming together in support of a single cause. The rally and its companion campaigns achieved a greater impact than the sum of their parts. The gains and benefits we attained—individually and as a bloc—continue to resonate today.

This chapter examines how the Let Freedom Ring (LFR) coalition emerged, what we accomplished, and how we altered the nature of international human rights activism by Washington-based nongovernmental institutions. I also discuss how various actors viewed the coalition. Finally, I consider if and how this mini-movement—this targeted expression of community power—can be said to demonstrate a "feminist approach."

In Solidarity

The LFR coalition began in early September 1997 with a commitment by five principal sponsoring organizations: the Robert F. Kennedy Memorial Center for Human Rights, Amnesty International USA, the International Campaign for Tibet, Human Rights in China, and the Greater Washington Network for Chinese Democracy. What motivated my colleagues and me to organize the campaign and rally was a deep desire to protest human rights violations in China and Tibet, and to do so in a high-impact, high-profile way. Our decision came after nearly five years of seeking to strengthen the Clinton administration's policy responses to continuing Chinese government repression in China and Tibet. Our earlier conciliatory, "semi-insider" efforts, based on access to White House, State Department, and National Security Council officials, had yielded minimal results.

As a candidate, Bill Clinton had promised to "use [America's] extensive economic and diplomatic leverage to increase material incentives to democratize and to raise the costs for those who don't." He criticized the incumbent administration for "extending [most-favored-nation] trade status to the PRC before it achieved documented progress on human rights," contending that "we should not reward China with improved trade status when it has continued to trade goods made by prison labor and has failed to make sufficient progress on human rights." Clinton pledged that, as president, he would "condition favorable trade terms with repressive regimes—such as China's Communist regime—on respect for human rights, political liberalization, and responsible international conduct."[2]

In a May 1993 executive order regarding extension of most-favored-nation (MFN) trade status to China, President Clinton required that the U.S. Secretary of State submit findings to his office by 3 June 1994 regarding China's progress in meeting the human rights conditions specified in the executive order. Yet despite clear evidence that the Chinese government continued to violate the emigration and forced labor provisions[3] of the order and had not made "overall, significant progress" with respect to the five additional human rights provisions,[4] Clinton opted in May 1994 to renew China's MFN status.[5] At the same time, he outlined a five-point plan for U.S.

foreign policy initiatives to promote human rights improvements in China and Tibet.[6]

More than three years later little had changed despite dozens of meetings with U.S. government officials, reports, letters, media announcements, and press conferences encouraging a stronger U.S. policy response. Thousands of Chinese prisoners of conscience remained behind bars, including high-profile dissidents such as Wei Jingsheng and Wang Dan.[7] The Clinton administration's promise to create a code of conduct for U.S. multinationals operating inside China had been watered down into a statement of global, voluntary business principles, and neither the United States nor China was enforcing a bilateral memorandum of understanding banning the importation of products made by Chinese prison labor. The administration had not established a proposed interagency task force on China to incorporate human rights considerations into all aspects of U.S. policy, and it had downgraded pursuit of a UN Commission on Human Rights (UNCHR) resolution criticizing the Chinese government's human rights violations.[8] Indeed, by the administration's own assessment, the Chinese government's crackdown on basic human rights was worsening: "All public dissent against the party and government was effectively silenced by intimidation, exile, the imposition of prison terms, administrative detention or house arrest. No dissidents were known to be active at year's end."[9] The human rights violations that we were protesting included arbitrary detention, torture and ill-treatment of prisoners, and severe restrictions on freedom of expression and association.

The rally was intended as an act of solidarity with the people of China and Tibet. As individuals living in the United States and as representatives of organizations comparatively free of government control, we were seeking to exercise our rights to freedom of expression, association, and assembly under conditions less oppressive than those faced by individuals living in China and Tibet. We would take advantage of our relative freedom to protest the Chinese government's abuses—and U.S. government complicity in them—in a way that the Chinese and Tibetans could not.[10]

The rally organizers adopted the slogan "Let Freedom Ring" to draw a sharp contrast between Chinese government practices and Jiang's intention to use his visit to improve China's image "by capitalizing on American symbols of democracy."[11] Some of the venues that Jiang would visit—such as the Liberty Bell and Independence Hall in Philadelphia, colonial Williamsburg, and Boston—are sites that most (non-Native) Americans equate with freedom and democracy:[12] principles enshrined in the constitutions of the United States and its first states, and associated with America's struggle for independence.

At the same time, the rally's focus on freedom of expression, religion, and association was broad enough to allow those representing a diversity of perspectives to participate. This was not a rally specifically in support of the rights of workers in China, of Tibetan rights to culture and religion, of Chinese citizens' pro-democracy activities, of the rights of minority groups such as the Uighurs living in China, of Taiwanese independence aspirations, of Chinese Christians' right to pursue their faiths independently of the Chinese government, or of the right to a healthy environment for all people living in China and Tibet. And yet, by placing the focus on these three internationally recognized rights, the LFR campaign united a wide array of nongovernmental organizations and concerned citizens behind a general human rights message and framework, while leaving space for each to protest specific human rights violations.

For the Robert F. Kennedy Memorial Center for Human Rights (RFK Center), one specific goal was the release from prison of noted Chinese pro-democracy dissident Wei Jingsheng, who had received the Robert F. Kennedy Human Rights Award in 1994. Other coalition members pursued different individual goals. For the International Campaign for Tibet (ICT), getting Beijing first to release eight-year-old Gedhun Choekyi Nyima, the eleventh Panchen Lama, and Ngawang Choepel, a Middlebury College ethnomusicologist and Fulbright Scholar, and second to begin talks with His Holiness the Dalai Lama were paramount objectives. ICT was also pressing for the appointment of the State Department Special Coordinator for Tibet mandated months earlier by the U.S. Congress. For Gary Bauer, executive director of the Family Research Council and candidate for the 2000 Republican presidential nomination, the rally was an opportunity to highlight his foreign policy positions and support for freedom of religion.

When "Professional" Activists Become Fed Up

For me, personally, and for many of my colleagues, the decision to organize a high-profile public demonstration represented a significant shift in our tactics. Until the rally, the organization for which I worked, the RFK Center, typically had employed a "paper and meetings" approach to seeking changes in U.S. foreign policy and in China's human rights practices. Since 1989 the RFK Center had written letters of petition and protest to the Chinese government urging prisoner releases, respect for basic civil and political rights, and rights-based law reform. Using our consultative status with the UN Economic and Social Council, we had also brought our concerns about human rights in China and Tibet to annual sessions of the UN Commission on Human Rights in Geneva. Every year without fail, we sponsored candlelight vigils and other demonstrations in front of the Chinese embassy in Washington to mark the anniversary of the Tiananmen Square massacre. These demonstrations were relatively small-scale, attracting up to one hundred or so protestors and little media attention.

The Center also had engaged in countless meetings with State Department and National Security Council staff urging stronger policy measures by the Clinton administration. In 1994, following Clinton's controversial renewal of China's most-favored-nation trade status, RFK Center Director Kerry Kennedy Cuomo had joined with directors of Amnesty International and the Lawyers Committee for Human Rights for a round of meetings with top Clinton administration officials. In discussions with Commerce Secretary Ron Brown, National Security Advisor Anthony Lake, and others, the three human rights organizations pressed for a more coordinated U.S. approach to promoting human rights through improved interdepartmental planning and policy development. Its access to administration officials as well as the Center's overall nonconfrontational advocacy style identified it as a "reasonable" NGO.[13]

In the run-up to the October summit, the RFK Center moved into new territory, exploring the use of more confrontational tactics, such as nonviolent civil disobedience. By becoming the primary coordinator of a major public demonstration, the RFK Center adopted a tactic that few other mainstream U.S.-based international human rights NGOs have pursued.[14]

After years of frustratingly slow progress and plenty of major setbacks, many of us in the Washington human rights community who focused on China were ready for a change. Our decision to hold a major public event to support Chinese and Tibetan activists was an explicit recognition of the limits to "insider" strategies. Our rally would be an energized popular gathering, in contrast to the formal toasts and speeches of praise between two governments. If the Clinton administration was going to hold summit-level talks with Jiang behind closed doors, then we would have an open airing of views outdoors across the street in Lafayette Park. If the White House was going to honor the Chinese government's repressive regime with a state dinner, then LFR coalition members would have their own party for those made stateless by the Chinese regime's occupation of Tibet.[15]

We also wanted to show that we were not alone in our protest against the Chinese government's repression and the U.S. government's complicity. The decision to hold a major public rally was a determined decision to shift gears to a grassroots, "outsider" strategy. It was based on the belief that thousands of other people in the United States shared our concerns. Indeed, according to a 1 May 1997 *Wall Street Journal*/NBC/Hart and Teeter poll, Americans believed by more than a two-to-one margin that the Chinese government should improve its human rights practices or lose its MFN trade status with the United States.

The rally—and the human rights campaign that preceded it—were also meant to place pressure on the administration to use the U.S.–China summit itself to achieve concrete improvements in the Chinese government's human rights practices and policies. Members of the U.S. Congress supported this goal. In late September 1997, a bipartisan group of senators introduced a resolution calling for significant progress toward improving human rights conditions in China and Tibet as a precondition for Jiang's visit. Introducing the resolution, Senator Russell Feingold (D-Wis.) noted that its intent was not to cancel discussions between the U.S. and Chinese leaders, but to advocate engagement at an appropriate level given China's poor human rights record. Stating that he would not object to working-level meetings between Clinton and Jiang, Feingold added that "the pomp and ceremony of a state-level visit is inappropriate given the current human rights situation in China."[16]

At the same time, members of the U.S. House of Representatives Committee on International Relations approved a bill denying U.S. visas to Chinese officials who had engaged in religious or political oppression. The committee also recommended a one-third increase in Congressionally appropriated funds for U.S. government-supported Radio Free Asia.[17] More significantly, on 30 September, the House passed a bill establishing a system of preferences for corporations that wanted U.S. Export-Import Bank support. This amendment to a bill reauthorizing the bank itself mandated that preference for assistance should be given to U.S. and Chinese corporations that had adopted and adhered to a code of conduct consistent with internationally recognized human and worker rights. These rights included providing a safe and healthy workplace, ensuring fair employment and avoiding child and forced labor, avoiding discrimination based on religion, complying with all environmental laws, and respecting free expression. The proposal also provided the Export-Import Bank with a checklist of procedures to help monitor corporate compliance as well as to report, discipline, and correct noncompliance.

In fact, a handful of large U.S.-based multinational corporations operating in China were benefitting from the Export-Import Bank's billions of dollars in corporate subsidies. During the period from 1992 to 1997, an average of 10.6 percent of all the bank's loans, grants, and guarantees went for business operations in China. Chief among the recipients of this U.S. taxpayer largesse were the Boeing Company, McDonnell Douglas Corporation, Westinghouse Electric Corporation, and Lucent Technologies. At the same time, these corporations led lobbying efforts to defeat the linking of human rights concerns to U.S. trade relations with China.

In announcing passage of the Export-Import Bank bill amendment, Rep. Lane Evans (D-Ill.) stated that the U.S.'s "China policy of 'constructive engagement' should not be merely a trickle-down initiative. It should be a policy that actively fosters human rights and democracy by encouraging global corporate responsibility." Evans also emphasized the fact that public funds—drawn from U.S. taxpayers—were at issue. "Every year, we provide multinationals with billions of taxpayer dollars so that they can break into the Chinese market," he said. "We should also ensure that the American taxpayer's [sic] hard-earned money is not contributing to the repression of democracy and human rights."[18]

Come Together

By the day of the rally, the LFR coalition had expanded from the original five sponsors to thirty-one groups with a collective membership of more than fourteen million Americans. This rapid growth reflected a relative lack of internal political disruptions. Some of the key sponsoring and supporting organizations had worked together on earlier projects and, because of consistency in staffing, most of the same individuals had already developed cooperative and collaborative working relationships. Some of our previous work together had centered on campaigns for the release of prisoners, advocacy regarding MFN trade status for China, and public-awareness-raising activities and solidarity work before, during, and after the UN Fourth World Conference on Women held in Beijing. All of our past work made the coming together of the LFR coalition much simpler.

I and my colleagues at the RFK Center had earned reputations as fair partners who embraced coalition work. The RFK Center itself was nonthreatening: it did not compete for funding from the sources upon which other organizations relied, and its program agenda was not seen as radical. Our approach to coalition-building was based on the principle of inclusivity. Because the primary goal of the rally was to demonstrate widespread concern about China's human rights practices and U.S. policy, we wanted to include as broad an array of organizations as possible. The fundamental test would be whether each potential cosponsor could support the LFR message without demanding an explicit focus on its own agenda.

Even within this low-bar framework, a significant challenge did arise: whether pro-independence Taiwanese organizations should participate. Amnesty International's mandate prevents it from taking a position on self-determination. Because of this, Amnesty International USA (AIUSA) objected to the inclusion of the Coalition for Taiwan Independence (CTI), ultimately forcing CTI to withdraw. The International Campaign for Tibet intervened formally on behalf of CTI, expressing its dismay that AIUSA had determined that CTI's involvement in the rally would compromise AIUSA. In a letter to AIUSA Executive Director Bill Schulz, ICT Director John Ackerly wrote, "[ICT] would have preferred that the organizing sponsors base their decision [about organizational sponsorship] on international human rights covenants which include the right to self-determination as an inalienable human right, rather than on Amnesty's in-house guidelines."[19]

Echo Lin of the Formosan Association for Public Affairs had participated in rally planning on behalf of CTI. She also expressed her concern at the decision to exclude CTI as an official sponsor: "The decision made by AI headquarters in London to exclude the Taiwanese group may leave the Chinese government an impression that China can dictate the operations of the other international organizations." Citing the Chinese government's relentless efforts to exclude Taiwanese government and civil society groups from international fora, Ms. Lin wrote, "Though we knew that there would be protest of our rally from the Chinese officials, we wished that we could defend our position with the understanding from these groups which represent universal human rights."[20]

Despite its best efforts at inclusivity, the LFR coalition failed to support CTI, and had thereby "self-policed" itself into condoning the Chinese government's rejection of an independent Taiwan. In hindsight, it would have strengthened the movement for human rights in China and worldwide if the coalition had more effectively challenged Amnesty International's position and had successfully mediated the inclusion of both organizations within its ranks.

Building Power

In addition to the core LFR coalition in Washington, D.C., affiliated coalitions evolved in the other cities that Jiang would visit: Honolulu, Williamsburg, Boston, Philadelphia, New York, and Los Angeles. AIUSA and ICT, the LFR-sponsoring organizations with national memberships, galvanized grassroots support to ensure that Jiang would face demonstrations at all stops on his United States tour. This decentralized, collaboratively coordinated national structure allowed the LFR to achieve a greater impact than would have been achieved by the D.C. rally alone. Each demonstration contributed momentum toward the next, keeping the media focused on human rights concerns. In the other cities also, the LFR banner was one around which diverse groups and local activists could unite. Activists designed protests that reflected and drew upon the strengths of their particular locales. At Jiang's first stop, Hawaii, local organizers held an "Aloha Welcome to Your Conscience" event at which they greeted Jiang with a traditional Hawaiian lei whose "flowers" were paper links constructed from strips cut from the Universal Declaration of Human Rights. In Boston, where Jiang addressed Harvard University faculty and students, local organizers turned out an estimated six thousand demonstrators. And in Philadelphia, Buddhist monks carried out a ritual cleansing of the Liberty Bell after Jiang's visit to the site.

Media Darlings, "Isolationists," "Terrorists"

From a media perspective, the LFR coalition offered excellent "copy." Journalists contacted coalition members for commentary and for background information about human rights conditions. The coalition's diversity was also a focus of extensive reporting. The media grasped the significance of the coalition and rally, correctly interpreting it as a sign of deep and widespread dissatisfaction amongst Americans with the administration's policies, and of moral outrage over China's brutality against its own citizens and against Tibet's.[21]

Dozens of media outlets covered the coalition's efforts, and the coalition received widespread positive coverage across the United States and abroad.[22] Spotlighting the central issue of human rights during the Clinton-Jiang summit, commentators challenged the administration's defense of its China policy. *Los Angeles Times* columnist Jim Mann put it succinctly, "When it comes to China, the Clinton Administration has developed its own theory of evolution. It is an almost religious belief that democracy will come to the world's most populous country after it gets richer. The theory was put on display in a congressional hearing one day last week in a way that underscored the strengths, weaknesses and dangers of the administration's approach."[23] Mann contrasted the U.S.'s China policy with previous U.S. policies toward South Korea and Taiwan, which were cited by the Clinton administration as models of its evolutionary democracy theory. Unlike China, Mann noted, Taiwan and South Korea were both aligned with the United States and were heavily dependent upon the United States for their security. China, by contrast, was an independent military power. Mann also cited the example of Singapore, another Asian country in which economic prosperity has not led to greater political freedom.

The intense media coverage did reach its target: President Clinton. At a Washington, D.C., speech on 24 October, Clinton sought to counter criticisms that his administration had weakened its stance against human rights violations by the Chinese government. He argued that cooperation rather than confrontation with China did not mean that the administration was abandoning its attention to human rights issues, suggesting that the debate within the United States about how to address human rights concerns in

China and Tibet was essentially a disagreement about means, not ends. He said that China was at a turning point between becoming "open and nonaggressive" or "inward and confrontational," and that "isolating" Chinese authorities because of human rights concerns would be "unworkable, counterproductive, and potentially dangerous."[24]

Human rights dominated Clinton's speech. According to administration aides, the speech was intended to persuade the U.S. public to take a broad view of the U.S. relationship with China, a relationship that should not be "held hostage to one issue." Clearly the coalition was hitting its mark. The fact that the White House felt compelled to devote the largest part of the President's major foreign policy address on U.S.–China relations to a justification of the U.S. approach to human rights concerns suggested that the administration was feeling the pressure generated by the coalition's organizing. However, Clinton's argument against isolating China over human rights concerns ignored the primary critique of coalition members: that the administration had failed to adopt effective policy tools—whether carrots or sticks—to encourage an improvement in the Chinese government's human rights practices. No member of the coalition was arguing that issues such as military security and trade were unimportant. We were arguing that the administration's policy of "constructive engagement"—and its resort to general statements of support for those seeking to exercise their civil liberties—had not achieved real results. Many in the coalition were not opposed to U.S. engagement with the Chinese leadership; we were concerned with the type of interactions and policy tools the Clinton administration employed. Isolationist charges directed at the coalition by the administration and by U.S.-based multinational corporations seeking to reap enormous profits from their business interests in China[25] apparently were attempts to marginalize the coalition's concerns by misrepresenting its positions in extremist terms.

At the same time, Chinese officials, worried about the LFR rally and related protests, adopted similarly exaggerated rhetoric. Some six months before the summit, concerns about public demonstrations against China's human rights practices had dominated the agenda of top-level Chinese officials during a preparatory visit to the United States.[26] In mid-October, authorities in Beijing urged the U.S. government to reign in demonstrators. One Chinese embassy official in Washington referred to protesters as "terrorists." Chinese government spokesman Shen Guofang told media that "The Chinese side will not interfere in any way. But we hope that the U.S. side will take a few steps to ensure that President Jiang's state visit goes smoothly."[27]

LFR coalition members were realistic about the impact the rally and previous human rights campaigns would have in China. We did not expect the official Chinese media to provide any coverage of LFR protest events. We did intend, however, to be seen and heard by Jiang Zemin, Foreign Minister Qian Qichen, and the legion of Chinese officials who would be part of the summit entourage. In the end, the subject of human rights reportedly figured prominently in the summit talks, and it indeed spilled over into the joint White House press conference Clinton and Jiang held following the meetings. During the press conference, which was broadcast live internationally on CNN, President Clinton commented on the Tiananmen Square crackdown and China's human rights record in general stating: "On so many issues, China is on the right side of history, and we welcome it. But on this issue, we believe the policy of the Chinese government is on the wrong side of history," adding that freedom of dissent and religious freedom were a birthright of "people everywhere."[28]

Celebrating Victory

What did the LFR coalition achieve?

The intense public focus on human rights issues and U.S. China policy spearheaded by the LFR led to several important developments: the Clinton administration's appointment, on 31 October 1997, of State Department Director of Policy Planning Greg Craig as U.S. Special Coordinator for Tibetan Issues;[29] the Chinese government's release on medical parole of leading Chinese dissident Wei Jingsheng;[30] and the Chinese government's signing of the International Covenant on Economic, Social and Cultural Rights.

The clearest victory achieved by the coalition was the widespread media coverage that made human rights, rather than trade, security, or other issues, the primary focus of Jiang's visit. This coverage educated the public and raised awareness in the United States about human rights issues in China and Tibet, and the media spotlight shone on us long enough to get our messages out to an international audience as well. The coalition and rally highlighted the activities of the sponsoring organizations for the media and public. For the main sponsoring organizations, the rally provided a high-profile platform for allies in the Congress and the U.S. labor movement. We put on an impressive show that far surpassed previous public gatherings in support of international human rights issues, and building the coalition significantly strengthened ties amongst the participating organizations and cemented already good working relationships.

The rally and the organizing leading up to it also offered all of us what is too often a rare commodity in Washington-based advocacy: fun.[31] Providing an opportunity to work proactively on our own project and agenda, the rally stood in stark contrast to our usual activities most often undertaken in reaction to and critical of government policy. Although we were still focused on criticizing government action—that is, human rights violations in China and

Tibet, and U.S. policy toward China—our tactics were separate from the actors we were protesting. We were not attempting to meet with Jiang Zemin or President Clinton. We were not attempting to "dialogue." We were expressing our outrage—in our own way and on our own ground.

In planning for the Jiang rally, I had my first introduction to street theater and nonviolent direct action. Recognizing both the effectiveness of these tactics and the strength of the diverse coalition that we had built—the LFR coalition represented one of the first seeds that would grow into the broad coalition of movements protesting the World Trade Organization in Seattle in November 1999—led us to identify the need for a training program. Social justice activists of all stripes need to acquire and master these powerful tools.

Working with the Ruckus Society, the RFK Center sponsored the first Human Rights Action Camp in June 1998. Participants included international environmental lawyers, student activists, human rights advocates from Burma, Nigeria, Indonesia, and Kenya, and an array of U.S.-based grassroots social justice and environmental activists. Participants put their new skills to use immediately: a day after the camp ended and on the eve of President Clinton's summit visit to China, they demonstrated and hung a banner across the street from the Chinese embassy in Washington. The banner read: "Clinton, Jiang: Free Tibet before Free Trade." The interpersonal and institutional relationships established at the Action Camp also led to the first defeat of a proposed World Bank loan to China. Employing an effective mix of nonviolent direct action tactics and "paper and meetings" advocacy, environmental lawyers and Tibet supporters worked together to block a $160 million loan that would have funded large-scale population transfers of Han Chinese into historically Tibetan territory.

The work that we did on U.S.–China policy also represented a cutting-edge analysis of the role of capitalist institutions by a human rights organization. We offered a critique of how multinational corporations' political influence had allowed their narrow economic interests to trump the U.S. government's obligation to uphold international human rights standards in China. In a variety of ways, then—from coalition building to substantive analysis—the LFR coalition broke new ground in the way that public-interest advocates conceptualized and practiced human rights advocacy inside the Beltway.

A Feminist Approach?

The LFR coalition did not articulate an explicitly feminist approach. Most of the organizations involved in the coalition lacked a clear feminist viewpoint, both in how they approached their work and in their internal organizational cultures. Indeed, even if feminism is understood only as "the principle that women should have political, economic, and social rights equal to those of men,"[32] then the U.S. human rights community in general has an uneven record. While international human rights instruments include specific commitments to gender equality, it is only recently that major U.S.-based human rights organizations have developed programs that focus on this goal. Integrating women's rights as human rights into all aspects of programmatic work continues to be a challenge. As feminist writers Jennifer Baumgardner and Amy Richards point out, "Women within other social justice movements—environmental, peace, *human rights*, and hip-hop, for example—often opt for the term 'humanist.' Although humanism includes men (and especially those who aren't white or otherwise privileged), in reality, it marks a retreat from feminism. Using humanism as a replacement for feminism is also a misuse of the term—theologically, humanism is a rejection of supernaturalism, not an embrace of equality between men and women."[33]

At the time of the LFR coalition and rally, the RFK Center did not embrace an explicitly feminist analysis. Its approach to human rights documentation and advocacy was—on the surface—gender neutral, focusing on the policies and practices of the United States and other governments, the release of (almost exclusively) male prisoners of conscience, and capacity-building for non-U.S. human rights advocates and organizations. The politics of the RFK Center and other LFR coalition members—to the extent that these are articulated—are best characterized as reformist rather than transformational.

In part, the approach of these organizations has developed as a reaction to U.S. foreign policy and the policies and practices of other governments, fields that are traditionally dominated by men and conducted in an implicitly—sometimes explicitly—patriarchal, militaristic manner. U.S. foreign policy, in particular, is intimately entwined with military power and the controlling, grasping masculinisms of international trade, investment, and finance. It is typically a dour field, dominated by somber, ultraserious men (and women!) in suits, prowling the halls of think tanks, and issuing enormous, deadly dull, "truth"-laden reports. The "Washington consensus" of support for "free markets" and democratic representational governance promotes a cosmology in which the standard of measurement is strictly economic and in which value is judged in dollars—not in human dignity.

As feminist author, scholar, and former New Zealand parliamentarian Marilyn Waring has noted, the economic statistics required by the UN System of National Accounts and presented in gross domestic product figures of nation-states do not reflect the well-being of humans or the planet.

They do not reflect social stability based on the functioning of healthy and just institutions.[34] At the same time, human rights issues and analysis traditionally have been viewed as "soft," and they have been dismissed as too "idealistic" to be central to foreign policy. Human rights organizations in the United States generally have implicitly accepted the patriarchal nation-state structure and lack a well-developed critique of neoliberal economic policies, and international capital and arms flows.

The LFR coalition's support for basic civil rights in China and Tibet was grounded in pragmatism and law rather than in moralistic appeals. The coalition broke ground in promoting an improved U.S. human rights policy toward China that included explicit criticism of a U.S.–China policy dominated by U.S. multinational corporations pursuing trade and foreign investment. An element of the LFR coalition that could be viewed as reflecting a feminist approach was the coalition's inclusion of organizations with diverse agendas and politics. In her chapter in this volume about the Northern Ireland Women's Coalition, Mary K. Meyer discusses the concept of "transversalist politics." Quoting NIWC member Monica McWilliams, Meyer describes transversalism as "a process of dialogue across differences, a respect for differences. . . . It leads," she writes, "to 'a different kind of coalition politics' where participants 'respect rather than bury differences'" (see page 184).

Similar transversalist dynamics were at play in the LFR coalition. An underlying principle of inclusivity guided the establishment and development of the coalition. As in the case of the NIWC, this was done for pragmatic and political reasons: simply, that the calls for change would have more impact if many parties, including those with different philosophies and programs, could participate. Perhaps one of the most revealing aspects of LFR transversalism was the acceptance of the socially conservative Family Research Council (FRC) as a coalition member.[35] Although this was controversial, it did not cause any other coalition member to reconsider its participation, standing in stark contrast to the "either them or us, but not both" position that Amnesty International USA took regarding the inclusion of the Coalition for Taiwan Independence. Including the FRC was the result of a conscious decision to prevent institutional differences on social policy from interfering with the pursuit of the coalition's common agenda.

The composition of the LFR coalition, then, reveals individual sponsors whose priorities are, arguably, non- or even anti-feminist. Differences on social policy (involving issues of gender equality and the rights of individuals to be sovereign in matters concerning their own bodies) apparently were of less importance than similarities on overtly political positions regarding the right to self-determination (involving the essentially patriarchal issue of what constitutes a self-governing nation-state and who controls it). In this regard, the LFR coalition yielded to the restrictive parameters of reformist, rather than transformative, politics.

If the coalition had been as committed to a feminist methodology as it was to a reformist program, it would have made a greater effort to include the CTI, refusing to support the political status quo as defined by the Chinese government. Or perhaps, the coalition would have excluded the Family Research Council because of its social policy positions. This possibility raises questions about the existence of tension within a feminist approach to coalition building that is based upon transversalism. When the differing positions of prospective coalition partners relate directly to underpinnings of contemporary Western feminism (for example, fundamental differences regarding "choice" or sexual liberation), is a respect for these differences possible? Is it preferable, in the face of some other oppression, to enter into a "strange bedfellows" alliance? Is a feminist approach equally capable of admitting "the warrior" as well as "the accommodator"? What are the limits to tolerance with respect to differing views? I find myself without clear answers to these questions.

In spite of the LFR coalition's lack of an explicitly feminist approach, I conclude that, overall, the coalition did demonstrate "feminist traits": its decentralized and horizontally and collaboratively coordinated national structure, its inclusivity and embrace of "transversalist politics," and its foundation in universal human rights values. In the face of entrenched power structures—represented by the U.S. and Chinese governments—the LFR coalition provided the vehicle for diverse communities to come together powerfully, effectively, joyfully, and energetically in solidarity with Chinese and Tibetan human rights defenders and victims. In the process, new synergies and relationships were born, new approaches to and models of human rights advocacy learned, and—perhaps most importantly—we all had fun. In these ways, the LFR coalition was a step towards transforming "inside the Beltway" activism, making it more proactive and enjoyable and, therefore, more sustainable. These elements do indeed represent an essential part of a feminist approach to social change.

Notes

The author is indebted to Jim Silk, Anjali Kochar, and Ayesha Rekhi, her colleagues at the Robert F. Kennedy Memorial Center for Human Rights, for their support and friendship. She also offers thanks to Harvard Law School's Human Rights Program, where she was a Visiting Fellow, for providing her with a home during the course of writing this piece. Special thanks to Prof. Henry Steiner, Peter Rosenblum, Susan Sessler, Christine Soh, Yosuke Yotoriyama, Dominic McGoldrick, Catriona Drew,

Leslie Sebba, K. Sritharan, Michael Ikhariale, Catherine LaMagueresse, Daniela Dohmes-Ockenfels, and Mary Cobb for their collegial support and good fellowship.

1. The Chinese military's violent crackdown on peaceful civilian protesters followed seven weeks of nonviolent demonstrations in Beijing in which more than one million people participated. The protesters, led by students, were calling for the elimination of government corruption and nepotism, and the ending of government campaigns against "spiritual pollution" and "bourgeois liberalization." They also appealed for a free press and freedom of speech, increased democratic participation in decision making, and better conditions in universities. For further information on Tiananmen and China's 1989 democracy movement, see, for example, the Special June Fourth Ten-Year Anniversary Issue of *China Rights Forum* (Summer 1999).

2. Quotes from Bill Clinton and Al Gore, *Putting People First: How We Can All Change America* (New York: Times Books, 1992).

3. These mandatory sections of the executive order were based on the Jackson-Vanik Amendment to the Trade Act of 1974 and on a 1992 memorandum of understanding between China and the United States regarding prison labor. Jackson-Vanik states that the president may not extend most-favored-nation trade status to a non-market-economy country if that country imposes more than a nominal tax, levy, fine, fee, or other charge on any citizen as a consequence of that citizen's desire to emigrate. The 1992 memorandum of understanding banned Chinese export of forced-labor-made goods to the United States and provided for U.S. inspection of suspected prison labor sites.

4. These provisions concerned (1) taking steps to adhere to the Universal Declaration of Human Rights, (2) releasing and providing an acceptable accounting of Chinese citizens imprisoned or detained for their nonviolent expression of their political and religious beliefs, (3) ensuring humane treatment of prisoners, (4) protecting Tibet's distinctive religious and cultural heritage, and (5) permitting international radio and television broadcasts into China.

5. For a detailed presentation of the issues and of China's lack of compliance with the executive order and underlying U.S. law, see Abigail Abrash, *China and Most-Favored-Nation Trade Status: A Public Hearing Featuring U.S. Government, Business, Academia and Human Rights Representatives: Summary and Findings* (Washington, D.C.: Robert F. Kennedy Memorial Center for Human Rights and the Washington College of Law, 1994).

6. The plan originally released by the State Department consisted of eleven points, but was publicized as a five-point plan by the President in his announcement on 26 May 1994 of the MFN trade status renewal. These administration commitments included increased broadcasts for Radio Free Asia and the Voice of America, increased support for nongovernmental organizations working on human rights in China, and the development with U.S. business leaders of a voluntary set of principles for business activity in China.

7. Both Wei and Wang had been imprisoned again for their pro-democracy activities. Wei, known for his prominent role in the 1979 Democracy Wall Movement, had already served nearly fifteen years in prison. Wang Dan, number one on the Chinese government's most-wanted list for his role as a Tiananmen Square student leader, had been arrested again in May 1995 for issuing petitions calling for tolerance of dissent, an end to the imprisonment of writers and activists, a reassessment of the events of 4 June 1989, and the establishment of democracy and the rule of law.

8. The administration had made passage of such a resolution a key policy commitment in its 1994 renewal of MFN trade status for China. At the fifty-first session of the UNCHR the following year, the resolution—cosponsored by the European Union and the United States—made an unprecedentedly strong showing. Despite this momentum, the United States failed to pursue vigorously a resolution at subsequent UNCHR sessions. For a detailed discussion, see Beatrice Laroche, "Dodging Scrutiny: China and the U.N. Commission on Human Rights," *China Rights Forum* (Summer 1997): 20–23.

9. U.S. Department of State, *Country Reports on Human Rights Practices: People's Republic of China* (Washington, D.C.: U.S. Government Printing Office, 1997).

10. The Chinese government suppresses dissenting opinions and has detained individuals for exercising their rights to freedom of association and expression. Although the Chinese constitution guarantees freedom of association and assembly, national regulations severely limit association and give the authorities absolute discretion to deny applications for public gatherings or demonstrations.

For more information about human rights conditions in China and Tibet in the mid-1990s, see "China Human Rights Fact Sheet," in *Going to Beijing with Open Eyes: China's Human Rights Situation and the U.N. Fourth World Conference on Women, Beijing, September 1995,* resource book for participants, prepared and published by Amnesty International USA (Washington Office), Human Rights in China, the International Human Rights Law Group, the International Campaign for Tibet and the Robert F. Kennedy Memorial Center for Human Rights, Washington, D.C., March 1995.

11. See Jack Kelley, "Protesters Prepare for Chinese Leader's Visit; China Officials Are Concerned about Images," *USA Today,* 17 October 1997, 8A. Also, Richard Halloran, "Jiang Plans Imperial Procession into the International Spotlight," *Washington Times,* 13 October 1997.

12. Sites associated with the American Revolution perhaps do not evoke notions of freedom or respect for basic rights for Native Americans. The consolidation of the United States of America—as a nation-state equipped with arms, military forces, and the "legal" power to acquire land and open it to non-Native settlers—has led to the dispossession and disempowerment of Native communities throughout North America.

13. The Center was reformist in its approach to social change. Its programs generally focused on gaining the release of individual prisoners of conscience, Washington-based "paper and meetings" advocacy, and documenting and reporting on civil and political rights violations by state actors. For a critical analysis of the RFK Center and other mainstream U.S. human rights groups, see Makau wa Mutua, "The Ideology of Human Rights," *Virginia Journal of International Law* 36 (1996): 589.

14. For example, Human Rights Watch, the Lawyers Committee for Human Rights, and the International Human Rights Law Group publish reports which are based on rigorous documentation of human rights violations and that generally incorporate a legal analysis and argument based on international human rights law. These organizations also engage in behind-the-scenes advocacy, relying on access to government officials. While the Law Group signed on as an LFR rally supporter, the Lawyers Committee and Human Rights Watch declined invitations to participate, indicating that their organizations' tactics do not include public protest, civil disobedience, or nonviolent direct action.

15. Key coalition member ICT hosted a "stateless dinner" at the Hotel Washington, across the street from the White House and the U.S. Treasury Department. The theme, an obvious contrast to the White House gathering taking place at the same time, was meant to emphasize the fact of Tibetans' statelessness; more than 250,000 Tibetan refugees—including His Holiness the Dalai Lama—live as stateless persons in Dharamsala, India, and elsewhere.

16. Democratic Party Senator Russ Feingold of Wisconsin introduced the resolution, cosponsored by Republican Party Senators Spencer Abraham of Michigan and Jesse Helms of North Carolina. It called for the release of political prisoners and other "significant progress towards improving human rights conditions in China and Tibet." See, "Feingold Introduces Resolution Calling for Human Rights Improvements in China as a Prerequisite to Planned State Visit," *News from U.S. Senator Russ Feingold,* 25 September 1997.

17. See, David Stout, "House Panel Takes a Slap at Clinton over China," *New York Times,* 1 October 1997, A1.

18. "House Approves Evans Amendment to Ex-Im Bank Reauthorization on China Trade; Gives Preference to Firms Whose Activities Respect Human, Worker Rights; Avoid Child Labor Abuses, Religious Discrimination," *News,* office of Congressman Lane Evans, 30 September 1997.

19. Letter from John Ackerly to William Schulz, 9 October 1997.

20. Letter from Echo Lin to Abigail Abrash, 10 October 1997.

21. Tibet is not considered an occupied area so it does not have "citizens."

22. See, for example, Norman Kempster, "Chinese Leader's Visit to U.S. Stirs Protesters; Rights: Activists Will Spotlight Beijing's Much-Criticized Record on Prisoners, Free Speech, Religion and Tibet," *Los Angeles Times,* 23 October 1997, A6; "Tibet: Americans Prepare to Give Jiang a Rough Welcome," *The Independent* (London), 20 October 1997, 14; Kelley, "Protesters Prepare"; David L. Marcus, "Groups Plan Protests during Jiang Visit to US," *Boston Globe,* 9 October 1997; Patricia Wilson, "Protesters Ready for Chinese Leader's US Visit," *Reuters,* 16 October 1997; Lena H. Sun, "Jiang Visit Helps Unite a Diverse Group of Foes; Protest Rally Spans Political Spectrum," *International Herald Tribune,* 29 October 1997, 2; Martin Kettle, "'Stateless' Make Meal of Jiang's Visit," *Guardian* (Manchester), 29 October 1997, 16; Sarah Jackson-Han and James Robinson, "Huge Protest against Jiang Expected as He Meets with Clinton," *Agence France Presse,* 28 October 1997. Television and radio spots included C-SPAN, Australian Broadcasting Corporation's "Lateline," BBC Radio World Service, Radio Free Asia, Voice of America and a number of U.S. radio and television stations.

23. Jim Mann, "Can Chinese Prosperity Yield Democracy?" *Los Angeles Times,* 24 September 1997.

24. I was a member of the audience at the speech, given at the Voice of America offices. The quotations are taken from John F. Harris's front-page news story on that event, "Clinton Vows to Bring Up Rights Issue," *Washington Post,* 25 October 1997, A1.

25. These corporations included Boeing, AT&T, Motorola, Caterpillar, and Cargill. See Ken Silverstein, "The New China Hands: How the Fortune 500 is China's Strongest Lobby," *The Nation,* 17 February 1997, 11–16.

26. Harvard Law School professor and China legal scholar William P. Alford noted that the Chinese delegation—which included Liu Ji, regarded by the *Far Eastern Economic Review* as one of Jiang Zemin's top advisors on political reform and

a prominent "liberal" thinker in the Chinese political establishment—spent several hours discussing these concerns with him during their visit to Harvard University in the spring of 1997. (Alford, conversation with Abigail Abrash, 12 October 2000.)

27. Kelley, "Protesters Prepare."

28. Jiang responded that, "concepts of democracy, on human rights and on freedoms are relative." *Newsweek* called the press conference an "unprecedented public exchange on democracy and human rights" (George Wehrfritz and Linda Liu, "A Noise in Jiang's Ears: Last Week's Summit, Dominated by Debate on Human Rights, Demonstrates Just How Far Apart Washington and Beijing Remain on Key Issues," *Newsweek*, 10 November 1997, 44–46).

29. The Clinton administration previously had dragged its feet in naming a person to fill the Congressionally mandated position. See G. C. Scott, "Toasted and Roasted in America . . . President Jiang Is Haunted by Tibet and Other Human Rights Issues He Had Long Ignored," *Tibetan Bulletin*, November–December 1997.

30. Wei's release was bittersweet as it was paired with his exile from China. He arrived in the United States in November 1997. Using similar tactics, the Chinese government released fellow Chinese dissident Wang Dan on medical parole, sending him to the United States in April 1998, six months after Jiang's visit and a few months prior to President Clinton's reciprocal summit visit to China in June 1998.

31. Robin Teske references Gwyn Kirk's description of a similar situation. Kirk describes the actions at Greenham Common as being "great fun—a good example of politics that enlivens and feeds the participants, as it must if we are to keep at it and not burn out" (cited in Teske, "The Butterfly Effect," in *Conscious Acts and the Politics of Social Change,* vol. 1 of *Feminist Approaches to Social Movements, Community, and Power,* ed. Robin L. Teske and Mary Ann Tétreault [Columbia: University of South Carolina Press, 2000], 122).

32. *Webster's New World Dictionary,* 2d college ed. (New York: Simon and Schuster, 1984).

33. Jennifer Baumgardner and Amy Richards, *Manifesta: Young Women, Feminism, and the Future* (New York: Farrar, Straus and Giroux, 2000). Emphasis added.

34. Dr. Waring's work is presented vividly in the 1995 documentary film *Who's Counting? Marilyn Waring on Sex, Lies and Global Economics,* which was directed by Terre Nash and produced by the National Film Board of Canada.

35. The Family Research Council opposes abortion and premarital sex. Its views on sexual orientation are equally conservative: the FRC views homosexuality as a sin and opposes "civil unions" between same-sex partners.

Chapter 11

Tilting at Closed Institutions

Marie Deans

Institutions that are closed to the public for security reasons are dangerously dependent on the mindset of those given power over them. One such closed institution is the prison. Quite often the managers of prisons believe that total control, including the complete suppression of individual free will, sanctions any action, no matter how inhumane, illegal, or immoral, toward inmates. In the minds of these managers, control is the only reason the institution exists, and the mandate to rehabilitate criminal offenders is an unattainable ideal.

Virginia's prison system is an example of a system based on the guideline "control at all costs." When I was considering coming to Virginia to open an office of the Southern Coalition on Jails and Prisons,[1] friends who ran prison systems around the country all told me the same thing: "Don't go. Virginia is a snitch system, and no system is more dangerous than a snitch system."

Anyone who works with prisoners knows how dangerous it is for a prisoner to be labeled a snitch, but I still didn't understand how a snitch *system* worked. Since most of my work was to be with death-row prisoners, who are isolated from the general prison population, I naively believed my clients and I would be relatively insulated from the dangers my friends warned me about. The story of Joe Giarratano shows how false this assumption was.

Joe Giarratano is a former death-row prisoner. While on death row, Joe had studied law and won two lawsuits that greatly improved access to courts for death-row prisoners nationwide. He studied history, comparative religion, and peacemaking, and practiced passive resistance to prison conditions, infuriating a new warden who, later, became one of Joe's strongest supporters. He also overcame his drug addiction. In February 1991, Joe was given a conditional pardon by Virginia Governor Douglas Wilder after the physical evidence in the brutal double murder for which he had been convicted failed to support his conviction. This evidence, found at the scene of the crime, included semen, body hairs, fingerprints, and bloody shoe prints. Joe's death sentence was commuted.

After he was taken off death row, Joe was placed with the general prison population and was eventually transferred to Augusta Correctional Center, a maximum security prison in Craigsville, Virginia. At Augusta, Joe's attempts to get a job failed; there were too few jobs and too many prisoners on the waiting list. After months of talking about the possibility, Joe and his cellmate, Kelly Stepp, decided to start a program to teach prisoners alternatives to violence. Joe contacted syndicated columnist Colman McCarthy's Center for Teaching Peace, which offered free course materials. Joe and Kelly then contacted me as executive director of the Virginia Coalition on Jails and Prisons and asked if VCJP would be an outside sponsor for what came to be known as Peace Studies/Alternatives to Violence (ATV).

Following many discussions about how the prison authorities might use or abuse such a program and what protections had to be in place, VCJP agreed to Joe and Kelly's request. At that time, I also was chair of Murder Victims' Families for Reconciliation (MVFR), a national organization that is opposed to the death penalty and advocates policies intended to lower the homicide rate. MVFR, whose voting members have all lost a family member to murder, addresses prison reform strictly from a rehabilitation viewpoint. When I brought the program to the attention of the board, MVFR also agreed to be an outside sponsor. We felt that ordinary citizens would be safer living among former prisoners who had gone through such a program than among those who had not. As an outside sponsor for Peace Studies/ATV in the Augusta Correctional Center, MVFR was represented on the organization's advisory board, met regularly with the prisoners' board, and kept in close touch with what the program was doing.

Joe and Kelly initially developed a twelve-week curriculum with classes that met three times per week. During these classes, the prisoners read and discussed the writings of peacemakers such as Mohandas Gandhi, Martin Luther King Jr., Leo Tolstoy, and Thomas Merton, and wrote essays about what they had learned. The essays were evaluated by the instructors at McCarthy's Center for Teaching Peace. Later, during a second twelve-week period, the men explored ways of applying the principles they had learned using actual examples from prison life.

Violence is a way of life in prison, and those who are nonviolent are seen as soft, as easy prey. Knowing they had to overcome this attitude, Joe and Kelly solicited twelve of Augusta's most violent prisoners for their first class. They also knew that some prisoners enter programs only to gain credit for parole, so they insisted that the program not count toward parole, that it remain self-supporting, and that it be run by the participants.

MVFR applauded these decisions. As Myles Horton, the director of the Highlander Folk School in Knoxville, Tennessee, taught generations of

Southern activists: it is the people who have the problems who best know how to solve them.[2] The decision not to allow the program to count toward parole made it clear that the prisoners were not going to be content with merely looking successful: they were aiming for genuine change in individuals and in the prison environment.

From September 1992 to May 1995, they accomplished significant changes. Prisoners come from violent backgrounds and environments. Many have been seriously abused and/or sexually molested as children. Most know nothing about the ideas, principles, or practices of nonviolence. Graduates of Peace Studies/ATV continually expressed amazement at the power of nonviolence.

To be accepted into the classes, prisoners had to fill out applications designed to elicit motive and need, and also had to submit to an interview conducted by the prisoner board. The prisoner board's priorities for acceptance were that the applicants had to have been convicted of particularly violent crimes, had to have extensive records of violence in the prison, and had to show themselves to be genuinely motivated to change their behavior. In spite of these hurdles, the waiting list climbed to 250 prisoners within the first two years of the program.

The program was evaluated by tracking disciplinary records. Most of the graduates had a long history of disciplinary charges for assault and fighting right up to the time they entered the program. During the years the program was running, not one graduate was charged with violent or aggressive behavior. In addition, program graduates began to be sought out by other prisoners to mediate disputes.

As Peace Studies/ATV became established at Augusta, VCJP closed due to lack of funds. MVFR, convinced of the program's potential for lowering the rate of recidivism, became more involved. MVFR members began introducing the program into prisons in their states. By the mid-1990s, programs teaching nonviolent conflict resolution were operating in sixty prisons in thirteen states.

When I was first approached by the editors of this volume to write an essay on my experiences with Peace Studies/ATV, I agreed because I believed the program showed the possibility of developing nonviolent programs and societies inside prisons, even inside maximum security prisons, where most of the inmates come from extremely violent backgrounds. But I no longer believe that such programs or societies are possible. My views have changed because of the events that ultimately led to the demise of Peace Studies/ATV at the Augusta Correctional Center and Joe's transfer to a prison in another state.

These events began in May 1995 when Governor George Allen's new director of the Virginia Department of Corrections (DOC), Ronald Angelone, ordered all prisoner-run programs at Augusta shut down. The Peace Studies/ATV board and the advisory board were informed that the shutdown was temporary, but rumors circulated that an investigation of drug smuggling was underway. These activities allegedly involved the chaplain at Augusta, who was very active in Peace Studies, and a prisoner who was not part of the program.

Shortly after the program was shut down, Joe was asked by a DOC investigator if he knew about the chaplain's smuggling drugs into the prison. Joe said no, that the chaplain wouldn't do such a thing. Joe was then questioned about a particular prisoner, and Joe said he had nothing to say. In June of 1995, Peace Studies/ATV was allowed to conduct normal classes and board meetings, but its office and computers were locked down until the computers could be inspected. The board was told that, after the inspection, Peace Studies/ATV could resume its full program activities. In July, however, the chaplain was suspended. Some time later he was indicted for bringing vitamins to a prisoner in another prison.

In late August the assistant warden at Augusta informed me that police at a drug bust in Norfolk had found a note saying that the way to get drugs into Augusta was through Peace Studies or the chaplain. The DOC Inspector General's Office then began an investigation at Augusta. The Inspector General also alleged that a check from the Peace Studies Program fund had been sent to someone known to be dealing drugs. A week later, a prisoner in the Peace Studies/ATV program told me that Joe had worn a wire and tried to implicate Kelly in the illegal activities. The prisoner said the DOC investigator had let Kelly hear the tape. When Joe's lawyer interviewed Kelly, Kelly said there was a tape with Joe's voice on it, along with another voice Kelly didn't recognize. Kelly believed the other voice had to be a prisoner's because there was prison background noise from at least four different areas of the prison. Kelly said Joe had not implicated anyone in anything.

In early October of 1995, Joe was transferred to the Buckingham Correctional Center's segregation unit. I received a call from another prisoner in the program saying that as soon as Joe was taken out of Augusta, Peace Studies was closed down completely and several prisoners were charged with dealing drugs. Rumors were rampant that Joe had sold out the program and his fellow prisoners.

Meanwhile, Joe stayed in segregation for some months. After he was returned to the general prison population, he was attacked several times. On 4 July 1996, Joe was stabbed six times by a prisoner who yelled, "Die, you m—— f—— snitch." He was immediately taken to the hospital in South Hill, Virginia. After being treated there, he was moved to the Augusta Correctional Center's medical treatment unit, where he was kept in strict isolation for two months.

When questioned by the press about the demise of Peace Studies/ATV, a DOC spokesman first claimed the program was shut down because the chaplain had been bringing contraband into the prison. When that was disputed, he then said the program was shut down due to the improper use of program funds by Joe and other prisoners. He also said that Joe was stabbed because he was such a high-profile prisoner. When I saw the article, I called the Center for Teaching Peace, which holds the audited books from the program. The director of the center told me the books were in perfect order, and that there were no improprieties with regard to the funds.

While Joe was in isolation, several prisoners from Augusta called to tell me that the DOC investigator had interviewed a number of prisoners, playing bits and pieces of tape for them, each time claiming that Joe was cooperating with the investigator by wearing a wire. However, in discussing what they had heard, one prisoner remembered being present during the conversation the investigator had played for another prisoner. Putting the pieces together, the prisoners noticed that the background noises during the conversations were different, and all of those noises came from open areas of the prison, not from any office. The investigator would have called prisoners into an office to talk with them; clearly, these tapes were being made by a prisoner, wearing a wire, recording conversations with other prisoners. They also realized that the voice doing the questioning was not the investigator's: it was the voice of a prisoner who had joined the program just one month before it was closed down. The prisoners concluded that Joe had been labeled as a snitch by the prison authorities because he had refused to provide information to convict the chaplain. Some who had helped spread the rumors realized they had been used to endanger Joe's life and to close the Peace Studies/ATV program.

This is the way the snitch system works. Such a system expects prisoners to snitch on one another. Those who cooperate are not rewarded; but those who do not cooperate are punished. More often than not, the punishment is being set up, labeled a snitch, and then "fed to the lions."

On 4 September 1996, Joe was removed from his isolation cell by a group of guards and three plainclothesmen from the Virginia DOC. They all boarded the state's small jet and were flown to Utah. During the flight, one of the men told Joe that none of this would be happening to him if he had just cooperated with them from the beginning.

Joe was allowed to bring the pages from a book he had been writing, clean paper, envelopes, stamps and a pen. After he arrived, all but the pages of the book were confiscated by the Utah prison system. He was allowed to call me and one of his attorneys. Both calls were short and both were monitored.

I notified colleagues in Utah, several of Joe's supporters, and reporters in Virginia. On 7 September, the director of the Utah Civil Liberties Union met with Joe. After her visit and after talking with the warden and others at the prison, she told me that Joe was practicing passive resistance. He had refused to cooperate while being processed into the Utah system and was on a hunger strike. She also told me he was in "the hole," a solid cell with a solid steel door, where he was kept twenty-four hours a day with no shower, no recreation time, and no communication. Ventilation in the cell is poor, and lighting is controlled by the guard—the cell is pitch black without the lights. The only amenities are an open toilet and cold water.

The Virginia Department of Correction's spokesman told reporters that Joe had requested the transfer. However, when told that Joe had sued to prevent the transfer, the spokesman then said that Joe had to be moved for his own safety. When asked if his safety had been endangered because he had been falsely labeled a snitch, the spokesman responded that he couldn't comment on the dynamics of an internal investigation. He insisted that the Peace Studies/ATV program had been shut down because of the chaplain, and when faced with claims that the chaplain's indictment had nothing to do with the program, he reverted to blaming bookkeeping improprieties for the program's demise.

A freelance journalist learned from an insider at Augusta that the prison officials had been pleased with the Peace Studies/ATV program. Orders to shut it down had come from Mr. Angelone. This insider also said that he had seen the allegations, including allegations of improprieties with the books, but to his knowledge there was no evidence to support them. It was the Utah press that learned the true story of why Joe was transferred. The Utah Department of Correction's spokesman told the Utah press that they had received a call from Mr. Angelone: "(He) called us and said, 'We've got this politically hot inmate and we need to get rid of him.'"[3]

Joe had committed the ultimate offense in this "control at any price" prison system. He had given prisoners the idea that they could control their own behavior and change their environment. Although the Peace Studies/ATV program brought praise to Augusta Correctional Center, lowered the level of violence in the prison, and created a place and an atmosphere where prisoners could rehabilitate themselves, it was clearly considered threatening by the system's managers. Those managers acted to discredit the program and its founder, making an example of Joe, so that other prisoners would realize just how futile such ideas were and how heavy the price would be should they try to carry them out.

As I write this, Joe has not eaten in thirteen days, and he remains in the hole in the Utah State Prison unable even to receive letters. The ACLU director's visit has been his only link to the outside world, and her ability to help is limited at best.

The demise of the Peace Studies/ATV Program and the cruelty inflicted on Joe Giarratano give those of us who attempt to reform closed institutions another lesson to study. How do we even begin to reform these institutions? How do we protect those inside such institutions who attempt reform? I don't know the answers to these questions, but I do know that we must continue to seek them.

(1996)

Epilogue, November 2000

Since I originally wrote this essay, the prison situation in Virginia has deteriorated further, and Ronald Angelone remains the director of the Virginia Department of Corrections.

Joe continued his hunger strike to pressure Utah to send him back to Virginia, where he believed his chances for a new trial were best. While he was hospitalized as a result of his hunger strike, he saw men put in the so-called devil's chair,[4] and learned of one dying as a result. He contacted numerous people to publicize and protest its use, and as a result the Utah prison system no longer uses the devil's chair. Joe's agitation received major attention in Utah, and the subsequent investigation of the Utah prison system led to the removal of the head of the state's Department of Corrections. At the time this was happening, Joe was moved to Illinois. There he tried to work within the prison system, while at the same time pressuring Illinois officials to return him to Virginia. After a few months, he again went on a hunger strike, and Illinois sent him back to Virginia.

Since Joe's return to Virginia, Angelone has kept him in the most restricted area of the most restrictive super maximum security prison—the Red Onion State Prison in Pound, Virginia. Even from there, Joe continues to draw attention to prison conditions, his efforts leading to a Human Rights Watch Report. Such attention is, directly or indirectly, responsible for a current investigation by the U.S. Department of Justice. In addition, since all this started, the Red Onion and Wallens Ridge prisons are being sued by two states, New Mexico and Connecticut, who sent prisoners to Virginia to alleviate overcrowding.

Joe still awaits a new trial.

Notes

1. Founded in the early 1970s, the Southern Coalition on Jails and Prisons was a coalition of thirteen state projects dedicated to working on prison and jail reform, the abolition of the death penalty, and providing legal services to prisoners, particularly those on death row.

2. The Highlander Folk School is known for training its students in the theory and practice of nonviolence.

3. Amy Donaldson, "Deal to Swap Inmates Turns Sour," *Salt Lake City Deseret News*, 9 September 1996, B1.

4. The devil's chair is a restraint device that keeps a prisoner immobile in a seated position. There are chest, arm, body, leg, and ankle restraints. The chair is not supposed to be dangerous, as long as the prisoner is allowed to get up and move around at regular intervals. In Utah prisoners were put in the chair nude and kept there for long periods of time—one prisoner told me as long as three days—without being allowed to move or leave, even to go to the bathroom.

Chapter 12

Finding Power in a Hegemonic Environment

Lessons on Surviving and Thriving from Five Women's Organizations in Poland

Diane M. Duffy

> . . . subjection is not equivalent to submission, and women, like members of other subordinate groups, have learned to use the blinders created by hegemonic ideologies to pursue their own liberation.
>
> —Tétreault and Teske

In 1988, when Poland was still ruled by a Communist regime, women's representation in the Polish Sejm amounted to 20 percent of that legislative body.[1] While representatives' policy input was limited and appointments were influenced by tokenism and ties to the Communist Party, women could have presence on the Parliamentary floor *if* they chose to play the game of politics as it was structured by the system in power.[2] On the eve of democratization and economic liberalization in 1989, one would have anticipated that women were well-positioned to enjoy even greater formal representation when Poland joined the cadre of Western industrialized democracies. Women would enter this new epoch demanding more than the lip service paid to women's rights by the Communist regime, trusting that extant laws would actually be enforced, and believing that representational credibility would really be achieved.[3]

As is well documented in the literature, women's expectations of transforming Poland were built on false hopes.[4] Women's representation in the Polish Parliament plummeted to 9.5 percent in the 1990–94 period, rebounding somewhat to 13 percent between 1994 and 1998, but never regaining Communist-era levels.[5] Women candidates faced many barriers in national elections: lack of family support; low sense of self-worth; historically rooted beliefs about women's proper roles; the stringent demands of political life; increased interest in local government activity; majoritarian rules in parliamentary voting; and reluctance of women to identify with other women as a group.[6]

In spite of the flagging figures, the barriers, and retrenchment, many women continue to be an integral part of Poland's public policy scene. They prod government to adhere to the Polish constitution's guarantees of equality;[7] they fill gaps in public services; and they speak out against injustices. In this essay, I describe how, with a minimum of resources, women have worked wonders, giving new meaning and importance to power and community. I examine how and why selected women's organizations direct their activities toward the "community"[8] and not toward the (center) state. Specifically, I discuss (1) the contemporary status of women in Poland, (2) political activities of five women's organizations in contemporary Poland, and (3) implications of the Polish case for understanding power and politics.

The Contemporary Scene in Poland

Status of Women

The transition period following the Communist era has not brought women parity with men in Poland. In many aspects of life, Polish women have borne a disproportionate burden incurred by the change from Communism's command economy to a market-based democracy. Representation of women in political elite circles has decreased significantly. While a few women have achieved highly visible political positions since 1989 (for example, Hanna Suchocka as prime minister, Zofia Kuratowska as senator, Hanna Gronkiewicz-Waltz as national bank president), their representation in the upper echelons of the Polish government, the party system, and executive power structures is markedly disproportionate to their educational levels. Women fill fewer than one-quarter of the high-level positions in the national government in spite of their greater education.[9]

While the drop in national legislative seats held by women at the beginning of the post-Communist era (1990–94) was disheartening, mobilization efforts produced modest electoral gains for women in both the Senate and Sejm (Poland's two legislative chambers). More interesting trends, though, are visible at the local level. Here, there has been a steady increase in representation, from 10 percent to nearly 16 percent. Grażyna Kopinska's analysis of the 1998 election indicated that the greatest gains by women were (a) in cities with populations of over 500,000, (b) in *gminas* (aldermanic districts) more than in *powiat* (county) and provincial elections, and (c) in the Unia Wolności (Freedom Union) Party and among independent candidates.[10] These findings tell us that women's gains at the governance level have come where women's organizations have been the most active and where there are the greatest numbers of well-educated women from which to draw a pool of candidates. Nonetheless, data indicate that men are ten times more likely to be listed first on party candidate lists than women.

Economic Status

We see the trend away from leadership roles for women in the job arena as well. Sixty-six percent of employed women but only 39 percent of employed men have a mid-level or higher education. Yet, women are not well represented in management and supervisory ranks, and men, on average, earn 26 percent more than women.[11] The government claims that the main reason for the trend is that women join "feminized" professions such as teaching and medicine, which are less well paid than jobs in sectors like mining and manufacturing.[12] The Federation for Women and Family Planning provides other reasons that put the situation in a broader perspective: vocational schools that women attended were more likely to be closed as the public education system responded to governmental budget cuts after 1989; the practice of denying women admission to technical schools has been common, resulting in fewer options for women at the high school level; blatant discrimination in hiring is rampant;[13] and women were the first to be laid off or fired when plants closed or workforces were trimmed during restructuring. Accordingly, women constituted 52 percent of the total *registered* unemployed at the end of 1993; in March 1997, the portion was 60 percent. These unemployed women are better educated than unemployed men. Moreover, nearly one-half of the women looking for employment have been doing so for more than a year, whereas only one-third of the men have been looking for so long.[14]

Women's Health Status

The *Demographic Situation of Poland,* a government report published in 1995, documented the general deterioration in the nation's health throughout the previous decade.[15] Among the factors contributing to this decline were the deterioration of health care services, inadequate preventive services, and the hardships of everyday life. The findings of a survey commissioned by Poland's Federation for Women and Family Planning illustrate the extent of this problem for women: nearly three-fourths of the women respondents reported that their gynecologists examine their breasts rarely, if at all; only 21.9 percent of the respondents conduct their own examinations on a regular basis; almost 15 percent of the women could not get Pap smears in spite of Poland having a national health program; and mammography was not available to 53 percent.[16] Forty-two percent of the respondents answered "I do not know" to the question about availability of prenatal examinations, and 6 percent did not respond at all. These data become even more dramatic when one considers that the Federation's respondents were skewed toward more educated women. Services for women of postreproductive age, for people with sexually-transmitted diseases, and for victims of domestic violence are not well integrated into the design of the health system. Indeed, data on violence against women and children are not systematically collected. Added to this, inattention to environmental and workplace pollution has translated into high cancer rates among workers during their most productive years (20–39 years of age) and, for pregnant women, into higher infant mortality rates and more premature births, low-birth-weight newborns, and babies with birth defects.

Family planning services are particularly underdeveloped. Few are provided by the national health system; there is a general lack of access to affordable contraception and a lack of education in these matters among members of the medical community and among women themselves. Parliamentary legislation in 1997 required the introduction of sex education in public school curricula, but the content was severely narrowed in scope by the AWS-led government[17] and presents a largely negative view of contraception and family planning (with the exception of periodic abstinence).

In March 1993, Poland implemented an abortion law that was far more restrictive than the law in effect during the Communist era. Legal abortions were permitted in public hospitals only if the pregnancy was a serious threat to the life or physical health of the woman, the fetus had irreversible damage, or there was justified suspicion (confirmed by a prosecutor) that the pregnancy was a result of an illegal act. In 1996 the law was liberalized to allow termination of pregnancy until the twelfth week if an argument could be made for personal hardship, but this liberalization was short-lived and was reversed in 1997. The lack of attention to reproductive health in the Polish health care system means that, on average, Polish women experience a higher incidence of maternal mortality than women in other European countries, undergo more abortions during their reproductive years and more abortions per live births, and face a growing incidence of sexually-transmitted diseases.

Social Benefits

Changes in benefit structures have hit women harder than men. Polish women still enjoy paid maternity leaves of sixteen to eighteen weeks—leaves that are fairly generous compared to those granted to women in the United States. This "benefit" has become a double-edged sword, however, because employers try to avoid the costs of the paid leaves by increasing the proportion of men in their workforce.[18] Some women have been illegally fired, and the high cost of benefits is increasingly used to justify hiring men instead of women and giving women "priority" in being laid off. Consequently, many women decide not to take full advantage of their entitlements in order to preserve their jobs.[19] In view of the excellent opportunity to seize the moral high ground while, in reality, pushing women out of the workforce, recent initiatives advocated by fundamentalist Catholics ("pro-family" policies) and liberals (policies to cut unemployment) have not only tried to double maternity leaves, but also to make leaves *obligatory* rather than optional.[20] It is the latter—the obligatory nature of the leaves in these initiatives—that is onerous to some women and is perceived as a restriction on their full rights as citizens.

New pension calculations add to women's difficulties in two ways: (1) the new formulas employed by government are based on the number of years of work and the level of wages earned, and (2) the second "pillar" of Poland's new retirement program allows private enterprise retirement program administrators to calculate women's retirement moneys using a larger denominator than they use for men due to women's greater longevity. Accordingly, women receive an average of 40 percent less than men in pension support every month. While these changes may, on the surface, appear to be a fair, objective means of calculating pensions (and not unlike what occurs in other countries), other factors undermine the justice of such calculations in Poland. First, pensions based on systematic and widespread discrimination in hiring, promotion, and remuneration institutionalize those injustices by incorporating them in calculations of a government benefit and thus extending them into the retirement years. (Indeed, some women in Poland today may even be ineligible for pensions that they would have had under the Communist regime.) Further, in the absence of a nursing home industry and with cutbacks in day care facilities,[21] Poland essentially relies *solely* on women to care for children, the elderly, and disabled and sick family members. Women's earlier retirement age historically provided a way to fill these societal needs. Although women in Poland provide a valuable *societal* service, one that is *institutionally* met in Western industrialized countries, they are punished for doing so by receiving lower retirement pensions. The government has barely moved toward establishing alternative institutional arrangements (such as nursing homes and day care centers) to free women to accumulate better/higher pension reserves via opportunities for longer and better-paid employment. Thus, women disproportionately bear society's burdens.

Other Impediments to Political Access

This overview shows women losing ground to men as a result of the economic and political transition in Poland that has ignored the nation's social needs. Many women—peasants, workers, and intellectuals—bemoan the current government's lack of interest in women's issues. They note that the government has done little to implement its own National Action Plan on Women, undertaken in accordance with the Convention on the Elimination of Discrimination Against Women (ratified by the Polish government in April 1997). Moreover, the government report for the United Nations outlining problems faced by women in Poland was so poorly prepared that the Federation for Women and Family Planning developed an independent (shadow) report to fill in the gaps.[22] So deficient was the government's report that this federation of women's groups was given special advisory status at the UN in matters concerning the status of women in Poland.[23]

The current, AWS-led government is fairly conservative. Previous, more liberal governments accomplished little more. While the earlier governments viewed women in social and public life more favorably, issues important to women were not given priority. Access to government funds has always been a problem. Emphasis on the market since 1989 leaves policy makers reluctant to make the connection between the status of women and the problems of the poor, the unemployed, the elderly, the handicapped, and children. Accordingly, much of the funding for women's rights and women's programs in Poland has come from abroad. Other factors also impede access to policy-making centers for many women's groups:

a) Since 1989 the Polish bureaucracy has continued to operate, as it had during the Communist period, on the basis of personal relationships. Whether nationally or locally, people in administrative positions help people and organizations they know, leaving the newly formed women's groups without access compared to established groups.
b) In the aftermath of Communism, controversial issues have been reframed as problems of morality and ethics. Political discourse and organizations themselves also became polarized and then labeled as either "good" or "bad." Thus, if a women's group was perceived as being in favor of, for example, legalization of abortion, it was uniformly labeled "bad" by those in power—no matter what other meritorious programs it advocated. Most activist women's groups eventually became so labeled.
c) After a period of influence in the early 1990s, the Women's Parliamentary Group became ineffective because it did not represent as broad a spectrum of views as it had earlier. Consequently, it lost power and credibility as an organization able to speak with authority on national issues of importance to women.

d) Women in Poland generally don't want to consider themselves targets of discrimination; they don't want to place themselves in the victim's role.[24] Hence, they focus on the present, have a hard time planning for the future, and tend to depend on people in government and in the parties to set policy for the nation. All of this impedes development of any mobilized women's initiative.

e) As government responsibility became decentralized and administrative reforms reconfigured the structures of provincial and district governance, there has been more opportunity to access decision-making structures at local levels. However, few women have the skills to intervene effectively at the local level, and most who do are concentrated in Warsaw, Kraków, and other large cities, rather than dispersed throughout Poland's new political landscape.

f) There has been no widespread, organized constituency in Poland to demand women's rights.[25] Poles simply do not conceptualize some things as explicitly women's issues, but rather see them as social issues. Thus, the higher unemployment rate for women is an unemployment problem; the large number of poor and elderly women is a demographic problem; and domestic abuse is a private, family affair that only becomes a public problem when it bothers the neighbors and the police are called.

In sum, the transition from Communism to a market-based democracy provided Polish women with a new set of fetters in place of the old ones, as a masculinist hegemony continued to pervade Poland throughout the early transitional period. R. W. Connell defines this kind of hegemony as a "social ascendancy achieved in a play of social forces [extending] beyond contests of brute power into the organization of private life and cultural processes."[26] This "hegemonic masculinity" created asymmetry between men's and women's access to political and economic opportunities. Thus, the new neoliberal fetters may be structurally more problematic than the old Communist fetters because, while the country as a whole has been making great economic and representational progress, Polish women have been constrained by institutional arrangements that force them into positions of dependency. Indeed, the asymmetry between men's and women's access to opportunities seems to be widening. In response, the organizations that represent women's interests have been forced to assume a defensive posture in reaction to governmental proposals (on birth control, cutbacks in benefits, and retirement formulas), a strategy that initially was largely ineffective, at least until some learned to play by the rules of the "free market."

Responses of Women's Organizations

Five Scenarios

Women's responses to the situation in Poland has been mixed. There have been few overt demonstrations—in contrast to the reactions of farmers and coal miners to analogous threats to their welfare. However, as time has passed and women have gained experience with the free market, we see a clear differentiation in mission and modes of operation among women's groups that reflects various forms of femininity, even within the confines of hegemonic masculinity.[27] Some of the women's groups that were not investigated for this essay were largely compliant with their reduced status and accommodated to their environment. They engage in what Connell calls "emphasized femininity." Others resorted to resistance and noncompliance. Still others used "complex strategic combinations of compliance, resistance, and cooperation."[28]

For this essay, I tried to interview women's groups that represent this entire spectrum of experiences but was unable to locate contacts—my calls were not returned, their phones were disconnected, and some expressed a preference not to be interviewed—or, in the case of government representatives, answers were vague and evasive. In the end, I interviewed members of five groups that represent Connell's third category, as demonstrated by their changing strategies and multifocal mode of operating. The five organizations—the Women's Rights Center, the Information Center on Women's Organizations and Initiatives, the Center for the Advancement of Women, the Batory Foundation's Women's Program, and the Federation for Women and Family Planning—all have academic and international contacts, and all are leftist in orientation. The sample is, then, a skewed sample but one that represents the broad repertoire of tactics available to groups operating in a hegemonic environment that is not receptive to their agendas.

All five organizations are service-oriented and use human rights to justify their existence. Their agendas have both ethical and pragmatic appeal, shaped by the need to address unsolved problems experienced by women. Ideological debates on issues such as public versus private ownership and provision of services don't generally surface in interviews. Each group, however, has unique features that set it apart from the others. The Federation for Women and Family Planning, in particular, presents an interesting contrast to the other groups with respect to autonomy, visibility, and the degree of controversy that surrounds it. Below, I discuss the organizations' main program concerns, coalitional work, locus of activity, and funding.[29]

Main Program Concerns

The Women's Rights Center (WRC, Centrum Prawo Kobiet) largely focuses on domestic legislative initiatives of importance to women and monitors compliance with international conventions and agreements signed by Poland. Over the past year, the WRC has provided input on legislative language for Poland's laws on legal separation, gender equity, and domestic violence. It participated in a critique of the Ministry of Family Affairs's *Report on Families* and of the law that allows physicians (even public sector physicians) to charge for documenting injuries to women and children who are victims of violence. It criticized abuses of women's human rights in local shelters for battered and homeless women, and the short sentences awarded by courts to rapists. Many of its earlier findings were published in *Situation of Women in Poland* in 1995.[30] Other advocacy activities include identifying and encouraging qualified women candidates to run for local offices, assisting women who encounter difficulties with public agencies and officials, authoring and promoting informational materials and programs on domestic violence, and providing limited individual legal representation.

The Information Center on Women's Organizations and Initiatives (Ośrodek Informacji Środowisk Kobiecych, OŚKa), in contrast, functions as a resource center on women's issues. It maintains a national database on over 250 women's organizations, institutes, and informal groups as well as a resource library and archive on women's issues, which is open to the general public. It disseminates a monthly calendar of events, a quarterly bulletin on feminist ideas, and informational handbooks such as *Women's Rights in United Nations' Documents.* It develops skills necessary to use the information by conducting conferences and workshops such as "The Role of Information Transfer for Women's Organizations—INFO OŚKa '96." Other training workshops have been offered on public relations, conflict resolution, leadership and organizational skills, and advocacy and lobbying. OŚKa funds basic research and surveys on women's status in Poland. In December 1998, for example, it commissioned OBOP Polling Center to conduct a survey on human rights, a portion of which explored women's rights issues. OŚKa facilitates contacts among women community leaders, nongovernmental organizations, government officials, and the public media to create a platform for dialogue about issues important to women.

The Center for the Advancement of Women (Centrum Promocji Kobiet, CPK), the third organization, focuses on women in the labor market. In 1996 approximately 2000 women used the CPK's "Employment Agency." The CPK helps women acquire the necessary skills for gainful employment, assists them with résumé preparation, and facilitates contact between employers and women seeking jobs. It makes available its telephones, fax and copying machines, and newspapers so that women can prepare and send job applications to prospective employers. At its Athena Center, the staff helps women acquire basic computer and bookkeeping skills, learn how to run small businesses, and practice public presentations. Summer traineeships are offered for single mothers from smaller towns and villages. CPK offers seminars such as "Women and Labor Markets from the Perspective of the Center for the Advancement of Women" and publishes the *Directory of Women's Organization and Initiatives in Poland.*

The Stefan Batory Foundation Women's Program functions mostly as a funder and facilitator of proposals submitted by *other* groups. Consequently, it appears to be the least controversial of the five organizations. Funded projects have addressed women's unemployment; women victims of domestic violence; women's health and sex education; women's legal rights and access to the judicial system; travel to international women's conferences; and training programs, seminars, and workshops dealing with women's issues. In 1996 the Women's Program awarded two institutional grants and fifty-two organizational grants totaling 1,140,998 złotys (approximately U.S. $500,000). The majority of grant applications have been from nongovernmental organizations (NGOs), many located in Warsaw.

Finally, the Federation for Women and Family Planning (Federacja na rzecz kobiet i planowania rodziny) provides information on family planning, sex education, and human sexuality; addresses women's health care issues, emphasizing preventive care and treatment of cancers of the reproductive system; and advocates for women's reproductive rights. Specific activities include management of the Hotline for Women;[31] individual counseling on contraception, human sexuality, and women's health and legal issues; "open house" discussions for women and teenagers; publication of pamphlets on sex education, contraceptives, and women's health, and a quarterly bulletin for Federation members; reports such as "Reproductive Health of Polish Women" prepared for advocacy purposes; and programs on reproductive health for health care personnel and teachers. The Federation has been critical of the current government's legislative agenda to limit the treatment of postpartum depression, access to amniocentesis, and access to abortion. The Federation was also responsible for the shadow report submitted to the UN Economic, Social, and Cultural Rights Committee.

Coalitional Behavior

While each organization's strategies vary, in four of the five groups I find commonalities rooted in bygone eras.[32] First, there is a preference for working in small, autonomous, cell-like groups rather than on a larger scale where the group might be more visible and powerful. There is a loose, nonhierarchical organizational style that encourages members to contribute to policy and programs.[33] While each group has a leader/director—indeed, this person appears central to the organization's dynamism—the trappings of hierarchy are decidedly missing. I saw, for example, no organizational charts. Directors' offices served multiple functions for the organization, and credit was readily given to staff members. There is a preference for operating at local levels, although their work has national relevance. The groups remain flexible enough to form ad hoc coalitions for strategy's sake and to optimize use of scarce resources. These coalitional activities, however, are usually short-lived and intended for very focused, coordinated action, such as during a recent antipornography campaign.

The particular operational pattern adopted by these organizations is intended to preserve their autonomy, that is, each group perceives its mission as slightly different from the others'. Moreover, they fear being coopted or having their agendas captured and redefined by others. Here, history has been an apt mentor. The Communist regime was a master at coopting groups and changing their agendas to suit its own interests.[34] Indeed, a preference for such cell-like activity was seen during the Solidarity era, in Poland's partisan resistance during World War II, and at various other stages in Poland's history when the country was partitioned.

In marked contrast, the Federation is the only one of the five that engages in consistent, long-standing, and large-scale collaborative work. The Federation is a coalition of nine organizations: the ProFemina Association; the Association for a Non-Ideological State, "Neutrum"; the Young Women's Christian Association (the Polish YWCA); the "Ewa" Section of the Democratic Union of Women; the Movement for the Protection of Women's Rights; the Association for Family Development; the League of Polish Women; the Center for the Protection of Women's and Families' Rights; and the Educational Association "Arbor." The reason for the Federation's different profile is its clear mission to promote family planning. In predominantly Roman Catholic Poland, this agenda is interpreted as proabortion and draws fire from conservatives, including the AWS party, and from the powerful Catholic Church. Accordingly, the Federation engages in few local activities in small communities. Director Nowicka believes that small communities are too politically sensitive and individual local supporters are too isolated to initiate activities at this time. Instead, the Federation uses the anonymity of aggregate data to push for policy changes from a national base.

The Federation is a clear, visible, and easy target for its opponents in the government. The latter require comparatively few resources to attack the group on moral grounds because other actors, especially the Catholic hierarchy, stand ready to mobilize against it. Therefore, the Federation's structure and its networking (both nationally and internationally) are critical to its mission and, even more, to its survival. It is no wonder that the Federation's constituent members, in contrast to other groups, are willing to give up some autonomy to protect one another by banding together.

Funding

The five organizations are similar in that little of their funding comes from Poland's central government. At one time, the Ministry of Family Affairs played a funding role but this has diminished and is nearly nonexistent at this time. Currently, the Ford Foundation, the Batory Foundation, the Šoroš Foundation, the United Nations Development Project, the UN Commission on Human Rights, the U.S. Agency for International Development, and PHARE Democracy are the most important supporters. Moneys have also come from various governments (Canada, Norway, U.K., Sweden, Switzerland, and Holland among others) for targeted programs; private Polish contributors (for example, Hortex and Polish Telecommunications); and various women's groups (such as the Women's International Group in Poland, UNIFEM, International Center for Research on Women). There are funding variations, however, that parallel the specific missions of the organizations. For example, the European Crime Prevention Institute funds a WRC program on violence against women; the local Warsaw government funds neighborhood-based programs; and the National Labor Office funds selected job initiatives at the CPK.

Locale of Activity

With the exception of the Federation, organizational activity for the women's groups has national import but is based on a pragmatic mindset that is locally based. Arguments are geared toward fixing local problems because needs are experienced individually and locally, and because using the rhetoric of local action is appealing to funders. Resources available to the groups are increasingly either community (*gmina*) funds or external funds for very specific, local projects. Indeed, the central government's neglect has made extensive nationwide activities impossible in recent years, driving the groups further toward local initiatives.

The WRC's local efforts address public safety and domestic violence. For example, the Safe Streets, Safe Houses project collected data and analyzed the neighborhood surrounding the Center, making specific recommendations to improve safety. Other activities include training criminal justice professionals about violence against women, establishing a hotline—STOP—to intervene against violence and discrimination, conducting "Learn Your Rights" meetings to educate Poles about violence against women, and raising funds for a shelter for victims of domestic violence in the Warsaw region. The WRC participates in international activities when external resources are available and when the topic is women's human rights. For example, it organized "Celebrate and Demand Women's Human Rights" and "Tribunal on Women's Human Rights Abuses," two international conferences to commemorate the fiftieth anniversary of the United Nations Universal Declaration of Human Rights.

OŚKa's activities, as well, are national in relevance but local in application. While its data on women's issues are drawn from around the country, local (that is, Warsaw) clientele have the easiest access. Conferences are usually geared to a Warsaw audience because the central government and major media outlets are located there. Internationally, OŚKa maintains a close networking association with the Regional Women's Program of the Open Society Institute in New York and the Center for Women's Global Leadership at Rutgers University.

Danuta Sowinska, CPK's director, reports that its employment services are available across Poland; however, women in Warsaw are the most frequent users of this assistance due to proximity. Moreover, the CPK staff knows more about the local (Warsaw) labor market. Plans are in process to develop two programs to broaden the center's scope: "Women's Political Academy," a program designed to teach women in smaller towns how to be active in public life in their communities; and "Springboard," a personal development program patterned after a successful British prototype.

Much of the funding awarded by the Batory Foundation's Women's Program has been for projects in cities; however, recently the foundation has been encouraging proposals from towns and villages where grants are sorely needed but applications have been few. Director Baraniewska has instituted outreach activities to such areas to facilitate proposal-writing.

Owing to its family planning agenda, the Federation is without a doubt the most controversial and the most attacked of the five organizations. To protect its supporters in small towns and villages, it must work from a broader support base than the other four groups. Consequently, 80 percent of its activities are geared to an explicitly national agenda, and it relies on the largest network of international contacts and coordinated activities of any of the five groups to press for reproductive health changes in Poland.

These cases illustrate what some Polish women have done when the central government has ignored their needs as citizens. All of them rely on international resources and institutions to some degree to leverage their position, optimize their chances to effect change, and provide credibility and legitimacy to their claims. Four of the five organizations—the WRC, OŚKa, CPK and the Batory Women's Program—operate in a nonhierarchical atmosphere, use human rights arguments as their refuge against critics, and design their agendas and programs to think globally but act locally. The Federation, in contrast, has a more complex organizational structure. Unlike the others, its human rights arguments draw fire from critics because its claim of reproductive rights is not embraced by either the current government or Poland's conservative power structure. Consequently, the Federation must capture and use a broader (national and international) base of support for its activities.

Discussion and Analysis

These Polish women's groups provide empirical evidence for Maxine Molyneux's argument that a "number of small associations even with very diverse agendas can in cumulative terms come to constitute a women's movement."[35] In a remarkably short period of time, the women acquired new skills allowing them to maneuver between local needs and the international community to put pressure on an uncooperative state. Their actions reflect considerable political dexterity and represent a way to take advantage of a women's movement that, in general, still lacks collective mobilization. Indeed, Poland's women's groups demonstrate how a number of small autonomous groups with diverse but overlapping agendas can become—in Molyneux's words—"a social and political phenomenon of some significance, that significance being given both by its numerical strength but also *by its capacity to effect changes* in some way or another whether this is expressed in legal, cultural, social, or political terms"[36] (emphasis mine).

Molyneux, however, also asks whether the autonomy demonstrated by such groups can marginalize them, reducing their political effectiveness.[37] In Poland's case, it is the tradition of autonomous existence that probably has allowed these groups to survive and thrive. Operating in their cell-like form, this network of women's organizations has been able to fill a niche in the policy arena. The network is such a diffuse target that it is difficult for the government to take effective aim without distracting attention from other problems (such as restructuring the economy or joining NATO and the European Community). Because each individual group is small, they are perceived as a relatively minor threat. The government can (or so it seems to think) marginalize them through inattention to their claims. In the meantime, though, these women's groups have made small but significant gains in training women, addressing domestic abuse, providing shelters, and so forth, and have endeared themselves to local officials because they address thorny, intractable problems that local officials are more than happy to contract out to NGOs run by and for women. They continue to survive because they fill a need. That need centers them and also liberates them because few other NGOs are interested in or care sufficiently about the problems they address. On that basis, solidarity is growing across these autonomous groups.

Nature of Engagement in Civic Life

Neglected by the central government, the women's groups reviewed in this essay demonstrate three often successful counterstrategies: ignoring the government and functioning "as if" one had visibility and clout; leveraging other resources and outflanking the government by utilizing international linkages to press for change; and operating at a different—lower—level of governance (that is, at the *gmina* level). The first strategy, ignoring the government and functioning "as if," continues what many activist Solidarity members did after that organization was declared illegal by the Communist government in the 1980s. Acting "as if" is more than passive resistance but less than taking to the streets. In the Solidarity era, acting "as if" Poland were a free country created a small "realm of liberty" around the actor that was perceived and replicated by others. The effect reverberated far beyond the individual to reach the whole society. Poles discovered that merely by proceeding with a normal free existence, the Communist regime became helpless, unable to defeat or control them. The sentiment in this approach is moral and stubborn in tone.

To contemporary women's groups in Poland, the "as if" strategy means testifying at hearings when others don't want them there, claiming the right (and therefore the power) to be present. It means using the media to voice their positions and present their cases, claiming access to the public ear. It means going time and again to the government to argue for a share of the budget for their constituents' needs, becoming a force that will not go away. Using this strategy, the women's groups have squeezed out small but consistent gains.

Leveraging other resources and circumventing the government by using an international platform has been particularly effective for the Federation, but the other organizations also use this strategy to garner funds for their projects. It works because the Polish government wants to solidify and strengthen its membership in the global community via institutional linkages and commitments. Poland desperately seeks to expand and institutionalize its democracy and its economic and strategic ties to the West. In March 1999, its application for membership in the North Atlantic Treaty Organization became a reality, and its European Union candidacy is well underway. As a condition of membership, though, Poland has had to comply with these communities' definitions of human rights as articulated in, for example, the Helsinki Agreement, the Women's World Congress Convention drafted in Beijing, and European Union admission requirements. In the process, the government (inadvertently) creates opportunities for Polish women. Women's organizations are able to exploit the government's desire to maintain a positive image abroad and the good standing required for membership in NATO and the EU in order to get action on issues women view as important.

When the government responds to the women's organizations, it is not necessarily sympathetic to the views of these groups. Indeed, the current government's preferences are not to bow to demands for reproductive rights, women's employment, or shelters for battered women. Rather, the government is responding to norms established by an international community it wishes to join, that is, to a collectively (internationally) constructed sense of what constitutes human rights and how those rights include women. Here, a global community—objectively existing in the form of international agreements and covenants and institutional structures—becomes a socially constructed instrument through which women's organizations can leverage domestic policy changes and hold the government accountable to commitments made in a public arena (the "global community"). Thus, the extranational contacts that Poland is making have become "enabling" for the women's groups interviewed for this essay.

The third strategy employed by these women's groups is to refocus their earlier (that is, immediate post-1989) national activities on local efforts. The rollback of the state in Poland after 1989 left room for an increased role for civil society and for the development of new institutional structures. The most discussed of the latter was the development of the market; however, the emergence of nongovernmental organizations also was a by-product. In addition, the process of decentralization that accompanied the curtailment of the central state devolved more responsibilities to local (*gmina*) authorities. Both of these developments opened spaces in which women could create NGOs and act in their neighborhoods to address needs heretofore neglected. Thus, the state inadvertently created a window of opportunity for women by virtue of its withdrawal.

Acting locally gives members of women's organizations more control over their agendas, provides them some measure of success within their localities, and is a psychological defense that allows them to redefine problems (and solutions) in spite of a state that essentially turns a deaf ear to their interests. Why has acting at the local community level succeeded? Some might say that the women know the problems in their neighborhoods, can articulate them in a manner that rings true with local politicians, and can design remedies that might actually work. Another reality is that there were so many other actors scrapping to position themselves in the market, in the new political and business order in Poland, that few others *wanted* to address the social needs that interested the women's organizations discussed here. Thus, as suggested by Tétreault and Teske and Evans and Boyte, women could act and not be acted upon, and the situation created space to act.[38]

What does the Polish case say about women's participation in civic life? It says that the way women have engaged in civic life is often constrained and shaped by historical and contemporary politics. It says that the women's groups discussed in this essay are cognizant of their impotence nationally and are making realistic decisions about when, where, and how to use their energies. This switching among loci of activity (international, national and local) is characteristic of the pragmatism that pervades these organizations, but it is also strategic. For example, activists currently appeal to social justice more than to democratic representation, and they use moral justifications for their arguments because these are the bases for political dialogue in their country right now.[39] However, they also network and lay groundwork that may be useful later using the democracy route, such as in electoral campaigns.

Critics, of course, may point out that entrenched power systems are simply using women and never will allow them into centers of power: once power or opportunities for profit filter down to the local communities, women's groups will be pushed out of their niche. This may be, but from the perspective of an outside observer, I can say that I have seen Polish women's sophistication and technological expertise (for computer networking and telecommunication, lobbying strategies and negotiation) grow at an astonishing rate. The skills and expertise they have acquired increase their adaptability to change and, in the meantime, thousands of women are benefitting from them directly. Moreover, women are cultivating the relational ties crucial to the functioning of Polish politics at the local level, ties that will provide a measure of insulation against any future attempts to displace them.

These women respond to *both* "practical" gender interests and "strategic" gender interests as defined by Molyneux. That is, they satisfy "needs arising from women's placement within the sexual division of labor" (practical) and "those involving claims to transform social relations in order to enhance women's position and to secure a more lasting re-positioning of women within the gender order and within society at large" (strategic).[40] Thus, they address problems such as unemployment, lower pensions, and special health care demands while, at the same time, seeking to locate a niche and to articulate a philosophy that can serve as a base for transcending existing power structures. The rhetoric of human rights and the locus of community-level work are key to this process and the heart of their empowerment.

Implications for Understanding "Power"

In their introduction to volume one, Tétreault and Teske argued that a reconceptualization of power is in order. Historically, international scholars have used a paradigm of power defined by realists as "domination"—or "power over"—and by idealists as "cooperation"—or "power with." The realists' and idealists' conceptualizations are founded on the idea of "differential capacities," in which capacity is defined in terms of prevailing values and preferences for what constitutes control and influence. Tétreault and Teske urged movement away from this dichotomous formulation of power to a much more complex understanding of the concept. They argue that in many cases, "a transcendent conception of power by a social movement accompanies a counter-hegemonic ideology along with a relative deficiency in the capacity to coerce physically."[41] They propose that "power against" is a new formulation used by those who "cannot hope to mount their challenge in an idiom dominated by the status quo forces." Specifically Tétreault and Teske suggest consideration of the "distribution and strategic location of capacities" so that the emphasis is changed from "one of force opposing force" to one that "mobilizes the force of the opponent in such a way that *they defeat themselves*" (emphasis mine). In this essay, an example of Tétreault and Teske's "power against" is the women's groups' use of the government's own record and position on the economic status of women to defeat the latter before the United Nation's Committee on Economic, Social, and Cultural Rights.

The Polish cases in this essay, however, also illustrate a fourth consideration of power: power in spite of—power "as if." Here the "distribution and strategic location of capacities" is affected by internal dynamics. The women employ their skills to improve their own conditions and not necessarily to engineer the explicit defeat of an *opponent*. That is, to act "as if" ignores the dominant regime's preferences *and* rejects attempts to marginalize one's group. It is to ignore what "must be" and create a new reality by acting as one chooses to act. This leaves behind a paradigm of oppression and conflict, and it takes on a sense of empowerment that comes from within, from the way a person conceptualizes strength and influence. Hence, there is not necessarily an intent to defeat or challenge an opponent, although defeat may be inadvertently achieved (as happened to the Communist regime when Solidarity members used the "as if" strategy). Rather, the power here comes from solving one's own problems and filling one's own unmet needs, thereby exerting control over one's destiny.

As mentioned above, this "as if" strategy is a direct descendent of the oppositional style used during the Solidarity era and during even earlier resistance eras in Poland, when "ideas of freedom took absolute precedence over reality and consciousness determined being."[42] Poles acted "as if" freedom of action and individual rights were the norm. The power gained in such a manner, as Jonathan Schell describes it, "was not power that had been wielded by others and had now been wrested from them, it was a new power, which had been created where there had been none before. The program, then, was not to seize political power from the state but to build up society."[43] In the course of proceeding "as if" they were living in a free society unencumbered by state prohibitions, the Poles defeated the Communist regime. Similarly, the women's groups have chosen to take matters into their own hands and create opportunities for women in the form of employment counseling centers, small business ventures, hotlines, and shelters, "as if" this is the logical and natural thing to do. They redefine their view of power and proceed with actions that will garner more and better opportunities for women and improve their conditions.

With regard to the groups' local activities, some critics might opine that the decision to act locally may be considered a "default choice" because it has been forced on women as the only viable route. Arguably, the Polish women's experiences merely demonstrate "differential capacities" found in the traditional realist ("power over") conceptualization. However, looking at the Polish value schema during Communist rule places the decision in another light. As documented by sociologists, the public and private spheres had been markedly split in Poland, with women dominating the private sphere.[44] Adding this to Polish women's historical proclivity to choose local, community activity, we might come to a different conclusion. Might not community work also demonstrate the positive choice of an arena in which women are comfortable, successful, and more influential? The central issue to address in answering this question becomes whether the choice to work at the local level is forced upon the groups because they are squeezed out at the national level, or is freely chosen because it is at the local level that the missions of these organizations can best be realized. Likely the answer to this question is as varied as the individuals who make up the organizations. Simply asking it, however, leads us to consider "power against" and "power in spite of" as viable alternate conceptualizations of power.

Conclusions

In the course of their efforts to play a role in shaping the condition of women in their country, the Polish women's groups presented here exhibit considerable paradigm dexterity. They actually walk in multiple worlds: they work at the community level to tackle problems introduced by the transition from a Communist system to a market-based democracy. Still, they react at the national level to the exclusionary tactics of the state. They strive for empowerment in the first setting (power in spite of) and policy change in the second (power against).

The women's groups in Poland demonstrate how, for both practical and strategic reasons, women switch between activity in the traditional circles of power in Poland (for example, promoting women candidates for office) and other empowerment activities outside the traditional political power venues (such as developing networks and creating tactics to address problems experienced by women). This is not merely a switch in the locus of activity. It is also a change in value orientations, skills, and emotional involvement—that is, a "cognitive switch" analogous to movement between two different cultures. The case of Poland's women's groups suggests that "capacities" may not only be differently located, but also differently constituted and defined. "Power in spite of" provides room for the creation of new forms of power alongside traditional forms of power (against, with, over). It should generate discussion about the three different scholarly traditions about women and politics outlined by Marianne Githens, Pippa Norris, and Joni Lovenduski in *Different Roles, Different Voices.*[45] Moreover, use of alternate conceptualizations of power paradigms may explain the incongruity between women's active participation in community affairs and their portrayal as politically passive:[46] researchers themselves have limited understandings of what constitutes power.

In the actions of these women's organizations, we also see what problems globalization has brought to state politics. Unlike Saskia Sassen's analysis of how local practices constitute and enable globalization,[47] we see how women in Poland have turned this image around using globalization to empower themselves at the local level. They have marshaled both objective structures (the UN, human rights treaties, the EU) and socially constructed processes (women's networking) to influence state politics. In doing so, they counter the state's arguments about economic expediency with arguments about human rights and equity. Hence, globalization is not embedded in a primarily economic framework as it usually is portrayed but, as the efforts of these women demonstrate, in basic understandings of universal rights. That is, these women's groups have shifted the state's attention and forced it to listen to them, bringing human rights issues to the foreground and raising their salience as conditions of membership in global regimes.

At the same time, concentrating their work at the local level—at the *gmina* or district level—means that in this increasingly globalized world the women's groups in Poland can also take advantage of multiple institutional venues. That is, as Clarke and Gaile argue, "social and cultural aspects of economic change associated with globalization leads to more numerous and more diverse local actors seeking cooperation in the face of greater complexity, the emergence of a third sector of non-profit organizations, and the reconstruction of the local institutional infrastructure to accommodate different bargaining and negotiation processes."[48] Poland's governmental decentralization process, shortage of funds for ambitious reforms, and administrative restructuring reflect such changes. They provide a fertile environment for creations of new opportunities for women because, while they shift responsibility to the local level, they do not provide the resources or skills to deal with extant problems. Women's NGOs attempt to fill the void by addressing those problems.

In contrast to Azza Karam's argument that the lack of information and analysis about how to maximize political impact, coupled with a global trend of rising conservatism vis-à-vis women's involvement in public life, has led to skepticism about women's contributions to politics in general,[49] the Polish women present another perspective. What the women in Poland show is that power and influence can be achieved and political inroads made *if* one is flexible in taking advantage of different sources of power, creative and innovative in program creation, and willing to operate on multiple levels. Thus, clinging to traditional empirical indicators of political power (such as, numbers of women in parliament) no longer suffices. This is especially true under conditions of rapid change where there are entrenched patterns of political behavior at the central but not necessarily the local level. Focusing too much on gains or losses at the national level may mask the nature and extent of influence locally. It may have led us to conclude that the Polish women's groups examined here have been fairly ineffective in influencing the direction of public policy. The groups, however, have made major gains at the international and local levels, as evidenced by their achievement of UN advisory status and also in the number of women who continue to seek and benefit from their assistance.[50] From them, we learn to consider the extent to which voice is effected and gains are made in those situations in which women find themselves. Thus, we can come back to Molyneux's definition of a "movement" for criteria to measure its success—that is, by its capacity to effect changes. By this standard, Poland's women's groups constitute a collective, nonmobilized movement. They use the rhetoric of equality to create new power. Their liberation comes both from winning battles (power over, power against) and also by following their own path (power in spite of, power as if) in creating a space in which to act. In discovering this space, they realize their own liberation and fulfillment.

Notes

The epigraph is from Mary Ann Tétreault and Robin L. Teske, "Introduction: Framing the Issues," in *Feminist Approaches to Social Movements, Community, and Power,* vol. 1, *Conscious Acts and the Politics of Social Change,* eds. Robin L. Teske and Mary Ann Tétreault (Columbia: University of South Carolina Press, 2000), 5.

1. Wendy Slater, "Women of Russia and Women's Representation in Russian Politics," in *Russia in Transition,* ed. David Lane (New York: Longman, 1995), 27–33.

2. If they chose otherwise, there was a vibrant underground network in which they could and did participate. See Shana Penn, "The National Secret," *Journal of Women's History* 5, 3 (Winter 1994): 55–69.

3. While Polish women enjoyed more extensive benefits under Communist rule than women in the West—guaranteed full employment, extensive maternity benefits, fairly extensive day care facilities, factory-run vacation facilities—these benefits were a poor compensation for the actual burdens they bore. Polish women under Soviet rule were "liberated" from vibrant, decentralized, and grassroots organizations, to be trapped in centralized, authoritarian, and ideological ones that did little to promote women's economic well-being. They were "liberated" from the burden of housework and readily permitted to join the workforce, only to be trapped in jobs that often paid poorly and gave few opportunities for professional development and enhancement. They were "liberated" from crowded rural housing to crowded, cement-block housing in urban industrial centers.

4. Barbara Einhorn, *Cinderella Goes to Market: Citizenship, Gender, and Women's Movements in East-Central Europe* (New York: Verso, 1993); and Barbara Einhorn, "Ironies of History. Citizenship Issues in the New Market Economies of East-Central Europe," in *Women and Market Societies: Crisis and Opportunity,* ed. Barbara Einhorn and Eileen Janes Yeo (Brookport, Vt: Edward Elgar, 1995), 217–33.

5. Grażyna Kopinska, "Ograniczenia i teriery w aktywnym uszestnictwie kobiet w życiu publicznym" (presented at *Kobiety w Samorządzie Terytorialnym,* Kraków, Poland, 8 March 1999).

6. Kopinska, "Ograniczenia i teriery."

7. Especially Article 33: "Men and women shall have equal rights in family, political, social and economic life in the Republic of Poland" (sec. 1) and "Men and women shall have equal rights, in particular, regarding education, employment and promotion, and shall have the right to equal compensation for work of similar value, to social security, to hold offices, and to receive public honours and decorations" (sec. 2).

8. In this essay, I use "community" to refer to a number of people living together and sharing common values, ties or interests, and subject to the same laws. While it generally refers to a local area (town, district, or neighborhood), it can take on a broader, international application if the ties, values, and interests are shared across national borders, as in the European Community.

9. Office of the Plenipotentiary of the Polish Government for Family Affairs, *Raport o Sytuacji Polskich Rodzin* (*Report on families*) (Warsaw, Poland, 1998), 190.

10. In the Unia Wolności Party, 25 percent of their elected representatives were women and, among independent candidates, nearly 17 percent of those elected to local seats were women.

11. Polish Central Statistical Office, *Monitoring the Labor Market: Reasons Differentiating Salaries in Poland* (Warsaw, Poland, February 1997); and Office of the Plenipotentiary of the Polish Government for Family and Women's Affairs, *Report to the Fourth UN World Conference on Women* (Warsaw, Poland, August 1995), 73–83.

12. The *Report on Families* points out that women represent 85 percent of the health care workforce and 75 percent in education, but only 11 percent of the miners and not even 9 percent in the building trades (p. 189). In neither health nor education are women among the decision makers.

13. Job advertisements in newspapers often specify that employers want male applicants, or that the applicant should have no children and not be pregnant or (even) of child-bearing age.

14. Office for Family Affairs, *Report on Families*, 190.

15. Government Population Commission, *Demographic Situation of Poland* (Warsaw, Poland, 1995).

16. See Wanda Nowicka, *Reproductive Health of Women in Poland* (Warsaw, Poland: Federation for Women and Family Planning, 1997). Only in 1999 was a visible campaign initiated to publicize the benefits of breast self-examinations. This campaign was given particular visibility owing to the help of high-profile personalities such as the wife of President Kwiaśniewski.

17. Poland has a parliamentary system. "AWS" refers to Akcji Wyborczej Solidarność (Solidarity Electoral Action), the party that currently heads the government.

18. Ursula Nowakowska, interview by Diane M. Duffy, 12 May 1999, Women's Right's Center, Warsaw, Poland.

19. Wanda Nowicka, "Factors Affecting Women's Health in Eastern and Central Europe with Particular Emphasis on Infectious Diseases, Mental, Environmental and Reproductive Health" (presented at Women and Health: Mainstreaming the Gender Perspective into the Health Sector, Expert Group Meeting, WHO, Tunis, 28 September–2 October 1998).

20. Barbara Limanowska, interview by Diane M. Duffy, 6 May 1999, Women's Center for Information, Warsaw, Poland.

21. For example, in 1995, *The Situation of Women in Poland* reported that between 1989 and 1993, the number of day care facilities and kindergartens fell by 20 percent in Poland. See Polish Committee of NGOs, *The Situation of Women in Poland* (Warsaw, Poland: Women's Rights Center, 1995).

22. Federation for Women and Family Planning, *Independent Report to the UN Committee on Economic, Social and Cultural Rights* (Warsaw, Poland: Federation for Women and Family Planning, April, 1998).

23. Other developments indicate that the neglect of women's issues is intentional and conscious rather than simply oversights. For example, the government has changed the Plenipotentiary name from "Family and Women's Affairs" to "Family Affairs." Dropping "women" from the title symbolizes what has been a policy of neglect under Kazimierz Kapura, head of this ministry. Moreover, the Plenipotentiary's major resource publication, *Report on Families* has a mere nine pages devoted explicitly to women's problems out of 201 pages.

24. Małgorzata Fuszara, interview by Diane M. Duffy, 8 June 1999, Center for the Social-Legal Studies of Women, University of Warsaw, Warsaw, Poland.

25. Limanowska interview.

26. R. W. Connell, *Gender and Power: Society, the Person, and Sexual Politics* (Stanford, Calif.: Stanford University Press, 1987), 267.

27. Connell, *Gender and Power,* p. 269.

28. Ibid.

29. Information in this section was obtained from informational materials from the respective organizations, and from interviews with the directors of each organization: Danuta Sowinska (Center for the Advancement of Women); Urszula Nowakowska (Women's Rights Center); Barbara Limanowska (OŚKa); Wanda Nowicka (Federation for Women and Family Planning); and Dagmara Baraniewska (Batory Foundation, Women's Program). The *Directory of Women's Organizations and Initiatives in Poland* is also useful and includes both Polish and English entries. See Małgorzata Jagiełło, ed., *Informator o organizacjach i inichatywach kobiecych w Polsce* (Warsaw: Center for the Advancement of Women, 1997). This directory is now available on-line at: http://free.ngo.pl/caw-cpk.

30. Polish Committee of NGOs, "Situation of Women."

31. The Warsaw hotline was established in 1992 to deal with issues related to reproduction and family planning. It currently receives approximately 1600 calls per year. Government funding was available for only one year.

32. See Małgorzata Fuszara, "Women's Movements in Poland," in *Transitions, Environments, Translations: Feminisms in International Politics,* ed. Joan W. Scott, Cora Kaplan, and Debra Keates (New York: Routledge, 1997), 128–42, for a historical overview. Fuszara argues that the "new" movements are, in a sense, in dialogue with movements of earlier generations because they draw from past achievements and "to some extent formulate their own goals in specific discussion with them" (128).

33. While the Batory Women's Program is part of a larger structure (foundation), there is a considerable degree of autonomy given to it. Moreover, its smallness works against a hierarchy. Hence, I've grouped it with the other three.

34. Fuszara, "Women's Movements in Poland," 132–33, 139–40.

35. Maxine Molyneux, "Analyzing Women's Movements," *Development and Change* 29 (1998): 223.

36. Ibid., 224.

37. Ibid., 228.

38. Tétreault and Teske, "Introduction," 5; and Sara M. Evans and Harry C. Boyte, *Free Spaces: The Sources of Democratic Change in America* (Chicago: University of Chicago Press, 1992).

39. The specific words chosen for the appeal are also important here. In Poland, many women avoid any association with the words "feminist" and "feminism" which

carry a connotation of confrontation with men and which could elicit a backlash against women's organizations. See Fuszara, "Women's Movements in Poland," 140, for a brief discussion on aversion to the use of "feminism." By emphasizing "equality" rather than "liberation," they avoid semantic arguments and instead use the platform of human rights, which resonates more effectively in a Poland emerging from the communist yoke.

40. Molyneux, "Analyzing Women's Movements," 232.

41. Tétreault and Teske, "Introduction," 7.

42. See Timothy Garton Ash, *The Uses of Adversity: Essays on the Fate of Central Europe* (New York: Random House, 1989) 105–7, 116. Garton Ash discusses this tradition of resistance among Poland's intellectuals that eventually gained a foothold among the entire population during the Solidarity era.

43. Jonathan Schell, Introduction to *Letters from Prison and Other Essays,* by Adam Michnik, trans. Maya Latynska (Berkeley: University of California Press, 1985), xxxi.

44. See Mirosława Marody, "Social Stability and the Concept of Collective Sense," in *Crisis and Transition: Polish Society in the 1980s,* ed. I. Bialecki, I. Koralewicz, and M. Watson (London: Berg 1987), 130–58; and Edmund Wnuk-Lipiński, "Social Dimorphism and Its Implications," in *Crisis and Transition,* 159–76.

45. See Marianne Githens, Pippa Norris, Joni Lovenduski, "Introduction," in *Different Roles, Different Voices. Women and Politics in the United States and Europe* (New York: Harper Collins, 1994), ix–xi. Githens et al. identify the three traditions as (1) concentration on women in the traditional political arena (for example, voting and electoral behavior, characteristics of women active in political affairs, office-holding, participation in political parties, gender gap); (2) the study of social movements (especially the relationship between women's activities and movements addressing issues in the public policy arena); and (3) the basis for the omission and subordination of women in political thought (that is, the nature of gender and the relationship of feminism with ideological divisions among liberals, socialists, radicals, and conservatives).

46. Ibid., x.

47. Saskia Sassen, "Cities and Communities in the Global Economy: Rethinking Our Concepts," *American Behavioral Scientist* 39 (March–April 1996): 630.

48. Susan E. Clarke and Gary L. Gaile, "Local Politics in a Global Era: Thinking Locally, Acting Globally," *Annals of the American Academy of Political and Social Science* 55 (May 1997): 33.

49. Azza Karam, "Shifting Focus: From the Road to Parliament to Making Inroads in Parliament," *Women in Parliament. Beyond Numbers,* available at: http://www.idea.int/women/parl/ch1b.htm (10 June 2002).

50. There are caveats to keep in mind, though. If power is transferred to the local level, and if those occupying traditional power centers become aware of the gains made by Polish women, they may redirect their attention and energy in a way that creates a backlash, undermining the inroads these women's groups have made. So, the imperative is to send out "tentacles of influence" in the form of contacts and support strong enough to counter any such efforts. These contacts and support networks may be critical to continuing success for the groups.

Part Five

Equal Justice

Chapter 13

Human Rights and the Rights of Women

Retrospects and Perspectives on Work in the United Nations

Agda Rössel

Fifty years ago the United Nations was created by the victors of the Second World War. It replaced the League of Nations, which had failed to maintain peace. Among those countries invited to participate as charter members of the new world organization—fifty-one countries in all—was Sweden. I had the privilege to start my involvement in UN affairs at the "construction phase." In 1951 I was appointed the Swedish delegate to the UN Commission on Human Rights. Sweden served as the Nordic member on that Commission between 1951 and 1953. Beginning in 1952 I was a Swedish delegate to the General Assembly, and in 1954 I began six years as the Swedish delegate to the UN Commission on the Status of Women. In 1958 I was appointed Sweden's Ambassador to the United Nations, the first female head-of-mission to the world organization. When I left the post of ambassador in 1964, there was still no other woman serving as head-of-mission to the United Nations. Luckily that situation changed during the following decades. Under President Bill Clinton, the U.S. permanent delegate to the United Nations was a forceful woman. I am referring to Ambassador Madeleine Albright. President Reagan also had appointed a woman, Jeane Kirkpatrick, to that post.

When I joined the United Nations, I faced the complications of the double—or triple—workload professional women still encounter today, more than fifty years later. I carried the woman's special responsibility for the family and the children. At the same time, I was a female civil servant—then, as today, we were a small minority in the male-dominated civil service. I worked with immigrant and refugee matters. At the same time, I was actively involved in the leadership of the women's movement, both nationally and internationally, as chair of the Swedish and, later, also of the International Federation of Business and Professional Women (IFBPW). That was a tall order. But it gave me a wealth of experience that I could apply to my work in the United Nations on behalf of women and children, and human rights in general.

From the start, the issue of human rights was given a permanent role in the work of the United Nations—it was written into the Charter. In 1946 the UN Commission on Human Rights was established. President Truman had mobilized one of the great women of the twentieth century, Mrs. Eleanor Roosevelt, as chairman of the Human Rights Commission. She had chaired the drafting of the UN Universal Declaration on Human Rights that was adopted in 1948. In that capacity, she was invited to Sweden in 1950 to speak to the Swedish branch of the IFBPW about the UN's work in the field of human rights. When I joined the UN, Mrs. Roosevelt chaired the drafting of the first legally binding international instrument on human rights, the first of what in 1966 became the two UN Covenants on Human Rights. At that time, the Cold War already had begun, complicating the work of the United Nations in the field of human rights. The Communist dictatorships in the Soviet Union and the Eastern European countries had in reality eliminated individual freedom of expression and all the democratic freedoms of their peoples. Consequently, they treated human rights activities as an attack on their social systems. The intensity of the fierce attacks that the Communist representatives directed at the United States, and Mrs. Roosevelt and the Human Rights Commission in 1952 is still fresh in my mind. They could not, however, stop the work in the UN in the same way that they had eliminated all the freedoms formally written into their own constitutions. However, they tried to "balance" the work by introducing economic human rights such as the right to a job and the right to livelihood into the discussion.

Today with the Cold War ended, these problems have been drastically reduced, but the remaining totalitarian states are still determinedly raising obstacles to progress in the promotion of human rights in the world by the United Nations. Progress is also being hampered by the many connections of human rights issues to the value systems of different religions, ethnic traditions, and civilizations throughout the world. We have no way of dealing with these issues in a concrete and constructive way. We must not do it the "male way," by using national identity against enemies, countries, or civilizations demonized as violators of human rights. That approach leads to polarization, to conflicts, and to wars between civilizations. That, in essence, is the crisis of male civilization, in all parts of the world, among all social and political systems, all religions and ethnic traditions, which have been based on centuries—millennia—of male domination and power. This has been realized not only by women today (see, for example, the excellent analyses by Rosiska Darcy de Oliviera of Brazil); this is also increasingly understood by men.

In his brilliant intellectual history of the world, *The Passion of the Western Mind,* the American professor Richard Tarnas maintains that the "*crisis of modern man is an essentially masculine crisis.*"[1] Humankind "faces the psychological and biological crisis of living in a world that has come to be shaped in such a way that it precisely matches the male world view." Tarnas describes that man-made environment of the world today: it is "increasingly mechanistic, atomized, soulless and self-destructive." To promote respect for human rights in such a world, it is, according to Tarnas, necessary "to achieve [a] reintegration of the . . . feminine" which has been repressed by the evolution over millennia of the Western mind. Humankind must choose to enter into a fundamentally new relationship of mutuality between the masculine and the feminine in all its forms.

Human rights problems are intimately linked to the growing social problems of poverty and underdevelopment as well as to the emerging global environmental crisis. They have to be dealt with politically, in combination with efforts to promote development and environmental rights, as well as with actions to fight poverty and to promote a better quality of life that can induce lower fertility.

Basic human rights problems are found in all political systems and among all civilizations. Capital punishment, the equality of women, the rights of children, and the rights of the many—and increasing numbers of —migrants and refugees in today's world are among these serious human rights problems. One of the provisions in the draft Covenant on Human Rights that we started to negotiate in the early 1950s, when I first joined the world of the United Nations, dealt with the right to life. The first sentence of the article read "Every man has the right to life." Unfortunately, the draft article did not end there. It continued with a list of exceptions about when states had the right to take a life.

Sweden had abolished capital punishment in the 1920s, so I questioned these exceptions and tried to have them deleted. That led to revealing statements by representatives of countries that upheld the death penalty. One of the limitations on the right of the state to take life concerned pregnant women. When I asked what would happen to a child who was born before the capital punishment of the mother took place, one answer was that the child belonged to the state. Those representatives who were of that view obviously had not reflected upon the provision forbidding slavery!

In 1959 I, along with representatives from eight other countries, proposed that the UN initiate a study of the question of capital punishment, of the laws and practices relating thereto, and of the effects of capital punishment and its abolition on the rate of criminality. That study was carried out in two phases, ending in 1965. The study confirmed that the abolition of the death penalty does not have the effect of significantly increasing the incidence of crime. The deterrent effect of capital punishment was not demonstrated, to say the least.

What happened after that study? There is good news, and there is bad news. Let me start with the good news. A Second Optional Protocol on the Abolition of the Death Penalty was adopted in 1989. A small number of states have ratified the Protocol, and it has entered into force. That is a crucial milestone in the protection and promotion of human rights because the right to life is the most fundamental of all human rights. Another piece of good news is that a few countries have taken encouraging steps toward abolishing the death penalty.

And now the bad news. In some countries the death penalty is being used more widely than before. It is also being applied to persons under the age of eighteen, in clear violation of the International Covenant on Civil and Political Rights. And, what is worse, some countries that had formerly abolished the death penalty have reintroduced it. Concerning the progress of the renewed efforts by the Nordic countries, inter alia, to abolish the death penalty, I am rather pessimistic. I base my assessment on the terrible trend towards a brutalization of societies that I see not only in the growing slums of the megacities of the Third World, but also in big cities in the developed countries. The brutalization of relationships between people also characterizes the many ethnic conflicts that have arisen after the end of the Cold War and the situation encountered by the soaring number of refugees.

These developments are caused by the growing gap between the increasing masses of very poor and underprivileged persons on the one hand and small groups of opulently consuming people on the other. These growing inequalities in all countries are leading to an increase in the number and brutality of crimes. The response of many governments has been to add more police and to implement more severe punishment—including wider use of the death penalty. We know, however, that this is not the right response. It will not deter crime. The correct response would be economic and social action to provide jobs to the increasing legions of unemployed young people who have no hope of ever getting a job in their lifetimes. This would give the millions of underprivileged—girls and boys, women and men—the chance of a worthy life; it would give hope to all those who despair.

During my years at the UN, I was often asked, "Why do we have to have both a Commission on Human Rights and a Commission on the Status of Women?" My answer used to be: "We will need this for as long as the position of women in the world does not reflect the fact that women are equal citizens with men. The process towards this self-evident goal will take decades, maybe centuries." Now, nearly fifty years later, I am sorry that my answer is still the same. I am saying this in spite of the many UN decisions and resolutions, as well as national legislation, policies, and decisions on different aspects of equal rights and equal opportunities for women and men. The fact, however, is that what we need is not more words and rhetoric. We need deeds. We need action by governments, municipal authorities, employers, trade unions, scientists, news media, cultural workers, and all other groups and individuals who influence attitudes on the position of women, among them perhaps primarily, their male spouses. We need to understand that the inequalities, in a variety of contexts, between opportunities and rights between men and women can only be explained in terms of an uneven distribution of power. It is really a question of power. This is how a leading Swedish politician, the former Deputy Prime Minister and Minister of Social Health and Welfare and of Equality, Mr. Bengt Westerberg put it in a series of speeches he made in 1994 and 1995. From this perspective an important strategy in the struggle for equal opportunities would be to make men's power and control over women visible. The reason for this is that power is often invisible. I would claim that today, and most likely for many years to come, this is a formidable task for the United Nations Commission on the Status of Women.

Bengt Westerberg highlighted the invisibility of this power relationship as a major cause of the difficulties in achieving equality. The well-known American journalist Susan Faludi suggests another motive. In *Backlash*, her major survey of the attacks that were made in the 1980s on the progress towards equality that American women had made in the postwar years, Susan Faludi stressed that the hard times of economic and social crises, characterized by high unemployment and social unrest, created a widespread fear of change in the opportunities and rights of women. She wrote that we, the women, live with the enemy. Most of us need men. But they also need us. And on top of that, I would say that we love them. And often they love us. Unfortunately, that love has not, as yet, led our men to yield more than a fraction of all their power to us. Sometimes that makes me feel strongly sympathetic towards a famous woman in the literature of one of the wonderful countries to which I was posted, Greece. I think of Lysistrata.

In 1952 the United Nations General Assembly adopted the text of a Convention on the Equality of Women. The Convention, which entered into force on 8 July 1954, stated that women shall be eligible for political assemblies on the same terms as men and that women shall have access to public office and public positions on the same conditions as men. I was asked why there was a need for a special treaty on these issues when they were already covered by the proposed UN Covenant on Human Rights. That text stated that every citizen should be eligible for political assemblies and have access to public office and official positions on the same terms. The problem was that in many old constitutions women were not considered citizens!

This is reflected in the wording of the Charter of the United Nations: The Rights of *Man!* Remember the phrases of the French Revolution. All the rights of that revolution were, as Mary Wollstonecraft stated, the rights only of men, "Droits de l'Homme"! The Great Revolution obviously didn't include women. All the major languages within which Western tradition has developed have tended to personify the human species with words that are masculine in gender.

The situation in most countries of the world today is not so very different from the one I tackled fifty years ago with regard to the position of women in public life, in government and in parliament. I still remember the situation in a non-European country where the Commission on the Status of Women held a meeting. The women were promised equal political rights. These rights, however, were conditional. Women could be elected only on condition that they could read and write, a condition not required of men. That would have led to the situation that women, had they been elected to the political assemblies (which of course they were not), would have been superior to many of the male members who didn't know how to read and write! In many countries, including the United States as well as the Nordic countries, we have seen positive developments in the political arena. In 1995 nearly half the members of the governments of Sweden and Norway were women. In the Nordic political assemblies, we are approaching a stage where half the membership is female. In 1995, 41 percent of the members of the Swedish parliament were women; in Norway the figure was 36 percent, in Finland 38 percent, and in Denmark 33 percent. By comparison, the figure in France at that time was a mere 5 percent.[2]

But in the bureaucracy, in advising politicians, and in being regularly instrumental in the real decision making, progress is much slower. Today, just as fifty years ago, offices are still headed by men to a large extent. Only a small minority of ambassadors are women, in my country as in all other countries, in the developed as well as in the developing world. And the situation in the United Nations and in the agencies of the UN system is the same. The General Assembly has reaffirmed its determination to see the number of women in the UN Secretariat increase. Even so, in 1995 less than 35 percent were women, and fewer than 10 percent of the persons in the four highest-level posts in the UN Secretariat were women. Thus, in the UN we also still have a long way to go to reach equality. We find a high level of inequality also in the private sector. Very few chief executive officers and "chairmen" of the board or, for that matter, board members, are women. The corporate world remains a male world.

A crucial issue concerning equal rights for men and women is the question of equal pay. When I started my work at the United Nations, a series of resolutions committing governments to adopt legislation securing equal pay for women were introduced. Even then I felt discomfort when these resolutions were adopted. I knew that my own country, in reality, was far from being able, or (if I wanted to be nasty) willing, to honor that commitment. So it was then, and so it is to a large extent now. In the 1990s in Sweden, the earnings of women still lagged one-third behind men of equal education and work experience. The most difficult problems to tackle, however, are perhaps equal evaluation and equal access to the better-paid jobs. The jobs that are traditionally occupied by women everywhere are the low-paid jobs. Women have less desirable jobs than men, jobs that are more monotonous and repetitive, and jobs with fewer opportunities for independent decision making. Fewer women than men have paid employment, even if the level in my own country in 1995 was high—at more than 80 percent. Among those who are part of the labor force, a higher percentage of women than men are unemployed.

An important factor is the equal right of women to professional education in all fields, academic as well as nonacademic. In this area also, too much remains the same today as fifty years ago. Among the underprivileged of the world, many girls still have no access to very basic education. Girls are not considered worth the costs of formal education because they are supposed to serve the men at home as wives and mothers. But at the same time, the positive effects of the tremendous resources invested in basic education in developing countries are noticeable among women. In the least developed countries, the share of women who have learned to read has doubled from 18 to 36 percent.[3] Among the "better offs," positive developments have also taken place in many countries. I am referring to the success of female students in high schools and in academia.

In 1954, when I chaired the International Federation of Business and Professional Women, we learned that many Arab women had completed their academic educations. We organized a conference in Beirut in 1956 and invited twenty-five of these women. We learned that their higher education had taken place in secret. They were allowed to attend a girls' secondary school in Beirut. However, they often continued in school for years until they received a college-level degree. When the fathers asked their wives in the harem about their daughters, they were informed that they were attending the girls' school in Beirut. These fathers could not officially allow their daughters to get academic training, an attitude that was similar to attitudes in many places in Europe at that time. In many countries, academically trained women, even if very successful in their academic studies, were exceptions to the general rule that academia was for men.

Of fundamental importance to female emancipation is the right of women to corporal integrity. That right is challenged in many ways in many parts of the world. I refer to the reproductive rights of women, the right to choose whether or not to have children, to control their own sexuality and fertility. It includes the right to abortion and to use contraceptives. I am also referring to the right to not be a victim of violence, including not to be a victim of female genital mutilation. Sweden was the first country to introduce the expression "family planning" in the UN. Behind family planning as a concept was a deep concern for the health of women, as well as for the well-being of the family and the welfare of society. Leading women and men in Sweden had taken action early to make life for women more bearable through spreading the use of contraceptives and thus allowing the spacing, and hopefully also limiting the number of children each woman would bear. Our efforts met with resistance, particularly in Catholic countries. Some developing countries such as Egypt, Ghana, India, and Pakistan cosponsored the resolution on family planning in the late '50s. Mind you, it was adopted. Over the years a series of UN conferences on population has been held, the latest one in Cairo in 1994.[4] We still encounter the same strong opposing attitudes from Catholic countries, and not least from the Holy See. In spite of this, the use of contraceptives is widely accepted in the world today, and ultimately even safe and legal abortions will be available worldwide.

One of the most disgusting violations of human rights is violence against women and children in all its forms. In this context, I would like to focus on female genital mutilation. As early as the 1950s, I was approached by African women at international conferences who asked if I could help them to bring that terrible practice before the UN. As chair of the Commission on the Status of Women, I saw to it that this horrible form of violence against women was discussed in the report of the Commission to the Economic and Social Council. In the Council, however, it was always voted down to the bottom of the agenda, meaning that a chronic shortage of time always resulted in the issue never being debated. In despair, I asked the Swedish delegate to the World Health Organization to introduce this urgent issue to the agenda of that organization. It took him four years to achieve this! However, it was dealt with, and today it is defined by the WHO as a major health problem. And it really is. Genital mutilation has been forced on over 136 million girls and women in the world, primarily in African countries.[5] It is being performed on small girls three to seven years of age. The physical and mental consequences are horrible.

Female genital mutilation is not a religious issue. It is a tradition that is millennia old among nomadic peoples. In this context, I would like to stress that it is not mentioned in the Qur'an. And it has been claimed that it is not even compatible with the Qur'an. No religious scripture in the world recognizes female genital mutilation. Through increasing migration, the problem has become real and pressing in Europe and North America. In 1982 a law was adopted in Sweden prohibiting female genital mutilation. We have learned that this is only the first of many steps necessary to stop this form of violence against women. What is needed is education and information to raise an awareness among women and men, girls and boys as to the terrible consequences of exercising this old tradition.

Much has happened over the years of my active participation at the United Nations. Today the issue of female genital mutilation is no longer taboo. Women are standing up for their right to not be mutilated. Even men are reacting and actively participating in efforts to stop it. Immigrant boys in Europe want to marry unmutilated girls. Human dignity demands that this terrible practice be eradicated from our planet.

Fifty years is normally a long-term perspective in society. We know about the formidable transformation of human practices and technologies that has taken place since World War II. We know of the phenomenal growth of the world economy. In comparison with this, it is easy to despair over the slow pace of change in approaching equality for women. But we are dealing with attitudes that took root thousands of years ago, in Western as well as Eastern traditions. The masculinity of the Western as well as the Eastern mind has been pervasive and fundamental, affecting every aspect of thought, determining the most basic conception of human identity and the human role in the world. From that perspective, a lot has happened in the last fifty years.

Sometimes I feel frustrated. Maybe particularly now because of the many global economic, social, and environmental crises, and the many ethnic conflicts and the growing masses of refugees. There is really no linear progress in the world towards respect for human rights. But often I feel hopeful. Especially when I feel the dedication, intelligence, and increasing force of the women's movements of the world, and also of the environmental movements.

I am not satisfied with many developments. But neither am I wholly dissatisfied. The United Nations continues to develop its tools for peacekeeping and for peacemaking. This is a cumbersome process. But progress has been made since the end of the Cold War. The UN must significantly strengthen its actions and support the efforts of the developing countries to escape the paralyzing grip of global economic, social, and environmental crises. It must avoid becoming an arena for struggles and fights between religions, ethnic groups, and civilizations. But the deliberations, decisions, and activities of the world organization must also contribute to necessary changes in the value systems of the religions and of the traditions in civilizations in order to "enter into a fundamentally new relationship of mutuality with the feminine in all its forms."[6]

Isn't the time ripe to elect a women as the next Secretary General of the United Nations? I think so. However, as important today as it was fifty years ago is that we must never give up in our efforts to promote respect for human rights and to achieve equal opportunities and rights for women and men.

Notes

Prepared for presentation at the Carrie Chapman Catt Center Conference on Women and Human Rights in the Middle East and Beyond, Washington, D.C., 3 March 1995.

1. Richard Tarnas, *The Passion of the Western Mind: Understanding the Ideas That Have Shaped Our World View* (New York: Harmony Books, 1993), 442–44.

2. More recent numbers remain similar with the positive exception of France. In 1998 the percentage of women in parliamentary seats was as follows: Denmark 33.0, Finland 33.5, Norway 36.4, Sweden 40.4, France 10.9 (Lane Kenworthy and Melissa Malami, "Gender Inequality in Political Representation: A Worldwide Comparative Analysis," *Social Forces* 78, 1 [September 1999]: 235–68).

3. For the most recent statistics, readers should refer to UNESCO's *Statistical Yearbook* or similar sources. See also the Population Concern's *The Population and Development Database,* available on-line at http://www.alsagerschool.co.uk Subjects/Geography/Geography Population Software (9 May 2002).

4. After a series of regional meetings, the UN held a special session of the General Assembly as a follow-up to the Cairo International Conference on Population and Development. This June 1999 meeting, nicknamed "Cairo + 5," focused on key actions needed to reach the goals set out in Cairo in 1994. For more information on Cairo + 5, please see http://www.unfpa.org/icpd (7 August 2002).

5. See the World Health Organization's "Female Genital Mutilation: An Overview," 1998, http://www.who.int/dsa/cat98/fgmbook.htm (9 May 2002) for more detailed information.

6. Tarnas, *Passion of the Western Mind,* 444.

Chapter 14

Speaking Out for Justice in Higher Education

The AAUW Legal Advocacy Fund Works to End Sex Discrimination in Academe

Patricia J. McCabe

"M.I.T. Acknowledges Bias against Female Professors" screamed the front page of the 22 March 1999 *New York Times.* When I read this headline I was stunned. Finally, an admission that sex discrimination does in fact occur within our nation's institutions of higher education. And the *New York Times* was carrying the story! In fact, the *New York Times, Boston Globe,* and other general circulation newspapers carried the story as headline news; coverage was not just relegated to the *Chronicle of Higher Education, Women in Academe,* or other outlets of the education press. Should I dare to hope that perhaps this will be the catalyst to eradicate sex discrimination in higher education once and for all?

The fact that there is bias against female professors came as no surprise to me. For the last eight years, I have been the director of the American Association of University Women (AAUW) Legal Advocacy Fund (LAF), a nonprofit organization dedicated to supporting women fighting sex discrimination in higher education. For twenty-one years, LAF has provided funding and a support system for female faculty, students, and administrators who challenge discrimination at colleges and universities across the country.

Sex discrimination is not just an M.I.T. problem—it is a national problem. Today, college campuses are still, by and large, men's clubs. Although women account for approximately 33 percent of higher education faculty nationwide, they represent only 14 percent of full professors and 12 percent of college presidents. In fact, the majority of women hold faculty positions, such as lecturer, adjunct professor, or researcher, that are less well paid, less stable, and less powerful than the positions men hold. There is a serious gap in female participation in the upper ranks of associate and full professors at our nation's colleges and universities.

Tenure rates are no more impressive. Only 48 percent of women faculty are tenured compared to 72 percent of male faculty. Moreover, in the last twenty years women's tenure rates have increased by a mere 1.5 percent while men's tenure rates have increased by 8 percent. This statistic is particularly alarming given that women earn almost half of all Ph.D.s awarded in the United States each year.

A study leading to M.I.T.'s admission demonstrated that even when women attain the rank of full professor, they do not attain equity. On the contrary, the senior female faculty members in M.I.T.'s School of Science suffered discrimination in the form of lower salaries, fewer resources (funding, laboratory space, etc.), heavier teaching loads, lower participation on committees of power (hiring/tenure committees), and hostile work environments when compared to male faculty members.

The university environment is supposed to foster groundbreaking research, innovative thinking, and the exchange of ideas. Despite hard work and small victories, women are still being denied equal opportunities and access in this forum, and their absence has far-reaching ramifications. A higher education system that reinforces gender bias has an important influence on the workplace as a whole, on individual families and relationships, and on society in general. If we do not reform these institutions entrusted with molding, teaching, and mentoring future generations, we prolong a legacy of gender inequity and complacency.

Speaking Out for Justice

Even more shocking than the statistics, however, are the individual stories of accomplished women who struggle against these barriers.

LAF-supported plaintiff Cynthia Fisher endured a thirteen-year tenure battle against Vassar College only to lose her case when the U.S. Supreme Court refused to hear her appeal in January 1998. Fisher, a biology professor, claimed in her lawsuit that she was denied tenure because she was an older married woman who had taken a leave from the laboratory to rear her children. Before beginning to teach at Vassar in 1977, Fisher had taken eight years off to care for her two daughters. She was denied tenure in 1985 by a departmental panel that, because of the voluntary hiatus in her career, questioned her scholarly independence, commitment to research, and mastery of her field.

Fisher was convinced that her colleagues denied her tenure not because she was unqualified but rather because of their bias against a woman who chose to take time off to care for her young children. She also felt that her colleagues did not take her seriously because she was a married woman with young children. At trial, Fisher presented statistical evidence documenting that although some single female faculty members succeeded in the sciences at Vassar, married faculty women with children were virtually blacklisted.

In 1994, after a three-week trial, federal district court Judge Constance Baker Motley agreed with Fisher. The decision was based on 111 findings of fact. It concluded that Fisher had been discriminated against on the basis of sex-plus (her gender and marital status), age (she was over 40), and pay equity (between men and women faculty). Fisher was awarded more than $600,000 in back pay and almost $400,000 in attorneys' fees.[1]

Judge Motley rested her opinion on evidence that compared Fisher's record with that of the four married men who had achieved tenure during the relevant period. She found that Fisher's record was superior to that of each of the men regarding scholarship and teaching and at least equal to each of the men regarding service to the college (the three criteria for judging promotion and tenure). Motley further found that Fisher's record was equal to that of the one unmarried woman who achieved tenure the year Fisher was rejected (and even superior to this unmarried woman in that she had a longer teaching career at Vassar). Judge Motley further noted, and Vassar conceded, that the college had not granted tenure to any married women in biology, chemistry, mathematics, physics, or geology from 1956 to 1985. Judge Motley concluded that Vassar had an affirmative intent to deny tenure to married women in the physical sciences and mathematics. In addition, Judge Motley said that denying tenure to Fisher reflected "a stereotype and bias that a woman with an active and ongoing family life cannot be a productive scientist, and, therefore, is not one, despite much evidence to the contrary."[2] The court ordered Vassar to reinstate Fisher.

The United States Court of Appeals for the Second Circuit overturned Judge Motley's decision. The Second Circuit Court held that universities *could* consider a faculty member's time off for child-rearing in making tenure decisions. Fisher petitioned the U.S. Supreme Court, but the court refused to hear her appeal, thereby upholding the Second Circuit Court's decision. Even before Fisher's appeal was denied, that decision was already affecting other sex-discrimination plaintiffs in the federal court system in New York.

Cynthia Fisher's case *should* have sparked a national debate about the rights and roles of working mothers, the tenure process on campus, and the continued oppression of female scientists. Instead, the case became a negative precedent that can and will be used against women in cases to come.

Less than a week after the U.S. Supreme Court denied Fisher's request for a hearing, a federal district court in New York rejected another tenure discrimination case against Vassar. In his decision, the judge noted his disagreement with the Supreme Court's ruling in *Fisher v. Vassar,* stating that it "can only bring confusion" to the court, and confessing "slight unease" in reaching the decision to dismiss the case before him. But because the precedent had been set, the judge felt he had to dismiss the case.[3]

Two other LAF-supported cases have been affected by the *Fisher* decision. In early 1997, a New York district court judge, citing *Fisher* and siding with the State University of New York–Buffalo, threw out Sharon Leder's claims of sex discrimination in the denial of tenure. Leder was allowed to pursue a pay equity claim, but the rest of her complaint was dismissed. Leder, a professor of women's studies/feminist literary criticism, had filed suit in 1988. Her lawsuit languished in the federal district court for nearly ten years before the court threw out the bulk of her case. In 1999 Leder settled her pay equity claim out of court.

More recently, a New York district court judge dismissed Shelley Weinstock's sex discrimination case against Columbia University. Weinstock was an assistant professor of chemistry at Barnard from 1985 to 1993. Because of Barnard's affiliation with Columbia University, the president and provost of Columbia University, in addition to committees and officials at Barnard, must approve Barnard professors seeking tenure. In 1993 Weinstock was denied tenure despite favorable recommendations from the departments of chemistry at both Barnard and Columbia; the College Appointments, Tenure and Promotion Committee (ATP); Barnard's president; and an ad hoc committee assigned to evaluate her candidacy. Apparently disregarding all of these recommendations, the provost of Columbia University denied her tenure. With support from the president of Barnard, Weinstock appealed the decision, but the appeal was denied in October 1993. She was terminated in June 1994.

Weinstock sued for sex discrimination alleging that, in the tenure review, the provost had devalued significant materials including the papers she published in prestigious refereed journals, the grants she won for her research in bioengineering, and her excellent teaching and service records. In July 1999, a federal district court judge granted summary judgment in favor of Columbia,[4] effectively ending the case without a trial. Dismissing all of Weinstock's sex discrimination arguments, the judge took Columbia at its word, accepting that Weinstock was denied tenure for the legitimate, nondiscriminatory reason that she lacked the requisite scholarship. Yet many of her peers agreed that she *did possess* the level of scholarship required. The approval from the Barnard chemistry department was unanimous. And the president of Barnard was so convinced that Weinstock deserved tenure that she appealed Columbia's decision, something she as president had never done before. So how could this happen?

It happened because the judge disregarded Weinstock's evidence that the two ATP committee members who voted to deny her tenure were sex-biased. (The ATP had voted 3–2 in favor of tenure.) He disregarded evidence that showed procedural irregularities in Weinstock's tenure review. For example, the provost had made phone calls to members of the ATP committee before the tenure review that at least two committee members attested were an improper attempt to sway the committee members to deny tenure. In ruling on the motion for summary judgment, the judge was supposed to look at the evidence in the light most favorable to Weinstock. Did he? Did not Weinstock at least deserve to have her evidence presented in a trial and have a jury decide the factual issues?

For women in New York, negative precedents have meant that the burden of proof in tenure cases has become insurmountable. However, a recent decision by the U.S. Supreme Court in *Reeves v. Sanderson Plumbing* may result in a shift in favor of the plaintiff.[5] Despite the difficulty, or perhaps because of it, LAF will continue to support Shelley Weinstock and others who are courageous enough to fight a sex discrimination tenure case in the currently unsympathetic second circuit of the federal court system. With perseverance, we anticipate that eventually one such case will make it to the U.S. Supreme Court, and we will have the opportunity to correct the negative legal precedent established in *Fisher.*

Working for Change
The AAUW Legal Advocacy Fund

The AAUW Legal Advocacy Fund was created to help courageous women, like Shelley Weinstock, stand up to higher education institutions and speak out for justice. LAF's primary program is to provide financial support to female litigants who are challenging sex discrimination by a college or university. Between 1981 and 2001, LAF gave more than $750,000 to over seventy women to support their sex discrimination lawsuits. To receive case support, a plaintiff must complete an application. These applications are reviewed by LAF staff to ensure that the applicant's case meets three basic criteria: that the case involves sex discrimination, that the defendant is a university or college, and that the case has been filed in state or federal court. If these criteria are satisfied, the application is forwarded to the LAF Advisory Committee.

The Advisory Committee conducts the second phase of the review cycle. The committee is composed of eight members, six of whom must be attorneys admitted and in good standing to practice law in one or more states. At least four committee members review each application and make recommendations to the LAF Board of Directors as to whether the case should be adopted and funded by LAF. The Advisory Committee looks at several factors in making its recommendations including the individual's financial need, the likelihood of success on the merits, and the case's potential significance for women in higher education.

In the third phase of the review cycle, the LAF Board of Directors reviews both the case and the Advisory Committee's recommendations. The LAF Board makes the final decision on which cases to adopt and fund. In assessing the committee's recommendations, the Board not only compares the applications to one another but also looks at the cases LAF is currently supporting. The LAF Board may reject all new applications in favor of granting more money to ongoing cases if the new cases are not as strong. Unfortunately, financial limitations mean LAF can fund only about one-quarter of the applications it receives. Although the decisions are often agonizing, LAF believes this process supports the strongest cases, those with the highest potential both for success and for having a significant impact on women.

A successful lawsuit does more than just hold the defending institution accountable; a favorable ruling can establish a legal precedent that affects the future of all women. For example, cases against colleges and universities that are filed under Title VII—federal legislation prohibiting discrimination in the workplace on the basis of sex, race, color, religion, and national origin—can establish law that applies to all workplaces and not just to institutions of higher education. Similarly, pay equity claims filed under the Equal Pay Act—federal legislation prohibiting sex discrimination in wages, salaries, benefits, and other forms of compensation—can establish legal precedent with consequences for all employed women. Winning lawsuits can help build a body of law that will eventually eradicate discriminatory practices in the workplace.

Many LAF-supported plaintiffs have successfully resolved their lawsuits. One example is the case of *James v. Virginia State and Polytechnic Institute* adopted by the LAF in 1994. Title IX is a federal law prohibiting sex discrimination in educational institutions and programs that receive federal funds. It protects women on the playing field and in the classroom. Since its passage in 1972, women and girls have made tremendous gains in athletic opportunities and resources, but, in many instances, it has taken litigation to secure those gains. This was a Title IX discrimination lawsuit brought by the National Women's Law Center on behalf of twelve female student athletes. The students alleged that they experienced discrimination in the process of seeking (and failing) to upgrade women's club sports to varsity status. The students were all outstanding athletes in field hockey, softball, lacrosse, and crew who each had paid hundreds of dollars, season after season, to play club sports. Their lawsuit asserted that they were denied equal access to athletic scholarships because women's sports had not been granted the same status as men's sports at Virginia Tech.

In the *James* case, Virginia Tech, like other colleges and universities that have defended similar lawsuits, argued that women and girls are simply not as interested in sports as men and boys and therefore need not be offered equal opportunity to participate in athletics. It is mind-boggling to think that schools still cling to this argument when, to the contrary, we have seen a huge surge of interest and participation in sports by women and girls in the quarter century since the passage of Title IX in 1972. The U.S. Women's National Soccer Team demonstrated this in its 1999 Women's World Cup victory. Likewise, the Women's National Basketball Association created dedicated fans and filled far more seats in its inaugural years than the National Basketball Association was able to do when it was first established.

There is no reason why men's collegiate and professional athletic teams should dominate weekend television programming. There is no reason why girls should not aspire to be collegiate and professional athletes—except that the opportunity is still denied them. We have made significant strides in athletics for women and girls but there is still much to be done to transform the male-dominated sports media and elevate women's collegiate and professional sports to the levels currently enjoyed by men's sports.

The female athletes and Virginia Tech were able to reach agreement and settle their lawsuit in April 1995. The settlement agreement, approved by the court, promised far greater athletic opportunities for female athletes at the university. It required Virginia Tech to achieve a female varsity athletic participation rate that is within three percentage points of the female share of full-time undergraduate enrollment at the university by the 1996–97 academic year. (Total women's enrollment in 1995 was 41 percent of the student body.) Prior to the lawsuit, Virginia Tech had only 18 percent female participation in athletics. The settlement changed this dramatically. By 1999 Virginia Tech boasted a female athletic participation rate of 39 percent.[6]

LAF has supported many women litigants. Their personal accounts of sex discrimination are moving and illustrative of the battles women must continue to fight to achieve equity. These battles cost more than money. They also drain an individual of her emotional reserves. Virtually all LAF-supported plaintiffs experience a chilling isolation from their peers and colleagues when they move forward with a lawsuit. Faculty members fear retaliation by their institution if they show support for a colleague who charges sex discrimination in the tenure process. University administrative staff members have been told not to talk to a plaintiff about her case.

In student sexual harassment cases, the student body may turn its back on the victim because the school's reaction (often a lack of any action) is interpreted to mean that the harassment did not occur. As for athletes seeking equal opportunity on the playing field, the administration and/or the student body often accuse them of unfairly taking opportunities and athletic funding away from men's athletic programs.

Because this chilling atmosphere creates an emotional drain on a plaintiff that can be just as significant as the financial drain a lawsuit creates, in addition to the financial support, LAF-supported plaintiffs are offered personal support. LAF asks AAUW members to support our plaintiffs with their contributions and also with notes of encouragement and even by their attendance at part or all of a local trial whenever possible. For instance, when LAF-supported plaintiff Vickie Dugan went to trial against Oregon State University, not only did AAUW members house her, her family, and her witnesses to cut down on Vickie's expenses (Dugan had relocated to another state after she was fired by the defendant institution), but numerous AAUW members also attended the trial. In fact, there was an AAUW presence at all sixteen days of the trial.[7]

The psychological boost these women receive from LAF's support is often as important as the monetary assistance. Knowing that a well-respected national association has backed their cases is just as valuable as financial assistance to women who find themselves embroiled in bitter litigation with little or no support from peers and colleagues. One plaintiff wrote, "It meant everything to me to know that AAUW and LAF believed in me at a time when it seemed that no one else did." Another wrote, "Even more than the money, your support has provided my case with a credibility it has been lacking."

Sex discrimination in higher education and elsewhere is no longer blatant. In fact, it is often very subtle and the result of socialized thinking and/or behavior that causes "unconscious" discrimination. Unfortunately, because of the changed nature of much of today's sex discrimination, many men and women react to "climate" studies like the one conducted at M.I.T. and to lawsuits brought by female faculty, staff, or students with disbelief and silence. Yet sex discrimination continues to pervade educational institutions of all sizes and reputations. Of the sixty cases that LAF has supported since its inception, more than ten have been brought against the nation's top twenty-five universities.[8] These cases receive little, if any, publicity. Often women plaintiffs who opt to settle their cases are pressured to sign a "gag order," a promise to keep silent about the nature of the lawsuit, the parties involved, and the amount of the settlement. Others choose to maintain a low profile because of the personal and professional damage already incurred. Yet these stories need to be told to protect subsequent generations of students and faculty from career-destroying discrimination.

Clearly not every LAF-supported case can win. Even so, virtually every LAF-supported plaintiff, win or lose, believes that, given the choice, she would pursue her claim all over again. Why? Most believe that their individual battles contribute to the greater good. These courageous women put their own financial, professional, and emotional well-being on the line for the benefit of others. To the last, these plaintiffs cite these future generations of women and girls as a significant motivating factor in bringing their lawsuits and seeing them to completion.

How many students, parents, and alumni would be outraged to learn that a favorite female professor was told, "You don't need this job. We're giving it to a man with a family"? How would women at one university react if they knew a male professor commented to a female colleague, "We all know women's brains are biologically inferior"? Two LAF-supported women faced comments like these as part of the sexual harassment each experienced on her campus.

Institutions need to be held accountable for sex discrimination. The AAUW Legal Advocacy Fund looks to newsworthy items like M.I.T.'s admission and other stories on successful sex discrimination lawsuits to raise awareness of this important issue. To its credit, M.I.T. implemented prompt action to redress the inequities disclosed within the School of Science. M.I.T.'s acknowledgment of discrimination not only sparked systemic change across its own campus, but it also serves as an institutional role model for other colleges and universities to follow. LAF knows all too well, however, that eradicating sex discrimination in higher education is a slow and arduous process. Gender equality in academe is possible, but it will take strong institutional leaders, courageous individuals willing to speak out for justice, and the vigilance of institutions of higher education and women's advocacy organizations to move us to that point.

Notes

1. *Cynthia J. Fisher v. Vassar College,* 852 F. Supp. 1193 (S.D.N.Y. 1994), Lexis 6376.
2. Ibid., section B: Findings of Fact, #87.
3. *Bickerstaff v. Vassar,* 992 F. Supp. 372 (S.D.N.Y. 1998).
4. Summary judgment is a pretrial motion by which the moving party (in this case, Columbia) argues that there are no disputes of fact, and when you apply appropriate law, the court must find for the party seeking summary judgment.

5. In *Reeves,* an age-discrimination lawsuit, the U.S. Supreme Court held that if a plaintiff makes a case and is able to provide sufficient evidence to show that the employer's asserted justification is a lie, the court may conclude that the employer discriminated unlawfully, even without a show of further evidence.

6. See *Chronicle of Higher Education,* "Gender Equity in Athletics," http://chronicle.com/free/equity/equitysearch.htm (7 May 2002).

7. Dugan, a former softball coach at Oregon State University, successfully sued the university for sex discrimination and for retaliating against her for speaking up for women's athletic opportunities at Oregon State. A jury awarded her $1.3 million. The university appealed but eventually settled the lawsuit out of court for $1.1 million.

8. Ranking based on *U.S. News and World Report's* 1998 Annual Guide to America's Best Colleges ("The Best National Universities," 1 September 1997, 100–114). Other cases have been against public and private four-year institutions of all sizes, as well as community colleges.

Chapter 15

In Search of Justice

Wartime Rape and Human Rights

Mary Ann Tétreault

Protection and justice are core obligations of the nation-state reflected, in the Western tradition, in two mythic stories of the state's origin. In *Leviathan,* Thomas Hobbes describes the social contract in a parable of the state as a protector of persons through the legitimate monopoly of force. This outlook is elaborated by contemporary analysts, such as Charles Tilly, who describe the early modern state as a kind of protection racket.[1] An alternative parable locates the origin of the state in its capacity to administer justice. Looking at the genesis of the nation-state form, some historians of the medieval period in Europe describe a trajectory that diverges from those traced by Hobbes and Tilly. For example, Joseph Strayer argues that the modern state coalesced around those contenders for leadership who displayed a capacity to provide superior judicial services.[2] There is some support for this proposition in premodern societies as well: for example, leaders such as Solon, Lycurges, Moses, Cyrus, Hammurabi, Mohammad, and Lekë Dukagjini are remembered chiefly for having been "lawgivers," even though several also were famous as military strategists and fighters, and two combined political authority with religious authority conferred by their special status as messengers of God.

Unfortunately, the protection of women by the state, both physically and legally, always has lagged far behind the protection of men. Indeed, state-formation in the ancient world occurred in tandem with the systematic denial of human rights, civil protection, and civil status to women.[3] Nation-states also have enforced female subjection, and it is not surprising that feminist claims to state protection during the modern era have been intertwined rhetorically and politically with movements intended to liberate subjected men.[4] The imperfect state of women's rights as citizens of their nations is echoed in the imperfect status of women in international law. As it is with respect to domestic law, the status of women in international law is also under revision: this revision is a response not only to the declarations of the United Nations Conferences on Women, the most recent of which met in Beijing in 1995, but also to a new awareness of violence against women that has arisen, in part, as a result of the systematic use of rape as an instrument of warfare and genocide in recent conflicts.[5] In this chapter, I examine wartime rape in three contemporary cases, Kuwait, Yugoslavia, and Rwanda, as indicative of the necessity for continued efforts to make women's human rights equal to men's. I also argue that international tribunals, despite their many flaws, continue to be the best venues for victims of sexual violence during armed conflicts to seek redress. Even so, much more needs to be done to raise sexual violence to the status of a grave violation of human rights and to prosecute vigorously those who commit such crimes.

War Crimes and Tribunals

The start of trials for war crimes committed in the former Yugoslavia followed on the heels of the fiftieth anniversary of the tribunals convened after the second world war. These venues are very different. The Nuremberg and Tokyo tribunals were victors' courts. The accused could be delivered from the ignominy of prosecution and judgment only by suicide; no "friendly" government stood prepared to shield defendants from appearing before the tribunals. This has not been the case for the Yugoslav war crimes trials.[6] And yet the example of Nuremberg in particular infuses the sensibilities of participants in the International Criminal Tribunal for Yugoslavia (ICTY), not so much with respect to the "convenience" of trying individuals whose persons cannot be withheld from justice other than by death, but because of what some see as the greatest good arising from the World War II tribunals: the attribution of individual, rather than collective, responsibility for atrocities. Richard Goldstone, the ICTY's first chief prosecutor, put it like this: "If individuals are not brought to book, then there is collective guilt. The victims and their survivors cry out for justice against a group. . . . Virtually every meeting I have [had with representatives of the various sides in the Bosnian conflict] starts with a history lesson. . . . In all those years, nobody has ever been held accountable for the horrors. That is why the history festers."[7]

The use of "history" to justify the suffering and death of individuals is especially common with respect to quarrels associated with cycles of atrocities and war.[8] Yet at the highest levels of government in powerful states, the commitment of political leaders to carrying through on war crimes trials is at best inconsistent. During the Dayton talks, for example, there was widespread press speculation that the United States would agree to close down the war crimes tribunal in exchange for an agreement to end hostilities and accept NATO peacekeepers. NATO military intervention in response to the threat of a new genocide in Kosova four years later led eventually to a change in government in Belgrade that finally resulted in the arrest of Slobodan Milošević in May 2001. However, the initial charges against him referred only to acts of genocide in Kosova. At this writing, indictments are promised that will cover his role in the wholesale murder of Bosnians and Croatians, but there is no indication that the indictments will cover his responsibility for the use of systematic rape as a primary tool of genocidal "ethnic cleansing" in the campaigns against non-Serb populations.

Rape is recognized as a crime against humanity, but it was not included as an explicit charge in the category of war crimes for which nationals of defeated states were prosecuted following World War II.[9] In her pathbreaking 1975 study of rape, Susan Brownmiller notes that at Nuremberg and Tokyo, where prosecutors could have introduced mountains of evidence of systematic rape, none of the charges brought before the tribunals included such an indictment. The rationales for this lack of attention to a crime, one that was widely publicized during war as a means to mobilize military and civilian populations against the enemy, are telling.

The conquest of Nanking (Nanjing) was marked by horrible atrocities committed by Japanese troops against the Chinese civilian population. Reports featured the trope "rape of Nanking" because it was so literally as well as figuratively true. Yet a 1938 report by a missionary group detailing the consequences of the Japanese invasion and conquest of the city "excluded rape per se" as a category of damage, despite its inclusion of many less damaging injuries.[10] The Tokyo prosecutors did not ask rape victims to testify, but witnesses testifying to other crimes also reported on the rapes they had seen, sometimes numbering into the hundreds.[11] From their testimony, the tribunal estimated that 20,000 rapes had occurred in Nanking during the first month of occupation alone, and that widespread rape continued, along with other crimes, "at least six weeks after the city had been taken."[12]

German officers also were not tried for rape at Nuremberg, but not because of flaws in evidence collection arising from the tender sensibilities of missionary witnesses. The allies were deterred from pressing such charges by the actions of Russian troops as they conquered Berlin. To indict Germans for systematic rape, even of concentration camp victims, while the orgy of Russian rapes of German women at the end of World War II went unremarked, would have invited comparisons the victorious allies preferred to leave unstated.[13]

The insensitivity of international tribunals to the injuries inflicted by rape is more than matched by the attitudes of domestic legislatures, police, and courts.[14] Indeed, despite the inclusion of state-mediated rape as a category of human rights violation in post–World War II international conventions, an unambiguous statement of a woman's absolute right to sexual integrity was not made prior to the 1995 United Nations Conference on Women held in Beijing.[15] Closely related to present-day controversies over a woman's right to control her reproductive capacity, the arguments of those who treat rape and forced childbearing as relatively minor inconveniences compared to forms of physical abuse and torture to which men and women are equally vulnerable,[16] reflect a system of values in which women's rights to corporal autonomy are vastly inferior to those of men.

I argue that the right to control one's own body is a fundamental human right, an essential element in the understanding and expression of moral and political equality as well as of individual freedom. Throughout history and throughout the world, various societies have denied this right to entire classes of persons, but, even among members of privileged classes, the rights of women to control their bodies have almost always been inferior to the rights of men. To illustrate this point, I trace the divergence in entitlements to control one's own body between women and men in the Western tradition. Such divergences occur in other cultures as well and help to explain the relative trivialization of sexual violence by international institutions as well as by nation-states.

A second level of argument examines the impact of cultural norms, which reflect women's inferior rights to control their own bodies, on the victims themselves. Using the Iraqi invasion and occupation of Kuwait, the wars of disintegration of the former Yugoslavia, and the 1994 Rwandan genocide as case examples, I argue that the internalization of such cultural norms not only inhibits the ability to prosecute those who commit war-related rapes and other forms of sexual violence but also blocks justice for the victims. Problems of justice as well as of accountability actually may be greater where international institutions try hardest to avoid them by employing extreme discretion to preserve the anonymity of victims. These cases also invite consideration of the question of individual versus collective guilt. In response to Iraq's invasion of Kuwait, the United Nations attributed to Iraq collective responsibility for all crimes committed in the course of the conflict. For the Bosnian conflict and the Rwandan genocide, the United Nations decided that responsibility for war crimes would be adjudicated individual by individual before international legal tribunals. Both the ICTY and the International Criminal Tribunal for Rwanda (ICTR) have brought indictments including rape as a war crime, and both have convicted defendants on this charge. The government of Rwanda also has tried genocide cases in national courts, but it has not, to my knowledge, produced even one indictment for rape in these courts, even though such behavior was widespread and widely reported, orders to commit genocide broadcast over Rwanda's infamous hate radio station (which was owned by members of the Rwandan president's inner circle[17]) were often heard as invitations to rape Tutsi women,[18] and rape was framed as an instrument of genocide in the indictments against defendants called before the ICTR.

I conclude with arguments supporting the inclusion of sexual violence as a category of war crime in the Yugoslav and Rwandan tribunals and also in the Rwandan and other national courts that have recently been asked to hear cases on human rights violations occurring in third countries (see below). This not only supports Richard Goldstone's analysis of the tragic consequences of collective guilt, but also highlights the fundamental injustice that persists in our collective understanding of basic human rights depending on whether we view these rights as women's or men's.

Whose Body?

Those who support and those who oppose the idea of universal human rights regard this concept as modern.[19] Yet a moral concern for human life predates the Enlightenment. It is reflected not only in Thomas Aquinas's writings about "just wars"[20] but in the moral bases of democracy and individual rights derived from the values and practices of early Christian communities. As Elaine Pagels points out, "For nearly the first four hundred years of [the common] era, Christians regarded *freedom* as the primary message of Genesis 1–3—freedom in its many forms, including free will, freedom from demonic powers, freedom from social and sexual obligations, freedom from tyrannical government and from fate; and self-mastery as the source of such freedom."[21]

Much of the religious revolution and counterrevolution associated with Christianity from the Apostles to Augustine took place on the battleground of the body and sexuality. The way that the concept of "men's human rights"[22] developed historically made freedom from sexual coercion among the most valued aspects of human rights from the perspective of women: not merely to be able to refuse to marry but also to be able to forbid absolutely that one's body be possessed by another.[23] Claims to individual ownership of the body, manifested in such peculiar practices as voluntary celibacy, were among the most basic assertions of Christians. For them, Pagels claims, "celibacy involved rejection of 'the world' of ordinary society and its multitudinous entanglements and was thereby a way to gain control over one's own life."[24] Christian ideology and practices such as these violated a strong and widespread norm that the bodies of subordinates were the instruments of the dominant.

This norm is described by Aristotle in *The Politics:*

> Now property is part of a household. . . . [and] in any special skill the availability of the proper tools will be essential for the performance of the task. . . . Any piece of property can be regarded as a tool enabling a man to live, and his property is an assemblage of such tools; a slave is a sort of living piece of property. . . . [and] is meant for action. . . . the slave . . . is one of the tools that minister to action. . . . Any human being that by nature belongs not to himself but to another is by nature a slave; and a human being belongs to another whenever, in spite of being a man, he is a piece of property, i.e. a tool having a separate existence and meant for action.[25]

Aristotle sees "man" and "slave" as composing a whole subsumed by the "man": "For the part and the whole, the soul and the body, have identical interests; and the slave is in a sense a part of his master, a living but separate part of his body."[26]

The natural inferiority that makes the slave the object of his master's rule is carried through in later sections of *The Politics* to explain why men also rule over women and children:

> Thus it becomes clear that both ruler and ruled must have a share in virtue, but that there are differences in virtue in each case, as there are also among those who by nature rule. An immediate indication of this is afforded by the soul, where we find natural ruler and natural subject, whose virtues we regard as different—one being that of the rational element, the other of the nonrational. . . . so that most instances of ruling and being ruled are natural. For the rule of free over slave, male over female, man over boy, are all different, because while parts of the soul are present in each case, the distribution is different. Thus the deliberative faculty in the soul is not present at all in a slave; in a female it is present but ineffective, in a child present but undeveloped.[27]

This juxtaposition of women and slaves as natural candidates for perpetual subjection is not fortuitous. In the ancient world, the majority of slaves were women, many taken as booty following the defeat of their city's military forces.[28] Related to their status as war prizes is both the role of women as producers of children and the ownership of those women and their children by persons other than themselves. "Women were used sexually by men who controlled or possessed them: neither the mores of pagan culture nor the precepts of most ancient religions hindered a man's sexual access to women under his power," John Boswell has claimed.[29] A similar norm governed the forced impregnation of African slaves by American plantation owners or their surrogates, and the subsequent enslavement or sale of the children by the mother's owner. It also underlies legal regimes dating back to Roman times that privilege birth parents over adoptive parents on the grounds that birth parents, particularly fathers, own children by virtue of having generated them biologically—that is, they have a *natural* right to these children.[30]

An additional element is the status metaphor through which body penetration was viewed, one that extended to men as well as to women. To be sexually penetrated was to be subordinate. A female "citizen" was a subject in part because it was expected that her body would, in the normal course of her life, be invaded by others, thereby signifying a *natural* absence of physical autonomy. Although homosexual relationships between boys and older men were idealized in ancient Greece, a man who permitted his body to be penetrated by another risked losing his citizenship.[31] So much of this complex of norms and values describing autonomy and ownership was played out sexually that sexuality and the individual's control of it became an assertion of individual freedom and the beginning of political notions of mass civil rights.

Pagels argues that the Augustinian counterrevolution reinscribed an ethic of physical and political subordination, particularly on women, through the doctrine of original sin: "Augustine draws so drastic a picture of the effects of Adam's sin that he embraces human government, even when tyrannical, as the indispensable defense against the forces sin has unleashed in human nature."[32] "Human government," says Augustine in *City of God,* begins in the household, where "the ordered agreement of command and obedience among those who live together . . . serves the ordered agreement of command and obedience among citizens."[33] Christians were encouraged to view the human condition generally but their own situations individually, as the result of divine retribution for their actions. In Pagels's reading of early Christianity, "pain, oppression, labor, and death are punishments that we (or our ultimate ancestors) *brought upon ourselves.*"[34]

The early Christians struggled to understand how human will could be used as a tool to reverse divine retribution and allow them to triumph over death. Augustine's contribution was to connect the promise of eternal life to an earthly existence characterized by sexual renunciation and political submission. Both were predicated on female subordination, resulting in a "blight of male domination . . . upon the whole structure of sexual relationships."[35] Although Christians continued to favor sexual practices such as celibacy that provided unmarried women with limited power over their own bodies, women's corporal autonomy in general was more tightly constrained than men's. For example, while all Christians were enjoined to fast, the denial of certain kinds of food to women, particularly meat and fat, was deeply embedded in Christian ideology and practice.[36]

The post-Augustinian tradition of religiously sanctioned hierarchy and subordination was challenged by the modern philosophy of liberalism. "Whether the individualism of the seventeenth century is deplored as having undermined the Christian natural law tradition, or applauded as having opened new vistas of freedom and progress, its importance is not disputed," notes C. B. Macpherson.[37] The strand of liberal thinking that reasserted the early Christians' conception of the body as belonging to the soul residing within it is associated with the Levellers, radical egalitarians who believed in individual freedom based on equal natural rights, including an equal right to life. Although their support of equal natural rights was cited by contemporary opponents as clear evidence that the Levellers aimed to destroy property rights, Macpherson argues that the Levellers were proponents of private property rights. For example, a 1646 tract by the Leveller John Lilburne listed as basic rights "Liberty of conscience in matters of Faith and Divine worship; Liberty of the Person, and liberty of Estate: which consists properly in the propriety of their goods, and a disposing power of their possessions."[38] The Levellers argued that the most fundamental possession of each person is himself:

> Not only has the individual a property in his own person and capacities, a property in the sense of a right to enjoy and use them and to exclude others from them; what is more, it is this property, this exclusion of others, that makes a man human: "every one as he is himselfe, so he hath a self propriety, else he could not be himselfe." What makes a man human is his freedom from other men. Man's essence is freedom. Freedom is proprietorship of one's own person and capacities.[39]

However, just as the contract theorists from Locke to the French revolutionaries applied their concepts of individual rights to men but not to women,[40] the concept of individual ownership of the body also was gendered. The natural law that the Levellers cited to justify each man's proprietorship of his own person and capacities was used to deny the same proprietorship to women, particularly married women, who were conceptualized legally as well as metaphorically as parts of their husbands under doctrines such as *feme de couverte*.[41] As extensions of their husbands' personhood, married women were tools in the Aristotelian sense, and their bodies, along with the issue of their production and reproduction, were naturally the rightful property of their husbands.[42] In the United States, where the extent of female autonomy in the nineteenth century was frequently remarked upon by foreign visitors such as Alexis de Tocqueville, historian Page Smith reminds us that it was in their capacity as daughters, not as wives and mothers, that American women enjoyed their still-limited rights.[43]

The assumption that men own women's bodies has a particular bearing on the question of wartime rape. Rape in war is intended to convey a set of messages. The social and symbolic connection between female chastity and group integrity is a strong motivation for wartime rape. *Women* are persons with private lives and civil statuses; *woman* is a concept that embodies complex constructions of family, community, and nationality.[44] Wartime rape, like other instances of state-mediated sexual assault, is a political crime against the concept, a means of destroying nations through shame, pollution, and the destruction of organized family and community life.

The deeply embedded ideology of male ownership of female bodies is starkly visible after the guns fall silent, when those charged with judging the actions of combatants shift to thinking of rape as a property crime: so many dead cows, burnt fields, destroyed homes, and raped women. "Rape in war is inevitable," George Patton is remembered as having said, just one of those regrettable things that happens as an epiphenomenon of the "real" business of war which is killing men and taking territory. Both perceptions—rape as a symbolic act and rape as a property crime—obscure the nature of rape as an egregious abuse of human rights and the dignity of persons. Also, and perversely, they lead to the personalization of wartime rape:

> Despite the pervasiveness of rape, it often has been a hidden element of war, a fact that is linked inextricably to its largely gender-specific character. The fact that the abuse is committed by men against women has contributed to its being narrowly portrayed as sexual or personal . . . a portrayal that depoliticizes sexual abuse in conflict and results in its being ignored as a war crime.[45]

It is true, of course, that rape is a crime committed by an individual against another individual. It probably is true as well that some individuals commit rape against members of enemy populations during war for personal reasons, just as it probably is true that some of the Germans who committed crimes against Jews during the reign of Hitler did so for personal reasons.[46] Yet it also is true that rape is a strategy of conflict, one ordered and orchestrated by political and military leaders.[47] Personalization of wartime rape removes the onus from the generals and their bosses. It also allows the victim's community to deny its loss of honor. That victims go along with this is a testimony to the internalization of cultural norms of honor and shame based on the assumption that men own and are responsible for the bodies of "their" women.[48]

Justice for Kuwaiti Rape Victims

As part of a strategy to terrorize and control the local population, Iraqi soldiers raped Kuwaiti women during their seven-month occupation of the country.[49] Most observers agree that, during the occupation, allegations of rape were exaggerated for political reasons by spokesmen for the Kuwaiti government. Even so, careful estimates compiled from the testimony of victims and doctors, medical records, and other sources conclude that about two thousand Kuwaiti women were sexually assaulted by Iraqi military personnel during the conflict.[50] Few rape victims are thought to have been killed. Consequently, one would expect that close to two thousand raped individuals remained in the community, having to come to terms with what happened to them and trying to rebuild their lives.

To reconcile war victims to their history, as Justice Goldstone notes, those responsible must be made accountable for the injuries they inflict. Like other victims of Iraqi war crimes, Kuwaiti victims of sexual assaults were urged to bring claims for damages under a novel and humane system of war crimes documentation and certification. This was made possible by the unusual international consensus charging Iraq with full responsibility for the invasion. The legal foundation establishing Iraq's culpability is United Nations Security Council Resolution 687, the comprehensive cease-fire resolution passed in April 1991, which reaffirmed Iraq's responsibility for all damages caused by its illegal invasion and occupation of Kuwait. This attribution of responsibility to an aggressor state rests on principles established under the laws of war, specifically the fourth Hague Convention (1907) and its provisions regarding the conduct of war on land, their interpretation by the International Military Tribunal at Nuremberg in 1946, and their reaffirmation in the 1949 Geneva Conventions.[51] Under these principles, "[the government of] Iraq is responsible for all acts of its armed forces in Kuwait, including acts contrary to military orders or discipline for which a state might not normally be responsible in peacetime."[52] As a result, the question of whether Iraqi rapes of Kuwaiti women were private crimes rather than war crimes never became an issue. The government of Iraq was accountable regardless.

The primary institution charged with collecting and assessing claims against Iraq for direct losses arising from the invasion and occupation of Kuwait is the United Nations Compensation Commission, the UNCC.[53] Created over the course of a year, the commission began sitting in July 1991 and received its first set of claims from governments in June 1992. Each government sending claims to the UNCC on behalf of its nationals had established special procedures for collecting them. In Kuwait, the Public Authority for Assessment of Compensation for Damages Resulting from Iraqi Aggression—PAAC—was created by emiri decree on 27 May 1991 "to serve as a national authority for Kuwaiti claims. PAAC has the responsibility to submit to the UNCC consolidated claims of Kuwaiti and certain [Gulf Cooperation Council] nationals, including claims of corporations and government institutions that suffered losses."[54]

PAAC opened five local offices to collect and process claims under six damage categories worked out by the UNCC. Its procedure was highly streamlined, requiring claimants to appear at one of the offices, complete a standard form describing their injuries and losses, and provide proof of damage such as medical reports, statements by witnesses, and/or other independent corroboration of their testimony. Each claim was then reviewed by a lawyer and evaluated with regard to its accuracy before being forwarded to the UNCC Governing Council in Geneva.[55]

Rape victims could apply for damages under Category B, which includes claims for serious personal injury or the death of a close family member. Ceilings were established for Category B damages, limiting their amount to token levels, most of which were specified in advance. For example, the UNCC set a ceiling of "$5,000 for each incident of sexual assault, aggravated assault, or torture."[56] The principle of fixed payments concentrates attention on the fact of damage rather than on such collateral—although certainly important—issues like the extent to which an individual might have suffered. And, however one might regard the low ceilings on damage claims, the relatively small amounts of the payments, particularly in light of the total funds available, ensured that compensation, with its strong implication of recognition of wrongs done to victims, could be awarded to a relatively large number of injured persons.[57]

The principles and procedures of UNCC/PAAC were intended to be humane and to guarantee that formal justice would be achieved for a large number of war victims. They seem particularly appropriate for the adjudication of claims of wartime rape. The crime was defined from the beginning as committed in pursuit of state policy. The victim was regarded as having been injured as the result of Iraqi government policy rather than as the result of a personal attack by a particular individual. The relative privacy of the proceedings gave social and emotional protection to victims and their families. Yet only a very small number of the estimated two thousand Kuwaiti rape victims ever claimed compensation.[58]

In the autumn of 1992, while I was in Kuwait to observe the parliamentary elections, I tried to find out about these Kuwaiti rape victims and what had happened to them. Among those I interviewed were human rights workers, clinical psychologists, and two of the investigators that the government had sent out in the first few months following the liberation to gather information and take testimony from Kuwaitis injured as the result of the invasion and occupation. The primary reason offered by all of these persons for the virtual disappearance of the rape issue from Kuwait's public agenda was the need to shield victims and their families from further shame. One of the clinical psychologists I interviewed put it this way: "Rape is a social and ethical stigma for the one and for their families. Many families keep their victims locked in the house. Married victims are being divorced. . . . Many cases with reactive anxiety are developing severe psychotic depression, even schizophrenia. . . . Virginity is a very precious concept to a Kuwaiti." How internalized concepts of family honor and shame as functions of female sexual behavior were was evident in further discussions with that psychologist, who said that men he knew had killed family members who had been raped during the war. In other instances, rape victims killed themselves.[59] The shame was equally intense for the few male victims of rape. For example, another clinical psychologist reported caring for a married couple, each of whom had been raped by Iraqi soldiers shortly after the invasion. Since liberation the husband had been hospitalized for mental illness, although the wife was living at home and caring for their children. Both of the investigators I interviewed were adamant in their refusal to disclose any details about the testimony they had taken from rape victims, including the number of victims each had questioned. The belief that the rapes must be hidden and denied for victims and their families to retain their reputations was very strongly voiced.

Sexual Torture in the Yugoslav Wars

Many Balkan communities are governed by social norms of family honor and shame similar to those that characterize Kuwaiti society. The willingness of so many rape victims in the Yugoslav conflict to recount their injuries to international investigatory bodies is, therefore, remarkable. As a result, despite the general absence of medically supervised post-traumatic care, the personal grief inflicted by many of the mostly well-intentioned interviewers gathering evidence for what they hoped would be future legal proceedings, and the social damage inflicted by the intrusion of television journalists during such fact-gathering expeditions, there is massive evidence based on direct testimony of systematic rape, forced pregnancy, and other forms of sexual degradation inflicted on civilians, especially in Bosnia, as a matter of military policy.[60] Rape in this conflict was so widespread, so egregious, and so clearly a deliberately chosen instrument of warfare that the "rape of Bosnia" has the same resonance for us as the "rape of Nanking" had for our parents and grandparents.

And yet, some of the same reasons so few claims of rape were actually presented for adjudication in Kuwait may inhibit claims in Yugoslavia. By now, many victims and witnesses are dead or mentally incapable of enduring the ordeal of testifying at a trial. An example of this problem comes from Antonio Cassese, the president of the ICTY:

> Famous guy, a Muslim. When he was captured, they said, "Aren't you So-and-So?" He admitted he was. So they broke both his legs, handcuffed him to a radiator, and forced him to watch as they repeatedly raped his wife and two daughters and then slit their throats. After that, he begged to be killed himself, but his tormentors must have realized that the cruellest thing they could possibly do to him now would simply be to set him free, which they did. Somehow, this man was able to make his way to some U.N. investigators, and told them about his ordeal—a few days after which, he committed suicide.[61]

It is noteworthy that Cassese does not name this "famous guy"—"aren't you So-and-So?"—he says when he tells his story to Lawrence Weschler. Among the victims and witnesses who were not killed by war criminals or by their own hands are no doubt many who are anxious that their shame remain hidden from public view. This anxiety is shared even by those who would like to have these crimes exposed and those who committed them punished. Jasmina Kuzmanović reports that physician Toni Carr had patients—some over seventy-five years of age—in Dubrovnik telling her that they had been raped by Serbian and Montenegrin soldiers: "All of these women begged Carr not to tell anyone nor even to speak of it to their families. The women's feeling of shame was even deeper than their hurt or anger."[62] However, as the interval of time between the sexual assault and the trial expanded and the recognition that rape was a strategic ploy rather than a personal matter grew, more victims came forward to testify than analysts originally predicted. This is borne out by a number of documentary films in which Bosnian rape victims recount the crimes committed against them and tell of their decisions to face their assailants rather than to contribute, by their silence, to the impunity allowing such crimes in the first place.

Still, there are difficulties. Many accusations of rape are brought by a single witness, the victim, whose testimony traditionally has not been seen as sufficient evidence for a conviction. Accusations documented with names, dates, and supporting evidence might also violate victims' rights if prosecuted: the Bosnian government knows, for example, the identities of the mothers who abandoned infants resulting from wartime rapes. The government forbade the surrender of these infants for overseas adoption, and they were placed instead in orphanages funded by foreign donors. A 1993 article in the *Los Angeles Times* reports that the mothers, many of whom had abandoned their infants to prevent their families from learning about their rapes or their pregnancies, were being pressured by the government to take these children into their homes to rear them.[63] Calling such women to be unwilling witnesses at a war crimes trial would present severe ethical problems.

Some of these difficulties are addressed in Rule 96, which the ICTY adopted to make the Tribunal more victim-friendly than many domestic venues with regard to rules of evidence governing admissible testimony. However, Hilary Charlesworth and Christine Chinkin conclude that it is too early to decide whether the rule will be applied in a way that preserves victims' rights. For example, it is not clear that Rule 96 can eliminate entirely the aggressive and humiliating questioning from defense attorneys designed to make women alleging rape look "immoral" and therefore unreliable as witnesses. Provisions specifying witness protection guarantees also are ambiguous in their results. Anonymous testimony by victims is at least technically possible under Rule 96, but its implementation so far has been so hedged by concerns for the rights of defendants that the benefit of the doubt has gone overwhelmingly to the latter. Even in instances where victims and their families do not fear retaliation from death squads or friends of the defendants, revealing their identities still leaves victims vulnerable to rejection by families and friends.[64]

A third difficulty is not shared by Kuwaiti rape victims. Regarding the Yugoslav wars, there is no United Nations decision holding a belligerent state responsible for every crime committed during the conflict. The Yugoslav Tribunal must bring formal indictments against individuals accused of specific crimes, request their arrest, hope they will be found and surrendered to the court's jurisdiction, and then try them for these crimes in open court following strict rules of evidence. Victims and witnesses are not able to confide their stories to a clerk and an attorney in an office near their homes. Virtually all of them must tell their stories in public, be questioned as to the details, and perhaps be harassed by defense counsel in spite of Rule 96. Telling one's story to a committee from Helsinki Watch or the European Union, even in the presence of television cameras, hardly compares to the grueling ordeal that testifying before the ICTY is or is imagined to be by traumatized victims of sexual violence.

Rape and Genocide in Rwanda

Still in the iron grip of negative sovereignty, the international norm recognizing a government's authority to do as it wishes on its own territory,[65] the international community took no action when news of the Rwandan genocide first broke. The availability of this norm, which underpins the international doctrine of nonintervention, was seized by the United Nations and its most powerful members as an excuse for standing by while Hutu officials, militia members, and average citizens accomplished the spectacular and internationally unimpeded murder of more than 800,000 persons, mostly Tutsis, in only one hundred days.[66] Rape was one of the tools of the Rwandan *genocidaires*. The prospect of raping Tutsi women was held out to entice Hutu citizens into killing their neighbors, and it terrorized Tutsis to the point of inhibiting their capacity to resist.[67] A small number of Hutu women, most of whom tried to protect Tutsis, also were raped.[68] In addition to the rapes, Tutsi women were subjected to organized sexual mutilation and deliberate impregnation similar to that imposed on Muslim women held in "rape camps" such as Foca in Bosnia.[69] In spite of the massive scale of sexual violence in Rwanda,[70] the scale of the genocide itself was so vast that observers worried that sexual crimes would be seen as insignificant in comparison, even though those crimes were "gender-specific manifestations of [genocide]."[71]

The United Nations set up an international tribunal in Arusha, Tanzania, to hear cases of human rights violations associated with the genocide, but the Rwandan tribunal (ICTR) faced many problems. The sheer scale of the genocide promised perpetual trials, a prospect strengthened by the tribunal's exceptionally slow progress in hearing and adjudicating cases. The tribunal, at first, also failed to investigate charges of sexual violence. The first case dealing with rape heard by the ICTR, *Akayesu, Jean Paul (ICTR-96–4)*, actually had omitted rape in the original indictment, but witness testimony divulged spontaneously at trial told of mass rape. The only female judge on the ICTR, Navanethem Pillay, also was one of the judges hearing this case. She pursued the rape issue, after which the prosecutor applied for and received permission to amend the indictment by adding rape to the charges.[72] Consequently, in spite of its inauspicious beginning, the ICTR was the first international tribunal to bring a conviction for rape "as a crime constituting genocide."[73]

The ICTR also broke new ground in defining rape. Criticizing what it dismissed as a "mechanical description" of objects and body parts, the Trial Chamber in *Akayesu* defined rape as "a physical invasion of a sexual nature, committed on a person under circumstances which are coercive. . . . Sexual violence, including rape, is not limited to physical invasion of the human body and may include acts which do not involve penetration or even physical contact," such as intimidation and duress.[74] In Judge Pillay's words, a conviction for rape under this definition "blows the myth that women won't speak about such crimes. We had witness J. J. in the courtroom who was gang-raped 16 times, and the lawyer asked, 'Tell me J. J. did he insert his penis in you?' She said, 'It's not only that. It's all the terrible things they did to me, and all the terrible things he said to me.' This is the voice of women saying what sexual violence means to women."[75]

In spite of these conceptual and legal breakthroughs, however, the ICTR remains a troubled institution. The ICTR procedure is still appallingly cumbersome and slow.[76] More problematic with respect to the stability of the trial court's convictions for rape was the decision by the appeals court in November 2001: it upheld the conviction of Alfred Musema (*Musema, Alfred, ICTR-96–13*) with regard to genocide but quashed his rape conviction on the grounds of "unreliable evidence."[77] The Musema case is not the only one in which technical difficulties caused a reversal on appeal,[78] adding to the anger of Rwandans and their government already disgusted with the ICTR for other reasons, such as the lack of a death penalty for convicted *genocidaires* whose crimes are seen as deserving punishment in kind.[79] Survivor disenchantment with international institutions began before the trials when the United Nations, which had ignored pleas for intervention to save Tutsis during the genocide, lavished food and medical care on *genocidaire* refugees in camps outside Rwanda; those remaining inside not only suffered from food and medicine shortages but also were victimized by cross-border Hutu raiders continuing their hit-and-run killings despite the presence of UN peacekeepers. Survivors also resent the lack of assistance from international bodies in disbanding the camps (indeed, the Rwandan government and military forces, but not the *genocidaires,* were castigated for the violence accompanying the camp closures) and in resettling refugees after the camps were closed.[80]

Yet the domestic trials for genocide in Rwanda also are problematic, as is the lack of support for Rwandan women most affected by the genocide. The trials began in December 1996 and by October 2001 had dealt with more than 3000 suspects, sentencing over 500 to death although only twenty-eight convicted persons were executed, all on 24 April 1998. The government also has instituted an amnesty program, loosely modeled on South Africa's Truth Commission, for those admitting their crimes. The amnesty program reflects both the impossibility of trying every murderer—

there are simply too many of them—and the government's desire to bring some sort of closure to low-level perpetrators and their victims. The total number of persons arrested for genocide is unknown but more than 100,000 were still estimated to be incarcerated in mid-October 2001, most of them under extremely inhumane conditions.[81] Both failing to arrest and releasing possible *genocidaires* also invite human rights violations. Survivors resent having to live with the people who tortured them and killed their families, and vigilante justice is not unknown—against persons who were arrested and released and against some who were tried and acquitted.[82]

Another deficiency with regard to the domestic courts is that the link between rape and genocide is salient neither to government prosecutors nor to *genocidaires*. Sexual crimes are rarely pursued by Rwandan prosecutors, not even in trials of accused *genocidaires,* and sexual violence remains a serious problem in post-genocide Rwandan society.[83] Female genocide survivors have had other problems: difficulties in claiming property rights, social isolation and ostracism as a result of their rapes, and—for some—the children conceived as a result of rape.[84] Women's health problems, including physical damage and HIV infection, receive far less government attention and resources than do projects such as the resettlement of Hutu refugees.[85] In spite of the provisions of Rwanda's constitution and international covenants to which it is a party, gender discrimination remains embedded in Rwandan civil law, and women have few avenues of judicial redress not only because of customary attitudes but because the courts continue to be choked with genocide cases.[86] The need for reconciliation is acute but unlikely under these conditions, especially given the indifference of the rest of the world.[87]

Why Sexual Violence in War Must Be Prosecuted as a War Crime

Despite the problems of prosecuting cases of rape and other forms of sexual violence before United Nations war crimes tribunals, these cases should be pursued as diligently as are the other claims the tribunals are authorized to adjudicate. This is not simply because the tribunals are one of the few avenues available for bringing justice to victims. It is also because some aspects of the tribunals are superior both to the UNCC/PAAC mechanism and to domestic courts.

The UNCC/PAAC model offers limited accountability and justice to victims through a procedure that guarantees maximum privacy and dignity. However, this procedure tacitly condones the traditional conception of rape as a crime against family and national honor rather than as a violation of an individual's human rights. The privacy intended to protect victims also sheltered family members who preferred to lock up, to divorce, and sometimes even to kill rape victims for what had happened to them, that is, to deal with crimes against honor in the traditional way—by punishing the victim. The ceiling on compensation had some virtues: many persons received compensation, more than would have if UNCC/PAAC had had to pick and chose among the many thousands of claims for hideous injuries and indescribable suffering those that were somehow more deserving than the rest. Yet to offer a rape victim $5000 as compensation for what is likely to be a lifetime of fear, rejection, and impairment is, at best, inadequate. From a practical perspective, this sum is too small to enable a repudiated wife or a rejected daughter to support herself. From an ethical perspective, it makes light of the long-term physical and emotional consequences of the rapes and is insulting as a measure of the value of the victims' lives.

Even more problematic is the effect of the blanket attribution of crimes to the government of Iraq. Although the UNCC devised a streamlined procedure that did, in fact, permit damages to be paid to thousands injured by Iraq's aggression, the process left intact the concept of collective guilt. One could argue that many of the Iraqi participants in the invasion were actually victims themselves. I've interviewed many Kuwaiti insiders—those who spent the invasion and occupation in Kuwait—who expressed pity for such Iraqi soldiers, noting their extreme youth, their lack of food and water, and the state of utter fear with which they regarded their government, their officers, and their immediate situations. But most Kuwaitis were outside the country during the occupation, and a large majority of these outsiders I have interviewed express a visceral hatred of Iraq and Iraqis. A Kuwaiti clinical psychologist reported similar findings, associating the strong feelings against Iraqis expressed by outsiders with their feelings of guilt at having escaped what the insiders had suffered. The complexity of these feelings and their motivations may actually increase their bitterness. The harsh scapegoating of Palestinians following liberation, many of whom had worked in the Resistance, is just one example of the irrational behavior that collective guilt supports.[88]

The problems that women have encountered taking complaints about sexual abuse to domestic courts are legion and well documented, and they occur not only in Rwanda.[89] Spike Peterson and Jacqueline Stevens both regard the state in any of its historical manifestations as what Stevens terms "the mother of gender."[90] Although attempts to adjudicate human rights violations associated with the Yugoslav and Rwandan genocides have been made in the national courts of third countries, the definition of rape developed by the Arusha tribunal and the rules of evidence adopted by the Hague tribunal do not apply in these national courts, many of which reflect sex-gender systems embedding gender discrimination in the politics and the economy of the countries in which they are located. While cases of genocide with respect to Yugoslavia and Rwanda have been brought in third countries (and at least one included rape among the charges),[91] the third-country mechanism is both more cumbersome and less obviously legitimate—as the controversy over attempts to try Augusto Pinochet in British courts for human rights violations committed in Argentina demonstrate.

There are other issues that argue for the vigorous prosecution of wartime rape and other forms of sexual torture associated with violent conflict in international tribunals. One is the need to keep faith with the many women who did come forward to testify about what had happened to them. They provided part of the basis for the establishment of the sitting tribunals; it is only fair that the crimes committed against them be an explicit part of the public accounting that the tribunals are pledged to make. It would be helpful if the tribunals consolidated the definitions and procedures each has adopted so that they apply equally in both venues. In addition, the international legal community—including the members of the tribunals—should reexamine the whole issue of "honor" and even of "dignity" as the foundation of criminal liability in cases of sexual assault. Here I agree with Hilary Charlesworth and Christine Chinkin: sexual violence should be classified as a "grave breach" of human rights along with "torture or inhuman treatment, wilfully causing great suffering, serious injury and unlawful confinement."[92] The presumption of universality in the application of human rights law resembles the presumption of universality in liberal principles generally. It falls far short of reality when comparisons are made between issues affecting men and those perceived as "only" affecting women. Treating rape as a grave breach of human rights in the public context of the tribunals removes it from the private space in which violations of women's human rights are both customary and protected, and begins what one hopes will be a thorough process of equalization of the human rights of women and men. Treating it as a violation of human rights should also detach rape from its connection to war and genocide and encourage its prosecution in situations, such as torture and treatment in detention, that might occur in the absence of armed conflict.

A final reason why rape and sexual torture should have the same status as other grave breaches of human rights is that these crimes are not confined only to women. As I noted above, men also are victims of wartime rape and other forms of sexual violence. The ubiquity of sexual mutilation and torture in armed conflict is evident not only in testimony from past conflicts but also in the current U.S.–Afghanistan war. The *New York Times* of 13 November 2001 featured a color photograph of a Taliban soldier whose pants had been stripped off by jubilant Northern Alliance forces, several of whom were shown aiming their weapons at his supine body. The photograph showed blood running down his legs, and although it was shot to screen the genital area, what had happened to this man is clear from what we can see. Testimony from male prisoners during the Yugoslav war also features stories of rape, castration, mutilation, and other forms of sexual torture inflicted on men. Indeed, Dubravka Zarkov argues that sexual violence directed toward men is an integral part of the "unmanning" of the enemy, linking "dominant notions of masculinity . . . with norms of heterosexuality and definitions of ethnicity,"[93] Even more often than with regard to women, whose sexual violation is used to goad populations to mobilize against an enemy, sexual violence against men is hidden from public view except in rare cases, and those few are centered on men who are outsiders to the group. This "feminization" of the enemy, especially when defeated, is yet another sign that the brutalization of women's bodies is seen as a masculine right, even when the "women" so violated are biologically men.[94]

The impunity that still characterizes incidents of sexual violence during armed conflict reflects the sorry history of gender discrimination by the very governments and international bodies whose diligence and forthrightness in other areas of international human rights law have done so much to bring human rights issues to the top of political agendas in scores of national and international forums. It constitutes a continued acceptance of "traditions" that sanction widespread violence against female human beings beginning with infanticide and extending through the abandonment, malnourishment, and mutilation of little girls to the enslavement, abuse, and murder of adult women.

It is time for the international community to recognize and promote the protection of the rights of women to sovereignty over their own bodies with the same seriousness as it recognizes the rights of men to sovereignty over theirs. The public prosecution of those indicted for wartime rape in Bosnia and Rwanda is one significant, and long overdue, indication that human rights are, indeed, *human* rights, to be cherished and protected by each of us for all of us. That bringing these criminals to justice would also bring relief to victims and to those whose sole connection to war crimes is that they share an ethnicity or a nationality with war criminals, only magnifies the humanitarian role of such tribunals as bodies seeking accountability for the horrors committed and justice for all those subjected to them.

Notes

Portions of this chapter originally appeared in Mary Ann Tétreault, "Justice for All: Wartime Rape and Women's Human Rights," *Global Governance: A Review of Multilateralism and International Organizations,* volume 3, number 2 (May–August 1997): 197–212. Copyright © 1997 by Lynne Rienner Publishers, Inc. Used with permission of the publisher.

1. Charles Tilly, "War Making and State Making as Organized Crime," in *Bringing the State Back In,* ed. Peter Evans, Dietrich Ruschemeyer, and Theda Skoçpol (New York: Cambridge University Press, 1985), 169–91.

2. Joseph R. Strayer, *On the Medieval Origins of the Modern State* (Princeton, N.J.: Princeton University Press, 1970).

3. V. Spike Peterson, "An Archaeology of Domination: Historicizing Gender and Class in Early Western State Formation" (Ph.D. diss., American University, 1988).

4. See, for example, Catherine A. MacKinnon, "Feminism, Marxism, Method, and the State: Toward a Feminist Jurisprudence," *Signs* 9, 4 (1983): 635–58; Amy Dru Stanley, *From Bondage to Contract: Wage Labor, Marriage, and the Market in the Age of Slave Emancipation* (New York: Cambridge University Press, 1998); Jacqueline Stevens, *Reproducing the State* (Princeton, N.J.: Princeton University Press, 1999); and the classic American work, Mary Wollstonecraft's *A Vindication of the Rights of Women,* first published in 1792 and, significantly, written in response to the reaction of conservatives such as Edmund Burke to her earlier work, *A Vindication of the Rights of Men.* For both, see Mary Wollstonecraft, *The Vindications: The Rights of Men; The Rights of Women,* ed. D. L. Macdonald and Kathleen Scherf (Peterborough, Ont.: Broadview Press, 1997). Men's movements opened what social movement theorists call a "political opportunity structure" that enabled women to join their claims to the claims of subjected men and also to learn techniques for activism as members of men's liberation movements such as the anticolonial movement in the American colonies.

5. Hilary Charlesworth and Christine Chinkin, *The Boundaries of International Law: A Feminist Analysis* (Manchester: Manchester University Press, 2000), 309.

6. U.S. military leaders seemed to be the most reluctant to arrest Yugoslavs under indictment for war crimes. Admiral Leighton Smith, the American military commander in the Balkans, "appeared to believe that his job was only to keep a military peace and had no interest in arresting anyone who might undermine it" (David Halberstam, *War in a Time of Peace* [New York: Scribner, 2001], 362).

7. Quoted in Anthony Lewis, "No Peace without Justice," *New York Times,* 20 November 1995, A11.

8. Yaron Ezrahi attributes the persistence of grand narratives of struggle in Israel to the victory of the state in the contest between collectivist narratives of Zionism and what he calls "the democratization of uniqueness . . . the idea that as an unrepeatable configuration of experience, emotions, sensations, thoughts, memories, biological traits, contingencies, aspirations, beliefs, and relations, each life is unique and, therefore, invaluable; the passing of each individual is, therefore, an irretrievable loss." See his *Rubber Bullets: Power and Conscience in Modern Israel* (Berkeley: University of California Press, 1997), 80.

9. Dorothy Q. Thomas and Reagan E. Ralph, "Rape in War: The Tradition of Impunity," *SAIS Review* 14, 1 (Spring 1993): 81–100.

10. Susan Brownmiller, *Against Our Will: Men, Women and Rape* (New York: Simon and Schuster, 1975), 57–58.

11. A similar story lies behind the first indictment for rape in the Rwandan tribunal—see page 299.

12. Ibid., 61. The Nuremberg tribunal did not include rape on the list of war crimes. During the war there was no rerun in the European theatre of allegations on the same level as stories of the World War I "rape of Belgium." Indeed, given both the volume of propaganda films produced by the allies during World War II and the volume of evidence amassed afterwards, contemporary charges of war crimes made against Germany during the war seem to have been vastly understated. Afterward, "sexual forms of torture, including rape, were documented at the [Nuremberg] trials" (Catherine A. MacKinnon, "Turning Rape into Pornography: Postmodern Genocide," *Ms.*, July/August 1993, 30).

13. Brownmiller, *Against Our Will,* 66–72; also Alfred P. Rubin, Letter to the editor, *New York Times,* 23 October 1992, A32; and, for a more recent historical treatment, see Antony Beevor, *The Fall of Berlin* (New York: Viking, 2002).

14. For a discussion in the context of U.S. law, see Caroline A. Forell and Donna M. Matthews, *A Law of Her Own: The Reasonable Woman as a Measure of Man* (New York: New York University Press, 2000).

15. Seth Faison, "Women's Meeting Agrees on Right to Say No to Sex," *New York Times,* 11 September 1995, A1.

16. However, as I shall discuss in the conclusion of this chapter, the idea that wartime rape is a crime directed only at women is unwarranted.

17. Robert Block, "The Tragedy of Rwanda," *New York Review of Books,* 20 October 1994, 9. The death of Rwandan President Juvenal Habyarimana in a suspicious plane crash was the event that triggered the genocide, but Block and others note that the Interahamwe and other militia groups, whose members formed the hard core of the *genocidaires,* had been preparing for at least two years, even engaging in a kind of dress rehearsal, a mini-slaughter of Tutsis in Bugasera in March 1992 (4).

18. Philip Gourevitch, *We Wish to Inform You That Tomorrow We Will Be Killed with Our Families: Stories from Rwanda* (New York: Picador, 1998).

19. Rhoda E. Howard, *Human Rights and the Search for Community* (Boulder, Colo.: Westview Press, 1995).

20. See, for example, Thomas Aquinas, *Summa Theologica,* STII, Question 40, "Of War," in Michael L. Morgan, ed., *Classics of Moral and Political Theory* (Indianapolis, Ind.: Hackett Publishing Company, 1992), 483–85.

21. Elaine Pagels, *Adam, Eve, and the Serpent* (New York: Random House, 1988), xxv; Pagels's italics.

22. Hilary Charlesworth, "Human Rights as Men's Rights," in *Women's Rights, Human Rights: International Feminist Perspectives,* ed. Julie Peters and Andrea Wolper (London: Routledge, 1995); also Charlesworth, "Alienating Oscar? Feminist Analysis of International Law," in *Reconceiving Reality: Women and International Law,* ed. Dorinda G. Dallmeyer, Studies in Transnational Legal Policy, no. 25 (Washington, D.C.: American Society for International Law, 1993).

23. Pagels and other scholars (for example, Sarah Pomeroy, *Goddesses, Whores, Wives, and Slaves* [New York: Schocken Books, 1975]; Eva C. Keuls, *The Reign of the Phallus: Sexual Politics in Ancient Athens* [Berkeley: University of California Press, 1985]; John Boswell, *The Kindness of Strangers: The Abandonment of Children in*

Western Europe from Late Antiquity to the Renaissance [New York: Vintage: 1988]) note that, in the ancient world, merchants reared children rescued from death by exposure in order to sell them as sexual slaves to wealthy persons. But even women who were nominal citizens of ancient states were expected to marry according to the wishes of their families, surrendering their bodies, the goods and services they produced, and the issue of their reproduction, to others. Chastity, thus, was an assertion of control over one's body, even though women could not control their civil status if their parents or others forced them to marry. See also Peter Brown, *The Body and Society: Men, Women, and Sexual Renunciation in Early Christianity* (New York: Columbia University Press, 1988).

24. Pagels, *Adam, Eve, and the Serpent,* 78.

25. Aristotle, *The Politics,* rev. ed. Trevor J. Saunders, trans. T. A. Sinclair (New York: Viking Penguin, 1981), 1253b23, 1254a1–9.

26. Ibid., 1255b4–15.

27. Ibid., 1259b32.

28. See, for example, Yvon Garlan, *Slavery in Ancient Greece,* rev. and expanded ed., trans. Janet Lloyd (Ithaca, N.Y.: Cornell University Press, 1988); and Roger W. Smith, "Genocide and the Politics of Rape: Historical and Psychological Perspectives" (paper presented at "Remembering for the Future: International Conference on the Holocaust and Genocide," 13–17 March 1994, Berlin). Thucydides' description of the end of Melos or Euripides' description of the end of Troy should be recalled in this context. The men and boys were put to death and the women taken back as slaves for the victors. Thus, we can see that even genocide has its roots in the ideology and practices of the ancients.

29. John Boswell, *Same-Sex Unions in Premodern Europe* (New York: Villard Books, 1994), 29.

30. This point is made several times by John Boswell in *Kindness of Strangers.*

31. Kenneth J. Dover, *Greek Homosexuality* (London: Duckworth, 1978), 103–4. This thesis is challenged by James Davidson who argues that it is, at least, overstated; see his *Courtesans and Fishcakes: The Consuming Passions of Classical Athens* (New York. Harper Perennial 1999). However, most scholars come closer to Dover's position than to Davidson's on this point. See, for example, David M. Halpern, "The Democratic Body: Prostitution and Citizenship in Classical Athens," in *One Hundred Years of Homosexuality and Other Essays on Greek Love* (New York: Routledge, 1990), 88–112. My analysis appears in "Frontier Politics: Sex, Gender, and the Deconstruction of the Public Sphere," *Alternatives* 26, 1 (January–March 2001): 53–72.

32. Pagels, *Adam, Eve, and the Serpent,* 113.

33. Quoted in ibid.

34. Ibid., 128; emphasis in the original.

35. Ibid., 133.

36. See, for example, Carolyn Walker Bynum, *Holy Feast and Holy Fast: The Religious Significance of Food to Medieval Women* (Berkeley: University of California Press, 1987).

37. C. B. Macpherson, *The Political Theory of Possessive Individualism: Hobbes to Locke* (Oxford: Oxford University Press, 1962), 1.

38. Quoted in Macpherson, *Possessive Individualism,* 137.

39. Ibid., 142.

40. Carole Pateman, "The Fraternal Social Contract," in *Civil Society and the State,* ed. John Keane (London: Verso, 1988): 101–27.

41. Carole Pateman, "'God Hath Ordained to Man a Helper': Hobbes, Patriarchy, and Conjugal Right," in *Feminist Interpretations and Political Theory,* ed. Mary Lyndon Shanley and Carole Pateman (University Park: Pennsylvania State University Press, 1991).

42. See, for examples, Jean Jacques Rousseau, *The First and Second Discourses,* ed. Roger D. Masters, trans. Roger D. and Judith R. Masters (New York: St. Martin's Press, 1964); and commentary on this and other philosophical works in this tradition in the following, all by Susan Moller Okin: *Women in Western Political Thought* (Princeton, N.J.: Princeton University Press, 1979); "Rousseau's Natural Woman," *Journal of Politics* 41, 2 (May 1979): 393–416; and *Justice, Gender, and the Family* (New York: Basic Books, 1989).

43. Page Smith, *Daughters of the Promised Land* (Boston: Little Brown, 1970).

44. Lynn Hunt, *Politics, Culture, and Class in the French Revolution* (Berkeley: University of California Press, 1984); George L. Mosse, *Nationalism and Sexuality: Respectability and Abnormal Sexuality in Modern Europe* (New York: Howard Fertig, 1985); Andrew Parker, Mary Russo, Doris Sommer, and Patricia Yaeger, eds., *Nationalisms and Sexualities* (New York: Routledge, 1992); Klaus Theweleit, *Male Fantasies,* vol 1, *Women, Floods, Bodies, History,* trans. Stephen Conway (Minneapolis: University of Minnesota Press, 1987); Nira Yuval-Davis and Floya Anthias, eds., *Woman-Nation-State* (London: Macmillan, 1989).

45. Thomas and Ralph, "Rape in War," 40.

46. This is explored in the context of the Rwandan genocide by Gourevitch, *We Wish to Inform You,* and Peter Uvin, *Aiding Violence: The Development Enterprise in Rwanda* (West Hartford, Conn.: Kumerian Press, 1998).

47. Examples of the use of rape as a strategy of conflict are described in Asia Watch and Physicians for Human Rights, *Rape in Kashmir: A Crime of War* (New York: Asia Watch, 1993); Human Rights Watch National Coalition for Haitian Refugees, *Rape in Haiti: A Weapon of Terror* (Washington: Human Rights Watch, 1994); Kanan Makiya, *Cruelty and Silence: War, Tyranny, Uprising, and the Arab World* (New York: Norton, 1993); Smith, "Genocide and the Politics of Rape."

48. J. G. Peristiany, ed., *Honor and Shame: The Values of Mediterranean Society* (London: Weidenfeld and Nicolson, 1965); Germaine Tillion, *The Republic of Cousins: Women's Oppression in Mediterranean Society,* trans. Quintin Hoare (London: Al Saqi Books, 1983).

49. Foreign women also were raped and, from all accounts, in far larger numbers. With respect to Kuwaiti victims, according to insiders I interviewed, the rape of Resistance women was publicized by their Iraqi captors to discourage women's participation in Resistance activities. One of the psychologists I interviewed in 1992 talked of a patient who had been raped repeatedly and sexually tortured in other ways as "punishment" for her participation in the Resistance. Afterward, she was released back into the community as an example of what would happen to other Kuwaiti Resistance women, rather than killed as so many other Kuwaiti victims of torture were.

50. Haya al-Mughni and Fawzia al-Turkait, "Dealing with Trauma: Cultural Barriers to Self-Recovery: The Case of Kuwaiti Women" (paper presented at the seminar on

Effective Methods for Encountering the Psychological and Social Effects of the Iraqi Aggression, sponsored by the Social Development Office of the Amiri Diwan, Kuwait City, 26–28 March 1994).

51. John R. Crook, "The United Nations Compensation Commission—A New Structure to Enforce State Responsibility," *American Journal of International Law* 87 (1993): 147; also W. Michael Reisman and Chris T. Antoniou, eds., *The Laws of War: A Comprehensive Collection of Primary Documents on International Law Governing Armed Conflict* (New York: Vintage Books, 1994).

52. Crook, "The UNCC," 148.

53. Governments of non-Kuwaiti nationals also processed claims brought by their citizens for transmission to the UNCC.

54. Adel Asem and Haya al-Mughni, "Claiming for Compensation Through the United Nations Compensation Commission: The Case of Kuwait" (paper presented at the International Conference on the Effects of the Iraqi Aggression on Kuwait, Kuwait City, 2–6 April 1994), 12.

55. Interviews in Kuwait, 1992 and 1994.

56. Crook, "The UNCC," 154.

57. The total available was effectively limited to the amount of assets sequestered under UN-directed economic sanctions against Iraq imposed on 6 August 1990, augmented by whatever monies would be collected as the result of assessing Iraq 30 percent of the proceeds from oil sales permitted for humanitarian purposes during the period of the sanctions (UN Security Council Resolution 706, 15 August 1991).

58. Two individuals working with PAAC told me that three claims for damages resulting from rape were received.

59. Mary Ann Tétreault, "Whose Honor? Whose Liberation? Women and the Reconstruction of Politics in Kuwait," in *Women and Revolution in Africa, Asia, and the New World,* ed. Mary Ann Tétreault (Columbia: University of South Carolina Press, 1994), 301; also Judy Mann, "Kuwaiti Rape a Doubly Savage Crime," *Washington Post,* 29 March 1991, C3.

60. Examples come from Helsinki Watch, *War Crimes in Bosnia-Hercegovina,* vol. 2 (New York: Human Rights Watch, 1993); MacKinnon, "Turning Rape into Pornography"; Anna Quindlen, "Gynocide," *New York Times,* 10 March 1993, A19; Alan Riding, "European Inquiry Says Serbs' Forces Have Raped 20,000," *New York Times,* 9 January 1993, 1, 4; Jasmina Kuzmanović, "Legacies of Invisibility: Past Silence, Present Violence against Women in the Former Yugoslavia," in *Women's Rights, Human Rights: International Feminist Perspectives,* ed. Julie Peters and Andrea Wolper (New York: Routledge, 1995); Jiřina Šiklová (member of the Helsinki Watch committee taking testimony from victims of war crimes in the Bosnian conflict), interviewed by Mary Ann Tétreault, Washington, D.C., 4 March 1995; Lawrence Weschler, "Inventing Peace," *New Yorker,* 20 November 1995, 52–68.

61. Quoted in Weschler, "Inventing Peace," 56.

62. Kuzmanović, "Legacies of Invisibility," 58.

63. Carol J. Williams, "Bosnia's Orphans of Rape: Innocent Legacy of Hatred," *Los Angeles Times,* 24 July 1993, A1, A12.

64. Charlesworth and Chinkin, *Boundaries of International Law,* 324–29.

65. Negative sovereignty and its consequences with respect to domestic human rights protections are discussed in Robert Jackson, *Quasi-states: Sovereignty,*

International Relations and the Third World (Cambridge: Cambridge University Press, 1990); Václav Havel, "Kosovo and the End of the Nation-State," *New York Review of Books*, 10 June 1999, 4, 6.

66. The mechanisms of denial and repertoires of excuses for inaction in the face of obvious brutality are examined for states (and other actors) in exquisite detail in Stanley Cohen, *States of Denial: Knowing about Atrocities and Suffering* (Cambridge, U.K.: Polity Press, 2001), especially chap. 4.

67. Gourevitch recounts several stories about this in *We Wish to Inform You*, and others can be found in Alison Des Forges, *"Leave None to Tell the Story": Genocide in Rwanda* (New York: Human Rights Watch, 1999). A heartbreaking example of terrorization can be seen in the PBS *Frontline* documentary, "The Triumph of Evil" (PBS FROL-1710, 1999), in itself a testimony that the events occurring in Rwanda were widely known and as widely denied by "the international community." (On this see also David Rieff, "Nothing Was Delivered," *New Republic*, 1 May 2000, 26–33.)

68. Human Rights Watch/Africa, Human Rights Watch Women's Rights Project, and Federation Internationale des Ligues des Droits de l'Homme, "Shattered Lives: Sexual Violence During the Rwandan Genocide and Its Aftermath," New York: Human Rights Watch, 1996), 65–68.

69. Des Forges, *"Leave None"*; Charlesworth and Chinkin, *Boundaries of International Law*, 323. Some of the violations inflicted on women in Foca are detailed in "Gang Rape, Torture and Enslavement of Muslim Women Charged in ICTY's First Indictment Dealing Specifically with Sexual Offenses," CC/PIO/093–E, The Hague, 27 June 1996.

70. Meredith Turshen, "The Political Economy of Rape: An Analysis of Systematic Rape and Sexual Abuse of Women during Armed Conflict in Africa," in *Victims, Perpetrators or Actors? Gender, Armed Conflict and Political Violence*, ed. Caroline O. N. Moser and Fiona C. Clark (London: Zed Books, 2001), 58. Turshen reports a 1996 UN estimate stating that a quarter of a million mostly Tutsi women had been raped in the genocide. A 2000 estimate by the World Health Organization puts the number at 15,700. Given the scale of the crimes and the number of women who were killed, raped or not, make all estimates merely that—estimates.

71. Ibid.

72. Judith Colp Rubin, "Judge of Genocide," *Women's International Net Magazine* 33, A (May 2000); Charlesworth and Chinkin, *Boundaries of International Law*, 323.

73. Rubin, "Judge of Genocide."

74. Quoted in Charlesworth and Chinkin, *Boundaries of International Law*, 323.

75. Rubin, "Judge of Genocide."

76. Andrew Harding, "Rwanda's Slow Justice," broadcast 19 May 2001, 12:04 GMT, BBC News Online.

77. Geraldine Coughlan, "Rwanda Genocide Conviction Upheld," broadcast 16 December 2001, 12:05 GMT, BBC News Online.

78. In November 1999, the ICTR's appeals court in The Hague ordered the release of Jean-Bosco Barayagwiza (*Barayagwiza, Jean Bosco, ICTR-96–7*). The defendant was a former political advisor in the Habyarimana foreign ministry, a founder of the *Radio télévision libre des Mille Collines*, the infamous hate radio station, and also a leader of an extremist party whose militia participated actively in the genocide. His conviction by the tribunal was put in question when the appeals chamber ordered him released because of procedural irregularities during his pretrial detention. Chris

Simpson, "Rwanda Tribunal's Shaky Progress," broadcast 16 February 2000, 13:31 GMT, BBC News Online.

79. PBS, "Valentina's Nightmare," *Frontline,* FROL-509, 1997.

80. Ibid.; also Gourevitch, *We Wish to Inform You.*

81. Helen Vesperini, "Rwanda Genocide Death Sentences," *BBC News,* 14 October 2001, http://news.bbc.co.uk/hi/english/world/africa/newsid_1598000/1598940.stm (7 May 2002); Amnesty International, "Rwanda: The Troubled Course of Justice," New York: Amnesty International, report no. AFR 47/15/00, April 2000, accessed at http://web.amnesty.org/ai.nsf/Index/AFR470152000/ (15 April 2002); "Rwanda," in the Amnesty International 2001 Annual Report, accessed at http://web.amnesty.org/web/ar2001.nsf/webafrcountries/RWANDA/ (15 April 2002).

82. "Rwanda," in the Amnesty International 2001 Annual Report, accessed at http//:web.amnesty.org/web/ar2001.nsf/webafrcountries/RWANDA/ (15 April 2002).

83. See, for example, Ibid.; Human Rights Watch, "Shattered Lives," 89–91 and Gourevitch, *We Wish to Inform You,* 313. Some of the sexual violence is a direct result of a government resettlement program that has forced hundreds of thousands of Rwandans to leave their homes for new and highly insecure "villages" called *imidugudu.*

84. Human Rights Watch, "Shattered Lives," 69–75; 79–82.

85. Ibid., 75–78.

86. Ibid., 83–91.

87. Ibid. Also, PBS, "Valentina's Nightmare."

88. This is not to say that such a ritual exorcism would be a perfect solution, especially if the attribution of personal responsibility is carried to extremes. See, for example Priscilla B. Hayner, "Digging Up the Past: Do Truth Commissions Cause Conflict?" (paper presented at the annual meeting of the International Studies Association, Chicago, 22 February 1995).

89. For examples, see MacKinnon, "Feminism, Marxism, Method"; and Forell and Matthews, *A Law of Her Own.*

90. Peterson, "An Archaeology of Domination"; Stevens, *Reproducing the State,* chap. 5.

91. See, for example, United States District Court, Southern District of New York, *Jane Doe I, on behalf of herself and all others similarly situated, and Jane Doe II, on behalf of herself, as administratrix of the estate of her deceased mother, and on behalf of all others similarly situated vs. Radovan Karadzić,* "Complaint for Genocide; War Crimes and Crimes Against Humanity; Summary Execution; Torture, Cruel, Inhuman or Degrading Treatment; Wrongful Death; Assault and Battery; and Intentional Infliction of Emotional Harm," No. 93 Civ. 0878 PKL. This case was initially dismissed for lack of jurisdiction, although the dismissal was overturned on appeal and a jury awarded damages to the plaintiffs in the summer and fall of 2000 (I thank Robin Teske for information updates on this case.). Although the likelihood that the plaintiffs can collect these damages is slight, the cases are significant in that they included rape and sexual torture among the crimes alleged against the defendant. A second example, a case involving four Catholic nuns, was brought in Belgium

92. Charlesworth and Chinkin, *Boundaries of International Law,* 315–17.

93. Dubravka Zarkov, "The Body of the Other Man: Sexual Violence and the Construction of Masculinity, Sexuality and Ethnicity in Croatian Media," in *Victims, Perpetrators or Actors?,* 69.

94. Ethnic/tribal conflicts are not the only ones where sexual violence is inflicted on male "losers." See, for example, Carolyn Nordstrom, *A Different Kind of War Story* (Philadelphia: University of Pennsylvania Press, 1997), 129–30.

Part Six

Philosophers' Stones

Chapter 16

Knowledge and Accountability in Global Governance

Justice on the Biofrontier

Clark A. Miller

At the onset of the twenty-first century, humanity inhabits a new biological frontier. This frontier is a realm of remarkable, if somewhat disturbing, technological potential. Around the world, life as we know it is changing as a result of new ideas and new products from the laboratory.[1] Advances in genomics, ecology, assisted reproduction, remote sensing, computer modeling, and other areas of research have transformed scientists' abilities to understand and manipulate nature on scales from the microscopic to the planetary. At the cellular level, new scientific and technological practices—cloning, gene therapy, in vitro fertilization, DNA fingerprinting, cross-species gestation, and the construction of transgenic varieties of plants and animals—are increasingly commonplace. On planetary scales, conservation biology and restoration ecology have become tools of global environmental management.

The biological frontier is also a realm of uncertain politics. Advances in biotechnology raise foundational questions about social order. Who will reproduce? Who will have access to the genetic material of human and non-human populations? Who will distribute the benefits of new genetic technologies? What rules will govern the release of new organisms into the environment? How will we manage the productive capacity of the biosphere to produce food and preserve disappearing ecosystems? Who will make such rules, and what procedures will they follow? Perhaps more importantly, advances in the biological sciences prompt reevaluations of the basic categories that characterize modern political imagination, categories such as race, gender, values, identity, rights, responsibilities, power, agency, and causality. In sites that range from in vitro fertilization clinics and zoological laboratories to courts and international treaty negotiations, these categories have acquired a contingent and unsettled character as people and institutions have sought to integrate scientists' new capabilities with existing social organization and practice.

My purpose in this chapter is to argue that, as humans grapple with the complexities and uncertainties of life on the biological frontier, we need to reassess institutional capabilities to reason and act in the new world of genomics, restoration ecology, and planetary management. The production, validation, and use of knowledge to inform policy choices lends considerable power to scientists and engineers in modern society.[2] Many democratic societies implicitly recognize the power wielded by those who depict and manipulate nature and have taken steps to constrain this power within existing political institutions.[3] However, the rapid transformations accompanying recent advances in the biological sciences have challenged the capacity of even the most robust democracies to respond adequately to new ideas and new technologies.[4]

Even more worrisome, while many of the challenges of the biological frontier are explicitly global in scope, international institutions are particularly poorly equipped to grapple with the underlying dynamics of power enmeshed in the new biology. In the newly emerging global governing regime for biodiversity, for example, little attention is given to the implications of how the production and application of knowledge affects the distribution of power and wealth. Since 1992, negotiations under the auspices of the UN Convention on Biological Diversity have sought to establish worldwide norms, rules, and procedures governing the mining and exploitation of genetic resources, the transfer and release of genetically-modified organisms, and the conservation of ecological systems. These negotiations have relied extensively on the biological sciences as both a source of factual information about nature and a model for how to produce reliable knowledge. Yet debates about biodiversity rarely if ever reflect a nuanced understanding of how the fairness, equity, and justice of global governing arrangements can become enmeshed in claims about how nature—and science—work.[5]

In the first two sections of the chapter, I argue that the concept of *organized skepticism* offers a fruitful starting point for exploring the production and use of policy-relevant knowledge on the biological frontier. This concept incorporates two ideas: subjecting knowledge claims and technological systems to critical review, and holding institutions accountable for how they produce and use knowledge.[6] In developing the concept of organized skepticism, I expand upon feminist theories of science and technology that have addressed questions of individual accountability and transparency in the production and application of knowledge. In the final section of the paper, I apply the concept of organized skepticism to the case study of conserving biological diversity planetwide.

Individual and Institutional Accountability

Many feminists are concerned about the potential for new genetic and reproductive technologies to fix women in a secondary position in modern society. In the name of science and objectivity, feminist critics argue, modern medical practices have helped to subjugate women in Western and non-Western societies by defining what is normal and abnormal, rational and irrational. Advances in biotechnology may eventually free women from diseases such as breast cancer and conditions such as infertility, but the continued framing of these issues in scientific and medical terms may also reduce further women's control over their own bodies and lives.

Responding to this possibility, feminist theorists offer resources for recognizing and resisting the value-laden assumptions enmeshed in the design and implementation of scientific and technological systems. In doing so, they have been careful to avoid simply replacing one reified version of objectivity with another. Instead, they have sought to teach people to see through the naturalistic discourses that surround science and technology to their *constructed* core, to understand that science and technology are the products of human ideas, interests, and institutions, and to grapple with the normative implications of the integration of science and technology into daily life. In plain words, they have tried to help women render scientific and technological aspects of their lives transparent to human reason and judgment.[7] At the same time, they ask women to hold themselves accountable for their own choices and beliefs regarding science, technology, the body, reproduction, and nature.[8]

In approaching transparency and accountability in scientific and technological systems through the empowerment of individual women, feminist scholarship has done much to illuminate life on the biological frontier and the complexities and ambiguities of its material, social, and ethical relationships. I believe it is necessary to extend this argument from individual choices to collective, institutional decision making. The ability to see the constructed character of scientific and technological systems is clearly important, but even highly skilled observers and interpreters of technoscience may, nonetheless, remain vulnerable to powerful institutions operating on the basis of preexisting models of objectivity, rationality, and normality. The choices made by firms, regulatory agencies, professional associations, and other corporate bodies carry enormous implications for how women and men live their lives. Consequently, these institutions should also be held accountable for the production and application of biological knowledge. Feminist theorists surely are correct to point to the individual's ability to reflect critically on her own life as an essential component of a just society within the liberal tradition, but a just society demands critical reflection from social institutions as well as from individuals.

The limitations inherent in focusing on questions of individual capacity can be observed readily in a modern fairy tale by author/anthropologist Charis Cussins.[9] The story, "Confessions of a Bioterrorist," offers a fictional interpretation, grounded in feminist theories of science and technology, of the challenges of life on the biological frontier. Cussins's protagonist, Mary, opens the story as a naive participant in modern life. She works as a technician in a zoological laboratory dedicated to freezing embryos of endangered species for future research. The daily activities of her life include collecting embryos from anaesthetized animals, giving tours to visiting dignitaries, going to lectures, and soliciting donations for the zoo. Mary befriends Gabriela, a young, black sociologist, and Eva, a doctor at a nearby in vitro fertilization clinic, and so begins a whirlwind series of events that shatters Mary's—and the reader's—sensibilities of normalcy. To cut a long, very well written short story even shorter, Mary first reveals and then ultimately acts upon a seemingly fantastic desire: she impregnates herself with an embryo from a bonobo chimpanzee.

Cussins's tale celebrates women's potential power on this new frontier. Radical opportunities exist for women and others for whom the biological realities of the past have often meant powerlessness and oppression, if they abide by the famous motto: *carpe diem*—seize the day. But as the story winds it way toward its shocking conclusion, Mary also learns how her life, and especially her reproductive choices, are hemmed in by modern society's norms, rituals, knowledges, and practices. Although cross-species gestation has become a reality in efforts to protect endangered species,[10] in the end Mary's decision is less a reasoned choice made to further the bonobo's chances of survival than a simple declaration of freedom. I am my own master, Mary declares, and I will choose to use my body and its potentials to carve out a future for myself according to self-selected and self-reasoned criteria.

Although she recognizes the challenges Mary faces, Cussins ends the story before Mary confronts the rest of the world: her family, the zoo, the media, and the government. As the day of birth approaches, Mary herself begins to worry about how her friends, family, and coworkers will react, but the problem goes well beyond these intimates with whom she shares bonds built up through daily interaction. What will happen when Mary returns to her family and her job, bonobo baby in tow? How will the media respond? Bill Clinton was shielded from predatory tabloid reporters—at least to a degree—by the fortress of the White House, but neither everyday individuals like Monica Lewinsky nor even Princess Diana enjoyed that much insulation. Will Mary's family survive the tensions of having a bonobo baby brother in the house, or the fact that Mary made her choice in complete secrecy, telling neither her husband nor her children? How will the zoo treat her decision? Officials will be vulnerable to enormous liability lawsuits and to the very real possibility that the ensuing scandal would scare off patrons and visitors. Will Christian groups denounce the zoo over Mary's choice? Powerful forces abound at the margins of Mary's story, never quite arriving at the center of our attention because the author ends the story before Mary's secret emerges from the womb.

It is interesting to compare "Confessions of a Bioterrorist" to other recent fictional accounts of the biological frontier. Surfing the edges of possibility in the slums and underworlds where anything goes in the mix of technology and body has become a common motif in science-fiction writing. Protagonists in stories like William Gibson's *Neuromancer* must look out, however, for agents of the vast, powerful institutions that dominate these dystopic societies. The governments, militaries, and corporations of these worlds seem poised to squash characters as if they were swatting flies. Such stories offer a powerful metaphor, I would suggest, that warns against focusing exclusively (or even predominantly) on creating a more technosocially sophisticated and aware self without also seeking ways to reconfigure and restructure the institutions that forge scientific and technological systems and narratives. Is it enough to create nimble subjects with protective, individual shells without finding ways to hold accountable the powerful collectives in society as well?

Consider, for example, the more dangerous dimensions of the biological frontier that emerge in "A Desperate Calculus" by Sterling Blake. As the story unfolds, we are introduced to Amy, a doctor working for the World Health Organization to track down the carrier of a novel epidemic. Todd, her lover, runs a transnational nongovernmental organization (NGO) that collects biological samples in the Brazilian Amazon, trying to stay one step ahead of the bulldozers and fires of local developers. The NGO's goal also is to create a frozen zoo, this time to preserve that part of the world's biological diversity wiped out on a daily basis as tropical rainforests disappear. The reader's notions of normal are turned upside down, once again, when the story reveals that Amy and Todd have used the resources of their employers to spread the viral agent in question—an agent which does not kill (except for the weakest of the elderly and children) but renders women sterile. Their goal is to end the threat to the environment posed by rapidly increasing world population. The story ends as Amy and Todd are executed for their "crimes" by a UN investigator who, aided by statistical analyses of the spread of disease and military spy satellites, has tracked them to their jungle hideout.[11]

Organized Skepticism

What distinguishes Amy and Todd's story from that of Mary is the way in which the central act of liberation—which stems, in both cases, from a creative, cyborg rearrangement of bodies and lives through the wonders of modern biology—is magnified billions-fold to encompass the entire human population. The ability of experts to work within the institutional forms of modern life to bring about widespread changes in human affairs is a staple of recent accounts of the biological frontier. Writing in *The Violence of the Green Revolution,* for example, and more recently in *Biopiracy,* Vandana Shiva has decried the destructive character of Western scientists' efforts to rationalize agricultural production in the Third World through scientific, technological, legal, and cultural standardization.[12] William Storey's account of British and French colonialism in Mauritius likewise highlights the deep connections between imperial power, social order, and the scientific efforts of British naturalists to enhance sugar cane production on the island.[13] Perhaps most ominous are the stories offered by James Scott in *Seeing Like a State.* Scott documents the historical disasters perpetrated in the name of what he calls the high-modernist impulse, social engineering on a grand scale. Agricultural collectivization, villagization, and urban planning all reflect, for Scott, the hubris of the scientific and technological mindset characteristic of elite planners in the modern state.[14]

The link between science and the state has not always resulted in exploitation and violence, however. In a recent critique of Shiva's work, and of constructivist and postcolonial studies of science and technology more generally, Indian feminist Meera Nanda offers a very different picture of the role of science in modern society. A veteran of the people's science movement in India, Nanda argues that science has offered women an effective alternative to traditionalist narratives of gender, race, and class (or caste) that have been used to enslave subjugated peoples throughout Indian history.[15] While there is much to take issue with in Nanda's account of the politics of science in India,[16] it is worth investigating her sense that it is possible to construct a very different relationship between the state, science, and society than the relationship described by Shiva and Scott.

This view also is shared by constructivist accounts of modern science and its role in the formation of political order. Yaron Ezrahi writes, for example, of American democracy: "The historical record of the fascist state and the communist dictatorship has more than confirmed [Edmund] Burke's fears of political engineers who would treat people like gassed mice. And, for their part, modern liberal-democratic governments have not been free of dreams of political engineering nor innocent of the morally and humanly costly uses of science and technology to augment their power to ameliorate, reconstruct, control and manipulate. . . . What has been widely ignored [however] are the efforts to use scientific knowledge and skills not so much to enhance the instrumental effectiveness of democratic governments as to ideologically defend and legitimate uniquely liberal-democratic modes of public action, of presenting, defending, and criticizing the uses of political power."[17]

Ezrahi is centrally concerned with the ways in which an instrumental model of state action (public policy) has been put to use in Western democracies to constrain the arbitrary exercise of power. In another book, *Rubber Bullets,* Ezrahi examines the efforts of the Israeli government to rein in its use of force by switching to rubber-coated bullets in its war against the Palestinians. He argues that, while this reasoning was fallacious (the bullets continued to kill Palestinians), it also constituted a form of instrumental reasoning—an effort to measure the use of force so as to apply only that amount of military power necessary to a given context—that expresses a growing liberal-democratic sensibility on the part of Israeli citizens.[18] Theodore Porter argues that American democracy deploys statistical information in much the same fashion, attempting to constrain the arbitrariness of bureaucratic decisions through the mechanical objectivity produced by following the rules of mathematics.[19]

These uses of science and technology to buttress liberal-democratic norms and institutions differ from similar applications of science and technology to strengthen state power in two important ways. First, in liberal democracies, instrumental logic is used in part to check the power of social planners. American law, for example, requires government agencies to make their reasoning public so that Congress, the media, courts, firms, and individuals can subject it to detailed scrutiny. In this way, the instrumental vision of social planning contributes to broader societal institutions for holding government accountable to the very people on and for whom the social planning is carried out.[20] While far from perfect, the use of science and technology as a means to measure policy ends has helped to constrain government action by forcing bureaucracies to defend their actions to an attentive public in nominally rational terms.[21] In contrast, the very worst atrocities of democratic governments (for example, the Tuskegee experiments, radiation tests on children in mental institutions, and releases of radioactive iodine from nuclear weapons facilities) have occurred when normal avenues of witnessing and accountability were closed off for one reason or another (racist institutions, forgotten children, or national security).

Likewise, when American planners operated abroad, as in Green Revolution and other international development projects, this fundamental chain of accountability also has been broken.[22]

Second, American democracy in particular is characterized by a decentralized approach to the production and use of science and technology in public policy making. Dorothy Nelkin, drawing upon sociological investigations of numerous public controversies, has noted that no single actor has a monopoly on scientific information. University, industry, and government laboratories all produce studies of controversial subjects available to scientists working for government agencies, industry trade groups, and nongovernmental organizations.[23] In her study of expert advisory processes, *The Fifth Branch,* Sheila Jasanoff finds that this pluralism is built into the institutional processes of American public policy making. Administrative hearings, expert advisory committees, congressional oversight, and judicial review of agency decisions all offer multiple entry points where divergent scientific viewpoints and competing interpretations of scientific data can be heard.[24] As Ezrahi has pointed out, the cacophony of voices generated by these encounters makes it extraordinarily difficult (if not impossible) to operationalize the concept of "the public interest" in modern democracies, effectively deconstructing grand narratives of social planning.[25]

To be sure, hegemonic narratives continue to pervade applications of science and technology, even in the United States. That is why, as feminist theorists suggest, it is necessary to expand the skills of individuals to interpret and deconstruct the discourses of technoscience in new and sophisticated ways. It is the informal, yet *organized skepticism* of American democratic institutions, however, that has made it possible for those on the receiving end of expert-conceived rational planning to confront government authorities with competing narratives of nature and society. Although the instrumental use of science and technology to rationalize policy choices first served as an impetus to strengthen the state,[26] American political institutions adapted it to more decentralized arrangements. These webs of accountability demand that policy makers defend their actions in explicitly instrumental terms (that is, in terms of the ends they will achieve), acting as a constraint on their discretion and choices. At the same time, the skeins of accountability reach down into the very production of policy-relevant knowledge itself as citizens, judges, administrators, industry representatives, and others regularly debate and dispute the adequacy of scientific studies in a variety of public forums.[27] Neither of these aspects of institutional accountability exists in the transnational settings of the biological frontier in which real-life stories are already taking place that are uncomfortably similar to those of Amy, Todd, and Mary.

Accounting for Knowledge in Global Governance

Organized skepticism has deep roots in American political culture. There is little evidence, however, that Americans have worked to incorporate similar constraints on the power of science and technology in international governance. Nor have the constructivist perspectives of feminist and other recent academic writings on science and technology been influential in the discursive frameworks of emerging arenas of global politics that characterize the biological frontier. Instead, unreflective portrayals of science as politically neutral have justified an expansion of the role of science in global governance.

Since World War II, diplomats, political officials, nongovernmental organizations, and industry groups have turned frequently to experts not only because of their seemingly unparalleled ability to find solutions to policy problems but also because of the perceived universality of science as a bridge to link distinct national perspectives. In the immediate postwar years for example, the presumed power of expertise to rationalize the conduct of international affairs led to the creation of a host of UN specialized agencies —the Bretton Woods institutions, the Food and Agriculture Organization, the World Health Organization, the World Meteorological Organization—centered around expert investigation and management of global-scale natural and social systems.[28] The rapid proliferation of global environmental agreements since the mid-1970s has produced a host of new international advisory bodies offering expert input into the negotiation and management of environmental regulatory regimes.[29] The World Trade Organization specifically vests the authority to overturn domestic environmental, health, and safety legislation in expert committees that decide whether such legislation is scientifically justified. Quantitative indicators of institutional performance and policy outcomes have emerged as key tools for ascertaining whether governments and international organizations are achieving publicly desired outcomes.[30]

In turning to experts and expert knowledge, however, neither global governing institutions nor scholars of international relations have given much attention to the moral questions that surround this growing dependence on science and technology.[31] A deeper awareness of how power is entwined in the practices of producing, validating, and using policy-relevant knowledge is missing. In the rest of the chapter, I want to show how insights drawn from feminist stories like "Confessions of a Bioterrorist" can be used to expand ideas of organized skepticism to fit the new *global* politics of biology. In particular, I use a case study of biodiversity conservation to explore how scientists conceptualize and frame "nature" in global politics and separate it off from "culture"; how people apply scientific depictions of nature to help construct social policy; and how notions of science and objectivity become symbolic resources in the creation of political order.

Defining Nature

Feminist and other critical scholarship has given a great deal of thought to how ideas of "nature" and "natural" are used to construct and maintain patterns of social activity and authority.[32] For Mary, in "Confessions of a Bioterrorist," cultural norms of childbirth led her to reveal her fantasy (and later her choice) to bear a bonobo child to only her closest friends—friends she knew understood and shared her own unconventional, very different ideals. As the story ends, Mary's fears about how her family, the zoo, and society will respond to the "unnatural" (or even monstrous) event nearly overwhelm her.

International efforts to conserve biological diversity offer a useful site for investigating how ideas about nature acquire power to shape people's lives through their production and application by political institutions. The biological frontier is a place where basic human ideas about nature are under revision. This is particularly true in global environmental governance. As I have argued elsewhere, changing conceptual frameworks increasingly depict nature as an integrated, global system (as in earth systems science) at risk from human activities. This planetary perspective underpins calls for a radical rearrangement of international political institutions to address these risks.[33]

In the mid-1980s, conservation biologists introduced the term "biodiversity" in a deliberate effort to reshape the conservation agenda in global policy making by reshaping people's ideas of nature. As David Takacs has described in his book *The Idea of Biodiversity,* conservation biologists used the term to de-emphasize piecemeal programs of nature conservation concentrating on individual locales and species (and especially the charismatic megafauna that had received priority attention in international affairs to that point). Instead, they sought to focus efforts on conserving the vast diversity of life on earth.[34] At the same time, some conservation biologists also initiated an intense campaign to attach economic value to biodiversity by introducing concepts such as ecosystems services (valuing services that ecosystems provide to human communities) and genetic prospecting (turning genes, chemicals, and products found in nature into economically valuable products, such as pharmaceuticals).

Their efforts worked. Early in 1990, international diplomats launched a series of negotiations intended to produce a biodiversity conservation treaty for the Rio Earth Summit in June 1992. Initially, the treaty was conceived as an umbrella or framework agreement to systematize and rationalize ongoing global conservation activities under existing treaties such as the Convention on International Trade in Endangered Species, the Ramsar Convention on Wetlands, and the International Convention on Migratory Species. As negotiations progressed, however, the idea that biological diversity constitutes an economic resource acquired considerable momentum. Particularly among developing countries, whose territories contained the vast majority of the world's species, anger emerged at the prospect of transnational corporations mining their natural resources to produce pharmaceuticals and other valuable commodities while returning little if any of the resulting wealth to the country that "owned" these resources. As the treaty took shape, therefore, developing countries demanded that an emphasis on biodiversity conservation be coupled with compensation for biological materials removed from their lands. The key phrase that emerged to capture this compromise was the "conservation and sustainable use of biological resources."

The ratification of the 1992 Convention on Biological Diversity (CBD) and the subsequent construction of its treaty-mandated institutional framework marked a further shift away from a global conservation focus. Particularly after 1995, momentum developed to pursue two protocols to the original treaty. One addressed "access and benefits sharing," a code phrase referring to rules for granting corporations access to the genetic and biological resources of biodiversity-rich countries on the condition that they share the benefits derived from the economic development of those resources. The other addressed "biosafety," referring to the risks associated with transnational transfers of genetically modified organisms. The second took precedence and resulted in the Biosafety Protocol in late 2000. Meanwhile, efforts to bring the conservation activities of other treaties under the CBD were shelved as opposition emerged from within those regimes.[35] Adding to the difficulty of coordinating global conservation activities, the CBD accorded all biodiversity priority-setting to national governments under the theory that biodiversity is a national resource. Although some treaty participants continue to push a global conservation agenda, their efforts have been limited primarily to providing technical assistance to help countries produce national biodiversity action plans.

By the end of the 1990s, many conservationists had grown dissatisfied with the CBD process and sought other avenues for promoting biodiversity conservation that was explicitly global in scope. In 1997, for example, the World Wildlife Fund (WWF) leveraged its $300 million annual conservation budget to launch what it calls its Living Planet Campaign. Working with local, regional, and national governments, business and religious organizations, and others, WWF's campaign hopes to catalyze planetwide conservation programs to protect habitats that sustain exemplars of all the world's varieties of life.[36] Taking a somewhat different tack, Conservation International (CI) began work to save the world's biodiversity "hotspots." Hotspots, a concept first articulated in the late 1980s, are regions that both contain high numbers of endemic species (species that exist only within that region) and are at extreme risk of degradation.[37] In late 2000, CI and the World Bank announced a joint, $150 million program through the Global Environment Facility to protect these hotspots.[38] By the turn of the millennium, therefore, two credible alternatives to the CBD had joined the competition to set global biodiversity conservation priorities.

The WWF and CI initiatives exemplify the turn to science-based, quantitative approaches to global policy making and also the need to strengthen organized skepticism in the production of policy-relevant knowledge in global governing arrangements. WWF's campaign is centered on its Living Planet Index, "a measure of the health of the world's natural ecosystems," and on the Global 200, a prioritized list of the 200-plus most important ecoregions for biodiversity conservation. WWF scientists constructed the Global 200 list using a complex grid scheme that divides the world into major habitat types and then looks for regions that contain high numbers of species endemic to those particular habitats. The goal is to guarantee that the priority list contains all major habitat types, from tundra and desert to tropical rainforests.[39] In contrast, CI's biodiversity hotspots are defined simply by measuring two quantities: the rate of habitat loss and the number of endemic species contained within the region. Any region that contains more than a specified number of endemic species (approximately 1500) and less than a specified amount of original habitat (10–25 percent) is designated a biodiversity hotspot. The result, according to the subtitle of CI's coffee-table volume *Hotspots*, is a list of "Earth's [twenty-five] biologically richest and most endangered terrestrial ecosystems."[40]

What is particularly striking about both WWF's and CI's priority lists (and the numbers they're based on) is the degree to which knowledge claims produced by scientists working directly for these two organizations have emerged, with little or no critical reflection by outsiders, to guide large-scale conservation programs. The differences between the two priority lists reflect differences not only in conservation values (whether to preserve the largest number of species or to preserve species from a diverse array of habitats—the vast majority of CI's hotspots are moist tropical rainforests) but also in policy approaches (whether to target regions most at risk or to adopt a longer-term perspective). Yet, despite these clear political choices shaping the global conservation agendas championed by WWF and CI, there has been little or no global political discussion of how their priorities were derived. Perhaps most important, people in developing countries—whose territories contain the majority of high priority conservation areas—have had little or no input in setting these priorities, despite the clear opposition of developing-country governments to global priority-setting within the CBD process.

The lack of critical review of biodiversity conservation agendas extends into the two organizations' active conservation programs. WWF's Living Planet Campaign is carried out through contractual arrangements between WWF and a variety of groups around the world—governments at all levels, business and religious organizations, and local and transnational non-governmental organizations. While this tactic has enabled WWF to bypass uncooperative national governments and the contentions of multilateral negotiating forums, the details of these agreements remain private and shielded from public view.

In contrast, in its agreement with the World Bank, CI promises to operate within established governmental frameworks, including requiring governments to submit proposals through traditional decision-making processes for international lending. However, CI's hotspots program also exemplifies a disturbing trend in bilateral and multilateral aid. Over the course of the past decade and a half, one of the major accomplishments claimed for the suite of global environmental treaties addressing ozone depletion, climate change, biodiversity loss, desertification, hazardous waste trade, and so on, has been the provision of "environmental aid." Beginning with the Montreal Protocol Fund, rich countries have pledged to help poor countries pay for efforts to move their economies closer to sustainability, and have allocated small but significant and increasing amounts to this kind of aid through several institutions. The Global Environment Facility, in particular, has become a multi-billion-dollar lending agency.[41]

Each of the treaties specifies that the aid provided as part of its commitments must be "new and additional"—it cannot simply be transferred from existing bilateral or multilateral development-aid programs. However, while these are new programs run out of new institutions like the Montreal Protocol Fund and the Global Environment Facility rather than existing lending agencies, they were launched during a period of slow but steady decrease in government-to-government aid.[42] The net result is that the new "environmental" aid almost exactly offsets decreases in aid in other areas, rendering the claim of "new and additional" meaningless. Moreover, environmental aid often comes with tight restrictions, and recipients must submit elaborate proposals to demonstrate that the money will be used to accomplish donor countries' environmental goals. Poor countries are thereby coerced into adopting the policy priorities of their rich counterparts.

Conservation International's new alliance with the World Bank to fund $150 million in biodiversity conservation initiatives through the Global Environment Facility falls exactly into this pattern of "environmental conditionality." Countries can apply for loans from the Facility—through the World Bank—only if they adopt Conservation International's "hot spots" agenda for biodiversity conservation. Thus, although governments agreed as part of the Convention on Biological Diversity that conservation priorities within their territories would remain subject to national sovereignty, Conservation International has found a way to overturn that decision and set its own "global" priorities that countries must accept if they wish to avail themselves of the new aid. Needless to say, poor countries had little or no opportunity to challenge (or even review) the expert claims with which these priorities were set.

Divorcing Nature from Culture

Knowledge and values also are intertwined in how communities construct the boundary between nature and culture. Donna Haraway, in particular, has highlighted the interpretive flexibility of this boundary in her concept of the *cyborg*. Each of us, Haraway argues, is a hybrid that mixes elements of the human and nonhuman, natural and artificial. Yet, societal ideas and practices often represent the two as easily distinguished.[43] Critical review of various biodiversity agendas demonstrates that this kind of boundary drawing can be a powerful tool in the hands of modern institutions.[44] Conservationists often ascribe blame for losses of biological diversity to human activities *directly* responsible for cutting down forests or other habitat destruction. As David Takacs puts it, "At places distant from where you are, but also uncomfortably close, a holocaust is underway. People are slashing, hacking, bulldozing, burning, poisoning, and otherwise destroying huge swaths of life on earth at a furious pace."[45] Placing blame on those whose actions directly affect plant and animal life reflects two characteristic aspects of American (and Western) political culture. First, Americans tend to draw a firm line of demarcation between humans and nature. For example, the concept of "wilderness" as a natural space undisturbed by humans has always been an important ideal in motivating American environmental policy making.[46] Second, Americans tend to ascribe responsibility on the basis of visual or surface causes rather than looking for hidden, underlying, or systemic explanations.[47]

Both are apparent in WWF's and Conservation International's biodiversity conservation programs. Of the over five hundred photographs contained in *Living Planet: Preserving Edens of the Earth*, the photo-documentary companion volume to WWF's biodiversity campaign, fewer than ten contain images of people. In those that do, humans are either photographers or ecotourists. Aside from cameras and clothing, no evidence of human civilization—buildings, automobiles, gardens—can be found in the book. Thus, although the Global 200 ecoregions contain vast stretches of human-dominated landscapes such as the southern California coastline and the bulk of China, and although WWF's conservation programs recognize that nature and humanity are often deeply integrated locally, WWF's representations of biodiversity at risk are of nature separated from humanity.[48] Figure 1 illustrates the kinds of landscape typical of *Living Planet.*[49] Figure 2 illustrates the kinds of images in which people do appear.[50]

Likewise, Conservation International's *Hotspots: Earth's Biologically Richest and Most Endangered Terrestrial Ecosystems* is dominated by photographs of nature—wildlife, flowering plants, flowing waterfalls, and expansive vistas. Unlike the WWF volume, however, approximately one in ten of the photographs in *Hotspots* contains people or evidence of civilization. The images of humanity favored in *Hotspots,* however, are depictions of people's destructive capacity: terraced coffee plantations, fire, logging, cattle farming, a mother and child (representing overpopulation), hunting, oil refining, charcoal production, and road construction.[51] Figure 3 illustrates the kind of photograph used to depict local people involved in destructive activities, in this case logging. In explicit contrast to recent scholarship that has sought to place the blame for nature's destruction on the institutions and practices of capitalism,[52] these photographs lay blame on the individuals who hack, slash, and burn.

Beyond its narratives of causation and responsibility, the cultural presumption that humans are separate from nature has insinuated itself even further into Conservation International's biodiversity programs. At the core of the CI policy agenda is the creation of new natural parks[53] and the strengthening of agencies that maintain and protect parks. The sole aspect of conservation policy measured for each hotspot is the "total area protected" by existing parks.[54] In the narratives accompanying each hotspot, natural parks also emerge as the heavily favored mode of nature conservation. Consider, for example, this statement describing the California Floristic Province: "Within the United States, the basic units of habitat and wildlife protection are the national parks, wilderness areas (in association with forest reserves), national wildlife refuges, state parks, and privately-managed lands, e.g., preserves under joint stewardship of federal agencies such as the Bureau of Land Management, organizations such as the Nature Conservancy, and a number of state universities."[55] The goal of the hotspots program is to expand this model of conservation policy globally.

Figure 1. "*Global 200 Ecoregion #64.* Oaks and maples turn red and gold as fall days shorten in the Blue Ridge Mountains. Early settlers named the mountains for the blue haze formed by natural terpenes from the trees. Now hydrocarbons from automobiles often form a haze, and pollution from many sources threatens the eastern forests." (*Living Planet,* 113) © Galen Rowell / Mountain Light

Figure 2. "*Global 200 Ecoregion #97.* In the Royal Chitwan National Park southwest of Kathmandu, where all rivers feed into the Ganges and wildlife thrives in protected habitat, ecotourists on Asian elephants from Tiger Tops Lodge view a one-horned Indian rhinoceros and its calf." (*Living Planet,* 193) © Galen Rowell / Mountain Light

Figure 3. "Timber cut illegally being removed from the Tai Forest National Park. According to a local truck driver, some 20 loads a day are being taken out using an unauthorized road built by a timber company, highlighting how difficult it still is to preserve West Africa's few remaining intact forests." (*Hotspots*, 250) © James Blair / National Geographic Society

The crisis atmosphere generated by the concept of hotspots—"Earth's biologically richest and most endangered terrestrial ecosystems"—drives preferences for the creation and strengthening of natural parks. These areas are portrayed as under extreme threat, and other options are presented as inadequate to the task of protecting nature from human interference. Only sequestering pieces for legal preservation will suffice: "So little remains in the hotspots, and what does persist represents so small a portion (1.44%) of the land surface of the planet, that we can no longer rationalize and make excuses for continued destructive exploitation in these areas, be it for timber extraction, mining, or anything else that produces short-term gain for the few to the long-term detriment of the many. . . . To begin assuming this great responsibility, we need to start by adopting a position of 'zero further deforestation' and 'zero further species loss' for the hotspots, and to make this a part of both a global imperative and the national psyche of all countries fortunate enough to have hotspot ecosystems within their borders."[56]

The project of classifying landscapes as either "human" or "natural" and then striving to maintain these categories is an example of what James Scott terms the effort of the state to render landscapes "legible."[57] Legibility refers to the tendency of the modern state to partition its territory into distinct land uses for ease of administration (such as the use of zoning by city planners). Here, although the agents of action are transnational nongovernmental organizations, the principle is the same. Efficient management and surveillance are achieved by excluding humans from certain areas. Although other solutions might ultimately be more sustainable and inflict less disruption on the lives of hotspots residents, such solutions inevitably require extensive local knowledge of both the people and the land.[58]

To be sure, Conservation International by itself has little power to enforce radical rearrangements of the social and biological landscapes of biodiversity hotspots. However, CI and other conservation organizations work closely with multinational institutions and developing-country governments. The major focus of Conservation International's partnership with the World Bank is to leverage the creation of new national parks in developing countries with money lent by the bank. Once parks are created, further demands are made to exclude humans by fashioning laws that outlaw or limit hunting inside park boundaries and training the new guards in park management. In a striking photograph in *Hotspots,* reproduced in Figure 4, two men with rifles are poled across a moonlit lake by two other guards.

Conservation organizations do not hesitate to acknowledge that their efforts involve strengthening the power of the state to exclude humans from protected areas. Describing the current state of biodiversity conservation in the Philippines hotspot, Conservation International notes:

> As of the late 1980s, the Haribon Foundation, the country's foremost conservation NGO, stated that none of the protected areas currently in existence met international standards for protection and management. As of 1992, Heaney's personal observations indicated that no national park boundaries had been demarcated, and law enforcement was lacking; an IUCN [International Union for the Conservation of Nature] report from 1988 estimated that two thirds of the parks contained human settlements and 27% of their cumulative area was covered by disturbed habitat or agriculture . . . We believe that a strong focus on creating effective protected areas is the best hope for what little remains in the Philippines, and needs to receive the greatest attention. Existing parks must have greatly improved management to prevent further logging or encroachment by farmers. Park wardens and guards need to be designated and given authority to do their jobs (which they currently lack).[59]

The Nature Conservancy, in conjunction with the U.S. Agency for International Development, operates a comparable program called Parks in Peril. The program helps to strengthen the management of Central and South American natural parks by providing funds to hire and train new

Figure 4. "Antipoaching patrol in the eastern range portion of Kaziranga National Park, Assam, in the Indo-Burma Hotspot. Poaching continues to be a serious problem in many protected areas, and threatens their long-term viability." (*Hotspots,* 52) © Michael Nichols / National Geographic Society

guards. Through the program, the Bolivian Fundacion Amigos de la Naturaleza (FAN) has hired, equipped, and trained numerous new guards for the Noel Kempff Mercado National Park, a park the size of Yellowstone National Park in the United States. FAN is a private, nongovernmental foundation that works in partnership with the Bolivian government. According to the Nature Conservancy: "From 1990 to 1994, FAN used Parks in Peril funds to equip and train park rangers, who then drastically reduced poaching, eliminated illegal logging, and drove covert drug operations out of the park."[60] Although statements like this reflect an effort to cast the actions of groups like FAN in the language of legitimate law enforcement, they cannot quite elide the use of force to conserve nature in parks around the world.

My point in this last section is not to argue that conservation programs should halt the construction of new natural parks or their efforts to improve park management. Rather, I simply point out that neither these programs nor the underlying scientific basis on which they've been constructed has been subjected to democratic oversight. Like Mary, Amy, and Todd, environmental NGOs have embarked upon ambitious projects without consulting those whose lives and livelihoods are likely to be deeply affected by their activities. WWF, Conservation International, and the Nature Conservancy derive their ultimate legitimacy from their ability to raise funds among environmentally conscious citizens of, principally, the United States and Europe. Their ability to raise funds depends, in turn, on their ability to convince supporters of the seriousness of the threat to biodiversity around the world. Only rarely are the people who inhabit hotspots or other ecoregions able to hold these organizations accountable for their actions. Nonetheless, these NGOs wield enormous influence and power, including the capacity to deploy deadly force in conflicts between preservationists and other potential "users" of land. Like Mary, Amy, and Todd they do so in pursuit of policy goals that stress a radical transformation of society and community. As Conservation International commented in regard to the Andean hotspot: "Everything possible must be done to stimulate fundamental changes in the attitudes and behaviors of the Andean people towards their natural surroundings."[61] Just how far does a standard like "everything possible" authorize governments, transnational NGOs, or groups like FAN to go? And who gave so few the sole authority to decide for the many who will be affected?[62]

Recent events have raised questions about the legitimate use of force in democratic societies around the world. In Israel, these concerns emerged out of conflict with the Palestinians. In the United States, they emerged in response to the actions of government agents in cases such as Ruby Ridge, Waco, and Elián Gonzales. In Europe, they were occasioned by the conflicts accompanying the disintegration of Yugoslavia. Yet no comparable concerns about rules of engagement have been raised by U.S. or European citizens with respect to the sponsorship of police action in developing countries. Traditions of autocratic behavior by state and parastatal organizations in some developing countries reinforce the desirability of institutions that can subject policies and the knowledge claims that ground them to organized skepticism from a variety of different perspectives, including those of the people whose lives these policies affect. Just governance of the biological frontier demands that we ask hard questions about policies and the reasons for them, especially when they permit and even encourage the use of force to change local people's lived practices and beliefs.

Conclusion

The twenty-first century is ushering in amazing and sometimes frightening new possibilities brought on by advances in the biological sciences. Efforts by feminists and others to help people learn how to read and interpret this new world in all of its moral complexity are critically important. This is not easy, as the stories of Mary, Amy, and Todd suggest. For each of us, these new technologies raise enormously difficult and ambiguous moral questions. Yet we also need to go further. Lurking just outside the lives of individual citizens on the biofrontier are powerful institutions—corporations, states, and international organizations—whose actions can have enormous consequences. Like individuals, these collective institutions also need to be attuned to the full moral complexity of the biological frontier.

Indeed, even as Amy and Todd are caught and executed at the end of "A Desperate Calculus," it becomes apparent that their power derives only in part from their creative rearrangements of moral and technological boundaries. Todd's NGO operates on money raised from a vast, rich elite seeking to protect nature. Amy's work and travels for the World Health Organization are funded by the same elites desiring protection from infectious tropical diseases like the Ebola virus. As Amy and Todd point out, these "Northern" elites support states that, after providing the instrumental bases for Amy and Todd to spread their virus (unknowingly, we presume), are likely to delay the distribution of any vaccine until the plague has done its work if they believe that their actions will curtail the population growth of the South:

> Loudly Segueno said, "You shall live just long enough to see the vaccine stop your plan."
>
> Amy kissed Todd, long and lingering, and then looked up. "Oh, really? And you believe the North will pay for it? When they can just drag their feet, and let it spread unchecked in the tropics?"
>
> Todd smiled grimly. "After they've inoculated themselves, they'll be putting their energy into a 'womb race'—finding fertile women, a 'national natural resource.' Far too busy. And the superflu will do its job."[63]

In her lectures on *Women and Human Development,* Martha Nussbaum argues that current institutions of global governance fall short in protecting important rights by failing to empower people to "participate effectively in political choices that govern one's life."[64] Feminist writers like Donna Haraway, looking at the role of science and technology in modern life, point out that one of the most important elements of effective participation is the ability to deconstruct expert claims about nature, reason, and objectivity that underlie the market and government policy.[65] I have argued in this essay that individual capacity to surf the networks of technoscientific civilization—while important—is unlikely to be sufficient to defend people and communities against the actions of powerful modern institutions like the state and transnational organizations. What is needed are opportunities to inject new and skeptical voices into the production, validation, and use of the knowledge on which government policies and international regimes are based. In the United States, many such opportunities exist.[66] Worldwide, few if any such opportunities exist. As global governing institutions acquire greater decision-making authority and power over the next half-century, institutional reforms to strengthen organized skepticism will be necessary.

Put simply, the crisis of biological diversity should be seen as an opportunity to strengthen justice on the biological frontier and not as a justification for imposing new forms of domination on impoverished communities around the world. A commitment to justice cannot be achieved so long as the global institutions that make knowledge and translate it into policy restrict rather than increase their accountability to all people. In creating new, more effective institutions to construct and implement global environmental policies, we can choose to create either what James Scott has called a "high-modernist" regime or what Yaron Ezrahi describes as "liberal-democratic centralism."[67] Activist organizations like WWF and CI have fought for a long time to open international political processes to greater democratic involvement. In their efforts to do so, they have relied heavily on scientific expertise to lend credibility to their voices. Now that they have become powerful in their own right, they should reflect carefully on how scientific ideas structure their policy proposals. Indeed, throughout emerging global governing regimes, the normative issues entailed in the production and use of expert knowledge need to be subjected to the same degree of review as are other aspects of the global political landscape.

Notes

1. Peter Taylor, Saul Halfon, and Paul Edwards, eds., *Changing Life: Genomes, Ecologies, Bodies, Commodities* (Minneapolis: University of Minnesota Press, 1997).

2. See, especially, several works by Bruno Latour: *We Have Never Been Modern* (Cambridge: Harvard University Press, 1993); *The Pasteurization of France* (Cambridge: Harvard University Press, 1988); *Science in Action* (Cambridge: Harvard University Press, 1987); "Give Me a Laboratory and I Will Raise the World," in *Science Observed,* ed. Karin Knorr-Cetina and Michael Mulkay (London: Sage Press, 1983).

3. Theodore Porter, *Trust in Numbers: The Pursuit of Objectivity in Science and Public Life* (Princeton, N.J.: Princeton University Press, 1995); Sheila Jasanoff, *Science at the Bar: Law, Science and Technology in America* (Cambridge: Harvard University Press, 1996); Jasanoff, *The Fifth Branch: Science Advisers as Policymakers* (Cambridge: Harvard University Press, 1990); Jasanoff, *Risk Management and Political Culture* (New York: Russell Sage Foundation, 1986); Yaron Ezrahi, *The Descent of Icarus: Science and the Transformation of Contemporary Democracy* (Cambridge: Harvard University Press, 1990); and see, especially, Jenny Reardon, "The Human Genome Diversity Project," *Social Studies of Science* 31, 3 (2001): 365–96.

4. Sheila Jasanoff, "Image and Imagination: The Emergence of Global Environmental Consciousness," in *Changing the Atmosphere: Expert Knowledge and Environmental Governance,* ed. Clark Miller and Paul Edwards (Cambridge: MIT

Press, 2001); Jasanoff, "Product, Process, or Programme: Three Cultures and the Regulation of Biotechnology," in *Resistance to New Technology,* ed. M. Bauer (Cambridge: Cambridge University Press, 1995).

5. See, for example, Marybeth Long-Martello, "A Paradox of Virtue? 'Other' Knowledges and Environment-Development Politics," *Global Environmental Politics* 1, 3 (2001): 114–41; and Aarti Grupta, "Framing 'Biosafety' in a Transnational Context: The Biosafety Protocol Negotiations under the Convention on Biological Diversity," ENRP Discussion Paper E-99–10, Kennedy School of Government, Harvard University, September 1999.

6. Robert K. Merton, *The Sociology of Science: Theoretical and Empirical Investigations* (Chicago: University of Chicago Press, 1973). Merton uses the phrase to refer to scientists' systematic efforts to subject knowledge claims to skeptical inquiry. My use of the phrase here is similar but incorporates a broader challenging of how scientific ideas are married to particular programs of social action.

7. Donna Haraway for example, describes her recent work, *Modest_Witness@ Second_Millennium.FemaleMan©_Meets_OncoMouse™: Feminism and Technoscience* (New York: Routledge, 1997) as "my exercise regime and self-help manual for how not to be literal minded, while engaging promiscuously in serious moral and political inquiry about feminism, antiracism, democracy, knowledge, and justice in certain important domains of contemporary science and technology" (15).

8. See Donna Haraway, *Simians, Cyborgs, and Women: The Reinvention of Nature* (New York: Routledge, 1991), 183–202.

9. Charis Thompson Cussins, "Confessions of a Bioterrorist: Subject Positions and Reproductive Technologies," in *Playing Dolly: Technocultural Formations, Fantasies, and Fictions of Assisted Reproduction,* ed. E. Ann Kaplan and Susan Squier (New Brunswick, N.J.: Rutgers University Press, 1999).

10. See Rick Weiss, "Cloning a Comeback?" *Washington Post,* 8 October 2001, A01.

11. Sterling Blake, "A Desperate Calculus," in *New Legends,* ed. Greg Bear (New York: Tom Doherty Associates, 1995). Similar themes of environmental terrorism are explored in other works of fiction, including Tom Clancy's *Rainbow Six* (New York: Berkley Group, 1999) and Edward Abbey's *The Monkey Wrench Gang* (New York: Harper Perennial Library, 2000).

12. Vandana Shiva, *Biopiracy: The Plunder of Nature and Knowledge* (Boston: South End Press, 1997); Shiva, *The Violence of the Green Revolution: Third World Agriculture, Ecology, and Politics* (London: Zed Books, 1991).

13. William Kelleher Storey, *Science and Power in Colonial Mauritius* (Rochester, N.Y.: University of Rochester Press, 1997).

14. James C. Scott, *Seeing Like a State: How Certain Schemes to Improve the Human Condition Have Failed* (New Haven, Conn.: Yale University Press, 1998). See also Shiv Visvanathan, *A Carnival for Science: Essays on Science, Technology, and Development* (Oxford: Oxford University Press, 1997); Loren R. Graham, *The Ghost of the Executed Engineer: Technology and the Fall of the Soviet Union* (Cambridge: Harvard University Press, 1993); Robert Proctor, *Racial Hygiene: Medicine under the Nazis* (Cambridge: Harvard University Press, 1988); Zygmunt Bauman, *Modernity and the Holocaust* (Ithaca, N.Y.: Cornell University Press, 1989).

15. Meera Nanda, "The Epistemic Charity of the Social Constructivist Critics of Science and Why the Third World Should Refuse the Offer," in *A House Built on Sand:*

Exposing Postmodernist Myths about Science, ed. Noretta Koertge (Oxford: Oxford University Press, 1998).

16. See, for example, Sheila Jasanoff, review of *A House Built on Sand: Exposing Postmodern Myths about Science,* edited by Noretta Koertge, *Science, Technology, and Human Values* 24, 4 (1999): 495–500.

17. Ezrahi, *Descent of Icarus,* 1.

18. Yaron Ezrahi, *Rubber Bullets: Power and Conscience in Modern Israel* (Berkeley: University of California Press, 1997), especially chap. 9.

19. Porter, *Trust in Numbers.*

20. Ezrahi, *Descent of Icarus,* especially chap. 3.

21. Porter, *Trust in Numbers;* see also Loren R. Graham, *What Have We Learned about Science and Technology from the Russian Experience?* (Stanford, Calif.: Stanford University Press, 1998), especially chap. 5. Graham points out, for example, that public participation in the design and oversight of large-scale technological projects is today the norm rather than the exception in the United States. In contrast, Chinese and Russian engineers plan projects with little public input and in consequence, Graham argues, these often have widespread and disastrous impacts on people's lives.

22. As an example, see John Perkins, *Geopolitics and the Green Revolution: Wheat, Genes, and the Cold War* (Oxford: Oxford University Press, 1997).

23. Dorothy Nelkin, *Controversy: Politics of Technical Decisions,* 3d ed. (Newbury Park, Calif.: Sage Press, 1992).

24. Jasanoff, *Fifth Branch.*

25. Yaron Ezrahi, "Technology and the Illusion of the Escape from Politics," in *Technology, Pessimism, and Postmodernism,* ed. Yaron Ezrahi, Everett Mendelsohn, and Howard Segal (Dordrecht, Netherlands: Kluwer Academic Publishers, 1994), 33.

26. See, for example, Samuel P. Hays, *Conservation and the Gospel of Efficiency: The Progressive Conservation Movement, 1890–1920,* 2d ed. (Cambridge: Harvard University Press, 1968), especially vii–xiii.

27. Jasanoff, *Fifth Branch;* see also Haraway, *Simians, Cyborgs, and Women,* 183–203, who points out the need to hold particular arrangements accountable for the way they intertwine knowledge and order and, to achieve that accountability, the necessity of examining in detail the specific practices of knowledge production, validation, and use.

28. Clark A. Miller, "Scientific Internationalism in American Foreign Policy: The Case of Meteorology (1947–1958)," in *Changing the Atmosphere;* Anne-Marie Burley, "Regulating the World: Multilateralism, International Law, and the Projection of the New Deal Regulatory State," in *Multilateralism Matters: The Theory and Praxis of an Institutional Form,* ed. John Gerard Ruggie (New York: Columbia University Press, 1993), 125–56.

29. Peter Haas, ed. *Knowledge, Power, and International Policy Coordination* a special issue of *International Organization* 46, 1 (1992); Haas, *Saving the Mediterranean: The Politics of International Environmental Cooperation* (New York: Columbia University Press, 1990); Clark A. Miller, "Undermining the Postwar Settlement: Climate Science and the Reconstruction of Global Order," in *States of Knowledge: Science, Power, and Political Culture,* ed. Sheila Jasanoff, forthcoming; Miller, "Challenges to the Application of Science to Global Affairs: Contingency, Trust, and Moral Order," in *Changing the Atmosphere;* Karen Litfin, *Ozone Discourses: Science and Politics in Global Environmental Cooperation* (New York: Columbia University Press, 1994).

30. See, for example, World Bank, *The State in a Changing World* (Washington, D.C.: World Bank, 1997); Manuel Contreras, "Capacity Building in the Bolivian Social Policy Analysis Unit: Reflections of a Practitioner," in *Getting Good Government: Capacity Building in the Public Sectors of Developing Countries,* ed. Merilee S. Grindle (Cambridge: Harvard University Press, 1997); Clive S. Gray, "Technical Assistance and Capacity Building for Policy Analysis and Implementation," in *Getting Good Government;* Ezrahi, *Rubber Bullets,* especially chap. 9; Porter, *Trust in Numbers;* Sheila Jasanoff, "Acceptable Evidence in a Pluralistic Society," in *Acceptable Evidence: Science and Values in Risk Management,* ed. Deborah Mayo and Rachelle Hollander (Oxford: Oxford University Press, 1991).

31. Sheila Jasanoff, "Science and Norms in Global Environmental Regimes," in *Earthly Goods: Environmental Change and Social Justice,* ed. Fen O. Hamson and Judith Reppy (Ithaca, N.Y.: Cornell University Press, 1996), 173–97.

32. Carolyn Merchant, *The Death of Nature: Women, Ecology, and the Scientific Revolution* (New York: Harper and Row, 1980); Mary Douglas and Aaron Wildavsky, *Risk and Culture: An Essay on the Selection of Technological and Environmental Dangers* (Berkeley: University of California Press, 1982); see also Michel Foucault, *The Birth of the Clinic* (New York: Pantheon Books, 1973).

33. Clark A. Miller and Paul N. Edwards, "Introduction: The Globalization of Climate Science and Climate Politics," in *Changing the Atmosphere.*

34. David Takacs, *The Idea of Biodiversity: Philosophies of Paradise* (Baltimore, Md.: Johns Hopkins University Press, 1996).

35. This opposition stemmed primarily from the fear that moving conservation policies into a centralized forum would enable opponents of conservation to reopen compromises achieved only after long and hard negotiations in each of the different treaty forums.

36. World Wildlife Fund, *Living Planet: Preserving Edens on Earth* (New York: Crown Publishers, 1999).

37. Russell Mittermeier, Norman Myers, and Cristina Goettsch Mittermeier, eds., *Hotspots: Earth's Biologically Richest and Most Endangered Terrestrial Ecoregions* (Mexico City: CEMEX International, 2000).

38. World Bank, "Critical Ecosystem Partnership Launches $150 Million Fund to Better Protect Biodiversity Hotspots," press release, 22 August 2000.

39. David Olson and Eric Dinerstein, *The Global 200: A Representation Approach to Conserving the Earth's Distinct Ecoregions* (Washington, D.C.: World Wildlife Fund, 1998).

40. Russell Mittermeier notes in the volume's introduction: "To summarize, the basic premises of our priority-setting approaches are as follows. The biodiversity of each and every nation is critically important to that nation's survival and must be a fundamental component of any national or regional development strategy. Nonetheless, biodiversity is by no means evenly distributed over the surface of our planet, and some areas, especially in the tropics, harbor far greater concentrations of biodiversity than others. Some of these high-biodiversity areas (e.g., tropical rain forests, coral reefs, deep ocean trenches, Mediterranean-type ecosystems) are under the most severe threat. To achieve maximum impact with limited resources, we must concentrate heavily (but not exclusively) on those areas richest in diversity and most severely threatened. Investment in them should be roughly proportional to their overall contribution to global biodiversity. And, finally, analyses of biodiversity priorities must be based on actual data, first and foremost on species diversity and

endemism, on phyletic diversity, and on ecosystem diversity, and subsequently on degree of threat, in order to be truly effective." See Mittermeier et al., *Hotspots,* 27.

41. Robert Keohane and Marc Levy, eds., *Institutions for Environmental Aid: Pitfalls and Promise* (Cambridge: MIT Press, 1996); Elizabeth DeSombre and Joanne Kauffman, "The Montreal Protocol Multilateral Fund: Partial Success Story," in *Institutions for Environmental Aid.*

42. World Bank, *World Development Indicators 2000* (Washington, D.C.: World Bank, 2000).

43. Haraway, *Simians, Cyborgs, and Women.*

44. See Thomas F. Gieryn, *Cultural Boundaries of Science: Credibility on the Line* (Chicago: University of Chicago Press, 1999); "Boundaries of Science," in *The Handbook of Science and Technology Studies,* ed. Sheila Jasanoff, Gerald E. Markle, James C. Petersen and Trevor Pinch (Thousand Oaks, Calif.: Sage Publications, 1996); Jasanoff, *Fifth Branch.*

45. Takacs, *Idea of Biodiversity,* 1.

46. William Cronon, "Getting Back to the Wrong Nature" in *Uncommon Ground: Rethinking the Human Place in Nature,* ed. William Cronon (New York: W. W. Norton and Company, 1996).

47. Ezrahi, *Descent of Icarus.*

48. World Wildlife Fund, *Living Planet.*

49. Ibid., 113.

50. Ibid., 193.

51. Mittermeier et al., *Hotspots.* Referenced photographs can be found on the following pages: terraced coffee plantations (145), fire (158–59), logging (146–47), cattle farming (84–85), a mother and child (83), hunting (62), oil refining (59), charcoal production (121), and road construction (134).

52. Shiva, *Biopiracy;* Wolfgang Sachs, *Planet Dialectics: Explorations in Environment and Development* (London: Zed Books, 1997).

53. Natural parks, as CI imagines them, are territorial regions formally set aside by law for the purpose of protecting nature within their boundaries.

54. Mittermeier et al., *Hotspots,* 58.

55. Ibid., 183.

56. Ibid., 67.

57. Scott, *Seeing Like a State.*

58. See, for example, the depiction of the biodiversity policies of the Costa Rican National Institute for Biodiversity, INBio, which has chosen to try to work with landholders rather than create new exclusive nature preserves, in Takacs, *Idea of Biodiversity,* especially chap. 6.

59. Mittermeier et al., *Hotspots,* 315.

60. Daniell Furlich, "From Peril to Progress," *Nature Conservation* 50, 5 (2000): 17.

61. Mittermeier et al., *Hotspots,* 82.

62. On 9 December 2001, Conservation International announced that it had received a $261 million gift from Intel cofounder Gordon Moore. The gift launches a $6 billion campaign to expand CI's programs to protect "hotspots" through the creation of new protected areas.

63. Blake, "Desperate Calculus," 70.

64. Martha Nussbaum, *Women and Human Development: The Capabilities Approach* (Cambridge: Cambridge University Press, 2000), 80.

65. Haraway, *Modest_Witness.*

66. Although the existence of opportunities for skeptical voices to be heard certainly doesn't preclude further critical attention; see Jasanoff, *Science at the Bar.*

67. Ezrahi, *Descent of Icarus;* Scott, *Seeing Like a State.*

Chapter 17

Thinking about Feminist Theology and Community

Robin L. Teske

> Knowledge that we are but a small part of life and death and transformation is the essential religious insight. The essential religious response is to rejoice and to weep, to sing and to dance, to tell stories and create rituals in praise of an existence far more complicated, more intricate, more enduring than we are.
>
> —Carol Christ

> The boys in the neighborhood had this game with rope . . . tug-o'-war . . . till finally some side would jerk the rope away from the others, who'd fall down. . . . Girls . . . weren't allowed to play with them in this tug-o'-war; so we figured out how to make our own rope—out of . . . little dandelions. You just keep adding them, one to another, and you can go on and on. . . . Anybody, even the boys, could join us. . . . The whole purpose of our game was to create this dandelion chain—that was it. And we'd keep going, creating till our mamas called us home.
>
> —Bess B. Johnson

> We said not a word about each other's wrongheadedness toward elephants. Not that we forgave the wrongheadedness, but something else was going on, something that set us adversaries suddenly into the same world with each other. After all, preservation of community is a first principle in all cultures. *Pfavira ngoma, usiku urefu,* the Shona say: Be patient with your drumming, the night is long.
>
> —Katy Payne

Introduction

In this essay I use feminist theology to explore the meaning of community and the relationship of community to power. I do not mind admitting that I find the subject more than a little intimidating. By training I am an attorney specializing in international law and a political scientist, not a theologian.

Perhaps the best way to begin is with a story from Rabbi Hanokh as related by Martin Buber:

> There was once a man who was very stupid. When he got up in the morning it was so hard for him to find his clothes that at night he almost hesitated to go to bed for thinking of the trouble he would have on waking. One evening he finally made a great effort, took paper and pencil and as he undressed noted down exactly where he put everything he had on. The next morning, very well pleased with himself, he took the slip of paper in his hand and read: "cap"—there it was, he set it on his head; "pants"—there they lay, he got into them; and so it went until he was fully dressed. "That's all very well, but now where am I myself?" he asked in great consternation. "Where in the world am I?" He looked and looked, but it was a vain search; he could not find himself. "And that is how it is with us," said the rabbi.[1]

William James tells the story of Margaret Fuller, a nineteenth-century transcendentalist, and Thomas Carlyle. One of Fuller's favorite sayings was "I accept the universe!" When Carlyle heard this comment, he rather sardonically replied, "Gad! She'd better!" But Fuller was right, for the manner of our acceptance of the universe serves as the foundation for the way a whole civilization lives, thinks, feels, acts. Our relations to things and beings form the heart of our existence.[2] At every stage of human development a new mystery or change in understanding and perception is involved. If humanity is regarded as essentially a maker of tools and an exploiter of nature, one conception of life follows. If we are regarded as seekers of visions, a very different conception is necessary. I agree with the theologians that "the image of God is the ultimate reference point for the values of a community," and that "speaking about God sums up, unifies, and expresses a faith community's sense of ultimate mystery, the world view and expectation of order devolving from this, and the concomitant orientation of human life and devotion."[3] As theologian Elizabeth Johnson notes, a religion that praises a warlike God, who destroys his enemies, would lead to a community based on aggressive behavior, while a religion based on a beneficent and loving God would lead to a very different kind of community and worldview. Religious imagery and social practice mutually reinforce each other. The "mystery of God" is always mediated through changing historical discourses and understandings; understandings of God are cultural creatures.[4]

Johnson claims, "Religions die when their light fails . . . when they lose the power to interpret convincingly the full range of present experience in the light of their idea of God."[5] This idea is expressed well in a Hindu story about a guru, an ashram, and the ashram's cat.

> When the Guru sat down to worship each evening, the ashram cat would get in the way and distract the worshipers. So he ordered that the cat be tied during evening worship. After the guru died the cat continued to be tied during evening worship. And when the cat expired, another cat was brought to the ashram so that it could be duly tied during evening worship.
>
> Centuries later learned treatises were written by the guru's scholarly disciples on the liturgical significance of tying up a cat while worship is performed.[6]

As feminist theologians and others reevaluate the meaning of the sacred, as they question the reasons behind "tying up the cat," they are challenging patriarchal structures and patterns of power and community that have long been central to our society, structures long taken to be "reality." Patriarchy is a pyramidal social organization that is sexist and hierarchical: power is in the hands of dominant men. One of the strongest forms of patriarchy is religious patriarchy, for it considers itself to be divinely established. The "power of the ruling men is said by them to be delegated by God (invariably spoken about in male terms)," according to Johnson, "and exercised by divine mandate."[7] Mary Catherine Bateson is right when she says that "there is a pattern that connects, and it is a pattern of dominance and exploitation, taught again and again in the most ordinary human arrangements."[8] In a sense, what feminist theologians are struggling toward "is not simply the solution to one problem, but an entire shift of world view away from patterns of dominance toward mutually enhancing relationships."[9]

There is a growing perception that "today's wars and violence, poverty and economic disparity, ecological devastation, and violation of human rights are rooted in a crisis that is moral in character and global in scope."[10] Or as the Baha'is put it: "No serious attempt to achieve world peace can ignore religion."[11] As we face the problems of the twenty-first century, there is a growing awareness that religious perspectives can play "an increasing role in providing auspices and a liberating sense of alternatives."[12] But what role religion might play, what these alternatives might be, has been surprisingly little studied. The subject is vast. In this essay I can explore only one small piece of the puzzle—the role of feminist theology in helping us understand the meaning of power and community.[13]

A Time to Tear Down and a Time to Build Up

What is theology? According to the *American Heritage Dictionary* it is "the study of the nature of God."[14] This is a standard definition, but perhaps a better one, as Kathleen Norris notes, comes from Evagrius of Pontus, a fourth-century Catholic monk who said, "If you are a theologian, pray truly; and if you pray truly, you are a theologian."[15] The traditional theological task is to reflect "on God and all things in the light of God." It is "a discipline of speaking which moves back and forth, spiraling around life and faith within the cultural context of a given time and place."[16] I am rather partial to Thomas Merton's definition. Merton said simply that "theology really happens in relations between people."[17] Feminist theology involves "discourses of emancipatory transformation, pointing to new ways of living together with each other and the earth."[18] As Elizabeth Johnson puts it, the crucial theological question today is "what is the right way to speak about God in the face of women's newly cherished human dignity and equality?" She goes on to say that "women, long considered less than adequate as human persons, claim themselves as active subjects of history and name toward God out of this emerging identity, to practical and critical effect."[19] Feminist theology begins with the assumption that women are active agents, not simply passive victims, in the historical process. It "seeks not just to undermine the legitimization of patriarchal religious structures but also to empower women in their struggle against such oppressive structures."[20]

Feminist theology is diverse both in substance and in methodology. Judith Plaskow and Carol Christ write that in feminist theology, there are "tensions between different views of women's experience, tensions between those who would reconstruct traditional religion and those who would create new religious forms, tensions between those who would name and celebrate women's body experience and those who would emphasize women's transcendence and freedom. These and other tensions have not only survived the decade but have festered and sometimes erupted into conflict as feminists have questioned each other's allegiances and choices, and as institutional resources have increasingly aligned themselves behind certain alternatives and not others."[21] Elizabeth Johnson points out that "even within North American feminist theology done by white, economically advantaged women, diversity abounds."[22]

Methodologically, feminist theological writing is both linear and nonlinear; it includes autobiography, academic writing, and nonacademic writing by writers and activists. What counts as resources is very broad. "That Shug and Celie's dialogue on God in Alice Walker's *The Color Purple* is one of the most widely quoted feminist theological texts indicates that feminist theology is not defined by what happens in the academy but draws on a wide range of sources that allow women's experiences to emerge," claim Plaskow and Christ. "Moreover, although this may seem paradoxical, it is often through the personal, through the articulation of particularity and what seems to be difference, that connection and universality are suddenly revealed. Indeed, one of the early insights of feminist theology was that, like a good novel, poem, or play, theology best illumines the universal in human experience through attention to the details in human life."[23]

Despite its broad and diverse nature and all the complexities that are involved, much of feminist theology is moving towards a common goal. This goal is "transformation into new community," a "genuine community of mutuality" between the oppressed and those who formerly dominated.[24] This mutuality includes not just men and women, but the earth itself, as well as species other than the human. Johnson writes that we are living in a very creative moment. It is "a time to tear down, a time to build up; a time to throw stones away and to gather them together—the season of feminist theology involves all of these at once."[25] Beverly Johnson puts it well when she says that "relationality is at the heart of all things."[26] To deepen relationship is to bring forth community. It is feminist theology's emphasis on relationality, community, and mutuality that has much to offer political scientists and international relations specialists as we, too, struggle to define and to build a community where human beings and the earth can flourish together.

A Pattern That Connects, or I Am Well If You Are Well

In Alice Walker's novel *The Color Purple,* Celie and Shug discuss the meaning of God. According to Shug:

> My first step from the old white man was trees. Then air. Then birds. Then other people. But one day when I was sitting quiet and feeling like a motherless child, which I was, it come to me: that feeling of being part of everything, not separate at all. I knew that if I cut a tree, my arm would bleed. And I laughed and I cried and I run all around the house. I knew just what it was. In fact, when it happen, you can't miss it. It sort of like you know what, she say, grinning and rubbing high up on my thigh. . . . I think it pisses God off if you walk by the color purple in a field and don't notice it. . . . Everything want to be loved. Us sing and dance, make faces and give flower bouquets, trying to be loved. You ever notice that trees do everything to git attention we do, except walk?[27]

Another widely quoted feminist theological "text" is from Susan Griffin, who writes: "We know ourselves to be made from this earth. We know this earth is made from our bodies. For we see ourselves. And we are nature. We are nature seeing nature. We are nature with a concept of nature. Nature weeping. Nature speaking of nature to nature."[28] Both Walker and Griffin experience God and the sacred through love and connection. Images of control, domination, sin, and salvation are absent. It is a vision of community, without hierarchy, in which human beings are part of the web of life, not separate from it; it is a community in which human beings "are no more valuable to the life of the universe than a field flowering in the color purple. . . . and no less."[29] It is a community in which all beings, not just humans, "including rocks and rain, corn and coyote, as well as the Great Spirit, have intelligence."[30] To have an "organic" sense of the world is to know things as we are a part of things. It is to realize that we can never speak of nature without at the same time speaking of ourselves.

Realization of such a community will, of course, require a revolution in thought. It will require us to rethink deeply ingrained notions of the sacred, deeply felt ideas of the relationship between humanity, god, nature, and other species. I recently read a book that has helped me to conceptualize how such a rethinking of what we mean by "community," and who is included in that community, might be both possible and necessary. The book is *Silent Thunder: In the Presence of Elephants,* by Katy Payne.[31] Payne is an acoustic biologist. Along with several colleagues, she discovered that elephants use powerful infrasound (sound pitched too low for humans to hear—that is, "silent thunder") to communicate and interact over long distances. The book is both an account of her field research among elephants in Kenya, Namibia, and Zimbabwe, and the story of how this research transformed her own ideas about the meaning of the sacred and the role of community. The book is beautifully written. I want to quote a passage that I think will give an idea of the argument Payne is making. Payne is describing a group of elephants on a hot summer afternoon:

> In the shade beside the calling mother's body, the enormous fluted ears of a very small male calf are slowly fanning, together, apart, together, apart, like a huge gray butterfly opening and closing its wings. From time to time his limber, stubby trunk stretches between his mother's front legs to touch one of her full breasts. After a time, his older sister ambles up beside him. He stills his ears and turns his head and lifts his trunk onto her head. The sister's trunk reaches to sniff his closer ear. The calf makes a faint growly sound and someone answers in a faint hum. The sister sniffs his farther ear, then lets her trunk fall loosely down, its weight resting on his neck.
>
> For a minute, all is still. Then a larger, broader-headed young male emerges from the grasses and joins the two siblings. His trunk sniffs inside their mother's mouth, then down into his sister's and brother's mouths, and in one motion the smaller animals reach their trunks into

> his mouth. This seems kind of like ants, I think, which exchange drops of regurgitated liquid when they meet, and so learn about the composition and condition of their colony. A colony's responsiveness to its own condition is a beautiful thing to think about. I wonder whether trunk checking in elephants is a variation on that theme . . . What cohesion! What unanimity! What relishing of one another![32]

In a similar vein, Bateson writes that for many people the singing of whales has become "a paradigmatic experience of the sacred, an encounter with another species living in a totally different medium, suddenly known as kin rather than as stranger." She notes that "the moment of recognition is a moment of self-knowledge as well."[33]

All of us live in a world defined by our associations, which are understood by many different criteria. And Bateson is right that today survival depends on our willingness to move away from familiar patterns, but that "new patterns must satisfy ancient needs for harmony. . . . The attention that looks for unfamiliar kinds of order even in behaviors that appear outrageous or bizarre may be a precondition for the capacity to generate new patterns from unfamiliar materials."[34] What we need are new patterns of mutual caring and respect. In her work on elephants, Payne writes that she sensed every elephant as a node in a network of bonds. She concluded that for elephants, there are several kinds of "we": "There is the 'we' in a family, whose members do everything together. There is the 'we' in a bond group, whose members stay within close range of each other but maintain separate family behaviors. . . . Finally, there is the 'we' in a clan, whose members share the use of the land but move about on it independently of each other." She said she never knew at what level she was seeing the whole organism, because "there was so much interdependence at each level and among and between levels."[35]

In talking about the meaning of "we," Payne tells the story of an incident when she was riding in the back of an open truck and was cut slightly on the head by a tree branch. When the other people in the back of the truck, mostly African trackers or scouts, saw her condition, they immediately, in one voice, moaned aloud.

> I said, "Aw, it's not bad," but they moaned again and again, in a chorus. . . . When my wound healed, there was no more moaning in my presence. But I kept thinking about what had happened. Clearly, it wasn't just I who had been hurt. It was we, the larger family of us, and we might have been worse hurt, and as we remembered our communal trouble, it was appropriate to make sounds that reminded us of our relationship.[36]

She learned from this experience that her American way of experiencing people as separate from herself was by no means universal. Indeed, the Shona response to "how are you?" is "I am well if you are well." The response back is then "I am well, so we are well." In arguing against the African ivory trade because she believes stopping the trade is better for the elephants, and that means better for all of us, Payne writes that "the community that includes us all is larger than any of us knows, and its health reflects the quality of the relations between all of its parts. I am well if you are well. I am well *only* if you are well, too."[37] In a similar vein, Mary Catherine Bateson argues that "no legal definition can free us from the need to bring one another into being. I am only real and have value as long as you are real and have value." She asks "what would happen if we learned to read Descartes's *cogito* beyond the first person concealed in the Latin verb forms: 'You think therefore I am. I think therefore you are. We think . . .'" As she notes, "it is an impoverished life that makes do with single vision."[38] It is not, after all, the individual organism that survives, "but the organism in the environment that gives it life." Bateson writes that "the world we live in is a biological, or, if you like a biologized world, a sacred process in which we share, a community to participate in, not an object to be used."[39]

Friendship and Mutuality, or Playing around the Beat

Ideas of self and the relationship between self and community are culturally constructed, dependent on context and point of view. Unlike the dominant Western view, which emphasizes the autonomous, isolated self, much of feminist ethics and theology argues that "the self is rightly structured not in dualistic opposition to the other but in intrinsic relationship with the other. Rather than 'we' meaning 'not they,' we and they are intertwined."[40] The stress is on the interrelationship of all creatures with each other; there is an intrinsic connectedness—all that exists in the universe is connected.[41] It is a community of equals, "interrelated in genuine mutuality, in theory as well as practice." The idea or a pattern of relationship based on "mutuality" is key. Duality becomes multiplicity; "mutual relationship of different equals appears as the ultimate paradigm of personal and social life."[42] Elizabeth Johnson emphasizes that she is ruling out both reverse sexism, which would place women in dominant positions over men, as well as sameness, because it would level out genuine and needed variety and uniqueness. She says that the goal is to make it possible for all beings, including both sexes, all races and social groups, and all creatures in the universe, to flourish in their uniqueness and interrelation. "This calls for a new model of relationship, neither a hierarchical one that requires an over-under structure, nor a univocal one that reduces all to a given norm. The model is rather inclusive, celebratory of difference, circular, feminist—we reach for the words."[43]

A metaphor often used to describe this mutuality, the reciprocity/independence dialectic that is at the heart of all caring relationships, is friendship—one "enters into a mutuality so profound that they may be called friends."[44] As Simone Weil described it, "Pure friendship is an image of the original and perfect friendship that belongs to the Trinity, and is the very essence of God."[45] Friendship is a relationship that is based on mutual, reciprocal love—the mutuality of *philia,* rather than the nonmutuality of *agape.* Much of feminist theology is in the process of retrieving the power of friendship, as well as the power of mutual, reciprocal love.[46] "The more just a personal relationship, the more loving this relationship, the more mutual, honest, beneficial, and creative for each friend, the more intense are the feelings of love between us." As Carter Heyward has written, "we act our way into new feelings, new emotions, new ideas. And the act is love."[47] Beverly Harrison agrees, and writes that: "I shudder to think how many times during my years of theological study I came upon a warning from a writer of Christian ethics not to confuse real, Christian love with 'mere mutuality.' One senses that persons who can think this way have yet to experience the power of love as the real pleasure of mutual vulnerability, the experience of truly being cared for or of actively caring for another. Mutual love, I submit, is love in its deepest radicality. It is so radical that many of us have not yet learned to bear it. To experience it, we must be open, we must be capable of giving and receiving. The tragedy is that masculinist reified Christianity cannot help us learn to be such lovers."[48] Heyward writes that the meaning of love has been so trivialized that one of the things we need to do is redefine what it means to say "I love you."[49] As Beverly Harrison puts it, radical love is a way of being in the world "that deepens relation, and embodies and extends community." She goes on to say that "we do not yet have a moral theology that teaches us the awful, awesome truth that we have the power through acts of love or lovelessness literally to create one another." Love is "the power to act-each-other-into-well-being"; it is the power of human and communal becoming.[50] It is a love based on mutual personal relations and shared responsibility; it is a love that can say to the other, "it is good that you exist!"[51] (Or, as Payne put it, "What cohesion! What relishing of one another!")

There is a sense in which love and compassion comprise the inner core of all religions. This is what Karen Armstrong has called practical compassion. Practical compassion involves feeling with others; approaching others with reverence; and acknowledging the true meaning of the word "holy," which in Hebrew is translated as "the other."[52] Indeed, in the words of Martin Buber, "Where two stand side by side on an equal footing and are open to each other without reservation, there God is."[53]

Love is not for cowards; to love is a great strength, not a weakness. Alice Walker is right when she writes that love is *the* revolutionary emotion, "partly because it cannot be limited, cannot be compartmentalized, cannot be controlled."[54] Heyward agrees, writing that "to really love is to topple unjust structures, bringing down the principalities and powers of domination and control at all levels of human social relations."[55] Those who love, says Harrison, "tend to develop a reluctance to accept anything less than mutuality and self respect, anything less than human dignity, anything less than authentic relatedness. It is for that reason that such persons become powerful threats to the status quo. As women have known, but also as men like Martin Luther King, Jr., and Archbishop Oscar Romero understood, as any must know who dare to act deeply and forcefully out of the power of love, radical love is a dangerous and serious business."[56]

Love involves mutuality and self respect, but it is important to remember that it also may involve anger. Anger is not the opposite of love. According to Harrison, "anger expressed directly is a mode of taking the other seriously, of caring. . . . Where feeling is evaded, where anger is hidden or goes unattended, masking itself, there the power of love, the power to act, to deepen relation, atrophies and dies."[57] Harrison argues that to deny anger subverts community.[58] One of my favorite Buddhist stories deals with love and anger or, in this case, "loving-kindness":

> A young female disciple undertook to develop the meditation on loving-kindness. Sitting in her small room, she would fill her heart with loving-kindness for all beings yet each day as she went to the bazaar to gather her food, she would find her loving-kindness sorely tested by one shopkeeper who would daily subject her to unwelcome caresses. One day she could stand no more and began to chase the shopkeeper down the road with her upraised umbrella. To her mortification she passed her teacher standing on the side of the road observing this spectacle. Shame-faced she went to stand before him expecting to be rebuked for her anger. "What you should do," her teacher kindly advised her, "is to fill your heart with loving-kindness, and with as much mindfulness as you can muster, hit this unruly fellow over the head with your umbrella."[59]

As I noted earlier, one model of mutuality, of the independent/reciprocal relationship between the self and something larger than the self, is friendship. Another way of examining these issues, of finding models of "the power of human and communal becoming" that show it is possible to deal creatively with conflict, to be inclusive, celebratory of difference, mutual, is described in an innovative essay by Karen McCarthy Brown.[60] In the essay she weaves together understandings of African drumming and Haitian voodoo. Brown writes that Haitian voodoo and African drumming are polyrhythmic. They are both essentially about balancing. A strong sense of self is needed (what Brown calls "metronome sense"—the ability to balance in the midst of opposing forces without missing the beat), yet relationships also are key. In African drumming, "no rhythm, not even the inner one, makes any musical sense in isolation." Likewise, the "moral wisdom of Vodou lies in teaching that it is precisely in responsive and responsible relation to others that one has the clearest and most steady sense of self . . . [but] developing a strong sense of self does not lead to self-sufficiency but to stronger and more sustaining social bonds."[61] Many Westerners have a difficult time understanding African music because the "main beat" is missing. "We can say that the musicians play 'around' the beat, or that they play on the off-beat, but actually it is precisely the ability to identify the beat that enables someone to appreciate the music. We begin to 'understand' African music by being able to maintain, in our minds or our bodies, an additional rhythm to the ones we hear. Hearing another rhythm to fit alongside the rhythms of an ensemble is . . . a way of being steady within a context of multiple rhythms."[62] It is the "metronome sense," the strong sense of self, that makes it possible to both identify and maintain the integrating beat. Similarly, "the participant in a Vodou ritual must pour his or her own life content into the polymorphic interplay of images found there, otherwise nothing will have meaning." In drumming and in ritual, "the community, individually and collectively, actually supplies the specific content." Balance is key, "but it is achieved not through resolving or denying conflict, but in finding a way to stay steady in the midst of it."[63] There is a "pattern that connects," but it is nonhierarchical and not based on domination. Such a pattern brings self and community together in ways that enrich and enhance both. "We" and "they," "you" and "I" are intertwined.

Power, Energy, Connectedness, or Relationality at the Heart of All Things

In voodoo, power is seen as energy, a kind of "life energy." There is a sense of "relationships (among people as well as between 'the living' and the spirits) and of how such relationships may be clarified and subtly changed to achieve a state that is at once dynamic and balanced."[64] Relationship and energy also are key to the understanding of power among many tribal peoples. For example, in *Buffalo Woman Comes Singing*, Brooke Medicine Eagle writes that the Creator's only law at the beginning of the world "was that we should be in good relationship with all beings and all things." She says this is "the ultimate call of the feminine": "to nurture and care for all things, for the whole of our universal family. This feminine energy within women, men, and all things is being called forth to rebalance a world that has forgotten or ignored this most basic and essential principle for the renewing of life. It represents for us, in profoundly simple form, an answer to our problems on Earth at this time. They are problems of relationship: relationship between peoples, races, tribes; relationship between two-leggeds and the other people of Earth; even relationships among family members and friends. We have forgotten the message she and other holy ones have brought us, which reminds us that whatever we do to any other creature or things, we do to ourselves."[65] Paula Gunn Allen, a Laguna Pueblo/Sioux Indian, agrees that "power inevitably carries with it the requirement that people live in cooperative harmony with each other and the beings and powers that surround them."[66] For Allen, to be sacred means to possess power.

Others who see power as the energy of connectedness, of relationship, are Starhawk, who writes from the Goddess or Wicca tradition, and Elizabeth Johnson, a Catholic theologian and member of the order Congregation of St. Joseph (C.J.S.). Starhawk emphasizes the ability of ritual to create community and to "build power by attuning the group to the values they share and the circle of life from which all energy is drawn." She defines ritual as "a patterned movement of energy to accomplish a purpose," and says that it is through ritual that we "become familiar with power-from-within, learn to recognize its *feel*, learn how to call it up, and let it go."[67] She writes that manifestations of power-from-within include the earth, fire, water, air, natural objects—and each other.

Elizabeth Johnson explores power "as the liberating power of connectedness that is effective in compassionate love," power as "vitality, an empowering vigor that reaches out and awakens freedom and strength in oneself and in others. It is an energy that brings forth, stirs up, and fosters life, enabling autonomy and friendship. It is a movement of spirit that builds, mends, struggles with and against, celebrates and laments. It transforms people and bonds them to one another and to the world. Such dynamism is not the antithesis of love but is the shape of love against the forces of nonbeing and death. And it operates in a relational manner."[68] As Johnson notes, "relational, persuasive, erotic, connected, loving, playful, empowering, resisting—such are some of the words we seek."[69] When one begins to talk, and to act, out of love, and when this love "is mutual, it signifies a respect, a prizing, and a bondedness that subvert the potential for domination. . . . Spoken of in terms of mutual love proceeding, God who is Spirit cannot be used to legitimize patriarchal structures but signals a migration toward reciprocity in community as the highest good."[70] This is not dominating power-over but power shared and power-from-within—the ability to empower oneself and others.[71] This is "sacred power as present in the whole complex web of life, not as power-taker but as empowerer."[72] Or, to go back to Beverly Johnson, "relationality is at the heart of all things." Such power does not reinforce patriarchal structures based on domination but may, on the contrary, be a catalyst in overcoming them.

Conclusion

Feminist theology is a process. I chose the second epigraph, the story of the dandelion chain, because I agree with Delores Williams and Marcia Falk that much of feminist (or in Williams's case, "womanist," or black feminist) theology is epitomized by such a chain. Feminist theological vision will grow as we "come together and connect piece with piece";[73] it involves a process, "the continual forging of links on an unending chain."[74] The dandelion is a metaphor for something larger. What that something larger might be is hinted at in a Sufi story:

> Mulla Nasrudin decided to start a flower garden. He prepared the soil and planted the seeds of many beautiful flowers. But when they came up, his garden was filled not just with his chosen flowers but also overrun by dandelions. He sought out advice from gardeners all over and tried every method known to get rid of them but to no avail. Finally he walked all the way to the capital to speak to the royal gardener at the sheik's palace. The wise old man had counseled many gardeners before and suggested a variety of remedies to expel the dandelions but Mulla had tried them all. They sat together in silence for some time and finally the gardener looked at Nasrudin and said, "well, then I suggest you learn to love them."[75]

Or as Rachel Remen and one of her students put it, "'a dandelion is just something that is happening at a place in the world.' And, I suppose, so are we all."[76]

This idea of theology as a process, as the continual forging of links on a chain that is unending and always changing distinguishes much of feminist theology from the stereotype of theology in general and, particularly, from fundamentalism. Before I began writing this essay I tended to define theology as the study of doctrine and dogma, the study of beliefs considered unchangeable and unchanging. I associated theology with words like rigidity, inquisition, orthodoxy, and boundaries rather than horizons. The Buddhist story about the devil and the "truth" summarized well my conception of the role of theology.

> One day Mara, the Buddhist god of ignorance and evil, was traveling through the villages of India with his attendants. He saw a man doing walking meditation whose face was lit up in wonder. The man had just discovered something on the ground in front of him. Mara's attendants asked what that was and Mara replied, "A piece of truth." "Doesn't this bother you when someone finds a piece of the truth, o evil one?" his attendants asked. "No," Mara replied. "Right after this they usually make a belief of it."[77]

The image here is of truth that is unchanging, of belief as "an insecure faith that has found sanctuary in a system."[78] Questioning orthodoxy is considered irreligious; complexity and ambiguity are "merely mystifications The world's ills should be overcome instead by the enforcement of hierarchies and systems inherited from the past."[79] But change is an inherent, inescapable part of life. As Bateson and others recognize, the weakness of fundamentalism "is that when some item is held constant while the context varies, constancy is an illusion, and those who resist change often suffer the reverse."[80] One of the reasons that feminist theology is so exciting to many people, and so threatening to others, is its willingness to challenge orthodoxy and its understanding that belief is a process. Rather than reviving the old forms, feminist theology recognizes the need to move on.[81]

I said at the beginning of this essay that much of feminist theology is moving toward a common goal, and that this goal is transformation into a new community, a genuine community of mutuality. This mutuality includes not just men and women, but the earth itself, and species beyond the human.[82] It is of course easy to talk about ideas like this, but it is much harder to put them into practice, or to visualize actual "communities of mutuality." I agree with those who say we must first visualize the future; then we can create it. We all "learn to understand the world by learning to invent it."[83] Two novels might help us with this visualization: *The Fifth Sacred Thing,* by Starhawk, and *Woman on the Edge of Time,* by Marge Piercy.[84] Both are "utopian" novels; both give us a vision, indeed multiple visions, of possible futures. While some may argue that these novels are "merely utopian," Philip Allott notes that it is useful to remember that utopian ideas "contain a future which is not only possible but also necessary, and that the human future is always an imaginary potentiality until it becomes a present actuality."[85] And as Bateson understands, "community, like the sacred, is an idea that becomes reality because we believe in it."[86]

In Starhawk's novel, the "fifth sacred thing" (in addition to air, fire, water, and earth) is spirit. She writes that "to honor the sacred is to make love possible."[87] The novel juxtaposes two societies, and one weakness of the book is the starkness of the contrast between the right-wing fundamentalist, military/industrial dominated society in the "Southlands," and the earth-and-environment centered, religiously pluralistic, mutually empowering society of the North. When the South invades the North, the North resists using the power of love. The South tries to control and take over the North; the North tries not to defeat the South, but instead to enlarge its own community to include those from the South willing to engage in genuine mutuality, a community in which power comes from connectedness, from relationships. It turns out that one of the hardest things for many of those from the South to accept is that the people of the North mean it when they say, over and over, "there is a place set for you at our table." I said that the stark contrast between the future symbolized by the North and the future symbolized by the South was one of the weaknesses of Starhawk's book. But perhaps this is not a weakness; perhaps the choice facing us really is that simple and stark.[88]

In her novel, Marge Piercy interweaves three societies—the present, and two possible futures. The main character, Connie, lives in the present where she is considered insane. Connie is committed to a mental institution, diagnosed as a paranoid schizophrenic. But perhaps Connie is not insane, or is insane only in the context of limited knowledge and imagination. Connie hears "voices" from the future and is able to project her consciousness into two possible futures which are not unlike Starhawk's two societies. One is Mattapoisett, a community where interconnectedness is recognized and valued, and mutual empowerment is a key characteristic. (Women even give up the power to give birth because they believed that monopolizing giving birth was a manifestation of power-over they would have to sacrifice for the good of a true community of equals.) The other is a society where domination and control are the essential characteristics, where power is held only by a few, and where "human beings" are almost unrecognizable. Piercy repeatedly argues that "control" is key—the Mattapoisett community recognizes that there is no such thing as the ability to control. The people in Mattapoisett also recognize that their community is only possible if the people of the present—the people of our and Connie's generation—will it to be so. The future existence or nonexistence of Mattapoisett is up to us. Indeed, there is a sense in which "part of what it is to be empowered is when people recognize that what happens in history is not independent of what they do."[89]

I have used a number of stories and poems in this essay. I would like to conclude with one more. I think the story is relevant as all of us try, in Carol Christ's words in the first epigraph, to make sense "of an existence far more complicated, more intricate, more enduring than we are."

> There's a monk who will never give you advice, but only a question. I was told his questions could be very helpful. I sought him out. "I am a parish priest," I said. "I'm here on retreat. Could you give me a question?"
>
> "Ah, yes," he answered. "My question is, "What do they need?"
>
> I came away disappointed. I spent a few hours with the question, writing out answers, but finally I came back to him.
>
> "Excuse me. Perhaps I didn't make myself clear. Your question has been helpful, but I wasn't so much interested in thinking about my apostolate during this retreat. Rather I wanted to think seriously about my own spiritual life. Could you give me a question for my own spiritual life?"
>
> "Ah, I see. Then my question is, 'What do they REALLY need?'"[90]

Whether or not this question is helpful will depend on us. It will depend on our ability to bring together theory and practice, our ability to imagine a new reality and to bring that reality to fruition. As Allott writes, it is religion that "seeks to integrate all value with all reality. . . . The religious instinct is a reflection of the capacity of imagination to form possible reality and the capacity of reason to bring order" to that reality.[91]

The original title of this essay was "For All of Us." The title came from the Shona word *tese,* which means "all of us." Katy Payne tells how she decided to learn Shona. At one point in her lessons she asked her teacher the proper way to congratulate her when the teacher's baby was born. The teacher responded "Oh, you can say '*Makorokoto*': that means 'congratulations.' And I will say, '*Tese.*' That means 'all of us.' The baby is for all of us."[92]

Notes

This chapter's epigraphs are taken from Carol Christ, "Rethinking Theology and Nature," in *Weaving the Visions: New Patterns in Feminist Spirituality.* ed. Judith Plaskow and Carol Christ (San Francisco: Harper, 1989), 321; Bess Johnson, quoted in Delores S. Williams, "Womanist Theology: Black Women's Voices," in Plaskow and Christ, *Weaving the Visions,* 186; and Katy [Katharine] Payne, *Silent Thunder: In the Presence of Elephants* (New York: Simon and Schuster), 268.

1. Martin Buber, *Hasidism and Modern Man* (New York: Harper and Row, 1958), 159.

2. William James, *The Varieties of Religious Experience: A Study in Human Nature* (New York: Modern Library, 1936), 41.

3. Elizabeth A. Johnson, *She Who Is: The Mystery of God in Feminist Theological Discourse* (New York: The Crossroad Publishing Co., 1992), 223, 4.

4. Johnson, *She Who Is,* 173, 6. In one of his books, Lewis Mumford quotes from a letter he received from his friend Roderick Seidenberg, the author of *Post Historic Man.* I wasn't sure whether to include an excerpt from this letter, but decided to do so because of what Seidenberg says about culture and our understandings of

God. Seidenberg's letter was in response to an article Mumford had published in the *New York Times:*

> Your plea in the *Times* brings to my mind an idea which haunts me: each culture evolves a characteristic bodily posture or gesture that symbolizes its essential values; thus Christianity brings to mind a suppliant figure on its knees in prayer; the Buddha sits in the calm of eternity with snails in his hair! The gods and Pharaohs of Egypt are seated—great granite figures of power. There is in these postures an element of the ultimate; an expression of a transcendent attitude. But what, pray, is our posture upon having miraculously touched the innermost sources of nature's power? Our school children here in the backwoods of the village of Tinicum are taught in daily drill to duck under their desks when they hear the siren blow. The citizenry have built themselves deep underground shelters where they are to cower while their civilization is blown to atoms. And those not fortunate enough to grovel in fear and trembling underground are taught to fall upon their faces in the gutters of their cities and await their doom. Prostrate, our heads deep in the mud, we face the future! Such is our posture.

Mumford writes that perhaps it is not by increasing our power, but rather by redeeming our humanity that we might be saved. Lewis Mumford, *In the Name of Sanity* (Westport, Conn.: Greenwood Press, 1954), 208–10.

5. Johnson, *She Who Is,* 15.

6. Christina Feldman and Jack Kornfield, eds., *Stories of the Spirit, Stories of the Heart: Parables of the Spiritual Path from around the World* (San Francisco: Harper, 1991), 249.

7. Johnson, *She Who Is,* 23.

8. Mary Catherine Bateson, *Peripheral Visions: Learning along the Way* (New York: HarperCollins Publishers, 1994), 142.

9. Johnson, *She Who Is,* 28.

10. William P. George, "Looking for a Global Ethic? Try International Law," in *Religion and International Law,* ed. Mark W. Janis and Carolyn Evans (The Hague: Martinus Nijhoff Publishers, 1999), 483.

11. National Spiritual Assembly of the Baha'is in the United States, *The Promise of World Peace to the Peoples of the World* 8 (1985), quoted in James A. R. Nafziger, "The Functions of Religion in the International Legal System," in *Religion and International Law,* 161.

12. Richard Falk, quoted in Nafziger, "Functions of Religion," 155.

13. I should note that the exploration of the meaning of power and community also is only one small piece of feminist theology, but it is the part of feminist theology on which this essay will focus.

14. Cited in Kathleen Norris, *Amazing Grace: A Vocabulary of Faith* (New York: Riverhead Books, 1998), 359.

15. Norris, *Amazing Grace,* 359.

16. Johnson, *She Who Is,* 5, 17.

17. Thomas Merton, quoted in Norris, *Amazing Grace,* 108.

18. Rebecca Chopp, quoted in Johnson, *She Who Is,* 5.

19. Johnson, *She Who Is,* 5. Also see the back cover. Johnson notes that "naming toward God" is a phrase used by Mary Daly in her book *Beyond God the Father: Toward a Philosophy of Women's Liberation* (Boston: Beacon, 1973), 37. Daly writes that women name toward God from the matrix of their own experience.

20. Elizabeth Schussler Fiorenza, "In Search of Women's Heritage," in *Weaving the Visions: New Patterns in Feminist Spirituality,* ed. Judith Plaskow and Carol Christ (San Francisco: Harper, 1989), 35. See also Plaskow and Christ, "Our Heritage is Our Power," in *Weaving the Visions,* 18.

21. Plaskow and Christ, introduction to *Weaving the Visions,* 6.

22. Johnson, *She Who Is,* 10.

23. Plaskow and Christ, introduction to *Weaving the Visions,* 5.

24. Johnson, *She Who Is,* 30, 31.

25. Ibid., 30.

26. Beverly Johnson, quoted in Plaskow and Christ, introduction to *Weaving the Visions,* 11.

27. Alice Walker, quoted in Carol Christ, "Rethinking Theology and Nature," in *Weaving the Visions,* 320. Walker writes, "it was years after writing these words for Shug that I discovered they were also spoken, millennia ago, by Isis, ancient Goddess of Africa, who as an African, can be said to be a spiritual mother of us all" (*Anything We Love Can Be Saved: A Writer's Activism* [New York: Random House, 1997], 3–4).

28. Susan Griffin, "This Earth Is My Sister," in *Weaving the Visions,* 109.

29. Plaskow and Christ, "Transforming the World," in *Weaving the Visions,* 272.

30. Ibid. Mary Catherine Bateson tells the story of the British evolutionist J. B. S. Haldane, "who was asked what, on the basis of his knowledge of the creation, he could infer about the mind of the Creator. His answer was perhaps a joke but surely a revealing one, 'an inordinate fondness for beetles,' he said. The patterns on the carapaces of the earth's multitude of beetles, thousands of species still undescribed and many threatened with extinction, are also epiphanies" (*Peripheral Visions,* 51).

31. Katy [Katharine] Payne, *Silent Thunder: In the Presence of Elephants* (New York: Simon and Schuster, 1998). In thinking about the relationship between human beings, nature, and other species it is perhaps useful to ponder that human beings are one of ten to twenty million species on planet Earth, yet use over 40 percent of the primary productivity (the amount of consumable energy from photosynthesis). See Paul Wapner, "Clinton's Environmental Legacy," *Tikkun,* March/April 2001, 11.

32. Payne, *Silent Thunder,* 51–52. Payne also tells the story of an attempt by herself and a colleague to record the sounds of male elephants. "A few days into this venture, we approached a large bull named M51. His face and legs streaming with evidence of musth [he was "in heat"], he walked up to the jeep that had driven offensively close to his drinking pool, put his right tusk slightly inside the window over Joyce's lap where she sat at the wheel, and made a fine musth rumble right in her face. Then he withdrew and stepped to the front of the vehicle, tapped the tusk on the hood of the vehicle three times, turned, and went back to splash in his pool" (93). Payne then relates the story of a whale which, during earlier research, also warned but didn't hurt her, and goes on to ask "why had the whale taken such care not to hurt us? It would have been easier to demolish the pram with a moderate slap of that huge tail. Why, in Amboselu, did the elephant M51 warn but not injure us?

Haven't I twice been given the benefit of the doubt during a moment of high handed intrusion?" She notes that such a question is a projection of human experience, and realizes that whales and elephants might not think in such ways at all. But she writes that she can say "that there was forbearance. That it was deliberate. And that it was communicated in a manner that was both subtle and clear" (95). Similarly, in the book *Woman on the Edge of Time,* the people in the "futuristic" community of Mattapoisett have a holiday, Washoe Day, when they "celebrate our new community, named for a heroine of your time—a chimpanzee who was the first animal to learn to sign between species" (Marge Piercy, *Woman on the Edge of Time* [New York: Fawcett Columbine, 1976], 92).

33. Bateson, *Peripheral Visions,* 231. In addition to the book *Silent Thunder,* I also recommend two articles that help in the process of reconceptualizing humanity's relationship to other species, and lead us to question whether "humankind is the sole creative (or constructive) agency in the earthly world." The articles are David Abram's "Reciprocity: Water-borne Reflections from the Northwest Coast," *Tikkun,* May/June, 2001, 21–26, 54–56; and Douglas Foster's "The Rise of the Fungus Farmers," *The Washington Post Magazine,* 15 April 2001, 30–34, 40. Abram explores whether the dams on the Colombia River should come down for the sake of the salmon (and maybe for our sake, too), and points out that in making this decision, perhaps it is time "to let another voice, another shape of intelligence, in on the conversation. It is an intelligence that speaks to us not in words, but in an elegant language of metamorphosis, and grace, and reciprocity. A fluid voice that, once we allowed it into the conversation, could not help but begin to heal the various rifts within our communities" (55). Foster's article explores the work of Ted Schultz, a research entomologist at the Smithsonian Institution's National Museum of Natural History. Schultz is an expert on farming ants—ants that actually grow their own food. "The nest extends down for six feet or more. It's the size of a cow. Those millions of gardening ants working below first trim and rough up the surface of the leaves, then lay them on the bottom of chambers dug into the dirt. They plant tiny fungi in neat little rows, like a string of cabbages. They cut and trim, remove unhealthy crops and use chemicals to control pathogens. When the fungi grow, they will provide food for the entire colony. It's the only nourishment they know" (40). In their farming, the ants use antibiotics. They "have used antibiotics for millions of years, yet there are no signs that resistance to the chemicals has posed a problem" (34). This is in contrast to humans, who have used antibiotics for only sixty years and already are faced with massive immunity on the part of the pathogens they are seeking to destroy. Schultz says that the "ants use antibiotics to knock pathogens back but not out," and the "system refined by the farming ants may hold useful clues to the smarter use of chemicals and the essential elements of sustainable agriculture for humans" (34).

34. Bateson, *Peripheral Visions,* 224.

35. Payne, *Silent Thunder,* 176, 68.

36. Ibid., 178.

37. Ibid., 273, 254.

38. Bateson, *Peripheral Visions,* 63, 55.

39. Ibid., 138, 74.

40. Johnson, *She Who Is,* 68. In her book *Woman on the Edge of Time,* Marge Piercy has an interesting description of the autonomous, isolated self:

> "See, there's a car," Connie said. "The red one. It's a Chevy Vega." "How come person inside has the windows all the way up when it's so hot? Is person scared of something?" Dawn asked.
>
> "He probably has the air conditioning on—a machine that makes it cool," Connie said, studying Dawn's hair and ears.
>
> "Only one person in that whole machine! So much energy spent! The sadness of it, the loneliness!" Luciente blew her nose.
>
> "Don't cry, Mama," Dawn said, kissing her cheek. "Why sadden? It just seems stupid." "All those people in metal boxes, alone and cut off!" Luciente shook her head. "How could you start to talk? Make friends? Once when I was returning from visiting my childhood family, I took ill suddenly. My fever rose and I felt dreadful. A person helped me lower my fever and the dipper rerouted to a hospital for me. . . . Traveling I always meet people I exchange pleasure with—a meal, a conversation, a coupling, interseeing, a making of music, drumming to their slide playing. . . . Locked in a metal box, how could I make contact? The accidents they had were bumping of metal on flesh. Our accidents are bumping of flesh against flesh, the brushing of lives—" (238)

41. Rita Nakashima Brock puts this well when she writes that "every cell in my body speaks to the ancients. I can understand in my body all the movements of faith that have been from the beginning. . . . We are all connected and feel the impact, literally and figuratively, of what happens on the other side of the globe." Rita Nakashima Brock, "On Mirrors, Mists and Murmurs: Toward an Asian American Theology," in *Weaving the Visions,* 295. Or in the words of the poet Francis Thomson:

> All things by almighty power
> Hiddenly
> To each other linked are,
> That thou cans't not stir a flower
> Without troubling of a star.

A widely used metaphor for this interconnectedness is the Gaia hypothesis, developed by American microbiologist Lynn Margulies and British biologist James Lovelock. The Gaia hypothesis argues that the planet is alive, and all things are interconnected. For a discussion of the Gaia hypothesis please see Robin L. Teske, "Power: An Interdisciplinary Approach," in *Reconceiving Reality: Women and International Law,* ed. Dorinda G. Dallmeyer, Studies in Transnational Legal Policy, no. 26 (Washington, D.C.: American Society of International Law, 1993), 243–45; and Bateson, *Peripheral Visions,* 127–43. Bateson asks the question "what would it be like to walk through the woods or the city in the presence of—aware of—Gaia? Part of that awareness . . . comes into being through the experience of loving and being loved, . . . attending patiently to things we do not understand" (140).

42. Johnson, *She Who Is,* 222, 166.

43. Ibid., 32.

44. Ibid., 97, 68.

45. Simone Weil, quoted in Johnson, *She Who Is,* 218.

46. Agape is nonmutual, nonreciprocal love—it is to will good for someone even if there is no basis for mutual affection. Love in the sense of agape is an important

component of the theory and practice of nonviolence. An example here is the call to love your enemies. For a discussion of agape and the power of nonviolence, please see Robin L. Teske, "The Butterfly Effect," in *Conscious Acts and the Politics of Social Change,* vol. 1 of *Feminist Approaches to Social Movements, Community, and Power,* ed. Robin L. Teske and Mary Ann Tétreault (Columbia: University of South Carolina Press, 2000), 107–23.

47. Carter Heyward, "Sexuality, Love, and Justice," in *Weaving the Visions,* 240.

48. Beverly Wildung Harrison, "The Power of Anger in the Work of Love: Christian Ethics for Women and Other Strangers," in *Weaving the Visions,* 222.

49. Heyward, "Sexuality, Love, and Justice," 294.

50. Harrison, "Power of Anger," 217, 223.

51. Johnson, *She Who Is,* 179, 197.

52. Karen Armstrong, interview with Bill Moyers on *NOW,* PBS, 1 March 2002.

53. Buber, *Hasidism and Modern Man,* 250. Or as David Kennedy asks, "Isn't the part of us that desires, that loves, that longs for encounter and connection—physical and psychic and every other way—also the part of us that knows something about God?" David Kennedy, "Losing Faith in the Secular: Law, Religion, and the Culture of International Governance," in *Religion and International Law,* ed. Mark W. Janis and Carolyn Evans (The Hague: Martinus Nijhoff Publishers, 1999), 317.

54. Walker, *Anything You Love Can Be Saved,* 160. See also Feldman and Kornfield, eds., *Stories of the Spirit, Stories of the Heart,* 144.

55. Heyward, "Sexuality, Love, and Justice," 300.

56. Harrison "Power of Anger," 223.

57. Ibid., 220. In a review of Peter Gabel's book *The Bank Teller and Other Essays,* Stephen Mo Hanan writes that "there is simply no depth of evil to which a society cannot sink once it abandons love as its governing principle." Stephen Mo Hanan, "The Source of Each Other's Completion," *Tikkun,* January/February 2001, 66.

58. Harrison, "Power of Anger," 220.

59. Feldman and Kornfield, eds., *Stories of the Spirit, Stories of the Heart,* 297.

60. Karen McCarthy Brown, "Women's Leadership in Haitian Vodou," in *Weaving the Visions,* 226–34.

61. Ibid., 231–32.

62. John Miller Chernoff, *African Rhythm and African Sensibility: Aesthetics and Social Action in African Musical Idiom* (Chicago: University of Chicago Press, 1979), 48–49, quoted in Brown, "Haitian Vodou," 229. For an interesting discussion of changing dance styles affecting changes in society and in culture please see Bateson, *Peripheral Visions,* 144–46.

63. Brown, "Haitian Vodou," 233.

64. Ibid., 234.

65. Brooke Medicine Eagle, *Buffalo Woman Comes Singing: The Spirit Song of a Rainbow Medicine Woman* (New York: Ballantine Books, 1991), 294.

66. Paula Gunn Allen, "Grandmother of the Sun: The Power of Woman in Native America," in *Weaving the Visions,* 26.

67. Starhawk, "Ritual as Bonding: Action as Ritual," in *Weaving the Visions,* 326. There is a sense in which "letting go" is an important part of spiritual life; Feldman and Kornfield argue it is the heart of spiritual practice. "Beginning to let go brings an immediate and profound revelation. We discover that it is when we are no longer full of opinions and expectations that we are truly receptive. It is when we are no

longer afraid of loss that we begin to open in a wholehearted way to the world around us. In the discovery of aloneness is the discovery of what it means to be truly together with others. Letting go is an expression of compassion for ourselves and of love for the universe we live in." Feldman and Kornfield, eds., *Stories of the Spirit, Stories of the Heart,* 331.

68. Johnson, *She Who Is,* 269–70.

69. Ibid., 270.

70. Ibid., 143.

71. This conception of power also is explored in Margaret Hrezo's essay in volume one. Please see Margaret Seyford Hrezo, "Composition on a Multiple Plane: Simone Weil's Answer to the Rule of Necessity," in *Conscious Acts*, 91–106.

72. Plaskow and Christ, introduction to *Weaving the Visions,* 10.

73. Williams, "Womanist Theology," 186.

74. Marcia Falk, "Notes on Composing New Blessings: Toward a Feminist-Jewish Reconstruction of Prayer," in *Weaving the Visions,* 136.

75. Feldman and Kornfield, eds., *Stories of the Spirit, Stories of the Heart,* 141.

76. Rachel Naomi Remen, *Kitchen Table Wisdom: Stories That Heal* (New York: Riverhead Books, 1996), 225.

77. Feldman and Kornfield, eds., *Stories of the Spirit, Stories of the Heart,* 250.

78. Ibid., 248.

79. Wendy Steiner, *The Scandal of Pleasure: Art in an Age of Fundamentalism* (Chicago: University of Chicago Press, 1995), quoted in Amanda Cross, *The Puzzled Heart* (New York: Ballantine Books, 1998), 107.

80. Bateson, *Peripheral Visions,* 88. Bateson gives as examples the clothing worn by Hasidic Jews and "creation science." "The long coats and fur-trimmed hats worn by Hasidic Jews, like the habits worn by nuns, were only slightly different from general patterns of dress when they were adopted, but freezing these styles created later situations of extreme differentiation. Christian fundamentalists claim they are practicing 'that old time religion,' but when they assert the literal truth of ancient words of scripture in the context of modern notions of truth and falsehood, they are in effect asserting something new. Translating the cosmology of the Old Testament into the format of 'creation science' turns the insight of an ordered universe into a caricature."

81. In a memoir of her brother's struggle with AIDS, Marcie Hershman has an interesting insight on "moving on," and on the role and renewal of ritual. She writes that "it seems right to add my brother's words to the Seder's layered traditions because rituals must encounter the present as well as the past. To be alive, to move across, rituals must not be enacted as if their meaning just stopped, preserved in year A or at juncture C. Rituals, like life, must be renewed so that they can renew." Marcie Hershman, "Here I Am," *Tikkun,* March/April 2001, 52.

82. A growing emphasis on relationship, on intrinsic interconnectedness, is not something that is happening only in theology. Other fields also are beginning to understand that there is a general interconnectedness of things. For example, despite appearances, physics, metaphysics, and religion strangely converge. Involved here is a grasp of infinitude, an appeal beyond boundaries, an understanding of the world not as events but as relationships. See Jacob Bronowski, *The Ascent of Man* (Boston: Little, Brown and Company, 1973), 254; and Alfred North Whitehead, *Adventures of Ideas* (New York: The Macmillan Company, 1933), 192, 367.

83. Bateson, *Peripheral Visions,* 226.

84. Starhawk, *The Fifth Sacred Thing* (New York: Bantam Books, 1993) and Piercy, *Woman on the Edge*.

85. Philip Allott, *Eunomia: New Order for a New World* (Oxford: Oxford University Press, 2001), xxvii. I like an answer Michael Lerner recently gave to the question "but what can we actually do?" His answer: "Don't just do something, sit there." He said what he means by this is that the most important thing to do is to help spread a new understanding. "A little meditation and a lot of new thinking would be useful. We must allow ourselves to develop a new way of understanding, because until that happens, we are just going to repeat and recycle the frustrations of the past." Michael Lerner, "Surviving the Bush and Sharon Years," *Tikkun,* March/April 2001, 7–8.

86. Bateson, *Peripheral Visions,* 42.

87. Starhawk, *Fifth Sacred Thing,* dedication page.

88. In regard to "simplicity," Pierre Teilhard de Chardin once said that "the true union is the union that simplifies. . . . the true fertility is the fertility that brings together in the engendering of spirit. . . ." Pierre Teilhard de Chardin, *Writings in Time of War,* quoted in Pierre Teilhard de Chardin, *Toward the Future* (New York: Harcourt Brace Jovanovich, 1975), 87.

89. Senator Paul Wellstone, paraphrasing Michael Lerner, in "An Interview with Senator Paul Wellstone," *Tikkun,* March/April 2001, 10. I like the way Philip Allott puts it: "To live is to choose the future. To exist as a human being is to choose to change the world." Allott, *Eunomia,* 41.

90. Father Theophane, quoted in Feldman and Kornfield, eds., *Stories of the Spirit, Stories of the Heart,* 152.

91. Allott, *Eunomia,* 94.

92. Payne, *Silent Thunder,* 276.

Bibliography

Abbey, Edward. 2000. *The Monkey Wrench Gang*. New York: Harper Perennial Library.

Abram, David. 2001. "Reciprocity: Water-borne Reflections from the Northwest Coast." *Tikkun*, May/June, 21–26, 54–56.

Abrash, Abigail. 1994. *China and Most-Favored-Nation Trade Status: A Public Hearing Featuring U.S. Government, Business, Academia and Human Rights Representatives: Summary and Findings*. Washington, D.C.: Robert F. Kennedy Memorial Center for Human Rights and the Washington College of Law.

Acker, Joan, Kate Berry, and Johanna Esseveld. 1991. "Objectivity and Truth: Problems in Doing Feminist Research." In *Beyond Methodology: Feminist Scholarship as Lived Research*, edited by Mary Margaret Fonow and Judith A. Cook, 133–53. Bloomington: Indiana University Press.

Adams, Henry. [1913] 1986. *Mont-Saint-Michel and Chartres: A Study of Thirteenth-Century Unity*. New York: Penguin Classics.

Adams, Parveen, and Jeffrey Minson. 1978. "The Subject of Feminism." *m/f* 2, no. 2: 43–61.

Agnew, John. 1993. "Representing Space: Space, Scale and Culture in Social Science." In *Place/Culture/Representation*, edited by James Duncan and David Ley, 251–71. London: Routledge.

Alasuutari, Pertti. 1995. *Researching Culture: Qualitative Method and Cultural Studies*. London: Sage.

Alexander, M. Jacqui, and Chandra Talpade Mohanty. 1997. "Introduction: Genealogies, Legacies, Movements." In *Feminist Genealogies, Colonial Legacies, Democratic Futures*, edited by M. Jacqui Alexander and Chandra Talpade Mohanty, xii–xlii. New York and London: Routledge.

Alexander, Norman, and Mary Glen Wiley. 1981. "Situated Activity and Identity Formation." In *Social Psychology Sociological Perspectives*, edited by Morris Rosenberg and Ralph Turner, 22–50. New York: Basic Books.

Alford, William P. 2000. Conversation with Abigail Abrash. 12 October.

Al-Hibri, Azizah. 1999. "Is Western Patriarchal Feminism Good for Third World/Minority Women?" In *Is Multiculturalism Bad for Women?* edited by Joshua Cohen, Matthew Howard, and Martha C. Nussbaum, 41–46. Princeton, N.J.: Princeton University Press.

Allen, Paula Gunn. 1989. "Grandmother of the Sun: The Power of Woman in Native America." In *Weaving the Visions: New Patterns in Feminist Spirituality*, edited by Judith Plaskow and Carol P. Christ, 22–28. San Francisco: Harper and Row.

Allott, Philip. 2001. *Eunomia: New Order for a New World*. Oxford: Oxford University Press.

Alpha Omicron Pi. "Mission." http://www.alphaomicronpi.org/ AOΠToday/Ideals/Mission (6 June 2002).

Amnesty International. 1993. *Bosnia-Herzegovina: Rape and Sexual Abuse by Armed Forces*. New York: Amnesty International.

Amnesty International. 1995. "Rwanda: The Troubled Course of Justice." Amnesty International, report no. AFR 47/15/00, April 2000. http://web.amnesty.org/ai.nsf/Index/AFR470152000/ (15 April 2002).

Amnesty International. 2001. "Rwanda." Annual Report. http://web.amnesty.org/web/ar2001.nsf/webafrcountries/RWANDA/ (15 April 2002).

Amnesty International USA (Washington Office), Human Rights in China, the International Human Rights Law Group, the International Campaign for Tibet, and the Robert F. Kennedy Memorial Center for Human Rights. 1995. *Going to Beijing with Open Eyes: China's Human Rights Situation and the U.N. Fourth World Conference on Women, Beijing, September 1995.* Resource book for participants. Washington, D.C.

Anderson, Benedict. 1991. *Imagined Communities: Reflections on the Origin and Spread of Nationalism.* Rev. and extended 2d ed. London: Verso.

Anderson, Perry. 1998. *The Origins of Postmodernity.* London: Verso.

Ang, Ien. "I'm a Feminist but . . . 'Other' Women and Postnational Feminism" In *Transitions: New Australian Feminisms,* edited by Barbara Caine and Rosemary Pringle, 57–73. Sydney: Allen and Unwin.

Arendt, Hannah. 1965. *On Revolution.* New York: Compass.

Ariès, Philippe. 1962. *Centuries of Childhood: A Social History of Family Life.* Translated by Robert Baldick. New York: Vintage.

Aristotle. 1981. *The Politics.* Rev. and re-presented by Trevor J. Saunders, translated by T. A. Sinclair. New York: Viking Penguin.

Armstrong, Karen. 2002. Interviewed by Bill Moyers on *NOW,* PBS, 1 March.

Asem, Adel, and Haya al-Mughni. 1994. "Claiming for Compensation through the United Nations Compensation Commission: The Case of Kuwait." Paper presented at the International Conference on the Effects of the Iraqi Aggression on Kuwait, Kuwait City, 2–6 April.

Ashley, Richard K. 1986. "The Poverty of Neorealism." In *Neorealism and Its Critics: The Politcal Economy of International Change,* edited by Robert O. Keohane, 50–70. New York: Columbia University Press.

Asia Watch and Physicians for Human Rights. 1993. *Rape in Kashmir: A Crime of War.* New York: Asia Watch.

Asia Watch and the Women's Rights Project. 1992. *Double Jeopardy: Police Abuse of Women in Pakistan.* New York: Human Rights Watch.

Axelrod, Robert. 1980. *The Evolution of Cooperation.* New York: Basic Books.

Ayubi, Nazih. 1995. *Overstating the Arab State.* London: Verso.

Baraniewska, Dagmara. 1999. Interviewed by Diane M. Duffy. Warsaw, Poland, 25 May.

Barash, David P. 1995. "Diplomacy, Negotiation, and Peaceful Settlement." In *Teaching about International Conflict and Peace,* edited by Merry M. Merryfield and Richard C. Remy, 185–216. Albany: State University of New York Press.

Bard, Morton, and Diane Sangrey. 1979. *Female Sexual Slavery.* Englewood Cliffs, N.J.: Prentice-Hall.

Bateson, Mary Catherine. 1994. *Peripheral Visions: Learning along the Way.* New York: HarperCollins Publishers.

Battersby, Christine. 1998. *The Phenomenal Woman: Feminist Metaphysics and the Patterns of Identity.* New York: Routledge.

Bauman, Zygmunt. 1989. *Modernity and the Holocaust.* Ithaca, N.Y.: Cornell University Press.

Baumgardner, Jennifer, and Amy Richards. 2000. *Manifesta: Young Women, Feminism, and the Future.* New York: Farrar, Straus and Giroux.

Beauvoir, Simone de. 1988. *The Second Sex.* London: Picador.

Beck, Julie. 2000. "(Re)Negotiating Selfhood and Citizenship in the Post-Communist Czech Republic: Five Women Activists Speak about Transition and Feminism." In *Gender and Global Restructuring,* edited by Marianne H. Marchand and Anne Sisson Runyan, 176–93. London and New York: Routledge.

Beevor, Antony. *The Fall of Berlin 1945.* New York: Viking, 2002.

Belfast Telegraph. January 1997–December 2001.

Benhabib, Seyla. 1999. "Sexual Difference and Collective Identities: The New Global Constellation." *Signs* 24, no. 2: 335–61.

Berlin, Isaiah. 1969. "Two Concepts of Liberty." In *Four Essays on Liberty.* Oxford: Oxford University Press.

Berman, Marshall. 1988. *All That Is Solid Melts into Air: The Experience of Modernity.* New York: Penguin.

Bickerstaff v. Vassar, 992 F. Supp. 372 (S.D.N.Y. 1998).

Blake, Sterling. 1995. "A Desparate Calculus." In *New Legends,* edited by Greg Bear, 45–71. New York: Tom Doherty Associates.

Block, Robert. 1994. "The Tragedy of Rwanda." *New York Review of Books,* 20 October, 3–4, 6–8.

Bordo, Susan. 1993. *Unbearable Weight: Feminism, Western Culture, and the Body.* Berkeley: University of California Press.

Bornstein, David. 1996. *The Price of a Dream: The Story of the Grameen Bank and the Idea That Is Helping the Poor to Change Their Lives.* Chicago: University of Chicago Press.

Boswell, John. 1988. *The Kindness of Strangers: The Abandonment of Children in Western Europe from Late Antiquity to the Renaissance.* New York: Vintage.

———. 1994. *Same-Sex Unions in Premodern Europe.* New York: Villard Books.

Boulding, Kenneth. 1964. *The Meaning of the Twentieth Century.* New York: Harper and Row.

Brah, Avtar. 1993. "Questions of Difference and International Feminism." In *Women's Studies: A Reader,* edited by Stevi Jackson et al., 29–35. New York: Harvester Wheatsheaf.

Braidotti, Rosi. 1992. "The Exile, the Nomad and the Migrant: Reflections on International Feminism." *Women's Studies International Forum* 15, no. 1: 7–10.

———. 1994. *Nomadic Subjects: Embodiment and Sexual Difference in Contemporary Feminist Theory.* New York: Columbia University Press.

———. 1996. "Figurations of Nomadism." Keynote address delivered at the 20th conference of the International Association for Philosophy and Literature (SOAS), George Mason University, 8–11 May; also forthcoming in John Burt Foster and Wayne Froman, eds., Series in Philosophy and Literature, Northwestern University Press.

———. 1997. "Uneasy Transitions: Women's Studies in the European Union." In *Transitions, Environments, Translations: Feminists in International Politics,* edited by Joan W. Scott, Cora Kaplan, and Debra Keates, 355–73. New York: Routledge.

Brennan, Teresa. 1994. Series preface to *The Spoils of Freedom: Psychoanalysis and Feminism after the Fall of Socialism,* by Renata Salecl, vi–vii. London: Routledge.

Brock, Rita Nakashima. 1989. "On Mirrors, Mists and Murmurs: Toward an Asian American Theology." In *Weaving the Visions: New Patterns in Feminist Spirituality,* edited by Judith Plaskow and Carol P. Christ, 235–43. San Francisco: Harper and Row.

Bronowski, Jacob. 1973. *The Ascent of Man.* Boston: Little, Brown and Company.

Brooks, David. 2001. "The Organization Kid." *Atlantic,* April, 40–46, 48–54.

Brooks, Paul. 1972. *The House of Life: Rachel Carson at Work.* Boston: Houghton Mifflin.

Brown, Karen McCarthy. 1989. "Women's Leadership in Haitian Vodou." In *Weaving the Visions: New Patterns in Feminist Spirituality,* edited by Judith Plaskow and Carol P. Christ, 226–34. San Francisco: Harper and Row.

Brown, Lyn Mikel, and Carol Gilligan. 1992. *Meeting at the Crossroads: Women's Psychology and Girls' Development.* Cambridge: Harvard University Press.

Brown, Peter. 1988. *The Body and Society: Men, Women, and Sexual Renunciation in Early Christianity.* New York: Columbia University Press.

Brownmiller, Susan. 1975. *Against Our Will: Men, Women and Rape.* New York: Simon and Schuster.

Buber, Martin. 1958. *Hasidism and Modern Man.* New York: Harper and Row.

Bulbeck, Chilla. 1998. *Re-Orienting Western Feminisms: Women's Diversity in a Postcolonial World.* Cambridge: Cambridge University Press.

Burley, Anne-Marie. 1993. "Regulating the World: Multilateralism, International Law, and the Projection of the New Deal Regulatory State." In *Multilateralism Matters: The Theory and Praxis of an Institutional Form,* edited by John Gerard Ruggie, 125–56. New York: Columbia University Press.

Burns, John F. 1992. "150 Muslims Say Serbs Raped Them in Bosnia." *New York Times,* 3 October, L5.

Burton, John W. 1972. "Resolution and Conflict." *International Studies Quarterly* 16, no. 1 (March): 5–30.

———. 1987. *Resolving Deep-Rooted Conflict: A Handbook.* Lanham, Md.: University Press of America.

———. 1990. *Conflict: Human Needs Theory.* New York: St. Martin's Press.

Butler, Judith. 1990. *Gender Trouble: Feminism and the Subversion of Identity.* New York: Routledge.

Bynum, Carolyn Walker. 1987. *Holy Feast and Holy Fast: The Religious Significance of Food to Medieval Women.* Berkeley: University of California Press.

Caine, Barbara, and Rosemary Pringle. 1995. *Transitions: New Australian Feminisms.* Sydney: Allen and Unwin.

Caparaso, James A. 1992. "International Relations Theory and Multilateralism: The Search for Foundation." *International Organization* 46, no. 6 (Summer): 45–66.

Cavalli-Sforza, Luigi Luca. 2000. *Genes, People, and Languages.* New York: North Point Press.

Charlesworth, Hilary. 1995 "Human Rights as Men's Rights." In *Women's Rights, Human Rights: International Feminist Perspectives,* edited by Julie Peters and Andrea Wolper, 103–13. London: Routledge.

———. 1993. "Alienating Oscar? Feminist Analysis of International Law." In *Reconceiving Reality: Women and International Law,* edited by Dorinda G. Dallmeyer, 1–18. Studies in Transnational Legal Policy, no. 26. Washington, D.C.: American Society of International Law.

Charlesworth, Hilary, and Christine Chinkin. 2000. *The Boundaries of International Law: A Feminist Analysis.* Manchester: Manchester University Press.

Chi Omega. "Chi Omega's Vision and Mission." http://www.chiomega.org/chiomega/AboutXΩ/Vision and Mission (6 June 2002).

Christ, Carol P. 1989. "Rethinking Theology and Nature." In *Weaving the Visions: New Patterns in Feminist Spirituality,* edited by Judith Plaskow and Carol P. Christ, 314–25. San Francisco: Harper and Row.

Clancy, Tom. 1999. *Rainbow Six.* New York: Berkeley Group.

Clarke, Susan E., and Gary L. Gaile. 1997. "Local Politics in a Global Era: Thinking Locally, Acting Globally." *Annals of the American Academy of Political and Social Science* 55 (May): 28–43.

Clinton, Bill, and Al Gore. 1992. *Putting People First: How We Can All Change America.* New York: Times Books (Random House).

Cohen, David. 1994. *The Combing of History.* Chicago: University of Chicago Press.

Cohen, Joshua, Matthew Howard, and Martha C. Nussbaum, eds. 1999. *Is Multiculturalism Bad for Women? Susan Moller Okin and Respondents.* Princeton, N.J.: Princeton University Press.

Cohen, Roger. 1993. "Two Serbs to be Shot for Killings and Rapes." *New York Times,* 31 March, A6.

———. 1994. "Ex-Guard for Serbs Tells of Grisly 'Cleansing' Camp." *New York Times,* 1 August, A1, A8.

———. 1995. "Tribunal Charges Genocide by Serbs." *New York Times,* 14 February, A1–A2.

Cohen, Stanley. 2001. *States of Denial: Knowing about Atrocities and Suffering.* Cambridge, U.K.: Polity Press.

Coll, Steve. 1994. "War Crimes and Punishment: Bosnia in the Shadow of the Holocaust." *Washington Post Magazine,* 25 September.

Connell, R. W. 1987. *Gender and Power: Society, the Person, and Sexual Politics.* Stanford, Calif.: Stanford University Press.

Contarino, Michael. 1990. "Agricultural Trade Liberalization and Food Security: Implications of the Quantitative Studies." United Nations World Food Council discussion paper. Rome: World Food Council.

———. 1991. "Implications for Food Security of the Uruguay Round of Multilateral Trade Negotiations." United Nations World Food Council document. Rome: World Food Council.

Contreras, Manuel. 1997. "Capacity Building in the Bolivian Social Policy Analysis Unit: Reflections of a Practitioner." In *Getting Good Government: Capacity Building in the Public Sectors of Developing Countries,* edited by Merilee S. Grindle, 199–228. Cambridge: Harvard University Press.

Cordes, Helen. 2000. "Battling for the Heart and Soul of Home Schoolers." *Salon,* 2 October. http://www.salon.com/mwt/feature/2000/10/02/homeschooling_battle/index.html (25 April 2002).

———. 2000. *Girl Power in the Classroom: A Book about Girls, Their Fears, and Their Future.* Minneapolis, Minn.: Lerner Publications.

———. 2000. *Girl Power in the Mirror: A Book about Girls, Their Bodies, and Themselves.* Minneapolis, Minn.: Lerner Publications.

———. 2000. "Kids Who Do Too Much." *Child* 15, no. 7 (September): 71–74.

———. 2000. "Overdoing Extracurriculars: How and When to Say 'When.'" *Britannica Online.* 7 September. http://www.britannica.com/bcom/original/article/0,5744,10020,00.html (20 November 2001).

———. 2000. "Sour Grapes, Anyone?" *Salon,* 6 June. http://www.salon.com/mwt/feature/tues/2000/06/06/homeschool/index.html (25 April 2002).

Cox, Robert. 1987. "Social Forces, States, and World Orders." In *Neorealism and Its Critics: The Politcal Economy of International Change,* edited by Robert O. Keohane. New York: Columbia University Press, 49–60.

Crane-Engel, Melinda. 1994. "Germany vs. Genocide." *New York Times Magazine,* 30 October, 56–59.

Crawford, Beverly, and Ronnie D. Lipschutz, eds. 1998. *The Myth of "Ethnic Conflict": Politics, Economics, and "Cultural" Violence.* Berkeley: International and Area Studies, University of California at Berkeley.

Cronon, William. 1996. "The Trouble with Wilderness, or Getting Back to the Wrong Nature." In *Uncommon Ground: Rethinking the Human Place in Nature,* edited by William Cronon. New York: W. W. Norton and Company.

Crook, John R. 1993. "The United Nations Compensation Commision—A New Structure to Enforce State Responsibility." *American Journal of International Law* 87: 114–57.

Cross, Amanda. 1998. *The Puzzled Heart.* New York: Ballantine Books.

Cushman, John H. 2001. "After 'Silent Spring,' Industry Put Spin on All It Brewed." *New York Times,* 26 March, A14.

Cussins, Charis Thompson. 1999. "Confessions of a Bioterrorist: Subject Positions and Reproductive Technologies." In *Playing Dolly: Technocultural Formations, Fantasies, and Fictions of Assisted Reproduction,* edited by E. Ann Kaplan and Susan Squier, 189–219. New Brunswick, N.J.: Rutgers University Press.

Davidson, James. 1999. *Courtesans and Fishcakes: The Consuming Passions of Classical Athens.* New York: Harper Perennial.

de Lauretis, Teresa, ed. 1986. *Feminist Studies/Critical Studies.* Bloomington: Indiana University Press.

Des Forges, Alison. 1999, *"Leave None to Tell the Story": Genocide in Rwanda.* New York: Human Rights Watch.

DeSombre, Elizabeth, and Joanne Kauffman. 1996. "The Montreal Protocol Multilateral Fund: Partial Success Story." In *Institutions for Environmental Aid,* edited by Robert Keohane and Marc Levy, 89–126. Cambridge: MIT Press.

DeVault, Marjorie. 1999. *Liberating Method: Feminism and Social Research.* Philadelphia: Temple University Press.

Di Stefano, Christine. 1991. *Configurations of Masculinity.* Ithaca, N.Y.: Cornell University Press.

Doe, In re Jane, et al. against Radovan Karadzic. 1993. United States District Court, Southern District of New York, Civ. 93–0878 PKL. October.

Donaldson, Amy. 1996. "Deal to Swap Inmates Turns Sour." *Salt Lake City Deseret News,* 9 September, B1.

Donnelly, Jack. 1993. *International Human Rights.* Boulder, Colo.: Westview Press.

Dougherty, J. E., and Robert L. Pfaltzgraff Jr. 1990. *Contending Theories of International Relations.* 3d ed. New York: Harper and Row.

Douglas, Mary, and Aaron Wildavsky. 1982. *Risk and Culture: An Essay on the Selection of Technological and Environmental Dangers.* Berkeley: University of California Press.

Dover, Kenneth J. 1978. *Greek Homosexuality.* London: Duckworth.

Drakulić, Slavenka. 1993. *How We Survived Communism and Even Laughed.* London: Vintage.

Dyson, Freeman. 1979. *Disturbing the Universe.* New York: Harper and Row.

Eagleton, Mary. 1996. *Working with Feminist Criticism.* Oxford: Blackwell.

Einhorn, Barbara. 1993. *Cinderella Goes to Market: Citizenship, Gender, and Women's Movements in East-Central Europe.* New York: Verso.

———. 1995. "Ironies of History. Citizenship Issues in the New Market Economies of East-Central Europe." In *Women and Market Societies: Crisis and Opportunity,* edited by Barbara Einhorn and Eileen Janes Yeo, 217–33. Brookport, Vt.: Edward Elgar.

Eisenstein, Zillah. 1996. "Stop Stomping on the Rest of Us: Retrieving Publicness from the Privatization of the Globe." *Journal of Global Legal Studies* 4, no. 59: 59–95.

Ejército Zapatista de Liberación Nacional. 1994. "EZLN Communique 31 January 1994." http://www.ezln.org/documentos/1994/19940131b.en.htm (25 April 2002).

Ejército Zapatista de Liberación Nacional, Clandestine Indigenous Revolutionary Committee General Command of the Zapatista Army of National Liberation. 1996. "First Declaration of La Realidad For Humanity and Against Neoliberalism," January 1996. http://www.ezln.org/documentos/1996/19960130.en.htm (25 April 2002).

Engelberg, Stephen. 1992. "Bosnians Provide Accounts of Abuse in Serbian Camps." *New York Times,* 4 August, A1.

———. 1992. "Clearer Picture of Bosnia Camps: A Brutal Piece of a Larger Plan." *New York Times,* 16 August, 1, 14.

———. 1992. "Refugees from Camps Tell of Agony and Terror." *New York Times,* 7 August, A5.

Evans, Sara M., and Harry C. Boyte. 1992. *Free Spaces: The Sources of Democratic Change in America.* Chicago: University of Chicago Press.

Ezrahi, Yaron. 1990. *The Descent of Icarus: Science and the Transformation of Contemporary Democracy.* Cambridge: Harvard University Press.

———. 1994. "Technology and the Illusion of the Escape from Politics." In *Technology, Pessimism, and Postmodernism,* edited by Yaron Ezrahi, Everett Mendelsohn and Howard Segal, 29–37. Dordrecht, Netherlands: Kluwer Academic Publishers.

———. 1997. *Rubber Bullets: Power and Conscience in Modern Israel.* Berkeley: University of California Press.

Faison, Seth. 1995. "Women's Meeting Agrees on Right to Say No to Sex." *New York Times,* 11 September, A1.

Falk, Marcia. 1989. "Notes on Composing New Blessings: Toward a Feminist-Jewish Reconstruction of Prayer." In *Weaving the Visions: New Patterns in Feminist Spirituality,* edited by Judith Plaskow and Carol P. Christ, 128–38. San Francisco: Harper and Row.

Fearon, Kate. 1999. *Women's Work: The Story of the Northern Ireland Women's Coalition.* Belfast: Blackstaff Press, Ltd.

———. 2000. Lecture delivered to the Eckerd College Study Group on the Northern Ireland Peace Process, at the Institute of Irish Studies, Queens University, Belfast, Northern Ireland, 20 January.

Fearon, Kate, and Monica McWilliams. 1999. "The Good Friday Agreement: A Triumph of Substance over Style." *Fordham International Law Journal* 22, no. 4 (April): 1250–72.

Federation for Women and Family Planning. 1998. "Independent Report to the UN Committee on Economic, Social and Cultural Rights." Warsaw, Poland, April.

Fein, Helen. 1990. "Genocide: A Sociological Perspective." *Current Sociology* 38, no. 1 (Spring).

Feldman, Christina, and Jack Kornfield, eds. 1991. *Stories of the Spirit, Stories of the Heart: Parables of the Spiritual Path from around the World.* San Francisco: Harper.

Felski, Rita. 1997. "The Doxa of Difference." *Signs* 23, no. 1: 1–21.

Ferencz, Benjamin B. Letter to the editor. *New York Times,* 23 October, A32.

Fiorenza, Elizabeth Schussler. 1989. "In Search of Women's Heritage." In *Weaving the Visions: New Patterns in Feminist Spirituality,* edited by Judith Plaskow and Carol P. Christ, 29–38. San Francisco: Harper and Row.

Fisher, Roger, William Ury, and Bruce Patton. 1991. *Getting to Yes: Negotiating Agreement without Giving In.* 2d ed. New York: Houghton Mifflin Co.

Fisher v. Vassar, 852 F. Supp. 1193 (S.D.N.Y. 1994), Lexis 6376.

Flax, Jane. 1993. *Disputed Subjects, Essays on Psychoanalysis, Politics and Philosophy.* New York: Routledge.

Fleischman, Suzanne. 1998. "Gender, the Personal, and the Voice of Scholarship: A Viewpoint." *Signs* 23, no. 4: 975–1016.

Fogelman, Eva. 1994. *Conscience and Courage: Rescuers of the Jews during the Holocaust.* New York: Anchor Books.

Fonow, Mary Margaret, and Judith A. Cook, eds. 1991. *Beyond Methodology: Feminist Scholarship as Lived Research.* Bloomington: Indiana University Press.

Forell, Caroline A., and Donna M. Matthews. 2000. *A Law of Her Own: The Reasonable Woman as a Measure of Man.* New York: New York University Press.

Foster, Douglas. 2001. "The Rise of the Fungus Farmers." *The Washington Post Magazine,* 15 April, 30–34, 40.

Foucault, Michel. 1973. *The Birth of the Clinic.* New York: Pantheon Books.

———. 1980. "Truth and Power." In *Power/Knowledge,* translated by Colin Gordon, 109–33. New York: Pantheon.

———. 1980. "Two Lectures." In *Power/Knowledge,* translated by Colin Gordon, 78–108. New York: Pantheon.

———. 1991. "Governmentality." In *The Foucault Effect: Studies in Governmentality,* edited by Graham Burchell, Colin Gordon, and Peter Miller, 87–104. Chicago: University of Chicago Press.

———. 1995. *Discipline and Punish: The Birth of the Prison.* New York: Vintage.

Fox, Richard Wightman, and T. J. Jackson Lears, eds. 1983. *The Culture of Consumption: Critical Essays in American History, 1880–1980.* New York: Pantheon.

Frazer, Elizabeth, and Nicola Lacey. 1993. *The Politics of Community: A Feminist Critique of the Liberal-Communitarian Debate.* Toronto: University of Toronto Press.

Freeman, Derek. 1999. *The Fateful Hoaxing of Margaret Mead: A Historical Analysis of Her Samoan Research.* Boulder, Colo.: Westview Press.

Funk, Nanette. 1993. "Feminism East and West." In *Gender Politics and Post-Communism: Reflections from Eastern Europe and the Former Soviet Union,* edited by Nanette Funk and Magda Mueller, 318–30. New York: Routledge.

Furlich, Daniell S. 2000. "From Peril to Progress." *Nature Conservation* 50, no. 5: 14–24.

Fuss, Diana. 1989. *Essentially Speaking: Feminism, Nature and Difference.* New York: Routledge.

Fuszara, Małgorzata. 1997. "Women's Movements in Poland." In *Transitions, Environments, Translations: Feminisms in International Politics,* edited by Joan W. Scott, Cora Kaplan, and Debra Keates, 128–42. New York: Routledge.

———. 1999. Interviewed by Diane M. Duffy. Warsaw, Poland, 8 June.

Gal, Susan. 1997. "Feminism and Civil Society." In *Transitions, Environments, Translations: Feminisms in International Politics,* edited by Joan W. Scott, Cora Kaplan, and Debra Keates, 30–45. New York and London: Routledge.

Garlan, Yvon. 1998. *Slavery in Ancient Greece.* Rev. and expanded ed., translated by Janet Lloyd. Ithaca, N.Y.: Cornell University Press.

Garner, Roberta. 1994. "Transnational Movements in a Postmodern Society." *Peace Review* 6, no. 4 (Winter): 427–34.

Gartner, Carol B. 1983. *Rachel Carson.* New York: Frederick Ungar.

Garton Ash, Timothy. 1989. *The Uses of Adversity: Essays on the Fate of Central Europe.* New York: Random House.

Gatto, John Taylor. 2000. *The Underground History of American Education.* New York: The Oxford Village Press.

"Gender Equity in Athletics." *Chronicle of Higher Education.* http://chronicle.com/free/equity/equitysearch.htm (7 May 2002).

George, William P. 1999. "Looking for a Global Ethic? Try International Law." In *Religion and International Law,* edited by Mark W. Janis and Carolyn Evans, 483–504. The Hague: Martinus Nijhoff Publishers.

Giddens, Anthony. 1987. *The Nation-State and Violence.* Vol. 2 of *A Contemporary Critique of Historical Materialism.* Berkeley: University of California Press.

———. 1990. *The Consequences of Modernity.* Stanford, Calif.: Stanford University Press.

Gieryn, Thomas F. 1996. "Boundaries of Science." In *The Handbook of Science and Technology Studies,* edited by Sheila Jasanoff, Gerald E. Markle, James C. Petersen, and Trevor Pinch, 393–443. Thousand Oaks, Calif.: Sage Publications.

———. 1999. *Cultural Boundaries of Science: Credibility on the Line.* Chicago: University of Chicago Press.

Gilligan, Carol. 1993. *In a Different Voice: Psychological Theory and Women's Development.* Cambridge: Harvard University Press.

Gills, Barry K. Forthcoming. "Globalization as Global History: Introducing a Dialectical Analysis." In *Rethinking International Political Economy: Emerging Issues, Unfolding Odysseys,* edited by Mary Ann Tétreault, Robert A. Denemark, Kurt Burch, and Kenneth P. Thomas. London: Routledge.

Girard, René. 1977. *Violence and the Sacred.* Trans. Patrick Gregory. Baltimore, Md.: Johns Hopkins University Press.

Githens, Marianne, Pippa Norris, and Joni Lovenduski. 1994. Introduction to *Different Roles, Different Voices: Women and Politics in the United States and Europe.* New York: HarperCollins.

Glenny, Misha. 1994. "Council of Despair." *New York Times,* 6 December, A15.

Goldberg, Ellis. 1992. "Smashing Idols and the State: The Protestant Ethic and Egyptian Sunni Radicalism." In *Comparing Muslim Societies: Knowledge and the State in a World Civilization,* edited by Juan R. I. Cole, 195–236. Ann Arbor: University of Michigan Press.

Golden, Ian, and Odin Knudsen. 1990. *Agricultural Trade Liberalization: Implications for Developing Countries.* Paris: OECD/World Bank.

Golden, Steve, and Jim Knudsen, eds. 1990. *Agricultural Trade Liberalization: Implications for Developing Countries.* Paris: OECD/World Bank.

Gordon, Linda. 1986. "What's New in Women's Studies." In *Feminist Studies/Critical Studies,* edited by Teresa de Lauretis, 20–30. Bloomington: Indiana University Press.

Gould, Carol C. 1988. *Rethinking Democracy: Freedom and Social Cooperation in Politics, Economy, and Society.* Cambridge: Cambridge University Press.

Gould, Stephen Jay. 1996. *The Mismeasure of Man.* Rev. and expanded ed. New York: Norton.

Gourevitch, Philip. 1998. *We Wish to Inform You That Tomorrow We Will Be Killed with Our Families: Stories from Rwanda.* New York: Picador.

Graham, Loren R. 1993. *The Ghost of the Executed Engineer: Technology and the Fall of the Soviet Union.* Cambridge: Harvard University Press.

———. 1998. *What Have We Learned about Science and Technology from the Russian Experience?* Stanford, Calif.: Stanford University Press.

Gray, Clive S. 1997. "Technical Assistance and Capacity Building for Policy Analysis and Implementation." In *Getting Good Government: Capacity Building in the Public Sectors of Developing Countries,* edited by Merilee S. Grindle, 413–34. Cambridge: Harvard University Press.

Grewal, Inderpal, and Caren Kaplan. 1994. "Introduction: Transnational Feminist Practices and Questions of Postmodernity." In *Scattered Hegemonies: Postmodernity and Transnational Feminist Practices,* edited by Inderpal Grewal and Caren Kaplan, 1–33. Minneapolis and London: University of Minnesota Press.

Grieco, John. 1988. "Anarchy and the Limits of Cooperation: A Realist Critique of the Newest Liberal Institutionalism." *International Organization* 42, no. 3: 485–507.

Griffin, Susan. 1989. "This Earth Is My Sister." In *Weaving the Visions: New Patterns in Feminist Spirituality,* edited by Judith Plaskow and Carol P. Christ, 105–10. San Francisco: Harper and Row.

Grunell, Marianne. 1995. "Feminism Meets Scepticism: Women's Studies in the Czech Republic." *European Journal of Women's Studies* 2: 101–11.

Grupta, Aarti. 1999. "Framing 'Biosafety' in a Transnational Context: The Biosafety Protocol Negotiations under the Convention on Biological Diversity." ENRP Discussion Paper E-99-10, Kennedy School of Government, Harvard University.

Guelke, Adrian. 2000. "Goodbye to All That." *Fortnight* (Belfast) No. 386 (June): 10–11.

Guinier, Lani. 1994. "No Two Seats: The Elusive Quest for Political Equality." In *The Tyranny of the Majority: Fundamental Fairness in Representative Democracy.* New York: Free Press.

Haas, Ernst B. 1983. "Words Can Hurt You: Or, Who Said What to Whom about Regimes." In *International Regimes*, edited by Stephen D. Krasner, 23–60. Ithaca, N.Y.: Cornell University Press.

——— 1990. *When Knowledge Is Power.* Berkeley: University of California Press.

Haas, Peter. 1989. "Do Regimes Matter? Epistemic Communities and Knowledge in World Politics." *International Organization* 43, no. 4: 377–404.

———. 1990. *Saving the Mediterranean: The Politics of International Environmental Cooperation.* New York: Columbia University Press.

———, ed. 1992. *Knowledge, Power, and International Policy Coordination*, a special issue of *International Organization*, vol. 46, no. 1. Also published as Haas, ed. 1997. *Knowledge, Power, and International Policy Coordination.* Columbia: University of South Carolina Press.

Haftendorn, Helga. 1991. "The Security Puzzle: Theory-Building and Discipline Building in International Security." *International Studies Quarterly* 35, no. 1: 3–17.

Halberstam, David. 2001. *War in a Time of Peace.* New York: Scribner.

Halloran, Richard. 1997. "Jiang Plans Imperial Procession into the International Spotlight." *Washington Times*, 13 October, A1.

Halpern, David M. 1990. "The Democratic Body: Prostitution and Citizenship in Classical Athens." In *One Hundred Years of Homosexuality and Other Essays on Greek Love.* New York: Routledge.

Hanan, Stephen Mo. 2001. "The Source of Each Other's Completion." *Tikkun*, January/February, 65–68, 79.

Haraway, Donna. 1991. *Simians, Cyborgs, and Women: The Reinvention of Nature.* New York: Routledge.

———. 1997. *Modest_Witness@Second_Millennium.FemaleMan©_Meets_Oncomouse™: Feminism and Technoscience.* New York: Routledge.

Harding, Sandra. 1986. *The Science Question in Feminism.* Ithaca, N.Y.: Cornell University Press.

———. 1991. *Whose Science? Whose Knowledge?* Ithaca, N.Y.: Cornell University Press.

———. 1993. "Rethinking Standpoint Epistemology: 'What is Strong Objectivity?'" In *Feminist Epistemologies*, edited by Linda Alcoff and Elizabeth Potter. New York: Routledge, 49–82.

———, ed. 1987. *Feminism and Methodology.* Bloomington: Indiana University Press.

Harris, John F. 1997. "Clinton Vows to Bring Up Rights Issue." *Washington Post*, 25 October, A1.

Harrison, Beverly Wildung. 1989. "The Power of Anger in the Work of Love: Christian Ethics for Women and Other Strangers." In *Weaving the Visions: New Patterns in Feminist Spirituality*, edited by Judith Plaskow and Carol P. Christ, 214–23. San Francisco: Harper and Row.

Hartman, Carol R., and Ann Wolbert Burgess. 1998. "Rape Trauma and Treatment of the Victim." In *Post-Traumatic Therapy and Victims of Violence*, edited by F. M. Ochberg, 152–74. New York: Brunner Mazel.

Harvey, David. 1989. *The Condition of Postmodernity: An Enquiry into the Origins of Cultural Change.* Cambridge, U.K.: Blackwell.

Hauser, Eva. 1992. "Mind the Gap! Women from Post-Communist Countries: Conservatism or Progressivism?" *Women: A Cultural Review* 3 (Winter): 238–44.

———. 1995. "How and Why Do Czech Women Organize? (Altos, Sopranos, and a Few Discordant Voices)." *Canadian Women's Studies/Les Cahiers de la Femme* 16, no. 1: 85–89.

Hauserová, Eva. 1997. "Cosmopolitan a harlequinky: plíživá emancipace ze Západu" (Cosmopolitan and Harlequin Books: Sneaky Emancipation from the West). Translated by Radka Zimová. *Jedním okem/One Eye Open, Women's Issues in Central and Eastern Europe* (Prague, Gender Studies Centre) 5 (Summer): 9–17.

Havel, Václav. 1997. "A Sense of the Transcendent: Address to the National Press Club in Canberra, Australia, 29 March 1995." In *The Art of the Impossible: Politics as Morality in Practice,* edited by Václav Havel and Paul Wilson. New York: Alfred A. Knopf.

———. 1999. "Kosovo and the End of the Nation-State." Translated by Paul Wilson. *New York Review of Books,* 10 June, 4, 6.

Havelková, Hana. 1996. "Abstract Citizenship? Women and Power in the Czech Republic." *Social Politics* 2, no. 3 (Summer/Fall): 243–60.

———. 1999. "Affidamento" (Trust). In *Nové čtení světa, feminismus devadesátých let Českýma očima (New readings of the world: feminism of the 1990s through Czech eyes),* edited by Marie Chřibková, Josef Chuchma, and Eva Klimentová, 46–64, Prague: One Woman Press.

Hayner, Priscilla B. 1995. "Digging Up the Past: Do Truth Commissions Cause Conflict?" Paper presented at the annual meeting of the International Studies Association, Chicago, 22 February.

Hays, Samuel P. 1968. *Conservation and the Gospel of Efficiency: The Progressive Conservation Movement, 1890–1920.* 2d ed. Cambridge: Harvard University Press.

Hekman, Susan J. 1999. *The Future of Differences: Truth and Method in Feminist Theory.* Cambridge,U.K.: Polity Press.

Helsinki Watch. 1993. *War Crimes in Bosnia-Hercegovina.* vol. 2. New York: Human Rights Watch.

Hershman, Marcie. 2001. "Here I Am." *Tikkun,* March/April, 51–54.

Heyward, Carter. 1989. "Sexuality, Love, and Justice." In *Weaving the Visions: New Patterns in Feminist Spirituality,* edited by Judith Plaskow and Carol P. Christ, 293–301. San Francisco: Harper and Row.

Hicks, Donna. 1990. "An Analysis of Global Security from the Perspective of Cognitive Development." Paper delivered at the annual meeting of the International Studies Association, Washington, D.C., 10–14 April.

Hicks, Donna, and Karen Walch. 1992. "Quality Relationships: Personal and Political." Paper delivered at the annual meeting of the International Society for Political Psychology, San Francisco, 4–8 July.

Hirsch, Marianne, and Evelyn Fox Keller, eds. 1990. *Conflicts in Feminism.* New York and London: Routledge.

Hobsbawm, Eric J., and Terence Ranger, eds. 1992. *The Invention of Tradition.* Cambridge: Cambridge University Press.

Honig, Bonnie. 1999. "My Culture Made Me Do It." In *Is Multiculturalism Bad for Women?* edited by Joshua Cohen, Matthew Howard, and Martha C. Nussbaum, 35–40. Princeton, N.J.: Princeton University Press.

Honoré, A. M. 1961. "Ownership." In *Oxford Essays in Jurisprudence,* edited by A. E. Guest, 107. Oxford: Oxford University Press.

hooks, bell. 1995. *Killing Rage, Ending Racism.* New York: Holt and Company.

Hooper, Charlotte. 1998. "Masculinist Practices and Gender Politics: The Operation of Multiple Masculinities in International Relations." In *The "Man" Question in International Relations,* edited by Marysia Zalewski and Jane Parpart, 28–53. Boulder, Colo.: Westview.

Horowitz, Irving Louis. 1980. *Taking Lives: Genocide and State Power.* New Brunswick, N.J.: Transaction Books.

Howard, Rhoda E. 1995. *Human Rights and the Search for Community.* Boulder, Colo.: Westview Press.

Human Rights Watch/Africa, Human Rights Watch Women's Rights Project, and Federation Internationale des Ligues des Droits de l'Homme. 1996. "Shattered Lives: Sexual Violence During the Rwandan Genocide and Its Aftermath." New York: Human Rights Watch.

Human Rights Watch National Coalition for Haitian Refugees. 1994. *Rape in Haiti: A Weapon of Terror.* Washington: Human Rights Watch.

Hunt, Lynn. 1984. *Politics, Culture, and Class in the French Revolution.* Berkeley: University of California Press.

Ikenberry, John, and Charles Kupchan. 1989. "Socialization and Hegemonic Power." *International Organization* 44, no. 4: 283–316.

Ingle, Róisín. 2000. "Meeting of All Pro-Agreement Parties Urged." *Irish Times* 20 November. http://scripts.ireland.com/special/peace/ . . . om/newspaper/ireland/2000/1120/north8.htm (3 January 2001).

Iowa State University Dean of Students Office. "Greek Affairs: Greek Facts . . . Did You Know?" http://www.dso.iastate.edu/ DSO Departments/Greek Affairs/Did You Know?/Greek Facts (6 June 2002).

Irish News (Belfast). January 1997–July 2001.

Irish Times (Dublin). January 1997–July 2001.

Jackson, Robert. 1990. *Quasi-states: Sovereignty, International Relations and the Third World.* Cambridge: Cambridge University Press.

Jackson-Han, Sarah, and James Robinson. 1997. "Huge Protest against Jiang Expected as He Meets with Clinton." *Agence France Presse,* 28 October.

Jagiełło, Małgorzata, ed. 1997. *Informator o organizacjach i inichatywach kobiecych w Polsce.* Warsaw: Center for the Advancement of Women.

James, William. 1936. *The Varieties of Religious Experience: A Study in Human Nature.* New York: Modern Library.

Jasanoff, Sheila. 1986. *Risk Management and Political Culture.* New York: Russell Sage Foundation.

———. 1990. *The Fifth Branch: Science Advisers as Policymakers.* Cambridge: Harvard University Press.

———. 1991. "Acceptable Evidence in a Pluralistic Society." In *Acceptable Evidence,* edited by Deborah Mayo and Rachelle Hollander, 29–47. Oxford: Oxford University Press.

———. 1995. "Product, Process, or Programme: Three Cultures and the Regulation of Biotechnology." In *Resistance to New Technology,* edited by M. Bauer, 311–31. Cambridge: Cambridge University Press.

———. 1996. *Science at the Bar: Law, Science and Technology in America.* Cambridge: Harvard University Press.

———. 1996. "Science and Norms in Global Environmental Regimes." In *Earthly Goods: Environmental Change and Social Justice,* edited by Fen O. Hamson and Judith Reppy, 173–97. Ithaca, N.Y.: Cornell University Press.

———. 1999. Review of *A House Built on Sand: Exposing Postmodern Myths about Science,* edited by Noretta Koertge. *Science, Technology, and Human Values* 24, no. 4: 495–500.

———. 2001. "Image and Imagination: The Emergence of Global Environmental Consciousness." In *Changing the Atmosphere: Expert Knowledge and Environmental Governance,* edited by Clark Miller and Paul Edwards, 309–37. Cambridge: MIT Press.

Jerdee, T., and Benson Rosen. 1974. "Effects of Opportunity to Communicate and Visibility of Individual Decisions on Behavior in the Common Interest." *Journal of Applied Psychology* 59, no. 5 (Summer): 55–77.

Jervis, Robert. 1988. "Realism, Game Theory, and Cooperation." *World Politics* 40, no. 3: 317–49.

Johnson, Elizabeth A. 1992. *She Who Is: The Mystery of God in Feminist Theological Discourse.* New York: The Crossroad Publishing Company.

Johnson, Miriam M. 1988. *Strong Mothers, Weak Wives: The Search for Gender Equality.* Berkeley: University of California Press.

Kačánová, Jitka, and Jarmila Pávková. 1999. "Život může být jako krasohled, Rozhovor s Jiřinou Šiklovou" (The world can be a beautiful kaleidoscope, interview with Jiřina Šiklová). *Incognito* 1: 9–11.

Kahler, Miles. 1992. "Multilateralism with Small and Large Numbers." *International Organization* 46, no. 7 (Summer): 33–40.

Kaplan, Caren. 1990. "Deterritorializations: The Rewriting of Home and Exile in Western Feminist Discourse." In *The Nature and Context of Minority Discourse,* edited by Abdul R. JanMohamed and David Lloyd, 357–68. Oxford: Oxford University Press.

———. 1994. "The Politics of Location as Transnational Critical Practice." In *Scattered Hegemonies: Postmodernity and Transnational Feminist Practices,* edited by Inderpal Grewal and Caren Kaplan, 137–52. Minneapolis: University of Minnesota Press.

Kappa Alpha Theta. "Kappa Alpha Theta Facts." http://www.kappaalphatheta.org/What Is Theta/Theta Facts (6 June 2002).

———. "Theta through the Decades—1870s." http://www.kappaalphtheta.org/What Is Theta/Theta through the Decades/1870 (6 June 2002).

Karam, Azza. "Shifting Focus: From the Road to Parliament to Making Inroads in Parliament." *Women in Parliament. Beyond Numbers.* http://www.idea.int/women/parl/ch1b.htm (10 June 2002).

Karpinski, Eva. 1995. "Do Polish Women Need Feminism?" *Canadian Woman's Studies/Les Cahiers de la Femme* 16, no. 1: 91–94.

Keck, Margaret E., and Kathryn Sikkink, eds. 1998. *Activists Beyond Borders: Advocacy Networks in International Politics.* Ithaca, N.Y.: Cornell University Press.

Keller, Evelyn Fox. 1993. *A Feeling for the Organism: The Life and World of Barbara McClintock.* San Francisco: W. H. Freeman.

———. 1996. *Reflections on Gender and Science.* New Haven, Conn.: Yale University Press.

Kelley, Jack. 1997. "Protesters Prepare for Chinese Leader's Visit; China Officials are Concerned about Images." *USA Today,* 17 October, 8A.

Kelman, Herbert. 1979. "An International Approach to Conflict Resolution and Its Application to Israeli and Palestinian Relations." *International Interactions* 6, no. 6 (Spring): 25–40.

Kempster, Norman. 1997. "Chinese Leader's Visit to U.S. Stirs Protesters; Rights: Activists Will Spotlight Beijing's Much-Criticized Record on Prisoners, Free Speech, Religion and Tibet." *Los Angeles Times,* 23 October, A6.

Kennedy, David. 1999. "Losing Faith in the Secular: Law, Religion, and the Culture of International Governance." In *Religion and International Law,* edited by Mark W. Janis and Carolyn Evans, 309–19. The Hague: Martinus Nijhoff Publishers.

Kenworthy, Lane, and Melissa Malami. 1999. "Gender Inequality in Political Representation: A Worldwide Comparative Analysis." *Social Forces* 78, no. 1 (September): 235–68.

Keohane, Robert. 1984. *After Hegemony: Cooperation and Discord in the World Political Economy.* Princeton, N.J.: Princeton University Press.

———. 1986. "Realism, Neorealism and the Study of World Politics." In *Neorealism and Its Critics: The Political Economy of International Change.* New York: Columbia University Press.

———. 1988. "International Institutions: Two Approaches." *International Studies Quarterly* 32, no. 4: 379–96.

———. 1990. "Multilateralism: An Agenda for Research." *International Journal* 45, no. 8: 731–50.

Keohane, Robert, and Joseph Nye. 1977. *Power and Interdependence: World Politics in Transition.* Boston: Little, Brown.

Keohane, Robert, and Marc Levy, eds. 1996. *Institutions for Environmental Aid: Pitfalls and Promise.* Cambridge: MIT Press.

Kettle, Martin. 1997. "'Stateless' Make Meal of Jiang's Visit." *Guardian* (Manchester), 29 October, 16.

Keuls, Eva C. 1985. *The Reign of the Phallus: Sexual Politics in Ancient Athens.* Berkeley: University of California Press.

Khong, Yuen Foong. 1992. *Analogies at War.* Princeton, N.J.: Princeton University Press.

Kilpatrick, Dean G., and Lois J. Veronen. 1983. "Treatment for Rape-Related Problems: Crisis Intervention is Not Enough." In *Crisis Intervention,* edited by L. H. Cohen, W. Claiborn and G. Specter, 165–85. New York: Human Sciences Press.

Kindleberger, Charles. 1983. "On the Rise and Decline of Nations." *International Studies Quarterly* 27, no. 6: 5–10.

Komorita, Samuel S., and C. Willia Lapworth. 1982. "Cooperative Choice among Individuals versus Groups in an N-prisoner's Dilemma Situation." *Journal of Personality and Social Psychology* 42, no. 3 (March): 487–96.

Kopinska, Grażyna. 1999. "Ogranizczenia i teriery w aktywnym uczestnictwie kobiet w życiu publicznym." Presented at *Kobiety w Samorzyądzie Terytorialnym,* Kraków, Poland, 8 March.

Krasner, Stephen D. 1983. "Structural Causes and Regime Consequences: Regimes as Intervening Variables." In *International Regimes,* edited by Stephen D. Krasner, 1–21. Ithaca, N.Y.: Cornell University Press.

Kriesberg, Louis. 1989. "Interpersonal Factors, Structural Factors, and Conflict Resolution Strategies." In *Peace: Meanings, Politics, Strategies,* edited by Linda Rennie Forcey, 163–75. New York: Praeger.

Kupchan, Charles, and Clifford Kupchan. 1991. "Concerts, Collective Security, and the Future of Europe." *International Security* 16, no. 1 (Summer): 114–61.

Kuzmanović, Jasmina. 1995. "Legacies of Invisibility: Past Silence, Present Violence Against Women in the Former Yugoslavia." In *Women's Rights, Human Rights:*

International Feminist Perspectives, edited by Julie Peters and Andrea Wolper, 57–61. New York: Routledge.

Kymlicka, Will. 1999. "Liberal Complacencies." In *Is Multiculturalism Bad for Women?* edited by Joshua Cohen, Matthew Howard, and Martha C. Nussbaum, 31–34. Princeton, N.J.: Princeton University Press.

Lairap-Fonderson, Josephine. 2002. "The Disciplinary Power of Micro Credit: Examples from Kenya and Cameroon." In *Rethinking Empowerment: Gender and Development in a Global/Local World,* edited by Jane L. Parpart, Shirin M. Rai, and Kathleen A. Staudt. London: Routledge.

Lancaster, John. 1993. "Administration Releases Report on Iraqi War Crimes in Kuwait." *Washington Post,* 20 March, A18.

Laroche, Beatrice. 1997. "Dodging Scrutiny: China and the U.N. Commission on Human Rights." *China Rights Forum* (Summer): 20–23.

Latour, Bruno. 1983. "Give Me a Laboratory and I Will Raise the World." In *Science Observed,* edited by Karin Knorr-Cetina and Michael Mulkay, 141–70. London: Sage.

———. 1987. *Science in Action.* Cambridge: Harvard University Press.

———. 1988. *The Pasteurization of France.* Cambridge: Harvard University Press.

———. 1993. *We Have Never Been Modern.* Cambridge: Harvard University Press.

———. 1999. *Pandora's Hope: Essays on the Reality of Science Studies.* Cambridge: Harvard University Press.

Lawless, Elaine. 1992. "'I Was Afraid Someone Like You . . . an Outsider . . . Would Misunderstand': Negotiating Interpretive Differences between Ethnographers and Subjects." *Journal of American Folklore* 105, no. 417: 302–14.

Lecheheb, Abdelkadar. 1993. "Les problèmes des pays en développement importateurs nets de produits alimentaires dans le cadre des négociations de l'Uruguay Round sur l'agriculture." New York: United Nations Commission on Trade and Development report.

Lerner, Michael. 2001. "An Interview with Senator Paul Wellstone." *Tikkun,* March/April, 9–10.

———. 2001. "Surviving the Bush and Sharon Years." *Tikkun,* March/April, 5–8.

Lewin, Tamar. 1993. "The Balkans Rapes: A Legal Test for the Outraged." *New York Times,* 15 January, B15.

Lewis, Anthony. 1994. "The Civilized World." *New York Times,* 1 July, A17.

———. 1995. "No Peace without Justice." *New York Times,* 20 November, A11.

Lewis, Justin. 1997. "What Counts in Cultural Studies." *Media, Culture and Society* 19: 83–97.

Lewis, Paul. 1992. "U.N. Sets Up War-Crimes Panel on Charges of Balkan Atrocities." *New York Times,* 7 October, A1, A6.

———. 1993. "Disputes Hamper U.N. Drive For a War Crimes Tribunal." *New York Times,* 9 September, A10.

———. 1993. "Security Council Establishes War-Crimes Tribunal for the Balkans." *New York Times,* 26 May, A13.

———. 1994. "If There Ever Were a Nuremburg for the Former Yugoslavia . . ." *New York Times,* 12 June, E7.

Limanowska, Barbara. 1999. Interviewed by Diane M. Duffy. Warsaw, Poland, 6 May.

Lin, Echo. 1997. Letter to Abigail Abrash. 10 October.

Lines, Patricia. 2000. "Homeschooling Comes of Age." *Public Interest* 140 (Summer): 74–85.

Lipschutz, Ronnie D. 1997. "From Place to Planet: Local Knowledge and Global Environmental Governance." *Global Governance* 3, no. 1 (January–April): 83–102.

———. 2000. *After Authority: War, Peace and Global Politics in the 21st Century.* Albany: State University of New York Press.

———. 2001. "Environmental History, Political Economy and Change: Frameworks and Tools for Research and Analysis." *Global Environmental Politics* 1, no. 3 (Fall): 72–91.

Lipschutz, Ronnie D., with Judith Mayer. 1996. *Global Civil Society and Global Environmental Governance.* Albany: State University of New York Press.

Lipsitz, George. 1990. *Time Passages: Collective Memory and American Popular Culture.* Minneapolis: University of Minnesota Press.

Litfin, Karen. 1994. *Ozone Discourses: Science and Politics in Global Environmental Cooperation.* New York: Columbia University Press.

Long, Norman. 1992. "From Paradigm Lost to Paradigm Regained? The Case for an Actor-Oriented Sociology of Development." In *Battlefields of Knowledge: The Interlocking of Theory and Practice in Social Research and Development,* edited by Norman Long and Ann Long, 16–43. London: Routledge.

Long-Martello, Marybeth. 2001. "A Paradox of Virtue? 'Other' Knowledges and Environment-Development Politics." *Global Environmental Politics* 1, no. 3: 114–41.

Lugones, Maria. 1990. "Playfulness, 'World'-Travelling, and Loving Perception." In *Making Face, Making Soul/Haciendo Caras: Creative and Critical Perpectives by Women of Color,* edited by Gloria Anzaldua, 390–402. San Francisco: Aunt Lute Foundation Books.

MacKinnon, Catherine. 1983. "Feminism, Marxism, Method, and the State: Toward a Feminist Jurisprudence." *Signs* 8, no. 4: 635–58.

———. 1993. "Turning Rape into Pornography: Postmodern Genocide." *Ms.,* July/August, 24–30.

Macpherson, C. B. 1962. *The Political Theory of Possessive Individualism: Hobbes to Locke.* Oxford: Oxford University Press.

Makau wa Mutua. 1996. "The Ideology of Human Rights." *Virginia Journal of International Law* 36: 589–657.

"Making the Crucial Leap to Mutual Trust." *Irish Times,* 8 May 2000. http://scripts.ireland.com/special/peace/...om/newspaper/ireland/2000/0508/north1.html (26 December 2000).

Makiya, Kanan. 1993. *Cruelty and Silence: War, Tyranny, Uprising, and the Arab World.* New York: Norton.

Mann, Jim. 1997. "Can Chinese Prosperity Yield Democracy?" International Outlook column. *Los Angeles Times,* 24 September.

Mann, Judy. 1991. "Kuwaiti Rape a Doubly Savage Crime." *Washington Post,* 29 March, C3.

Mansbridge, Jane. 1990. *Beyond Self-Interest* Chicago: University of Chicago Press.

Marchand, Marianne H., and Anne Sisson Runyan, eds. 2000. *Gender and Global Restructuring: Sightings, Sites and Resistances.* London and New York: Routledge.

Marcus, David L. 1997. "Groups Plan Protests during Jiang Visit to US." *Boston Globe,* 9 October, A2.

Marody, Mirosława. 1987. "Social Stability and the Concept of Collective Sense." In *Crisis and Transition: Polish Society in the 1980s,* edited by I. Bialecki, I. Koralewicz, and M. Watson, 130–58. London: Berg.

Marshall, John. 1992. "Why Rational Egoism Is Not Consistent." *Review of Metaphysics* 45, no. 4 (June): 713–37.

Martin, Patricia Yancey. 1990. "Rethinking Feminist Organizations." *Gender and Society* 4, no. 2 (June): 182–206.

Marx, Karl. 1967. *Capital: A Critique of Political Economy.* 3 vols. Edited by Frederick Engels. New York: International Publishers.

Mayer, Ann Elizabeth. 1995. "Rhetorical Strategies and Official Policies on Women's Rights: The Merits and Drawbacks of the New World Hypocrisy." In *Faith and Freedom: Women's Human Rights in the Muslim World,* edited by Mahnaz Afkhami, 104–32. Syracuse, N.Y.: Syracuse University Press.

McCabe, Barbara. 1997. Address to the Women's Studies Centre Seminar Series, at University College, Galway, Ireland, 15 May.

McCay, Mary A. 1993. *Rachel Carson.* New York: Twayne Publishers.

McWilliams, Monica. 1991. "Women in Northern Ireland: An Overview." In *Culture and Politics in Northern Ireland, 1960–1990,* edited by Eamonn Hughes, 81–100. Philadelphia. Open University Press.

———. 1995. "Struggling for Peace and Justice: Reflections on Women's Activism in Northern Ireland." *Journal of Women's History* 6/7 (Winter/Spring): 13–39.

———. 1997. "Women and Society in Northern Ireland." Address to the CIEE International Faculty Development Seminar: Conflict Resolution: On the Threshold of Peace in Northern Ireland, Council on International Educational Exchange and University of Ulster, Coleraine, Ireland, 7 January.

Medicine Eagle, Brooke. 1991. *Buffalo Woman Comes Singing: The Spirit Song of a Rainbow Medicine Woman.* New York: Ballantine Books.

Meighan, Roland. 1995. "Home-Based Education Effectiveness Research and Some of Its Implications." *Educational Review* 47, no. 3 (November): 275–87.

Melvern, Linda. 1995. *The Ultimate Crime: Who Betrayed the UN and Why.* London: Wilson and Day Ltd.

Merchant, Carolyn. 1980. *The Death of Nature: Women, Ecology, and the Scientific Revolution.* New York: Harper and Row.

Mernissi, Fatima. 1991. *The Veil and the Male Elite: A Feminist Interpretation of Women's Rights in Islam.* Translated by Mary Jo Lakeland. Reading, Mass.: Addison Wesley.

Merton, Robert K. 1973. *The Sociology of Science: Theoretical and Empirical Investigations.* Chicago: University of Chicago Press.

Meyer, Mary K. 2000. "Ulster's Red Hand: Gender, Identity, and Sectarian Conflict in Northern Ireland." In *Women, States, and Nationalism: At Home in the Nation?* edited by Sita Ranchod-Nilsson and Mary Ann Tétreault, 119–42. New York: Routledge.

———, and Elisabeth Prügl, eds. 1999. *Gender Politics in Global Governance.* Boulder, Colo.: Rowman and Littlefield.

Miller, Clark A. 2001. "Challenges to the Application of Science to Global Affairs: Contingency, Trust, and Moral Order." In *Changing the Atmosphere: Expert*

Knowledge and Environmental Governance, edited by Clark A. Miller and Paul N. Edwards, 247–86. Cambridge: MIT Press.

———. 2001. “Scientific Internationalism in American Foreign Policy: The Case of Meteorology (1947–1958).” In *Changing the Atmosphere: Expert Knowledge and Environmental Governance,* edited by Clark Miller and Paul Edwards, 167–218. Cambridge: MIT Press.

———. Forthcoming. “Hybrid Management: Boundary Organizations, Science Policy, and Environmental Governance in the Climate Regime.” *Science, Technology and Human Values.*

———. Forthcoming. “Undermining the Postwar Settlement: Climate Science and the Reconstruction of Global Order.” In *States of Knowledge: Science, Power, and Political Culture,* edited by Sheila S. Jasanoff.

Miller, Clark A., and Paul N. Edwards. 2001. “Introduction: The Globalization of Climate Science and Climate Politics.” In *Changing the Atmosphere: Expert Knowledge and Environmental Governance,* edited by Clark A. Miller and Paul N. Edwards, 1–30. Cambridge: MIT Press.

Mitchell, George J. 1999. *Making Peace.* New York: Alfred A. Knopf.

Mittermeier, Russell, Norman Myers, and Cristina Goettsch Mittermeier, eds. 2000. *Hotspots: Earth's Biologically Richest and Most Endangered Terrestrial Ecoregions.* Mexico City: CEMEX International.

Mohanty, Chandra Talpade. 1986. “Feminist Politics: What's Home Got to Do with It?” In *Feminist Studies/Critical Studies,* edited by Teresa de Lauretis, 190–211. Bloomington: Indiana University Press.

———. 1989. “On Race and Voice: Challenges for Liberal Education in the 1990s.” *Cultural Critique* 14: 179–208.

———. 1991. “Cartographies of Struggle: Third World Women and the Politics of Feminism.” In *Third World Women and the Politics of Feminism,* edited by C. Mohanty, A. Rosso, and L. Torres, 1–43. Bloomington: Indiana University Press.

———. 1992. “Feminist Encounters: Locating the Politics of Experience.” In *Destabilizing Theory, Contemporary Feminism Debates,* edited by Michele Barrett and Anne Phillips. London: Polity Press.

———. 1997. “Women Workers and Capitalist Scripts: Ideologies of Domination, Common Interests, and the Politics of Solidarity.” In *Feminist Genealogies, Colonial Legacies, Democratic Futures,* edited by M. Jacqui Alexander and Chandra Talpade Mohanty, 3–29. New York and London: Routledge.

Molnar, Alex. 1996. *Giving Kids the Business.* Boulder, Colo.: Westview Press.

Molyneux, Maxine. 1985. “Mobilization without Emancipation? Women's Interests, the State, and Revolution in Nicaragua.” *Feminist Studies* 11, no. 2: 227–54.

———. 1998. “Analyzing Women's Movements.” *Development and Change* 29: 219–45.

Morgan, Edmund S. 1997. “America's First Great Man.” *New York Review of Books,* 12 June, 42–44.

Morgan, Valerie, and Grace Fraser. 1994. *The Company We Keep: Women, Community, and Organisations.* Coleraine: Centre for the Study of Conflict and Centre for Research on Women, University of Ulster.

Morganthau, Hans. 1948. *Politics among Nations: The Struggle for Power and Peace.* New York: Alfred A. Knopf.

Mosse, George L. 1985. *Nationalism and Sexuality: Respectability and Abnormal Sexuality in Modern Europe.* New York: Howard Fertig.

Al-Mughni, Haya, and Fawzia al-Turkait. 1994. "Dealing with Trauma: Cultural Barriers to Self-Recovery: The Case of Kuwaiti Women." Paper presented at the seminar on The Effective Methods for Encountering the Psychological and the Social Effects of the Iraqi Aggression, sponsored by the Social Development Office of the Amiri Diwan, Kuwait City, 26–28 March.

Mumford, Lewis. 1954. *In the Name of Sanity.* Westport, Conn.: Greenwood Press.

Myers, Charles N. 1997. "Policy Research Institutes in Developing Countries." In *Getting Good Government: Capacity Building in the Public Sectors of Developing Countries,* edited by Merilee S. Grindle, 177–98. Cambridge: Harvard University Press.

Nafziger, James A. R. 1999. "The Functions of Religion in the International Legal System." In *Religion and International Law,* edited by Mark W. Janis and Carolyn Evans, 155–76. The Hague: Martinus Nijhoff Publishers.

Nanda, Meera. 1998. "The Epistemic Charity of the Social Constructivist Critics of Science and Why the Third World Should Refuse the Offer." In *A House Built on Sand: Exposing Postmodernist Myths about Science,* edited by Noretta Koertge, 286–311. Oxford: Oxford University Press.

Narayan, Uma. 1997. *Dislocating Cultures: Identities, Traditions, and Third World Feminism.* New York and London: Routledge.

Nelkin, Dorothy. 1992. *Controversy: Politics of Technical Decisions.* 3d ed. Newbury Park, Calif.: Sage.

New York Times. 1992. "Rape—And Soldiers' Morale." Editorial, 7 December, A18.

News. Office of Congressman Lane Evans. 30 September 1997.

News from U.S. Senator Russ Feingold. 25 September 1997.

Newstone, David. 2001. "Democracy, the State, and the Political Imagination: The Power of Sovereign Stories in the Context of 'Globalization.'" Paper presented at the 42nd annual convention of the International Studies Association, 20–24 February, Chicago.

Nicholls, Todd R. 2000. "Breaking Barriers for Political Acceptance." *Irish News,* 11 December. http://www.irishnews.com/archive2000/11122000/politics1.html (11 December 2000).

Niou, Emerson, and Peter Ordeshook. 1991. "Realism vs. Neoliberalism: A Formation." *American Journal of Political Science* 35, no. 6 (Spring): 481–511.

Nitzan, Jonathan. Forthcoming. "Mergers, Stagflation, and the Logic of Globalization." In *Rethinking International Political Economy: Emerging Issues, Unfolding Odysseys,* edited by Mary Ann Tétreault, Robert A. Denemark, Kurt Burch, and Kenneth P. Thomas. London: Routledge.

Nolan, Janne E., and John D. Steinbrunner. 1994. "A Transition Strategy for the 1990s." In *Global Engagement: Cooperation and Security in the 21st Century,* edited by Janne E. Nolan, 573–93. Washington, D.C.: Brookings Institution.

Nordstrom, Carolyn. 1997. *A Different Kind of War Story.* Philadelphia: University of Pennsylvania Press.

Norris, Kathleen. 1998. *Amazing Grace: A Vocabulary of Faith.* New York: Riverhead Books.

Northern Ireland Forum for Political Dialogue. 1997. *Record of Debates.* No. 38. Friday, 11 July. Castle Buildings, Stormont. Belfast, Northern Ireland.

Nowakowska, Ursula. 1999. Interviewed by Diane M. Duffy. Warsaw, Poland, 12 May.

Nowicka, Wanda. February 1997. "Reproductive Health of Women in Poland." Report of the Federation for Women and Family Planning, Warsaw, Poland.

———. 1998. "Factors Affecting Women's Health in Eastern and Central Europe with Particular Emphasis on Infectious Diseases, Mental, Environmental and Reproductive Health." Paper prepared for Women and Health: Mainstreaming the Gender Perspective into the Health Sector, Expert Group Meeting, WHO, Tunis, 28 September–2 October.

———. 1999. Interviewed by Diane M. Duffy. Warsaw, Poland, 20 May.

Nussbaum, Martha C. 1977. "Kant and Stoic Cosmopolitanism." *Journal of Political Philosophy* 5, no. 1: 1–25.

———. 1995. *Poetic Justice: The Literary Imagination and Public Life*. Boston: Beacon Press.

———. 2000. *Women and Human Development: The Capabilities Approach*. Cambridge: Cambridge University Press.

Okin, Susan Moller. 1979. "Rousseau's Natural Woman." *Journal of Politics* 41, no. 2 (May) 393–416.

———. 1979. *Women in Western Political Thought*. Princeton, N.J.: Princeton University Press.

———. 1989. *Justice, Gender, and the Family*. New York: Basic Books.

———. 1999. "Reply." In *Is Multiculturalism Bad for Women?* edited by Joshua Cohen, Matthew Howard, and Martha C. Nussbaum, 117–31. Princeton, N.J.: Princeton University Press.

Olson, David, and Eric Dinerstein. 1998. *The Global 200: A Representation Approach to Conserving the Earth's Distinct Ecoregions*. Washington, D.C.: World Wildlife Fund.

Onuf, Nicholas. 1989. *World of Our Making*. Columbia: University of South Carolina Press.

Orfield, Gary, and John Yun. 1999. "Resegregation in American Schools." The Civil Rights Project, Harvard University. June 1999. http://www.law.harvard.edu/civilrights/publications/resegregation99/resegregation99.html (25 April 2002).

Owen, Barbara. 1998. *"In the Mix": Struggle and Survival in a Women's Prison*. Albany: State University of New York Press.

Pagels, Elaine. 1988. *Adam, Eve, and the Serpent*. New York: Random House.

Paisley, Rhonda. 1992. "Feminism, Unionism, and 'The Brotherhood.'" *Irish Reporter* 8, no. 4: 32–33.

Parker, Andrew, Mary Russo, Doris Sommer, and Patricia Yaeger, eds. 1992. *Nationalisms and Sexualities*. New York: Routledge.

Pateman, Carole. 1988. "The Fraternal Social Contract." In *Civil Society and the State*, edited by John Keane, 101–27. London: Verso.

———. 1988. *The Sexual Contract*. Stanford, Calif.: Stanford University Press.

———. 1991. "'God Hath Ordained to Man a Helper': Hobbes, Patriarchy, and Conjugal Right." In *Feminist Interpretations and Political Theory*, edited by Mary Lyndon Shanley and Carole Pateman, 53–73. University Park: Pennsylvania State University Press.

Payne, Katy [Katharine]. 1998. *Silent Thunder: In the Presence of Elephants*. New York: Simon and Schuster.

PBS. 1997. "Valentina's Nightmare." *Frontline*. FROL-509.

———. 1999. "The Triumph of Evil." *Frontline.* FROL-1710.

Penn, Shana. 1994. "The National Secret." *Journal of Women's History* 5, no. 3 (Winter): 55–69.

Peristiany, J. G. 1965. *Honor and Shame: The Values of Mediterranean Society.* London: Weidenfeld and Nicolson.

Perkins, John. 1997. *Geopolitics and the Green Revolution: Wheat, Genes, and the Cold War.* Oxford: Oxford University Press.

Peterson, V. Spike. 1988. "An Archaeology of Domination: Historicizing Gender and Class in Early Western State Formation." Ph.D. diss., American University.

———. 1994. "Gendered Nationalisms." *Peace Review* 6, no. 1: 77–83.

———. 2000. "Sexing Political Identities/Nationalism as Heterosexism." In *Women, States, and Nationalism: At Home in the Nation?* edited by Sita Ranchod-Nilsson and Mary Ann Tétreault, 54–80. New York: Routledge.

———. Forthcoming. "Analytical Advances to Address New Dynamics." In *Rethinking International Political Economy: Emerging Issues, Unfolding Odysseys,* edited by Mary Ann Tétreault, Robert A. Denemark, Kurt Burch, and Kenneth P. Thomas. London: Routledge.

Phillips, Anne. 1995. *The Politics of Presence.* Oxford: Clarendon Press.

Piaget, Jean. 1965. *The Moral Judgment of the Child.* New York: Free Press.

Piercy, Marge. 1976. *Woman on the Edge of Time.* New York: Fawcett Columbine.

Plaskow, Judith, and Carol P. Christ, eds. 1989. *Weaving the Visions: New Patterns in Feminist Spirituality.* San Francisco: Harper and Row.

Poland. Government Population Commission. 1995. *Demographic Situation of Poland.* Warsaw.

———. Office of the Plenipotentiary of the Polish Government for Family Affairs. 1995. "Report to the Fourth UN World Conference on Women." Warsaw, August.

———. Office of the Plenipotentiary of the Polish Government for Family Affairs. 1998. *Raport o Sytuacji Polskich Rodzin (Report on families).* Warsaw.

Polanyi, Karl. 1944. *The Great Transformation.* New York: Farrar and Rinehart; reprint, Boston: Beacon Press, 1957.

Polish Central Statistical Office. 1997. "Monitoring the Labor Market: Reasons Differentiating Salaries in Poland." Warsaw, Poland, February.

Polish Committee of NGOs. 1995. "The Situation of Women in Poland." Warsaw, Poland: Women's Rights Center.

Pomeroy, Sarah. 1975. *Goddesses, Whores, Wives, and Slaves.* New York: Schocken Books.

Population Concern. *The Population and Development Database.* Available on-line at http://www.alsagerschool.co.uk Subjects/Geography/Geography Population Software (9 May 2002).

Porter, Elizabeth. 1997. "Diversity and Commonality: Women, Politics and Northern Ireland." *The European Journal of Women's Studies* 4: 83–100.

Porter, Theodore. 1995. *Trust in Numbers: The Pursuit of Objectivity in Science and Public Life.* Princeton, N.J.: Princeton University Press.

Prestowitz, Clyde. 1994. "Comment." In *The New GATT: Implications for the United States,* edited by Susan M. Collins and Barry P. Bosworth, 78–80. Washington: Brookings Institution.

Proctor, Robert. 1988. *Racial Hygiene: Medicine under the Nazis.* Cambridge: Harvard University Press.

Protz, Roger. 1964. "Millions of Britons See Malcolm X in TV Broadcast of Debate at Oxford." *The Militant,* 14 December, 2.

Putnam, Robert D. 1993. *Making Democracy Work: Civic Traditions in Modern Italy.* Princeton, N.J.: Princeton University Press.

———. 2000. *Bowling Alone: The Collapse and Revival of American Community.* New York: Simon and Schuster.

Quindlen, Anna. 1993. "Gynocide." *New York Times,* 10 March, A19.

———. 1993. "The Rescuers." *New York Times,* 5 May, A23.

Ranchod-Nilsson, Sita, and Mary Ann Tétreault, eds. 2000. *Women, States, and Nationalism: At Home in the Nation?* New York: Routledge.

"Rape after Rape after Rape." 1992. *New York Times,* 13 December, E17.

Reardon, Jenny. 2001. "The Human Genome Diversity Project." *Social Studies of Science* 31, no. 3: 365–96.

Reisman, W. Michael, and Chris T. Antoniou, eds. 1994. *The Laws of War: A Comprehensive Collection of Primary Documents on International Laws Governing Armed Conflict.* New York: Vintage.

Remen, Rachel Naomi. 1996. *Kitchen Table Wisdom: Stories That Heal.* New York: Riverhead Books.

Riding, Alan. 1993. "European Inquiry Says Serbs' Forces Have Raped 20,000." *New York Times,* 9 January, 1, 4.

Rieff, David. 2000. "Nothing Was Delivered." *New Republic,* 1 May, 26–33.

Rierden, Andi. 1997. *The Farm: Life inside a Women's Prison.* Amherst: University of Massachusetts Press.

Riley, Denise. 1988. *"Am I That Name?" Feminism and the Category "Women" in History.* London: Macmillan.

Robbins, Carla Anne. 1993. "Balkan Judgments: World Again Confronts Moral Issues Involved in War-Crimes Trials." *Wall Street Journal,* 13 July, A1, A8.

Rosen, Ruth. 1990. "An Interview with Jiřina Šiklová." *Peace and Democracy News,* Fall, 33–38.

Ross, Karen. 2000. "Unruly Theory and Difficult Practice: Issues and Dilemmas in Work with Women Politicians." *International Feminist Journal of Politics* 2, no. 3 (Autumn): 319–36.

Rothman, Jay. 1991. "Negotiation as Consolidation: Prenegotiation in the Israeli-Palestinian Conflict." *Jerusalem Journal of International Relations* 13, no. 1 (March): 22–44.

———. 1992. *From Confrontation to Cooperation: Resolving Ethnic and Regional Strife.* Newbury Park: Sage Publications.

Rousseau, Jean Jacques. 1964. *The First and Second Discourses.* Edited, with introd. and notes, by Roger D. Masters, translated by Roger D. and Judith R. Masters. New York: St. Martin's Press.

Rowbotham, Sheila. 1989. *The Past Is before Us: Feminism and Action since the 1960s.* London: Pandora Press.

Roy, K. K. 1975. "Feelings and Attitudes of Raped Women of Bangladesh Towards Military Personnel of Pakistan." In *Exploiters and Exploited: The Dynamics of Victimization,* edited by Israel Drapkin and Emilio Viano, 65–72. Victimology: A New Focus, vol. 5. Lexington, Mass.: Lexington Books.

Ruane, Joseph, and Jennifer Todd. 1996. *The Dynamics of Conflict in Northern Ireland: Power, Conflict and Emancipation.* New York: Cambridge University Press.

Rubin, Alfred P. 1992. Letter to the editor. *New York Times,* 23 October, A32.

Rubin, Gayle. 1975. "The Traffic in Women: Notes on a Political Economy of Sex." In *Toward an Anthropology of Women,* edited by Rayna Reiter, 157–210. New York: Monthly Review Press.

Rubin, Judith. 2000 "Judge of Genocide." *Women's International Net Magazine* 33, A (31 May); this Internet journal is no longer on-line, page last accessed December 2001.

Ruggie, John G. 1992. "Multilateralism: The Anatomy of an Institution." *International Organization* 46, no. 6 (Summer): 35–46.

Runyan, Anne Sisson. 1999. "Women in the Neoliberal 'Frame.'" In *Gender Politics in Global Governance,* edited by Mary K. Meyer and Elisabeth Prügl, 210–20. Lanham, Md.: Rowman and Littlefield Publishers.

Sachs, Wolfgang. 1997. *Planet Dialectics: Explorations in Environment and Development.* London: Zed Books.

Sadker, Myra, and David Sadker. 1994. *Failing at Fairness: How Our Schools Cheat Girls.* New York: Touchstone.

Sagar, Pearl. 1997. Address to the Women's Studies Centre Seminar Series, 15 May, University College, Galway, Ireland.

Said, Edward. 1986. "Intellectuals and the Post-Colonial World." *Salmagundi* 70–71 (Spring–Summer): 44–81.

———. 1994. *Culture and Imperialism.* New York: Vintage.

Salecl, Renata. 1994. *The Spoils of Freedom: Psychoanalysis and Feminism after the Fall of Socialism.* London: Routledge.

Sales, Rosemary. 1997. *Women Divided: Gender, Religion and Politics in Northern Ireland.* London and New York: Routledge.

Sassen, Saskia. 1996. "Cities and Communities in the Global Economy: Rethinking Our Concepts." *American Behavioral Scientist* 39, no. 5 (March–April): 629–40.

———. 1999. "Culture Beyond Gender." In *Is Multiculturalism Bad for Women?* edited by Joshua Cohen, Matthew Howard, and Martha C. Nussbaum, 76–78. Princeton, N.J.: Princeton University Press.

Saunders, Harold. 1993. "Enlarging US Policy Toward 'Ethnic' Conflict: Rethinking Intervention." Paper presented at the symposium on Ethnic Conflicts: Threat to Domestic and International Peace, National Defense University and the Joint Center for Political and Economic Studies, Washington, D.C., 3 November.

Schell, Jonathan. 1985. Introduction to *Letters from Prison and Other Essays,* edited by Adam Michnik and translated by Maya Latynska, xvii–xlii. Berkeley: University of California Press.

Schorske, Carl E. 1980. *Fin-de-Siècle Vienna: Politics and Culture.* New York: Knopf.

Scott, G. C. 1997. "Toasted and Roasted in America . . . President Jiang Is Haunted by Tibet and Other Human Rights Issues He Had Long Ignored." *Tibetan Bulletin,* November–December, 29–30.

Scott, James C. 1998. *Seeing Like a State: How Certain Schemes to Improve the Human Condition Have Failed.* New Haven, Conn.: Yale University Press.

Scott, Joan W. 1991. "The Evidence of Experience." *Critical Inquiry* 17, no. 4 (Summer): 773–97.

———. 1992. "Experience." In *Feminists Theorize the Political,* edited by Judith Butler and Joan W. Scott, 22–41. New York: Routledge.

———. 1996. *Only Paradoxes to Offer: French Feminists and the Rights of Man.* London: Harvard University Press.

———, ed. 1989. *Feminism and History.* Oxford: Oxford University Press.

Selbin, Jesse Cordes. 2001. "Reading between the Lines: Why Are So Many Books Still Sexist." *New Moon: The Magazine For Girls and Their Dreams* 8, no. 4 (March/April): 40–42.

Selman, Robert L. 1980. *The Growth of Interpersonal Understanding: Developmental and Clinical Analyses.* New York: Academic Press.

Selman, Robert L., Charles Stone, and Edward Phelps. 1983. "A Naturalistic Study of Children's Social Understanding." *Developmental Psychology* 19, no. 15: 92–102.

Sen, Gita. 1997. "Globalization in the 21st Century: Challenges for Civil Society." Presented as the University of Amsterdam Development Lecture, University of Amsterdam, 20 June.

Sheffer, Susannah. 1995. *A Sense of Self: Listening to Homeschooled Adolescent Girls.* Portsmouth, N.H.: Boynton/Cook Publishers.

Shiva, Vandana. 1991. *The Violence of the Green Revolution: Third World Agriculture, Ecology, and Politics.* London: Zed Books.

———. 1995. *Trading Our Lives Away: An Ecological and Gender Analysis of "Free Trade" and the WTO.* Penang, Malaysia and New Delhi, India: PAN Asia and Pacific and Research Foundation for Science, Technology and Natural Resource Policy.

———. 1997. *Biopiracy: The Plunder of Nature and Knowledge.* Boston: South End Press.

Šiklová, Jiřina. 1990. "The Grey Zone and the Future of Dissent in Czechoslovakia." *Social Research* 57, no. 2 (Summer): 363–67.

———. 1991. "Rozumí Západ na im ženám?" (Does the West understand our women?). *Listy* (Prague) 5: 14–17.

———. 1992. "Dilemmas of Transition: A View From Prague." *Peace Review,* Winter, 24–28.

———. 1992. "Women in Politics in the CSFR." Conference report for Women in Leadership: Politics and Business, Vienna, 9–22 November; available at the Foundation for Gender Studies, Prague.

———. 1993. "Are Women in Eastern Europe Conservative?" In *Gender Politics and Post Communism, Reflections from Eastern Europe and the Soviet Union,* edited by Nanette Funk and Magda Mueller, 74–83. New York: Routledge.

———. 1993. "Feminism and Citizenship." Conference Paper for the Third HCA Assembly, Fourth Commission: Women and Citizenship, Ankara, Turkey.

———. 1993. "McDonalds, Terminators and Coca Cola Ads and Feminism? Imports from the West." In *Bodies of Bread and Butter: Reconfiguring Women's Lives in the Post-Communist Czech Republic,* edited by Susanna Trnka and Laura Busheiken. Prague: Prague Gender Studies Centre, 7–12. Reprinted 1997 in *Ana's Land: Sisterhood in Eastern Europe,* edited by Tanya Renne, 76–81. Boulder, Colo.: Westview.

———. 1993. "Moderní feminismus" (Modern feminism). *Playboy* (Czech Edition) 1: 29.

———. 1994. "Factors Inhibiting the Development of Feminism in the Czech Republic." Paper presented at the conference Crossing Borders: International

Dialogues on Gender, Social Politics, and Citizenship, Stockholm, Sweden, 27–29 May.

———. [1994?] "Identity and Traditions of Women's Rights in the Czech Republic." Unpublished paper; available at the library of the Foundation for Gender Studies, Prague.

———. 1994. "Women and the Welfare State in Transition." Paper presented at the Prague School for Economics/Institut für Gesellschaftspolitik-Abteilung Sozialpolitik, Linz, 29–30 November.

———. 1995. "Inhibition Factors of Feminism in the Czech Republic after the 1989 Revolution." In *Women, Work and Society,* edited by Marie Čermárková, 33–45. Prague: Academy of Sciences of the Czech Republic, Institute of Sociology.

———. 1996. "Jiný kraj, jiné ženy—proč se v Čechách nedaří feminismu" (Different region, different women—Why feminism isn't successful in the Czech Republic, translated by Dagmar Halama and Angela Argent). *Respekt* (Prague) 13, 25–31 May, Civilizace section.

———. 1996. "O feminismu women a gender studiích u nás a na západě" (About feminism, women and gender studies in our country and in the West, translated by Dagmar Halama and Angela Argent). In *Documenta pragensia, Žena v dějinách Prahy.* vol. xiii, edited by Václav Ledvinka, 21–25. Prague: Scriptorium.

———. 1996. "Report on Women in the Post-Communist Centre of Europe (Personal View from Prague)." Translated by Sona Kunová. In *She and He in Slovakia. Gender Issues in Public Opinion,* edited by Zora Bútorova et al., 7–18. Bratislava: USPO Bratislava.

———. 1997. "Feminism and the Roots of Apathy in the Czech Republic." *Social Research* 64, no. 2 (Summer): 1–23.

———. 1997. "Gender and Citizenship: Contentions and Controversies in the East/West Debates." Unpublished paper.

———. 1997. "McDonalds, Terminators, Coca Cola Ads—and Feminism? Imports from the West." In *Ana's Land: Sisterhood in Eastern Europe,* edited by Tanya Renne, 76–81. Boulder, Colo.: Westview.

———. 1998. "Moderní doba je krizí muže" (The modern time is a crisis for men) *Právo,* 5 March, Salon section, pp. 1, 4.

———. 1998. "Why We Resist Western-Style Feminism." *Transitions: Changes in Post-Communist Societies* 5, no. 1 (January): 30–35.

———. 1998. "Why Western Feminism Isn't Working in the Czech Republic." *The New Presence: The Prague Journal of Central European Affairs,* January, 8–10.

———. 1999. "Únava z vysvětlování" (Tiredness from explanations). In *Nové čtení světa, feminismus devadesátých let Českýma očima* (New readings of the world: feminism of the 1990s through Czech eyes), edited by Marie Chřibková, Josef Chuchma, and Eva Klimentová, 128–41. Prague: One Woman Press.

———. 1999. "Women and Human Rights in Post-Communist Countries: The Example of the Czech Republic." In *Gender, Planning and Human Rights,* edited by Tovi Fenster, 153–67. London: Routledge.

Silverstein, Ken. 1997. "The New China Hands: How the Fortune 500 is China's Strongest Lobby." *The Nation,* 17 February, 11–16.

Simons, Marlise. 1994. "Bosnian Rapes Go Untried by the U.N." *New York Times,* 7 December, A8.

Slater, Wendy. 1995. "Women of Russia and Women's Representation in Russian Politcs." In *Russia in Transition,* edited by David Lane, 27–33. New York: Longman.

Šmejkalová-Strickland, Jiřina. 1995. "Revival? Gender Studies in the 'Other' Europa." *Signs* 20, no. 4: 1000–6.

Smith, Anthony. 1991. *National Identity.* Reno: University of Nevada Press.

Smith, Dorothy. 1987. *The Everyday World As Problematic.* Boston: Northeastern University Press.

Smith, Page. 1970. *Daughters of the Promised Land.* Boston: Little, Brown.

Smith, Roger W. 1994. "Genocide and the Politics of Rape: Historical and Psychological Perspectives." Paper presented at Remembering for the Future: International Conference on the Holocaust and Genocide, Berlin, 13–17 March.

———. 1994. "Women and Genocide: Notes on an Unwritten History." *Holocaust and Genocide Studies* 8, no. 3 (Winter): 315–34.

Sober, Elliot. 1989. "What Is Psychological Egoism." *Behaviorism* 17, no. 2 (Summer): 3–25.

Social Studies Center for Educational Development. "Texas Essential Knowledge and Skills—Questions and Answers." http://www.tea.state.tx.us/resources/ssced/teks/teksqa.htm (25 April 2002).

Sowinska, Danuta. 1999. Interviewed by Diane M. Duffy. Warsaw, Poland, 13 May.

Soysal, Yasemin N. 1994. *Limits of Citizenship: Migrants and Postnational Membership in Europe.* Chicago: University of Chicago Press.

Spivak, Gayatri Chakravorty. 1990. *The Post-Colonial Critic: Interviews, Strategies, Dialogues.* Edited by Sarah Harasym. New York: Routledge.

———. 1998. "Gender and International Studies." *Millennium: Journal of International Studies* 27, no. 4: 809–31.

Stacey, Judith. 1988. "Can There Be Feminist Ethnography?" *Women's Studies International Forum* 11, no. 1: 21–27.

Stanley, Amy Dru. 1998. *From Bondage to Contract: Wage Labor, Marriage, and the Market in the Age of Slave Emancipation.* New York: Cambridge University Press.

Starhawk. 1989. "Ritual as Bonding: Action as Ritual." In *Weaving the Visions: New Patterns in Feminist Spirituality,* edited by Judith Plaskow and Carol P. Christ, 326–35. San Francisco: Harper and Row.

———. 1993. *The Fifth Sacred Thing.* New York: Bantam Books.

Staudt, Kathleen. 1998. *Policy, Politics and Gender: Women Gaining Ground.* West Hartford, Conn.: Kumarian Press.

Stein, Janice Gross, ed. 1989. *Getting to the Table: The Processes of International Prenegotiation.* Baltimore, Md.: Johns Hopkins University Press.

Stenzler, Jon. 1997. "Protesters Target Visit of Leader; China's Totalitarian Rule Object of Scorn." *Houston Chronicle,* 27 October. www.chron.com/cgi-bin/auth/story/content/chronicle/nation/97/10/28/china-protests.2.110/29/97.

Stevens, Jacqueline. 1999. *Reproducing the State.* Princeton, N.J.: Princeton University Press.

Storey, William Kelleher. 1997. *Science and Power in Colonial Mauritius.* Rochester, N.Y.: University of Rochester Press.

Stout, David. 1997. "House Panel Takes a Slap at Clinton over China." *New York Times,* 1 October, A1.

Strayer, Joseph. 1970. *On the Medieval Origins of the Modern State*. Princeton, N.J.: Princeton University Press.

Sulloway, Frank J. 1996. *Born to Rebel: Birth Order, Family Dynamics, and Creative Lives*. New York: Pantheon.

Sun, Lena H. 1997. "Jiang Visit Helps Unite a Diverse Group of Foes; Protest Rally Spans Political Spectrum." *International Herald Tribune*, 29 October, 2.

Takacs, David. 1996. *The Idea of Biodiversity: Philosophies of Paradise*. Baltimore, Md.: Johns Hopkins University Press.

Tarnas, Richard. 1993. *The Passion of the Western Mind: Understanding the Ideas That Have Shaped Our World View*. New York: Harmony Books.

Taylor, Charles. 1989. *Sources of the Self: The Making of Modern Identity*. Cambridge: Harvard University Press.

Taylor, Mark. 1999. "Ignaz Semmelweis: 'Please Wash Your Hands.'" *Singapore Microbiologist* April–June, http://www.np.edu.sg/dept-bio/ssm/news/apr_jun99/ignaz.htm (10 May 2001).

Taylor, Peter J. 1999. *Modernities: A Geohistorical Interpretation*. Minneapolis: University of Minnesota Press.

Taylor, Peter, Saul Halfon, and Paul Edwards, eds. 1997. *Changing Life: Genomes, Ecologies, Bodies, Commodities*. Minneapolis: University of Minnesota Press.

Teilhard de Chardin, Pierre. 1975. *Toward the Future*. New York: Harcourt Brace Jovanovich.

Teske, Robin L. 1993. "Power: An Interdisciplinary Approach." In *Reconceiving Reality: Women and International Law*, edited by Dorinda G. Dallmeyer, 231–65. Studies in Transnational Legal Policy, no. 26. Washington, D.C.: American Society of International Law.

Teske, Robin L., and Mary Ann Tétreault, eds. 2000. *Conscious Acts and the Politics of Social Change*. Vol. 1 of *Feminist Approaches to Social Movements, Community and Power*. Columbia: University of South Carolina Press.

Tessler, Mark, and Ina Warriner. 1997. "Gender, Feminism, and Attitudes toward International Conflict: Exploring Relationships with Survey Data from the Middle East." *World Politics* 49, no. 2 (January): 250–81.

Tétreault, Mary Ann. 1993. "Civil Society in Kuwait: Protected Spaces and Women's Rights." *Middle East Journal* 47, no. 2 (Spring): 275–91.

———. 1994. "Whose Honor? Whose Liberation? Women and the Reconstruction of Politics in Kuwait." In *Women and Revolution in Africa, Asia, and the New World*, edited by Mary Ann Tétreault. Columbia: University of South Carolina Press, 296–315.

———. 1994. "Women and Revolution: A Framework for Analysis." In *Women and Revolution in Africa, Asia, and the New World*, edited by Mary Ann Tétreault, 3–30. Columbia: University of South Carolina Press.

———. 1994. "Women and Revolution: What Have We Learned?" In *Women and Revolution in Africa, Asia, and the New World*, edited by Mary Ann Tétreault, 426–41. Columbia: University of South Carolina Press.

———. 1997. "Justice for All: Wartime Rape and Women's Human Rights." *Global Governance* 3, no. 2 (May–August): 197–212.

———. 2000. *Stories of Democracy: Politics and Society in Contemporary Kuwait*. New York: Columbia University Press.

———. 2000. "Women's Rights in Kuwait: Bringing in the Last Bedouins?" *Current History*, January, 27–32.

———. 2001. "Frontier Politics: Sex, Gender, and the Deconstruction of the Public Sphere." *Alternatives* 26, no. 1 (January–March): 53–72.

———. 2001. "A State of Two Minds: State Cultures, Women, and Politics in Kuwait." *International Journal of Middle East Studies* 33, no. 2 (May): 203–20.

———. Forthcoming. "Contending Fundamentalisms: Religious Revivalism and the Modern World." In *The International Political Economy of Religious Revivalism,* edited by Mary Ann Tétreault and Robert A. Denemark. Boulder, Colo.: Lynne Rienner.

———, and Haya al-Mughni. 1995. "Women, Citizenship, and Nationalism in Kuwait." *British Journal of Middle Eastern Studies* 22, no. 1 & 2: 64–80.

Theweleit, Klaus. 1987. *Male Fantasies.* Vol. 1, *Women, Floods, Bodies, History.* Translated by Stephen Conway. Minneapolis: University of Minnesota Press.

Thomas, David Hurst. 2000. *Skull Wars: Kennewick Man, Archaeology, and the Battle for Native American Identity.* New York: Basic Books.

Thomas, Dorothy Q., and Regan E. Ralph. 1993. "Rape in War: The Tradition of Impunity." *SAIS Review* 14, no. 1 (Spring): 81–100.

Thomas Aquinas. 1992. *Summa Theologica,* STII, Question 40, "Of War." In *Classics of Moral and Political Theory,* edited by Michael L. Morgan. Indianapolis, Ind.: Hackett Publishing Company.

Thorne, Barrie. 1993. *Gender Play: Girls and Boys in School.* New Brunswick, N.J.: Rutgers University Press.

Thorson, Esther. 1997. *Summary Report: The Impact of Greek Affiliation on College and Life Experiences.* Indianapolis, Ind.: National Interfraternity Conference and National Panhellenic Conference.

Thurman, Judith. 2001. "The Queen Himself." *New Yorker,* 5 May, 72–77.

"Tibet: Americans Prepare to Give Jiang a Rough Welcome." 1997. *The Independent* (London), 20 October, 14.

Tierney, Patrick. 2000. *Darkness in El Dorado: How Scientists and Journalists Devastated the Amazon.* New York: Norton.

Tillion, Germaine. 1983. *The Republic of Cousins: Women's Oppression in Mediterranean Society.* Translated by Quintin Hoare. London: Al-Saqi Books.

Tilly, Charles. 1985. "War Making and State Making as Organized Crime." In *Bringing the State Back In,* edited by Peter B. Evans, Dietrich Reuschemeyer, and Theda Skoçpol, 169–91. New York: Cambridge University Press.

Tocqueville, Alexis de. 1990. *Democracy in America.* The Henry Reeve Edition. New York: Vintage.

Trinh, T. Minh-ha. 1989. *Woman, Native, Other: Writing Postcoloniality and Feminism.* Bloomington: Indiana University Press.

Tripp, Aili Mari. 2000. "Rethinking Difference: Comparative Perspectives from Africa." *Signs* 25, no. 3: 649–75.

Trivers, Robert. 1990. "The Evolution of Reciprocal Altruism." *Quarterly Review of Biology.* 46, no. 2: 35–50.

Tronto, Joan. 1993. *Moral Boundaries: A Political Argument for an Ethic of Care.* New York: Routledge.

Tsing, Anna Lowenharpt. 1997. "Transitions as Translations." In *Transitions, Environments, Translations: Feminisms in International Politics,* edited by Joan W. Scott, Cora Kaplan, and Debra Keates, 253–72. New York and London: Routledge.

Turshen, Meredith. 2001. "The Political Economy of Rape: An Analysis of Systematic Rape and Sexual Abuse of Women during Armed Conflict in

Africa." In *Victims, Perpetrators or Actors? Gender, Armed Conflict and Political Violence,* edited by Caroline O. N. Moser and Fiona C. Clark. London: Zed Books.

UNESCO *Statistical Yearbook.*

United Nations Commission on Trade and Development. 1990. *Agricultural Trade Liberalization in the Uruguay Round: Implications for Developing Countries.* New York: United Nations.

United States Trade Representative. 1993. *Final Act Embodying the Results of the Uruguay Round of Multilateral Trade Negotiations.* Washington, D.C.: U.S. Government Printing Office.

U.S. Department of Justice, Bureau of Justice Statistics. "Correction Statistics." http://www.ojp.usdoj.gov/bjs/correct.htm (2 August 2002).

U.S. Department of Justice, Bureau of Justice Statistics. "Prison and Jail Inmates at Midyear 1999." http://www.ojp.usdoj.gov/bjs/abstract/pjim99.htm (2 August 2002).

U.S. Department of Justice. 2001. "Prisoners in 2000." *Bureau of Justice Statistics Bulletin.* Washington, D.C.: Government Printing Office. Also available at http://www.ojp.usdoj.gov/bjs/abstract/p00.htm (2 August 2002).

U.S. Department of State. 1997. *Country Reports on Human Rights Practices: People's Republic of China.* Washington, D.C.: U.S. Government Printing Office, January.

U.S. News & World Report. 1997. "The Best National Universities." 1 September, 100–114.

Uvin, Peter. 1988. *Aiding Violence: The Development Enterprise in Rwanda.* West Hartford, Conn.: Kumerian Press.

Veblen, Thorstein. [1923] 1997. *Absentee Ownership: Business Enterprise in Recent Times: The Case of America.* New Brunswick, N.J.: Transaction Publishers.

Vesperini, Helen. 2001. "Rwanda Genocide Death Sentences." *BBC News,* 14 October. http://news.bbc.co.uk/hi/english/world/africa/newsid_1598000/1598940.stm (7 May 2002).

Visvanathan, Shiv. 1997. *A Carnival for Science: Essays on Science, Technology, and Development.* Oxford: Oxford University Press.

Vodrážka, Mirek. 1993. "Před Velkým Exodem, Kořen Českého Antifeminismu" (Before the great exodus, the root of Czech antifeminism), translated by Pavla Slaba and Anne Petrov. Lecture delivered at the Bechtel International Center at Stanford University.

Walker, Alice. 1997. *Anything We Love Can Be Saved: A Writer's Activism.* New York: Random House.

Walker, Alice, and Pratihba Parmar. 1993. *Warrior Marks: Female Genital Mutilation and the Sexual Blinding of Women.* New York: Harcourt Brace.

Walker, R. B. J. 1990. "Sovereignty, Identity, Community: Reflections on the Horizons of Contemporary Political Practice." In *Contending Sovereignties,* edited by R. B. J. Walker and Saul Mendlovitz, 159–95. Boulder, Colo.: Lynne Rienner.

Walton, John. 1992. *Western Times and Water Wars: State, Culture, and Rebellion in California.* Berkeley: University of California Press.

Waltz, Kenneth. 1959. *Man, the State and War.* New York: Columbia University Press.

———. 1979. *The Theory of World Politics.* Reading, Mass.: Addison Wesley.

Walzer, Michael. 1965. *The Revolution of the Saints: A Study in the Origins of Radical Politics.* Cambridge: Harvard University Press.

Wapner, Paul. 2001. "Clinton's Environmental Legacy." *Tikkun,* March/April, 11–14.

Watterson, Kathryn. 1996. *Women in Prison: Inside the Concrete Womb.* Rev. ed. Boston: Northeastern University Press.

Weber, Steve. 1992. "Shaping the Postwar Balance of Power: Multilateralism in NATO." *International Organization* 46, no. 3 (Summer): 633–80.

Webster's New World Dictionary. 1984. 2d college edition. New York: Simon and Schuster.

Wehrfritz, George, and Linda Liu. 1997. "A Noise in Jiang's Ears: Last Week's Summit, Dominated by Debate on Human Rights, Demonstrates Just How Far Apart Washington and Beijing Remain on Key Issues." *Newsweek,* 10 November, 44–46.

Weiss, Penny A., and Marilyn Friedman, eds. 1995. *Feminism and Community.* Philadelphia: Temple University Press.

Weiss, Rick. 2001. "U.S. Fertility Expert Announces Effort to Clone a Human." *Washington Post,* 27 January, A3.

———. 2001. "Cloning a Comeback?" *Washington Post,* 8 October, A01.

Wendt, Alexander. 1987. "The Agent-Structure Problem in International Relations Theory." *International Organization* 41, no. 3 (Summer): 335–70.

———. 1992. "Anarchy Is What States Make of It: The Social Construction of Power Politics." *International Organization* 43, no. 2 (Spring): 391–425.

Wendt, Alexander, and Raymond Duvall. 1983. "Institutions and International Order." In *Global Changes and Theoretical Challenges: Approaches to World Politics for the 1990s,* edited by Ernst-Otto Czempiel and James N. Rosenau, 51–71. Lexington, Mass.: Lexington Books.

Weschler, Lawrence. 1995. "Inventing Peace." *New Yorker,* 20 November, 52–68.

Whitehead, Alfred North. 1933. *Adventures of Ideas.* New York: The Macmillan Company.

Who's Counting? Marilyn Waring on Sex, Lies and Global Economics. Directed by Terre Nash and produced by the National Film Board of Canada. 94 min. Bullfrog Films, 1995. Film and videocasette.

Wilford, Rick. 1996 "Representing Women." In *Democratic Dialogue.* Report No. 4. Belfast: 48–55.

Williams, Carol J. 1993. "Bosnia's Orphans of Rape: Innocent Legacy of Hatred." *Los Angeles Times,* 24 July, A1, A12.

Williams, Delores S. 1989. "Womanist Theology—Black Women's Voices." In *Weaving the Visions: New Patterns in Feminist Spirituality,* edited by Judith Plaskow and Carol P. Christ, 179–86. San Francisco: Harper and Row.

Wills, Garry. 1978. *Inventing America: Jefferson's Declaration of Independence.* Garden City, N.Y.: Doubleday.

———. 1984. *Cincinnatus: George Washington and the Enlightenment.* Garden City, N.Y.: Doubleday.

———. 1992. *Lincoln at Gettysburg: The Words That Remade America.* New York: Simon and Schuster.

———. 2000. *Papal Sin: Structures of Deceit.* New York: Doubleday.

Wilson, Patricia. 1997. "Protesters Ready for Chinese Leader's US Visit." *Reuters,* 16 October.

Winham, Gilbert. 1990. "GATT and the International Trade Regime." *International Journal* 45, no. 4 (Autumn): 796–882.

Wnuk-Lipiński, Edmund. 1987. "Social Dimorphism and Its Implications." In *Crisis and Transition: Polish Society in the 1980s,* edited by I. Bialecki, I. Koralewicz, and M. Watson, 159–76. London: Berg.

Wolf, Diane, ed. 1996. *Feminist Dilemmas in Fieldwork.* Boulder, Colo.: Westview Press.

Wolf, Eric R. 1982. *Europe and the People without History.* Berkeley: University of California Press.

Wolfers, Arnold. 1962. *Discord and Collaboration: Essays on International Politics.* Baltimore, Md.: Johns Hopkins University Press.

Wolin, Sheldon. 1996. "Fugitive Democracy." In *Democracy and Difference,* edited by Seyla Benhabib, 31–45. Princeton, N.J.: Princeton University Press.

Wollstonecraft, Mary. 1997. *The Vindications: The Rights of Men; The Rights of Women.* Edited by D. L. Macdonald and Kathleen Scherf. Peterborough, Ont.: Broadview Press.

World Bank. 1997. *The State in a Changing World.* Washington, D.C.: World Bank.

———. 2000. "Critical Ecosystem Partnership Launches $150 Million Fund to Better Protect Biodiversity Hotspots." Press release. August 22.

———. 2000. *World Development Indicators 2000.* Washington, D.C.: World Bank.

World Health Organization. "Female Genital Mutilation: An Overview." 1998. http://www.who.int/dsa/cat98/fgmbook.htm (9 May 2002).

World Wildlife Fund. 1999. *Living Planet: Preserving Edens on Earth.* New York: Crown Publishers.

Young, Oran R. 1989. "The Politics of International Regime Formation." *International Organization* 43, no. 3 (Summer): 349–75.

Yuval-Davis, Nira. 1997. *Gender and Nation.* Thousand Oaks, Calif.: Sage.

Yuval-Davis, Nira, and Floya Anthias, eds. 1989. *Woman-Nation-State.* London: Macmillan.

Zalewski, Marysia, and Jane Parpart, eds. 1998. *The "Man" Question in International Relations.* Boulder, Colo.: Westview.

Zarkov, Dubravka. 2001. "The Body of the Other Man: Sexual Violence and the Construction of Masculinity, Sexuality and Ethnicity in Croatian Media." In *Victims, Perpetrators or Actors? Gender, Armed Conflict and Political Violence,* edited by Caroline O. N. Moser and Fiona Clark, 69–82. London: Zed Books.

Zartman, William. 1989. "Prenegotiation: Phases and Functions." In *Getting to the Table: The Process of International Prenegotiation,* edited by Janice Gross Stein, 1–17. Baltimore, Md.: Johns Hopkins University Press.

Zeta Tau Alpha. "Mission Statement." http://www.zetataualpha.org/mission.htm (26 April 2002).

About the Contributors

Abigail Abrash is a human rights researcher, writer, activist, and educator. She has worked on U.S. foreign policy issues for more than a decade with organizations including the International Human Rights Law Group, the Robert F. Kennedy Memorial Center for Human Rights, and the Indonesia Human Rights Network. Abi has taught courses on international human rights, citizen advocacy, and social movements at James Madison University and Antioch New England Graduate School. She is the director of ActionWorks, a New England–based public interest consulting firm, and served as a visiting fellow at Harvard Law School's Human Rights Program during 2000.

Angela Argent is a doctoral student at Monash University in Melbourne, Australia. In 1998 she lived in Prague while conducting research for her dissertation about intellectual women's relationships with feminism. During that year Angie worked part-time at Prague's Gender Studies Centre, attended conferences, and studied the Czech language at Charles University. Until recently she taught contemporary European history in the School of Historical/Gender Studies and European Studies at Monash University. Currently she is living in Sydney.

Helen Cordes and ***Eric Selbin*** are involved in several communities and networks, both on-line and face-to-face, which focus on learning, progressive politics, revolution, and feminism. They also tag along with their two homeschooled daughters, **Jesse**, 15, and **Zoe**, 9, as they interact with various multiage communities ranging from Brownie Scouts to teen Shakespeare thespians to neighborhood block parties where octogenarians predominate. Helen is a freelance writer, editor, and author of *Girl Power in the Mirror* and *Girl Power in the Classroom* (Lerner Publications, 2000). Eric is Brown Distinguished Research Professor and Associate Professor of Political Science at Southwestern University and the author of *Modern Latin American Revolutions,* 2d ed. (Westview, 1999) and numerous articles and chapters on matters revolutionary. Jesse is the author of several articles, including "Reading Between the Lines: Why Are So Many Books Still Sexist" (*New Moon,* 2001) and Zoe recently published "Why Me, And When Can I Get This SEXIST SHIT Off Me? (*The Rag,* 2001). Both write for the Austin, Texas, area homeschoolers newsletter.

Marie Deans is a mitigation specialist and the executive director of the Virginia Mitigation Project. She is the founder of Murder Victims' Families for Reconciliation, a national organization of those who have lost a family member to murder and who work for abolition of the death penalty and for programs that effectively reduce crimes. Marie founded the Virginia Coalition on Jails and Prisons and served as its executive director until 1993, when it folded due to lack of funds. She is a past president of the Southern Coalition on Jails and Prisons and has served on numerous nonprofit boards, including Amnesty International USA.

Diane M. Duffy is an independent scholar living in northern Wisconsin. She has written on different aspects of public policy in the United States, Sweden, and Poland, and on patriotism among Native Americans. She has been deeply interested and involved in health care policy for some years and spent the 1998–99 academic year in Poland teaching and consulting with health care professionals in Warsaw and Kraków. It was during that year that she did the research for her chapter in this volume.

Beate Gersch is assistant professor in the Department of Communication at the University of Texas in San Antonio, Texas. She also continues to teach as a volunteer at the Bexar County Jail.

Ronnie D. Lipschutz is a professor of politics at the University of California, Santa Cruz. His most recent books are *After Authority: War, Peace, and Global Politics in the 21st Century* (SUNY Press, 2000) and *Cold War Fantasies: Film, Fiction and Foreign Policy* (aka, *What Did You Do in the Cold War, Daddy?*) (Rowman and Littlefield, 2001). He is a community-of-one-among-many but also a staunch believer in both his bioregion and a global ethos.

Patricia J. McCabe, an attorney, is director of the AAUW Legal Advocacy Fund. She is responsible for program development and execution, budgeting, financial planning and developing LAF resources. In her eight years at LAF, Patty has talked with thousands of women facing disparate treatment at colleges and universities. She has provided hours of technical assistance and dozens of strategies for addressing discrimination on campus through the following initiatives: a Campus Outreach program to educate institutions about sex discrimination; a national public education campaign to bring the issue of sex discrimination to a broader audience; the securing of significant grants from national foundations; and the tripling of annual funding to individual plaintiffs. She is a member of the District of Columbia, Massachusetts, and Virginia bars.

Mary K. Meyer is an associate professor of political science at Eckerd College, where she teaches courses in international relations and women and gender studies. She has been a long-time peace activist and, professionally, is a founding member and past chair of the Women's Caucus for International Studies, a section of the International Studies Association. Her publications include *Gender Politics in Global Governance* (Rowman and Littlefield, 1999), which she coedited with Elizabeth Prügl. Mary travels regularly to Ireland, both for research on the peace process and politics in the north and to learn more about Irish traditional music.

Clark A. Miller is assistant professor of public affairs and science and technology studies at the University of Wisconsin–Madison. He is an electrical engineer and atmospheric physicist by training and a sometime commentator on globalization and international science policy. His work includes *Changing the Atmosphere: Expert Knowledge and Environmental Governance* (MIT Press, 2001, with Paul N. Edwards). Clark belongs to an eclectic and growing community of scholars whose studies examine how people in particular cultural and historical contexts come to regard knowledge as "scientific" and use that knowledge in fashioning their collective political imagination.

Agda Rössel is a long-time feminist activist who was appointed Sweden's delegate to the UN Commission on Human Rights in 1951. She also served in several other positions in the United Nations and then became Sweden's Ambassador to that body in 1958. She was the first female head-of-mission to the world organization. In 2000 Ambassador Rössel celebrated her ninetieth birthday at an international gala held in Stockholm.

Anne Sisson Runyan is director and associate professor of women's studies at the University of Cincinnati. Other professional communities she has helped to build include the Women's Studies Programs at Wright State University and the State University of New York at Potsdam, and the Feminist Theory and Gender Studies Section of the International Studies Association. Anne hopes that she has added to the literature on more just communities by coauthoring *Global Gender Issues* (Westview Press, 1993 and 1999), coediting *Gender and Global Restructuring: Sightings, Sites and Resistances* (Routledge 2000), and serving on the editorial board of the International Feminist Journal of Politics.

Karla Scheele is currently a graduate student at the University of Nebraska–Lincoln. A long-time student of gender issues with academic training in political science, she has done research on such topics as women in the Iowa judiciary and women in Muslim countries. Karla is an alumna of the Kappa Alpha Theta chapter at Iowa State University; as a member, she was given opportunities to develop the leadership skills necessary to be a successful teacher and activist, and to refine her conceptions of feminism to encompass both the "feminine" and the "feminist" tendencies she observed in herself and others.

Robin L. Teske is a professor of political science at James Madison University in Harrisonburg, Virginia, where she teaches courses in international law and organizations, U.S. foreign policy, and peace studies. She previously worked as an attorney with the Washington, D.C.–based International Human Rights Law Group and as a Peace Corps volunteer in the Republic of Korea.

Mary Ann Tétreault is the Una Chapman Cox Distinguished Professor of International Affairs at Trinity University in San Antonio, Texas, where she is delighted to belong to an "academic community" which pays equal attention to academic values and community life.

Karen S. Walch is an associate professor at Thunderbird, the American Graduate School of International Management, where she teaches graduate courses on negotiation, mediation, and dispute resolution. She is a board member of Peace Initiatives, a nonprofit organization involved in training and facilitation of international ethnic conflict. Karen is also a member of several organizations involved in the promotion of commercial alternatives to international dispute resolution.

Marjorie L. Zap was trained as an economist and worked for the U.S. Treasury Department during and just after World War II on economic issues relating to post-war Japan. From there she went to the United Nations, where she worked as an economist on economic development in third world countries. After she left the UN, Marge and her husband established one of the first international handcraft shops in the U.S., traveling to many countries to find one-of-a-kind handcrafts, supporting indigenous workers, and making their products available to a larger market.

Index